Foreign Direct Investment

In 2000 foreign direct investment (FDI) broke through the trillion-dollar level and its annual growth rate over the last decade has exceeded the growth of both international trade in goods and services and output. This rapid growth has led to wide-ranging policy changes at national and international level. In the 1960s and 1970s, FDI and indeed multinational corporations in general were viewed with heightened levels of suspicion by governments in developing countries. Today, those same governments seem to fall over one another in attempts to attract FDI.

Foreign direct investment: research issues examines the different approaches to explaining the growth, impact and distribution of FDI in the world. Pulling together contributions from an array of international experts, this study combines theoretical with empirical work on issues such as computable general equilibrium modelling, trade, intellectual property, environment, labour, services and development.

By analysing different aspects of the growth and impact of FDI the book is able to balance areas where research is well advanced with areas, such as the role of FDI in development, where many questions remain. This insightful and important book will be useful to students of development and international economics as well as policy makers and researchers.

Bijit Bora is a Counsellor in the Economic and Research Analysis Division of the World Trade Organisation and formerly a Senior Lecturer in the School of Economics at the Flinders University of South Australia.

Development Economics/International Business.

Routledge Studies in International Business and the World Economy

1 **States and Firms**
Multinational enterprises in institutional competition
Razeen Sally

2 **Multinational Restructuring, Internationalization and Small Economies**
The Swedish case
Thomas Andersson, Torbjörn Fredriksson and Roger Svensson

3 **Foreign Direct Investment and Governments**
Catalysts for economic restructuring
Edited by John H. Dunning and Rajneesh Narula

4 **Multinational Investment and Economic Structure**
Globalization and competitiveness
Rajneesh Narula

5 **Entrepreneurship in a Global Context**
Edited by Sue Birley and Ian Macmillan

6 **The Global Structure of Financial Markets**
An overview
Edited by Dilip K. Ghosh and Edgar Ortiz

7 **Alliance Capitalism and Global Business**
John H. Dunning

8 **Multinational Enterprises from the Netherlands**
Edited by Roger van Hoesel and Rajneesh Narula

9 **Competition, Growth Strategies and the Globalization of Services**
Real estate advisory services in Japan, Europe and the United States
Terrence LaPier

10 **European Integration and Foreign Direct Investment in the EU**
The case of the Korean consumer electronics industry
Sang Hyup Shin

11 **New Multinational Enterprises from Korea and Taiwan**
Beyond export-led growth
Roger van Hoesel

12 **Competitive Industrial Development in the Age of Information**
The role of co-operation in the technology sector
Edited by Richard J. Braudo and Jeffrey G. MacIntosh

13 **The Global Restructuring of the Steel Industry**
Innovations, institutions and industrial change
Anthony P. D'Costa

14 **Privatisation and Liberalisation in European Telecommunications**
Comparing Britain, the Netherlands and France
Willem Hulsink

15 **Multinational Corporations**
Emergence and evolution
Paz Estrella Tolentino

16 **Foreign Direct Investment in Emerging Economies**
Corporate strategy and investment behaviour in the Caribbean
Lou Anne A. Barclay

17 **European Integration and Global Corporate Strategies**
Edited by François Chesnais, Grazia Ietto-Gillies and Roberto Simonetti

18 **The Globalisation of Corporate R&D**
Implications for innovation systems in host countries
Prasada Reddy

19 **Globalization of Services**
Some implications for theory and practice
Edited by Yair Aharoni and Lilach Nachum

20 **A Century of Foreign Investment in the Third World**
Michael J. Twomey

21 **Global Capitalism at Bay**
John H. Dunning

22 **Foreign Direct Investment**
Research issues
Bijit Bora

23 **Ford and the Global Strategies of Multinationals**
The North American auto industry
Isabel Studer Noguez

24 **The World Trade Organization Millennium Round**
Freer trade in the next century
Klaus Deutsch and Bernhard Speyer

25 **Consultancy and Innovation**
The business service revolution in Europe
Edited by Peter Wood

26 **Knowledge Economies**
Clusters, learning and co-operative advantage
Philip Cooke

27 **The Role of Resources in Global Competition**
John Fahy

28 **Globalization, Employment and the Workplace**
Diverse impacts
Edited by Yaw A. Debrah and Ian G. Smith

29 **Transnational Corporations**
Fragmentation amdist integration
Grazia Ietto-Gillies

Foreign Direct Investment

Research issues

Edited by
Bijit Bora

London and New York

First published 2002
by Routledge
2 Park Square, Milton Park, Abingdon, Oxon, OX14 4RN

Simultaneously published in the USA and Canada
by Routledge
270 Madison Ave, New York NY 10016

Routledge is an imprint of the Taylor & Francis Group

Transferred to Digital Printing 2005

Typeset in 10/12 pt Times New Roman by
Newgen Imaging Systems (P) Ltd, Chennai, India

British Library Cataloguing in Publication Data
A catalogue record for this book is available
from the British Library

Library of Congress Cataloging in Publication Data
A catalog record for this book has been requested

ISBN 0-415-23814-5

Contents

List of figures ix
List of tables x
List of contributors xii
Acknowledgments xiv

1 **Introduction** 1
BIJIT BORA

PART I
Theory and measurement of FDI **5**

2 **International business research: steady-states, dynamics and globalisation** 7
STEPHEN NICHOLAS AND ELIZABETH MAITLAND

3 **FDI: strategic issues** 28
RON EDWARDS

4 **The international distribution of multinational production** 46
BIJIT BORA

5 **A method for improved international and intertemporal comparisons of US MNCs' overseas gross product in manufacturing** 63
RAYMOND J. MATALONI, JR.

6 **Research issues in Japanese FDI** 75
ROGER FARRELL

PART II
Structural issues related to the impact on FDI **91**

7 **FDI and trade** 93
JAMES R. MARKUSEN

8 **Cross-border investment and effects on competition in the telecommunications sector** 113
EDWARD M. GRAHAM

9 **Outsourcing jobs and enterprise-level bargaining: 'Cheshire cat' unions revisited?** 132
NOEL GASTON

10 **FDI and the structure of home country production** 152
ARI KOKKO

11 **Host-country impact of FDI in East Asia** 168
PREMA-CHANDRA ATHUKORALA AND HAL HILL

12 **IPRs and FDI** 195
KEITH E. MASKUS

13 **FDI and the environment: the link between FDI and the environment** 211
BIJIT BORA

PART III
Analytical and policy issues **231**

14 **Modelling FDI in a computable general equilibrium framework** 233
SUSAN F. STONE AND PATRICK A. JOMINI

15 **Measuring and modelling barriers to FDI** 252
ALEXIS HARDIN AND LEANNE HOLMES

16 **The impact of tax policy and incentives on FDI** 273
JACQUES MORISSET AND NEDIA PIRNIA

17 **Options for collecting globalisation statistics: Australia** 292
MARK LOUND AND GEOFF ROBERTSON

18 **Multilateral investment rules** 310
DAVID ROBERTSON

19 **FDI and development: research issues in the emerging context** 325
SANJAYA LALL

Index 346

Figures

5.1 Gross product of majority-owned German affiliates in manufacturing in current dollars and in current marks and the dollar–mark exchange rate 67
5.2 Current dollar and real gross product of MOFAs in manufacturing and foreign currency price of the US dollar, 1982–94 71
5.3 Current dollar and real gross product of majority-owned Japanese affiliates in manufacturing and dollar price of yen, 1982–95 72
6.1 Japanese cumulative FDI by industry, March 1998 77
6.2 Japanese cumulative FDI by country, March 1998 77
6.3 Changes in Japan's overseas production ratio, 1985–97 78
7.1 Equilibrium regime with high trade costs 100
7.2 Trade regime with high trade costs 101
7.3 Volume of affiliate production: 25 percent trade costs 102
7.4 Equilibrium regime with low trade costs 103
7.5 Trade regime with low trade costs 103
7.6 Investment liberalization and the direction of trade 105
7.7 Investment liberalization and the volume of trade 105
7.8 Investment liberalization and the return to skilled labour 107
7.9 Effect of trade liberalization on the volume of affiliate production 109
13.1 Share of pollution intensive manufacturing production in total manufacturing production 216
13.2 Share of United States MOFA GDP in manufacturing pollution intensive industries in total United States manufacturing GDP, by region, 1982–96 217
13.3 Share of pollution intensive production by affiliates of United States parent companies in host country production 218
14.1 Input–output table structure 238
14.2 Adding FDI into a GE framework 240
15.1 FDI restrictiveness indices for communications services in selected APEC economies 264
15.2 FDI restrictiveness indices for telecommunications services in selected APEC economies 265
15.3 FDI restrictiveness indices for financial services in selected APEC economies 266

Tables

4.1	Specification of the dependent variable	51
4.2	Specification of market characteristics	53
4.3	Specification of cost characteristics	55
4.4	Specification of government policy	57
5.1	Components of the gross product of MOFAs, 1994	66
5.2	Categories used for price deflation and currency translation of the gross product estimates	69
6.1	Distribution of Japanese FDI in manufacturing, by country, 1951–95	79
6.2	Waves of Japanese FDI 1966–97, by sector	81
6.3	Japanese FDI by industry, 1966–97	84
6.4	Internationalisation of Japanese industry, 1966–97	86
11.1	FDI inflows: East Asia in the global context (1980–98)	172
11.2	Net resource flows to East Asia and the Pacific, 1970–98	175
11.3	FDI in Korea, Malaysia and Thailand, 1995–99	176
11.4	Share of foreign affiliates in total manufactured exports from developing host countries in East Asia	181
11.5	Export–sales ratio and home-country export shares of MOFAs of US multinationals, 1982–93	183
11.6	R&D expenditure of MOFAs of US multinationals, 1989–93	189
12.1	Percentage of firms claiming that the strength or weakness of IPRs has a strong effect on whether direct investments will be made, by type of facility, 1991	198
12.2	Percentage of firms claiming that intellectual property protection is too weak to permit types of investment, 1991	199
12.3	Elasticities of modes of supply with respect to domestic characteristics and policies	203
14.1	Motivations of FDI and consequent modelling considerations	239
14.2	Direct barriers	243
14.3	Sample input structure for an industry with FDI located in Australia	244
14.4	Main sources of data	247
14.5	Models distinguishing between foreign and domestic firms	248

15.1 Components of an index of FDI restrictions 261
15.2 FDI restrictiveness indices, selected APEC economies and GATS sectors and sub-sectors 262
16.1 Types of incentives used by region 273
17.1 *SNA93* definition of foreign control 297
17.2 Globalisation indicators under consideration by the OECD Working Group on Industry Statistics 297
17.3 Extended classification of foreign ownership 300
17.4 Alternative classification of foreign ownership 301
17.5 Theoretical data items required to measure trade of foreign owned businesses in Australia 305
17.6 Theoretical data items required to measure foreign affiliates trade of Australian owned businesses abroad 306

Contributors

Prema-chandra Athukorala is Professor of Economics at the Research School on Pacific and Asian Studies, Australian National University.

Bijit Bora is a Counsellor at the Economic and Research Analysis Division of the World Trade Organisation and formerly a Senior Lecturer in the School of Economics at the Flinders University of South Australia.

Ron Edwards is a Senior Lecturer at the School of Management at Monash University.

Roger Farrell is a Research Fellow at the Australia Japan Research Centre at the Australian National University.

Noel Gaston is Professor of Economics at Bond University.

Edward M. Graham is a Senior Research Fellow at the Institute for International Economics in Washington, DC.

Alexis Hardin is a Principal Consultant with the Network Economics Consulting Group.

Hal Hill is a Professor at the Research School of Pacific and Asian Studies at the Australian National University.

Leanne Holmes is an Economist with the Productivity Commission.

Patrick A. Jomini is Senior Economist at the Productivity Commission.

Ari Kokko is a Professor at the European Institute for Japanese Studies at the Stockholm School of Economics.

Sanjaya Lall is Professor of Development Economics at Queen Elizabeth House, Oxford University.

Mark Lound works for the Australian Public Service. At the time of writing this article he was with the Australian Bureau of Statistics.

Elizabeth Maitland is Associate Director of the Australian Centre for International Business, University of Melbourne.

James R. Markusen is Professor of Economics at the University of Colorado, Boulder.

Keith E. Maskus is Professor of Economics at the University of Colorado, Boulder.

Raymond J. Mataloni, Jr. is a Research Economist at the US Bureau of Economic Analysis.

Jacques Morisset is Lead Economist and Program Manager with the Foreign Investment Advisory Service of the World Bank and the International Finance Corporation.

Stephen Nicholas is Professor of International Management at the University of Melbourne and Director, Australian Centre for International Business, University of Melbourne.

Nedia Pirnia is an independent consultant and formerly a Senior Economist with the Foreign Investment Advisory Service of the World Bank and the International Finance Corporation.

David Robertson is a Commissioner of the Productivity Commission, and was formerly John Gough Professor of International Trade at the Melbourne Business School.

Geoff Robertson works for the Australian Public Service. At the time of writing his article he was with the Australian Bureau of Statistics.

Susan F. Stone is a Research Economist with the Productivity Commission.

Acknowledgments

I am greatly indebted to the Australian Research Council for generously funding this project through their Special Research Initiatives program. No project on research issues on the interface of theory, evidence and policy would be complete without the participation and cooperation of a central statistical agency. The Australian Bureau of Statistics, through Dennis Trewin now the Chief Australian Statistician was open to investigating and listening to avenues through which the quality and depth of research on FDI issues in Australia could be improved. Strong support from other Australian departments was also received from the Productivity Commission, through Gary Banks, and the Australian Department of Foreign Affairs and Trade, through Pam Fayle and Geoff Raby.

The project was a joint one with Kym Anderson at the University of Adelaide's Centre for International Economic Studies and Peter Lloyd at the University of Melbourne's Asia Business Centre. It also adds to many previous joint projects and hopefully many more.

Most of the preparation of the manuscript was done while I was in Geneva at UNCTAD. Throughout the period of the project. I was fully dependent on Sonja Beagly. Sonja not only helped with the workshop where authors discussed drafts of their papers she also handled the accounts of the project. The project was also greatly assisted by Robert Langham and Terry Clague at Routledge. Finally, I am grateful and indebted to Laura Brewer for not only her overall support, but also with the preparation of the final manuscript.

1 Introduction

Bijit Bora

In the past decade there has been considerable interest in the 'forces for globalisation'. Of these, the international trade in goods and services and the increase in international production through multinational corporations have been identified as being important factors. In 2000 global private foreign direct inflows (FDI) reached US$1.1 trillion compared to US$159 billion in 1991. In fact, the annual growth rate of FDI during the past decade exceeded the growth of both the international trade in goods and services and output.

This rapid growth in FDI has raised a number of policy issues at the national and international level. During the 1960s and 1970s FDI and multinational corporations were generally treated with suspicion, as they were seen to use their economic strength to take advantage of developing countries. During the same period many developed countries enacted legislation to monitor and control the flow of FDI and the activities of multinational corporations. Their concern was less in the context of economic exploitation, but more in the context of economic sovereignty.

Today, however, the general policy position of most countries is to be receptive to FDI. As a result, national governments are actively seeking a better understanding of its determinants, impacts and implications. At the international level, considerable discussion has taken place on the topic of incorporating rules on investment in the World Trade Organisation (WTO). Indeed, at the Fourth WTO Ministerial held in Qatar in November 2001, a decision was taken to orient discussions on this topic with a view to negotiating such rules at a later date. Many see such an initiative as complementing the existing set of multilateral rules on trade in goods and services and on trade related investment measures and intellectual property rights. At the same time, there is also some scepticism of the benefits of such rules.

While at its most basic level foreign direct investment is a dollar of capital crossing an international border, in reality the issues surrounding FDI are more complex. FDI is essentially a package of potentially wealth creating assets that can have a significant impact on home and host countries. The issues relating to FDI range from theories of commercial presence and management issues to the impact of FDI on trade employment, wages, intellectual property and development. As a result representatives from the management field, international trade theorists and international macroeconomists are active in the field of FDI research. Each particular sub-discipline brings with them a particular insight into FDI.

The purpose of this book is to bring together representatives from these three different areas to take stock of the literature in their particular area and identify future research areas and impediments to fulfiling this research agenda. The book examines and reviews the role played by FDI in areas such as international trade, employment, technology transfer, economic growth, the environment and development in general. Understanding these transmission channels of the impact of FDI is critical for the development of appropriate policies.

The book is divided into three key subject areas. The first examines some of the theories as to why foreign direct investment takes place and the empirical work on measuring the degree of foreign presence. The chapters by Edwards (Chapter 2) and Nicholas and Maitland (Chapter 3) examine the orthodox models of why multinationals emerge from the point of view of the firm. These papers are from the particular perspective of the international business field and hence focus on organisational and management issues at the level of the firm. Three empirical chapters that examine some key aspects of the international distribution follow these chapters. Chapter 4 (Bijit Bora) is a survey of the empirical work on location and draws conclusions about the generality of the results and some of the key determinants of the distribution of foreign direct investment. Raymond Mataloni (Chapter 5) examines the measurement of foreign presence in an economy using US data while the last chapter in the section by Roger Farrell (Chapter 6) examines issues related to Japanese foreign direct investment.

The second section of the book covers structural issue related to FDI. These relate to the impact of foreign direct investment on international trade by James Markusen (Chapter 7), industry structure, with a special focus on telecommunications, by Edward M. Graham (Chapter 8), the labour market by Noel Gaston (Chapter 9), home country by Ari Kokko (Chapter 10), the host country by Prema-chandra Athukorala and Hal Hill (Chapter 11), intellectual property rights by Keith Maskus (Chaper 12) and environment by Bijit Bora (Chapter 13).

The last section covers analytical and policy issues. It starts with Chapter 14 on how to incorporate multinational corporations into a general equilibrium policy framework by Patrick Jomini and Susan Stone. A key element of this research area, however, is access to reliable data on the barriers to foreign direct investment. Chapter 15 by Alexis Hardin and Leanne Holmes takes up this issue in the context of the services industries. They develop a methodology to construct indices of barriers to FDI that can be used in CGE models in addition to painting a landscape of the pattern of such barriers across countries and sectors.

Equity restrictions on FDI are only one element of government policy that affects the flow and composition of FDI. Tax policy and incentives are also important. Jacques Morisset and Nedia Pirnia take up their role and impact on FDI in Chapter 16.

Chapters 2 to 16 cover many of the analytical issues related to foreign direct investment. In the context of doing good applied research in these and other FDI related areas, researchers require access to data. The United States has excellent data. Indeed, this explains the bias in applied FDI research on American companies. However, other countries are interested in developing statistical databases that will accommodate the research needs of academics and policy makers. Chapter 17 by Mark Lound and Geoff Robertson addresses these issues. Their paper takes up the problem of how to augment the Australian statistical database to help address issues related to FDI and globalisation in general.

Chapter 18, by David Robertson, takes up the question of multilateral rules on investment. The failure of the negotiations on a Multilateral Agreement on Investment at by the members of the Organisation for Economic Cooperation and Development, the discussions surrounding the Agreement on Trade Related Investment Measures and the investment provisions in the North American Free Trade Agreement have raised questions about modality and composition of multilateral investment rules. Robertson examines these issues from the context of identifying avenues for further research.

What is fast becoming one of the most important areas of research is the intensification of the debate on the sign and magnitude of the link between FDI and development. Sanjaya Lall, in Chapter 19, takes up this issue within what he calls the new context.

Research themes

There are two broad themes that run throughout the book. The first is the different approaches that researchers can take when analysing the same question. In other cases, the approach is an aggregate or national one. The second is the nexus between theory, evidence and policy and the third is the identification of impediments to research.

Research methodologies

As discussed in Chapters 2 and 3 the decision to invest in another country is taken at the level of the firm. However, many researchers take an aggregate approach to analysing the pattern of FDI and its impact, such as the work on determinants or the link between FDI and other variables. While considerable insights can be obtained from the aggregate approach there is a need to reconcile results from the different approaches. In some cases, as discussed in the chapters on the environment and development, results from firm level surveys sometimes contradict findings at a more aggregate level. Attempts also need to be made to identify ways to cross-fertilise findings from one particular approach with other approaches. A good example of the benefits of such activities can be found in the chapter on international trade. There, James Markusen, highlights that neglect of international trade theory to account for the multinational firm. He points out that the formal modelling of the multinational corporations in the trade literature relied heavily on the insights of literature from the business perspective, which is covered in Chapters 2 and 3. Similar types of cross-fertilisation can be found in the chapter on intellectual property. Keith Maskus cites firm level evidence on how such rights affect the location decision.

Impediments to research

One of the main reasons for obtaining a better understanding of the determinants and impact of foreign direct investment is to formulate more efficient policies that will assist the development process. In this context, there has to be a link between theory, evidence and policy making. This, however, is difficult to do without good quality data. Researchers can collaborate and work jointly on ideas, but in reality, policy guidance requires solid empirical work. When discussing a future research agenda many of the chapters in this book identify impediments to conducting research. Of these, the most frequently cited impediment is access to good quality data.

Indeed, improving the quality and accessibility of data, should be a priority, but researchers cannot do this. Data on foreign direct investment flows is collected by national statistical agencies. In annual form these are quite good now that there is some standardisation to the data collection. However, as pointed out in the chapters in this book, FDI flow data needs to be disaggregated if there is to be a better understanding of its determinants and impacts. Many countries publish disaggregated statistics of FDI flows, but only to the two digit industry level. This is not sufficient.

A related point that is made strongly in the second section of this book is that flow data is not sufficient for proper analysis of impacts. Since impacts are determined by decisions at the level of the firm, what is required is data at that level. This is difficult to do. However, if such data can be collected the insights gained from research and the quality of research output can increase. This is evidenced by the types of new issues that are investigated in Chapter 5 in terms of measuring the contribution of US multinational corporations in a host country.

How do you proceed to start collecting statistics at the level of disaggregation that is currently done in the United States to meet the research demands set out in this book? This question is taken up to a significant degree in Chapter 17 within the specific context of Australia. It highlights that the task is quite large and argues for the most part that it has to be undertaken by a national statistical agency. The chapter discusses what is required in order to collect such statistics.

The imperative to improve the infrastructure, and hence quality of research on FDI issues is getting stronger as the policy debate on FDI continues to intensify. As David Robertson outlines in Chapter 18 the increased visibility of non-governmental organisation and critics of globalisation is forcing governments to think harder about rules at the multilateral levels. While this book does not take up this specific issue, it does argue that research on FDI has an important role to play in improving the literacy level of the debate on FDI.

Part I

Theory and measurement of FDI

2 International business research

Steady-states, dynamics and globalisation

Stephen Nicholas and Elizabeth Maitland

Introduction: internationalisation, globalisation and management strategies

The strategic direction of national and international business organisations lies at the heart of wealth creation in modern industrial societies. Stephen Hymer (1976) formulated research on internationalisation by recasting foreign direct investment (FDI) in micro analytic terms.[1] Since Hymer's pathbreaking conceptualisation of the multinational corporation (MNC), a generic model of the international activities of firms has slowly evolved. While the model's lineage is multidisciplinary, it draws heavily on new industrial economics and new institutional economic theories of internalisation, challenging neoclassical economic models of international capital flow.

Recently, interest in international business research has been boosted by popular and scholarly fascination with globalisation. Since Levitt (1983) highlighted the trend of increasing integration of national intermediate, factor (particularly finance) and product markets, globalisation, as a word, has assumed many different guises. For some, globalisation is an economic and technological phenomena; for others, globalisation is as much a social and cultural force, threatening national independence, self-determination, individual rights and diversity. Governments seek to understand the new global economy, and the enhanced role of host and home country MNCs in shaping the world economic order.

Yet, globalisation and internationalisation are frequently misunderstood and misused terms. Internationalisation is the process of increasing involvement in international operations, which requires adapting the firm's strategy, resources, structure and organisation to international environments (Welch and Luostarinen, 1988; Calof and Beamish, 1995). Divestment and exit, as well as growth and expansion, form part of internationalisation. Globalisation is a subset of internationalisation. Globalisation stems from interdependencies across the subsidiaries within an international firm, which need to be actively managed and where corporate dominates subunit maximisation. Internationalisation and globalisation differ from other growth strategies, such as product diversification, because they involve transacting in goods, services and know-how across national borders.

This chapter tracks the theoretical and applied research on the internationalisation of firms. The research focus has been on the growth strategies of MNCs.

MNCs grow by expanding their web of contractual arrangements, including market contracts, intermediate arrangements (licenses, franchises and alliances) and internal activities. Until recently, internal expansion has preoccupied researchers. The choice between green field investments and acquisitions has been the predominant focus of empirical studies in international business research. Shortcomings in the generic model of internationalisation and in its empirical testing are identified. The paper reformulates the transaction cost-agency model, linking dynamic capability theory to economic models of the MNC. A reconceptualisation on how MNCs grow is also presented.

The theory of the MNC and internationalisation

Prior to Stephen Hymer's benchmark doctoral thesis on the pattern of FDI, international business was international economics, with attention directed to trade flows and portfolio investments. Such traditional neoclassical economic models of cross-border transactions were seen to lack explanatory power with respect to the phenomenon of enterprises manufacturing, as well as selling, goods and services in more than one country. Dunning's (1970) early work using location theory and studies by Knickerbocker (1973) and Graham (1974) on MNC strategic interaction, defined international business as a separate area of study.

Hymer (1976: 23) observed '(t)he important theoretical shortcoming of the interest-rate theory is that it does not explain control ... If we wish to explain direct investment, we must explain control'. Within the Coasean paradigm, internalisation initially focused on the MNC as the alternative contractual form to transacting in the market (McManus, 1972; Buckley and Casson, 1976; Hymer, 1976; Dunning, 1977). Following Williamson (1979), Casson (1979) and Hennart (1982), internalisation was widened into a transaction cost-agency perspective, incorporating a range of intermediate forms of overseas involvement (such as licenses, franchises, alliances and long-term contracting), as well as markets and hierarchy. The MNC is a firm which transfers know-how between operating entities in two or more countries, through a clear decision-making system linked by ownership or other form of control, with the sharing of knowledge and resources, which allows coherent and common policies and strategies.

While the inclusion of internalisation in the theory of MNC placed international business research at the cutting edge of new schools of thought in economics, the transaction cost-agency approach only explains alternative forms of transacting. As a minimum, the theory of the MNC must explain two simultaneous and interdependent decisions: the choice of contractual form for operating abroad and the location of overseas activity. Alternative theories, such as comparative advantage and location theory, are required to explain the location decision.

Form of overseas involvement

At the centre of the transaction cost-agency approach to international involvement is the concept of internalising market transactions within hierarchical firms or intermediate contracts (including franchises, licenses and alliances), when firms face imperfections in market exchange (Buckley and Casson, 1976; Casson, 1979; Rugman, 1981; 1982; Caves, 1982; Hennart, 1982; Teece, 1986). Firms grow by internalising market transactions. Intermediate product markets frequently are subject to uncertainty and asymmetric information that allow potential opportunistic behaviour by input sellers (agents), who have better and different information than buyers. It is costly for the principal to write market contracts to monitor, bond and enforce input purchases, given potential moral hazard and adverse selection problems. Firms, as principals, are vulnerable to post-contractual opportunistic 'hold-up' by input suppliers, when transaction-specific physical and human capital assets, with low or scrap value in second best uses, are present.

Arm's-length markets also fail to secure the full value of the firm's tangible and intangible assets (ownership advantages or capabilities), including product and process technology, network co-ordination, work and managerial expertise, advertising, marketing and distribution skills, and brand name and parent reputation advantages. The problem arises from the public good characteristics of the assets, when their use in several different applications and locations does not diminish their value in their original use or location (Johnson, 1970; Teece, 1980; Caves, 1982; Hennart, 1982). Markets fail to value correctly firm-specific ownership advantages. Given the high costs of arm's-length market contracting, firms select alternative contractual forms for securing inputs, including franchises, licenses, alliances, long-term contracts and intrafirm FDI (the multinational firm).

Transaction cost-agency theory takes a comparative organisational perspective, since all contractual forms have costs of writing, bonding, monitoring and enforcing incentive contracts for the exchange of property rights in goods, services and know-how (capabilities). Firms 'go international' to appropriate the rents from firm-specific intangible assets, whether through licensing, franchising, strategic alliances or intrafirm FDI. MNCs are frequently superior to intermediate contractual arrangements, especially when transferred capabilities are tacit knowledge, concentrated in teams of skilled workers and involve network co-ordination, work practices and advertising. Compared to franchises, licenses and strategic alliances, the internal organisation of MNCs provides superior mechanisms for managerial control, dispute resolution and goal alignment (Williamson, 1975; Hennart, 1982). Yet, intangible asset transfers within MNCs are costly, requiring complex incentive contracts between the parent and its overseas managers and workers that are monitored by sophisticated organisational structures, including internal accounting systems and information reporting devices (Chandler, 1962; Williamson, 1975; Carlos and Nicholas, 1993).

Transaction cost theory provides only a partial explanation for the form of overseas involvement, a limitation frequently forgotten both by transaction cost supporters and its critics. Production and other real costs are integral elements in the overseas involvement decision. Hierarchy might be selected because ownership allows better control and co-ordination of global MNC strategies (Hill *et al.*, 1990); extends market power (Teece, 1981); appropriates a larger share of investment returns (Anderson and Gatignon, 1986); allows follow-the-leader and oligopolistic exchange-of-threat responses (Graham, 1974; 1978; Rose and Ito, 1996); or reflects the preferences of decision makers. For example, Erramilli and Rao (1993) and Nicholas *et al.* (1996), found from mail surveys that American service firms investing abroad and Japanese manufacturing, financial services and tourism firms investing in Australia preferred full ownership to alternative forms, such as licensing and long-term contracting. Location factors also impact on the form of overseas involvement. Host governments may specify or exclude certain forms of involvement, for example, in exempt sectors, such as mining, communications and residential housing, non-equity alliances may be second best forms to exclude hierarchy.

Entry mode choice

As an alternative to intermediate contracting, there are three possible hierarchical entry mode choices: full equity control through greenfield investment (called greenfield); full equity control through acquisition/merger (called acquisitions); and JVs, either greenfield investment or acquisition (denoted JVs). The theory of entry mode choice is rarely specified in empirical work, although most of the empirical literature focuses on market entry choices and not forms of involvement (see Hennart, 1988; Kogut, 1988; Hennart, 1991; Hennart and Park, 1993 for exceptions).

The nature of firm-specific assets and inputs determines whether the firm chooses greenfield wholly owned operations, JV or acquisition. When the ownership advantages are characterised by non-separability, particularly associated with tacit knowledge and embedded know-how, and all complementary local inputs can be relatively efficiently procured through local markets then greenfield is the selected mode. Inversely, JVs and acquisitions occur when the firm encounters difficulties in procuring complementary assets and inputs through market exchange and intermediate contracting, particularly when the investor requires know-how that is bundled within an existing firm or when requirements exist for inputs that cannot be procured through intermediate or market contracting. The firm also may elect to acquire assets and/or inputs, even when the firm can replicate those capabilities, if the costs of replication exceed the costs of acquiring complementary assets.

However, acquisition requires the hierarchical firm to use its incentive structures, monitoring and enforcement regimes to efficiently exploit the know-how embodied in the acquired firm, which implies high internal transaction-agency costs (Williamson, 1975; 1985; Teece, 1985; 1986). These agency costs include integrating, incentivising and monitoring different management practices, administrative structures and cultures embedded in the acquired firm. While high internal transaction-agency costs are incurred in JVs and acquisitions, an advantage of JVs is the lower expense of termination of the investment. When complementary assets are hard to disentangle, acquisition involves the purchase of all the target firm's assets, irrespective of whether only a subset of assets is required. JVs allow the partner firm to contribute only those assets required by the MNC

(Hennart and Reddy, 1993). JVs also embody an efficient incentive structure for attenuating opportunism. Both parties are rewarded for their complementary assets and/or inputs according to their share of the venture's residual, rather than payment for inputs, reducing opportunistic rent dissipation (Hennart and Reddy, 1993). In the presence of transaction-specific assets, both parties have an incentive to continue the JV relationship, when the second-best use for specialised assets is low or scrap value.

Non-transaction cost factors also contribute to the choice of mode. For example, acquisition may be a source of market power, governments may require JVs, late entrants may seek speedy entry through acquisition, and economies of scale may make greenfield unprofitable in a small or saturated market.

Empirical literature on form and entry mode

The literature on internationalisation of firms is now extremely large, yet, much of the empirical work is dependent on *ad hoc* model theorising. A discursive survey of the literature that generates either a 'new integrated model' or a series of hypotheses typifies the methodology in much of the empirical literature. Similarly, there is a large measure of *ex post* theorising even in the best empirical work. For example, the process of staged involvement through exporting, agents, licensing and franchising to sales and production subsidiaries, what Teece (1985) called 'transitioning', is entrenched in the empirical literature, but poorly motivated by theory. Staged involvement is a particularly important strand in research because of its early attempt to introduce dynamics into studies of MNC growth.

Based on historical studies, case studies and questionnaires, empirical studies of staging have revealed contradictory evidence on whether MNCs grow by sequentially passing through or even adhere to stages of overseas involvement at all. While a number of studies (Johanson and Vahlne, 1977; Luostarinen, 1977; Nicholas, 1983; Kwon and Hu, 1995) have found empirical support for Stopford and Wells (1972: 38) original description of progressive steps in international involvement by US firms, others have found little evidence for the stages process (Newbould *et al.*, 1978; Bureau of Industry Economics, 1984; Hedland and Kverneland, 1985; Turnbull, 1987; Millington and Bayliss, 1990; Ayal and Raban, 1997).

Staged growth is a subset of the larger empirical literature on the choice of form and mode of overseas involvement. While informed by theory, this wider empirical research has been marred by poor model specification and a tendency to blur the distinction between the forms of overseas involvement (market-intermediate-hierarchy) and the choice of market entry mode (greenfield-acquisition-JV). This poor model specification has also hindered model development. For example, experience has been used to explain greenfield investment, when market-specific know-how allows the MNC to enter the market without complementary resources, and acquisition, when knowledge of routinised processes of expanding internationally allow the MNC to assess and manage acquisitions. 'Experience' is typically employed as a proxy for knowledge-based ownership advantages, central to all transaction cost models of internationalisation, but with little uniformity regarding its definition. Stopford and Wells (1972), Hennart and Park (1993), Hennart and Reddy (1993) and Andersson and Svensson (1994) measured country-specific experience, estimated by the number of years in a particular country. Wilson (1980), Zejan (1990) and Nicholas (1991) measured firm-specific experience, using the length of time the firm operated abroad or the number of overseas branches. Dubin (1976), Kogut and Singh (1988) and Caves and Mehra (1986) specified experience as the number of countries in which the MNC-operated subsidiaries. Not surprisingly, these different types of experience and, hence, different types of knowledge of operating multinationally, lead MNCs to select different entry forms and modes.

The problem with 'experience' is not theoretical, but with its specification and interpretation as a proxy in empirical international business studies. Nationality poses a similar problem, being tested in various ways in a transaction cost framework. For example, nationality can be tested by studying firms from several countries investing in a single host market (Kogut and Singh, 1988), one nationality investing in several countries (Belderbos and Sleuwaegen, 1996) or nationality held constant, as in Hennart's (1991) study of Japanese JV market entry into a single market. Each of these measures has tended to return different results. Kogut and Singh (1988) found that nationality mattered for Japanese MNCs in the US, while Hennart (1991) found that it did not.

Differences across industry categories are frequently ignored, with most empirical work focusing on manufacturing MNCs. Erramilli and Rao (1993) suggested that service firms have lower costs of internal administration than manufacturing firms, with low levels of transaction-specific investments. The implication is that service and manufacturing MNCs will choose different forms of international involvement. Further, high degrees of inseparability between production and consumption in health services, hotel accommodation, consulting and advertising, mean these service firms may be particularly sensitive to cultural distance and host country risk factors. Industry-specific factors requiring continuous contact between producer and buyer may force service firms to design different types of incentive contracts than manufacturing MNCs. This is not only an empirical problem, since it raises the question of the applicability of the generic transaction cost model across firms, irrespective of size, nationality, industry segment or product type.

Before 1985, very little empirical research was done at the level of the firm, with the emphasis on country (the inflow and outflow of investment) and industry (what industry sectors attracted FDI). Yet, the crucial growth choices occur at firm-level, requiring an understanding of managerial decision-making models. The use of host-country variables to the exclusion of source-country variables and the use of broad industry-level proxies for firm-level variables are unsatisfactory explanators for the choice of the form of overseas involvement, as opposed to the level of overseas investment. The poor results of their partial ownership equation led Gatignon and Anderson (1988) to argue that long versus short-term decision-making criteria of executives need to be integrated into their model. Kogut and Singh (1988) called for further studies of culturally determined managerial decision-making and Hennart and Park (1993) identified the need to assess the judgements of top executives, since objective economic factors ignore the complex process of decision-maker's responses to external stimuli.

Kim and Hwang (1992) introduced global strategic variables (global concentration, global synergies and global strategic motivations) into a transaction cost framework of internationalisation. Using survey data on US-based MNCs, they found high global concentration favoured wholly owned modes over licenses, and when global strategic motivations and global synergies were ranked high, firms chose JVs and wholly owned over licenses. Culturally distant and high-risk countries favoured licenses and the greater the tacit knowledge, the more likely firms selected wholly owned or JVs over licenses. Kim and Hwang (1992) claimed their results contributed to management, reinforcing in executives' mindsets the importance of expanding entry decision-variables to include global strategic factors, something of which Kogut and Singh (1988) and Hennart and Park (1993) claimed executives were already well aware. Recognition of strategic decision-making variables complements the growing emphasis on the need to model international firm growth as a dynamic process, subject to constant pressures of adaptation.

Dynamics

Transaction cost theory is static. Calvert (1981: 56) recognised the static nature of the markets-hierarchy paradigm when he called for the need to analyse the forces which moved economic transactions to be internalised or externalised. Making the same point, Buckley (1983; 1988; 1990) labelled the internalisation model a 'concept in search of a theory largely because of its failure to explain the transition from one mode (internal or external) to the other'. Similarly, Teece (1985) argued that the literature on the MNC, whether emphasising market power or efficiency, suffered from a common deficiency: under emphasis on dynamics.

Equally disappointing has been the lack of progress at uncovering the dynamics of overseas involvement empirically. Generally, static transaction cost models have been applied to systematically changing data, without analysing the process of change. Caves (1995) and Calof and Beamish (1995: 115) noted that 'little empirical research has examined the dynamics of internationalization' and more recently, Andersen (1997: 29–38) argued that internationalisation was a time-dependent process, but that 'most research … has, however, been static in nature'. Hennart and Reddy (1993) complained that their analysis was static, and Madhok (1997) recommended dynamic resource-based approaches to entry choice over static transaction cost theory.

Dynamic capabilities and internationalisation

Transaction cost models of internationalisation are under challenge, with organisational capability, international management, path dependency, evolutionary and radical political economy approaches providing alternative conceptualisations of international involvement. Organisational capability models focus on firms competing on the basis of capabilities and resources, which are heterogeneous across firms (Wernerfelt, 1984; Reed and DeFillippe, 1990; Peteraf, 1993; Teece *et al.*, 1997). In order for monopoly and Ricardian rents to be earned, organisational capability models impose *ex post* limits to competition, either through imperfect imitability or imperfect substitutability of the firm's capabilities. Imperfect imitability means that competitors cannot reproduce the firm's heterogeneous and firm-specific resources, which are linked to specialised (idiosyncratic) assets that earn quasi-rents. The model also assumes *ex ante* limits to competition, which ensures that the competitive advantages are not immediately competed away, since capabilities are imperfectly mobile. The framework is then used to explain business strategy (what product markets to enter on the basis of identifying competitive advantages from the firm's internal resources) and corporate strategy (boundaries of the firm, including diversification).

There is significant overlap with transaction cost theorising. Resource models emphasise the failure of markets to define property rights in non-imitable and non-tradable firm-specific resources (Barney, 1986; Wernerfelt and Montgomery, 1988; Peteraf, 1993). Resource and internalisation models both emphasise the failure to assemble or transfer a firm's capabilities through the market (Teece, 1982; 1986; Kogut and Zander, 1993). In resource-based theory, vertical integration and diversification are strategies for earning rents on scarce, firm-specific capabilities, which are difficult to sell in intermediate markets (Teece *et al.*, 1997). Resource-based models emphasis scope economies derived from firm-specific knowledge from one activity which are used to enter new activities (Peteraf, 1993), which borrows from transaction cost theory (Willig, 1979; Teece, 1980). In a spirited defense of the generic transaction cost model, Williamson (1999) has identified tautological definitions of key terms and a failure of operationalisation in the dynamic capability approach.

Despite these limitations, the focus on capabilities in resource approaches has introduced a dynamic element into models of firm growth. Borrowing from path dependency and evolutionary approaches, organisational capability models explain both the accumulation of heterogeneous resources of the firm and the constraints on the use of those resources in selecting business and corporate strategies (Penrose, 1959; Nelson and Winter, 1982; David, 1986; North, 1990). In contrast, the transaction cost-agency approach remains a comparative contractual undertaking. Firms select forms and modes of international involvement by selecting across an unconstrained spectrum of contractual choices, ranging from markets, through intermediate contractual forms to hierarchy, neglecting organisational evolution and history.

Resource-based approaches emphasise maximising rents accruing from capabilities and resources, rather than economic profits from market positioning (Teece *et al.*, 1997). In contrast, competitive dynamic models focus on monopoly rents arising through impediments to the operation of factor or product markets, as discussed above. Combining both approaches, dynamic capability models asks how new capabilities could be created, while exploiting existing capabilities in a competitive external environment (Itami and Roehl, 1987). Dynamic capabilities reflect the MNCs skill in learning, integrating, building and augmenting existing organisational and intangible assets as a platform for future growth.

The introduction of dynamics also overcomes the problem of the inception of competitive advantage. History matters, and transaction cost economics is ahistorical, taking the firm's ownership advantages as given. The transaction cost model of the MNC starts mid-flight, with a domestic firm with a set of capabilities looking to expand the scope of its activities beyond its current national boundaries. The firm's origins and innovative capabilities are the starting point of the firm's evolution. By begging the questions of origin and entrepreneurship, it is unlikely that the path dependent nature of the firm's form and mode choice can be understood. The result is to impose a comparative-static mode choice decision on an inherently dynamic process, with serious implications for understanding globalisation. Archival research has underlined the limitations of the 'generic' model, revealing the existence of 'brass-plate companies' born international, rather than evolving from an existing domestic entity (Wilkins, 1988; Hennart and Park, 1994).

Integrated theories and neglected areas of research

Enhanced theories of international involvement provide greater scope for modelling particular aspects the dynamics of internationalisation, which have been relatively neglected areas of research. Focusing on transactions and firm-specific advantages, transaction cost models have rarely adequately addressed the nature of the MNC's operating competitive environment, or determinants of performance, divestment and exit. In the following section, a dynamic model of MNC with directions for empirical testing is presented.

Sequential entry and investment clustering

Research on re-investment, clustering and dynamic capabilities, in particular, has revealed new research avenues for achieving an integrated theory of international involvement. Kogut (1983) differentiated between the initial reason for establishing plants and sequential investment decisions. Rather than a stages approach, the sequential literature focused on re-investment within an entry form or mode. Kogut (1983; 1993) viewed the MNC as a set of resource options that could be allocated to different locations due to the firm's organisational experience gained through co-ordinating a network of international subsidiaries. Expanding the sequential approach, Chang's (1995) empirical results showed that Japanese electronic firms in the US made small core FDI before re-investments into more distant fields on a bigger scale, on the basis of learning from prior entries. Chang explained the sequential entry pattern in terms of learning gained from past entry experience, a recurring theme in the work by Kogut and Zander (1993) and Zander and Kogut (1995).

While the extant literature has highlighted many aspects of firms' international expansion paths, a necessary, but neglected, precursor to modelling the dynamics of internationalisation is an examination of patterns in the timing of MNCs' initial FDI entries into individual countries. Several authors have identified bunching in investment activities. The early studies on inter-firm rivalry by Knickerbocker (1973) noted the bunching of foreign investment by US MNCs. Using a sample of 448 pre-1939 British MNCs, Nicholas (1991) found that nearly 60 per cent invested in two or more countries in the same year. Archival case studies of British MNCs revealed that plant investment decisions were concentrated within a very few years (Nicholas and Maitland, forthcoming). Preliminary studies of Japanese MNCs in the 1950s–1980s by Nicholas and Maitland (Nicholas and Maitland, forthcoming) also uncovered evidence that some firms tended to invest in several countries in the same year.

In a related study, Maitland *et al.* (forthcoming) analysed the Harvard MNC database using the methodology of statistical process control to identify non-random patterns in the manufacturing investments through time of US MNCs. Two patterns of MNC growth were identified. While some firms displayed random variation in the timing of their first investments into a host country, others displayed non-random variation, clustering their investments. Experience, learning and multinational co-ordination and network flexibility advantages provide one avenue to explore the dynamics behind investment clustering (see Bartlett and Ghoshal, 1989; Bartlett *et al.*, 1990). Maitland *et al.* (forthcoming) also hypothesised that clustering reduces the administrative disruptions to the parent's structure and organisation caused by new investments.

Competitive dynamics

Integrating competitive dynamics into the transaction cost framework is a relatively simple task for international business researchers. While international management perspectives elevate market structure and inter-firm rivalry to centre stage (Porter, 1980; 1990), competitive strategic behaviour has a long transaction cost background, beginning with Hymer's (1976) observation that ownership advantages give rise to monopoly advantages through market entry barriers in a world of international oligopolistic competition. Graham's (1974; 1978) exchange-of-threat and Knickerbocker's (1973) follow-the-leader inter-firm behaviours emphasise the importance of competitive dynamics, elegantly modelled by Rose and Ito (1998).

While the international management school has undertaken much of the recent running on competitive dynamics, there are important synergies between the two approaches. For example, Porter's (1980; 1990) value chain defines a geographical scope for MNCs in terms of the relationships with suppliers and buyers. Transaction cost-agency economics operationalises the value chain, providing a rationale for selecting the appropriate contractual arrangement (including markets, intermediate modes and vertical integration) along the chain.

Performance, divestment and exit

Internationalisation involves both investment and divestment. Caves (1995: 20) asked whether there is any reason 'other than temperamental positivism why researchers' attention has stayed away from international divestment'? While comparative static, transaction cost predicts that MNCs shift between forms, including from hierarchy to intermediate arrangements or markets. Recently, Benito (1995), Benito and Welch (1997) and Benito and Larimo (1998) have begun to conceptualise and test divestment by Nordic MNCs.

Managerial growth strategies of entry form and mode choice are risky, and our data are almost always on survivors. This biases our data, truncating the samples to existing firms. But, our data do not identify successful exit from failure, although the high rates of joint venture terminations have been interpreted as failure. Analysing the high termination rates of Japanese manufacturing JVs in the US, Hennart *et al.* (1997) found that Japanese JVs were more likely to be sold than affiliates, but not more likely to be liquidated. Terminations in Hennart *et al.* (1997) study involved take-over by the Japanese partner. These results raise the question of whether JVs are an efficient way to learn about a country (learning model), a superior form to access resources, and whether they allow foreign investors to exploit local partners.

Modelling divestment and exit decision requires recognition of the importance of the subjectivity and bounded rationality of managerial decision-making. In a study of 38 Canadian firms, Calof and Beamish (1995) identified an international adaptation staged model, where the attitudes of executives, and not objective environmental factors, drove form changes. Managers' perceptions of their resource capabilities, experiences and skills and opportunity were important in anti-staging (divesting) or skipping stages.

Uncovering the determinants of divestment and exit decisions focuses attention on an equally neglected area of research, the performance of entry forms and modes. Woodcock *et al.* (1994) theorised that the total resource and control costs of greenfield entry was lowest, with JV entry the next highest and acquisition posing the highest total costs. Testing whether alternative market entry modes performed differently, Woodcock *et al.* discovered that Japanese greenfield FDI in North America performed better than JVs which performed better than acquisitions. For firms operating in the Asia-Pacific, Nicholas and Maitland (1998) undertook a similar performance test for Japanese MNCs in Australia. They found no differences in performance across greenfield, JV and acquisition, despite greater parent control over greenfield and acquisitions than JVs. Recently, Hennart *et al.* (1997) found that Japanese manufacturing MNCs who entered in the market via JVs did not perform any better than those entering via wholly owned affiliates.

Globalisation and organisational design

Dynamic capabilities bring managerial globalisation strategies centre stage, especially the decision-making criteria of executives (Gatignon and Anderson, 1988; Kogut and Singh, 1988; Hennart and Park, 1993). Globalisation involves the MNC creating an interdependent subsidiary network with cross unit learning (Doz, 1986; Prahalad, 1987; Bartlett and Ghoshal, 1989; Bartlett *et al.*, 1990). Dynamic capabilities focus on the MNCs capacity to renew capabilities by learning across the network, in order to compete in a changing competitive external environment. From their empirical work, Caves and Mehra (1986) found that entry mode choice was dependent on the entrant's configuration of activities outside the US and the prospects for co-ordinating its new American facilities with its existing overseas units. Technology transfer, Kogut and Zander (1993) argued, was shaped by the opportunities to accumulate and recombine knowledge across the network of subsidiaries, providing a platform for further growth.

The subsidiary–parent relationship literature is grounded in the transaction cost model, where parents transfer know-how to subsidiaries (see Jarillo and Martinez, 1990 for reviews of the literature; Birkinshaw and Morrison, 1996). But the assumption that the MNC's firm-specific ownership advantages originate in the parent is no longer true, since subsidiaries can play an important part in the maintenance and creation of capabilities (Bartlett and Ghoshal, 1986). But, transaction cost economics provides a powerful analytical framework for analysing organisational structures and architecture, especially by Williamson's (1975) analysis of U- and M-form structures (Jones and Hill, 1988). The creation and structuring of knowledge flows within the firm is a transaction cost undertaking, but transaction cost modelling of organisation design has been neglected in the entry mode literature (Carlos and Nicholas, 1993). Transaction cost approaches must model globalisation and organisational design issues in the analysis of entry form and market entry choice.

The state and MNCs

The gathering pace of globalisation has also focused attention on the implications of state sovereignty for MNCs entry form and mode choice. Following the success of establishing rules and disciplines for international trade through the WTO, efforts are being made to frame a binding multilateral treaty that protects foreign investors. At a superficial level, as more countries become both source and host countries for foreign investment, a confluence of interests should emerge, facilitating the establishment of a multilateral investment treaty. However, the strength of such a possibility will be tested by the nature of sovereignty. Unlike the WTO trade agreements, accepting a binding multilateral investment agreement requires states to forgo sovereign powers. Existing non-binding investment instruments have been plagued by problems of consensus. In the case of the OECD Liberalisation Code, twenty-five years passed from its adoption until the right of establishment was confirmed. The OECD negotiations on a multilateral agreement on investment also faltered (see Chapter 18).

Efforts to frame multilateral agreements are also weakened by their focus on liberalisation of entry standards and dispute settlement rather than limiting *ex post* opportunistic behaviour by the state. For example, rather than protecting investors from the legality or undesirability of nationalisation, these draft multilateral treaties uphold the right of the state to nationalise and control MNCs, providing compensation is made. Even if competition between states for investment attenuates obvious state opportunism, such as expropriation and blocked profit remittance, less visible state manipulations, including delays in approving zoning permits, issuing of visas and granting import and export licenses, impose constraints on entry form and mode choice. State opportunism has not been integrated into transaction cost-agency models, despite its implications for global strategies of MNC growth.

Improving the quality of data

Finding the necessary data for the testing of enhanced transaction cost models of entry form and market entry mode is a daunting task. Perhaps the most challenging is the need to collect longitudinal data. Firm-specific data sources fall into several categories.

Government statistics

The Canadian Census of Manufacturers provide rich firm-specific data on industry sector, entry mode (greenfield, merger and JV), size, performance and nationality (Baldwin, 1995). The Canadian statistics are unique, providing data both on foreign and domestic incumbents and entrants, over-time.

University databases

Second, there are university databases on representative samples of MNCs. Perhaps the most famous is the Harvard Database on American and Foreign MNCs. These data have been the source of much of the empirical work on MNCs over the past three decades, including entry form and mode studies. Unfortunately, the Harvard Database terminates in 1975. The Industrial Institute for Economic and Social Research in Stockholm collects data on Swedish MNCs about every four years, providing a consistent database since, 1965 (Andersson and Svensson, 1994).

Researcher's databases

Databases are frequently constructed from published material. For example, Hennart (1991), Hennart and Reddy (1993) and Hennart and Park (1993) constructed a database on Japanese investment in the US. Using *Toyo Keizai*, Japan Economic Institute, Lexis-Nexis news retrieval service, Nikkei database, Japan Company Handbook and the US Census of Manufacturers, Hennart derived variables on advertising and R&D expenditures, entry form and mode, year of entry, number of subsidiaries and years in the US, SIC industry categories, first-tier supplier, sales and concentration levels.

The Australian Centre of International Business at the University of Melbourne and UNSW has surveyed Japanese and Korean foreign investment in Australia and Australian investment in India, Philippines, Vietnam, Indonesia and China, as well as surveys of parent–subsidiary relationships. Similar surveys have been undertaken at other universities. One problem is the duplication of surveys, the lack of standardisation, the failure to amalgamate the surveys into a consistent database and the limits of user access. Recently, Hennart has collaborated with European researchers, combining European and American databases on Japanese MNCs (Hennart and Larimo, 1998). Such collaboration is rare. But, it seems unlikely that a single or small group of researchers can collect data sets of sufficient size for cross-country comparisons. The mechanisms for international collaborative data collection are not well developed.

Longitudinal databases

Both the Canadian Census of Manufacturers and the Harvard Database provide longitudinal or panel data, and the Swedish database collected by the Industrial Institute for Economic and Social Research in Stockholm seems to offer similar data (Andersson and Svensson, 1994). If the dynamics of global managerial strategies are to be analysed, then we need to control for changing data in our empirical estimation (Caves, 1995). The Australian Centre for International Business has just completed two longitudinal surveys of Japanese MNCs, 1993/4 and 1997/8 and Korean MNCs 1996 and 1998. Yan and Zeng (1999) argued that longitudinal data were necessary to resolve the debate over the instability of joint venture performance. The maintenance of longitudinal databases is a massive undertaking for private researchers, and might be more profitably undertaken in collaboration with Government statistical bureaux. This would require protocols for data access and co-operation in survey design and data analysis.

Interview data

Interview data is high cost data, limited by interview resources, access to firms and the constrained scope of the research agenda. Open-ended questions also pose data analysis challenges for econometric model estimation. Government departments regularly undertake qualitative interviews in Australia to assess the 'climate' of business and peak (interest group) body opinion, especially for policy making and briefings to ministers.

Archival databases

Archival based data falls into two categories, samples of firms and case studies. Turning first to archival data sets of firms, Nicholas (1982; 1983; 1991) has collected archival data, supplemented with published firm histories to construct a database on 119 pre-1939 British MNCs. Second, business history research relies on aggregating case studies, especially the work of Chandler (1962; 1977; 1990). The case study approach also underpins the Harvard management or process approach, especially work by Bartlett and Ghoshal (1989).

Data and policy

Data problems present the greatest obstacle to researching MNC management strategies, globalisation and internationalisation. In the Australian context, the lack of adequate empirical data for model testing has major public policy implications. Re-evaluating industry policy has become urgent in view of the Goldsworthy (1977) and Mortimer (1997) and the Industry Commission Reports that claim that foreign firms are 'bid away' from Australia. Mortimer and Goldsworthy recommend a more pro-active and interventionist industry policy to capture multinational investment which transfers know-how to Australia. The decision to continue tariff protection at current levels until 2005 in the automotive and textiles, clothing and footwear (TCF) industries, the discussion of free trade (export) zones and the *Government Investing for Growth* policy reflect a significant shift in the direction of Australian industry policy. But framing 'good' incentive policies require empirical studies of entry form and mode choice by MNCs investing in Australia. Both the data and empirical studies are sadly lacking.

Conclusion

The transaction cost-agency theory of the MNC faces significant challenges. Giving strategic, locational and path dependent factors a more prominent role, requires a re-conceptualisation of the transaction cost-agency model. The central focus becomes the strategic question of how firms build and enhance ownership advantages in a competitive external environment, with form and mode of market entry subsidiary questions. 'Modelling' this strategic question based on a discursive discussion of the extant literature is all too common in studies of international involvement by MNCs. Without a clear exposition of the underlying theory, the explanatory power of discursive models is weak. Using transaction cost-agency theory to formally integrate dynamic capabilities and competitive dynamic is a major challenge, and the way ahead will not be easy. But formally modelling the MNC entry and exit form and mode, in the context of the strategic questions of how firms create and use capabilities in a competitive external environment, promises exciting new understandings of firm growth.

The second limitation facing empirical work on MNCs is data constraints. The need for collaborative data collection and analysis provides the best option for developing databases that will allow foreign involvement in the Australian economy to be analysed and understood. Such collaboration should include Government departments and statistical bureaux in order to ensure the collection of high quality data. Collaboration will also ensure unbiased and independent data analysis, which will contribute to Government policy making.

Notes

1 Although Hymer's 1960 doctoral dissertation (Massachusetts Institute of Technology) was not published until 1976, two years after his death in an automobile accident,

Kindleberger noted in an introduction to the 1976 edition that photocopies of the thesis were circulating widely from the early 1960s.

References

Andersen, O. (1997) 'Internationalization and Market Entry Mode: A Review of Theories and Conceptual Frameworks'. *Management International Review* 37(2): 27–42.

Anderson, E. and H. Gatignon (1986) 'Modes of Foreign Entry: A Transaction Cost Analysis and Propositions'. *Journal of International Business Studies* 17(Fall): 1–26.

Andersson, T. and R. Svensson (1994) 'Entry Modes for Direct Investment Determined by the Composition of Firm-Specific Skills'. *Scandinavian Journal of Economics* 96(4): 551–60.

Ayal, I. and J. Raban (1997) *Export Management Structure and Successful High Technology Innovation. Managing Export Entry and Expansion*. S. R. P. J. Rosson (ed.). New York, Praeger.

Baldwin, J. (1995) *The Dynamics of Industrial Competition: A North American Perspective*. Cambridge, Cambridge University Press.

Barney, J. B. (1986) 'Strategic Factor Markets: Expectations, Luck, and Business Strategy'. *Management Science* 32: 1231–41.

Bartlett, C. A., Y. Doz *et al.* (1990) *Managing the Global Firm*. London and New York, Routledge.

Bartlett, C. A. and S. Ghoshal (1986) 'Tap your Subsidiaries for Global Reach'. *Harvard Business Review* (November–December 1986): 87–94.

——(1989) *Managing Across Borders: The Transnational Solution*. Boston, Harvard Business School Press.

Belderbos, R. and L. Sleuwaegen (1996) *Japanese Firms and the Decision to Invest Abroad: Business Groups and Regional Core Networks*. Massachusetts, Harvard College and the Massachusetts Institute of Technology.

Benito, G. (1995) 'Divestment of Foreign Production Operations'. Working Paper *12th Annual National Conference of Business Economics* (FIBE-XII). Bergen, Norway.

Benito, G. and L. Welch (1997) 'De-internationalization'. *Management International Review* (37): 7–25.

Benito, G. R. G. and J. Larimo (1998). 'Divestment of Foreign Production Operations: The Case of Foreign Direct Investments from Two Nordic Counties'. *Global Competition and Market Entry Strategies*. J.-F. Hennart (ed.). Amsterdam, Elsevier Science.

Birkinshaw, J. M. and A. J. Morrison (1996) 'Configurations of Strategy and Structure in Multinational Subsidiaries'. *Journal of International Business Studies* (26): 729–94.

Buckley, P. J. (1983) 'New Theories of International Business: Some Unresolved Issues'. *The Growth of International Business*. M. Casson (ed.). London, George Allen and Unwin.

——(1988) *Organisational Forms and Multinational Companies. Internal Organisation, Efficiency and Profit*. S. T. M. Wright (ed.). Oxford and New Jersey, Philip Allan: 126–44.

——(1990) 'Problems and Developments in the Core Theory of International Business'. *Journal of International Business Studies* (21): 657–66.

Buckley, P. J. and M. Casson (1976) *The Future of Multinational Enterprise*. London, Macmillan.

Bureau of Industry Economics (1984) *Australian Direct Investment Abroad: Effects on the Australian Economy*. Canberra.

Calof, J. L. and P. W. Beamish (1995) 'Adapting to Foreign Markets: Explaining Internationalization'. *International Business Review* 4(2): 115–31.

Calvert, A. (1981) 'A Synthesis of Foreign Direct Investment Theories and Theories of the Multinational Firm'. *Journal of International Business Studies* (12): 43–60.

Carlos, A. and S. Nicholas (1993) 'Managing the Manager: An Application of the Agent Principal Model to the Hudson's Bay Company'. *Oxford Economic Papers* (45): 243–56.

Casson, M. (1979) *Alternatives to the Multinational Enterprise*. London, Macmillan.

Caves, R. E. (1982) *Multinational Enterprise and Economic Analysis*. Cambridge, Mass., Cambridge University Press.

——(1995) 'Growth and Decline in Multinational Enterprises: From Equilibrium Models to Turnover Processes'. *Corporate Links and Foreign Direct Investment*. E. K. Y. Chen and P. Drysdale (eds). Pymble, NSW, HarperEducational Pacific Trade and Development Conference: 9–28.

Caves, R. E. and S. K. Mehra (1986) 'Entry of Foreign Multinationals into US Manufacturing Industries'. *Competition in Global Industries*. M. E. Porter (ed.). Boston, Mass., Harvard Business School Press, 449–81.

Chandler, A. D. (1962) *Strategy and Structure: Chapters in the History of the Industrial Enterprise*. Cambridge, Mass., MIT Press.

——(1977) *The Visible Hand: The Managerial Revolution in American Business*. Boston, Mass., The Belknap Press of Harvard University Press.

Chandler, A. D. (1990) *Scale and Scope: The Dynamics of Industrial Capitalism*, Cambridge, Boston, Mass., The Belknap Press of Harvard University Press.

Chang, S. J. (1995) 'International Expansion Strategy of Japanese Firms: Capability Building Through Sequential Entry'. *Academy of Management Journal* 38(2): 383–407.

David, P. (1986) Understanding the Economics of QWERTY: The Necessity of History. Oxford, Blackwell.

Doz, Y. (1986) *Strategic Management in Multinational Companies*. Oxford, Pergamon Press.

Dubin, M. (1976) *Foreign Acquisitions and the Spread of the Multinational Firm*. B.BA thesis, Graduate School of Business Administration, Harvard University.

Dunning, J. H. (1970) *Studies in International Investment*. London, Allen and Unwin.

——(1977) Trade, Location of Economic Activity and the MNE: A Search for an Eclectic Approach. *The International Allocation of Economic Activity: Proceedings of a Nobel Symposium Held at Stockholm*. P. H. a. P. M. W. B. Olin. London, Macmillan.

Erramilli, M. K. and C. P. Rao (1993) ''Service Firms'' International Entry Mode Choice: A Modified Transaction-Cost Analysis Approach'. *Journal of Marketing* **57**: 19–38.

Gatignon, H. and E. Anderson (1988) 'The Multinational Corporation's Degree of Control over Foreign Subsidiaries: An Empirical Test of a Transaction Cost Explanation'. *Journal of Law, Economics, and Organization* 4(2).

Goldsworthy Report (1977) *The Global Information Economy: The Way Ahead*. Canberra, Commonwealth of Australia Government Printing Office.

Graham, E. (1974) *Oligopolistic Imitation and European Direct Investment in the United States*. Boston, Mass., Graduate School of Business Administration, Harvard University, Boston.

——(1978) 'Transatlantic Investment by Multinational Firms: A Rivalistic Phenomenon'. *Journal of Post-Keynesian Economics* (Fall): 82–99.

Hedland, G. and A. Kverneland (1985) 'Are Strategies for Foreign Markets Changing? The Case of Swedish Investment in Japan'. *International Studies of Management and Organization* (25): 41–59.

Hennart, J.-F. (1991) 'Control in Multinational Firms: The Role of Price and Hierarchy'. *Management International Review* 31(Special Issue 1991): 71–96.

——(1991) 'The Transaction Costs Theory of Joint Ventures: An Empirical Study of Japanese Subsidiaries in the United States'. *Management Science* 37(4): 483–97.

——(1982) *A Theory of Multinational Enterprise*. Ann Arbor, University of Michigan Press.

——(1988) 'A Transaction Cost Analysis of Equity Joint Ventures'. *Strategic Management Journal* (9): 361–88.

Hennart, J.-F. and J. Larimo (1998) 'The Impact of Culture on the Strategies of Multinational Enterprises: Does National Origin Affect Ownership Decisions'. *Journal of International Business Studies* (29): 515–38.

Hennart, J.-F., D.-J. Kim, *et al.* (1997) *Why are Joint Ventures Short-lived? An Investigation of Japanese Affiliated in the United States*. Illinois, University of Illinois.

Hennart, J.-F. and Y.-R. Park (1993) 'Greenfield vs Acquisition: The Strategy of Japanese Investors in the United States'. *Management Science* 39(No. 9, September 1993): 1054–70.

——(1994) Location, Governance, and Strategic Determinants for Japanese Manufacturing Investment in the United States. CCC 0413-2095/94/060419-18, College of Commerce and Business Administration, University of Illinois at Urbana-Champaign 15: 419–36.

Hennart, J.-F. and S. Reddy (1993) The Choice Between Mergers/Acquisitions and Joint Ventures: The Case of Japanese Investors in the United States. CIBER.

Hennart, J.-F., T. Roehl, *et al.* (1997) *Are Joint Ventures with Local Firms an Efficient way to Enter a Culturally Distant Market? The Case of Japanese Entry into the United States*. Champaign, University of Illinois.

Hill, C. W. L., P. Hwang, *et al.* (1990) 'An Eclectic Theory of the Choice of International Entry Mode'. *Strategic Management Journal* (11): 117–28.

Hymer, S. H. (1976) *The International Operations of National Firms: A Study of Direct Foreign Investment*. Cambridge, Mass., MIT Press.

Itami, M. and T. W. Roehl (1987) *Mobilizing Invisible Assets*. Cambridge Mass., Harvard University Press.

Jarillo, J. C. and J. I. Martinez (1990) 'Different Roles for Subsidiaries: The Case of Multinational Corporations'. *Strategic Management Journal* (15): 579–601.

Johanson, J. and J.-E. Vahlne (1977) 'The Internationalization Process of the Firm: A Model of Knowledge Development and Increasing Foreign Market Commitments'. *Journal of International Business Studies* (8): 23–32.

Johnson, H. G. (1970) *The Efficiency and Welfare Implications of the International Corporation*. The International Corporation. C. P. Kindleberger (ed.). Cambridge, Mass., MIT Press: 35–56.

Jones, G. and C. Hill (1988) 'Transaction Cost Analysis of Strategy-Structure Choice'. *Strategic Management Journal* (9): 159–72.

Kim, W. C. and P. Hwang (1992) 'Global Strategy and Multinationals' Entry Mode Choice'. *Journal of International Business Studies* (First Quarter 1992): 29–53.

Knickerbocker, F. T. (1973) *Oligopolistic Reaction and Multinational Enterprise*. Division of Research Graduate School of Business Administration, Harvard University, Boston, Mass.

Kogut, B. (1983) 'Foreign Direct Investment as a Sequential Process'. *The Multinational Corporation in the 1980s*. C. P. K. a. D. Audretsch. Cambridge, Mass., MIT Press.

Kogut, B. (1988) 'Joint Ventures: Theoretical and Empirical Perspectives'. *Strategic Management Journal* (9): 319–32.

Kogut, B. (1993) 'Learning, or the Importance of Being Intert: Country Imprinting and International Competition'. *Organisation Theory and the Multinational Corporation.* S. G. a. D. E. Westney. New York: 136–54.

Kogut, B. and H. Singh (1988) 'The Effect of National Culture on the Choice of Entry Mode'. *Journal of International Business Studies* (Fall 1988): 411–32.

Kogut, B. and U. Zander (1993) 'Knowledge of the Firm and the Evolutionary Theory of the Multinational Corporation'. *Journal of International Business Studies* (24): 625–46.

Kwon, Y.-C. and M. Y. Hu (1995) 'Comparative Analysis of Export-oriented and Foreign Production-oriented Firms' Foreign Market Entry Decisions'. *Management International Review* (35): 325–36.

Levitt, T. (1983) 'The Globalisation of Markets'. *Harvard Business Review* (May–June): 92–102.

Luostarinen, R. (1977) *The Internationalization of the Firm.* Helsinki, Acta Academic Oeconomica Helsingiensis.

Madhok, A. (1997) 'Cost, Value and Foreign Market Entry Mode: The Transaction and the Firm'. *Strategic Management Journal* (18): 39–61.

Maitland, E., E. Rose, *et al.* (2001) 'Patterned Growth? The Dynamics of Multinational Expansion'. *Asia-Pacific Issues in International Business.* S. S. Gray, McGaughey and W. Purcell (eds). Cheltenham, Edward Elgar.

McManus, J. (1972) 'The Theory of the Multinational Firm'. *The Multinational Firm and the Nation State.* G. Paquet (ed.). Ontario, Collier Macmillan.

Millington, A. and B. Bayliss (1990) 'The Process of Internationalisation: UK Companies in the E.C'. *Management International Review* (30): 151–61.

Mortimer (1997) *Going for Growth: Business Programmes for Investment, Innovation and Export.* Canberra, Commonwealth of Australia Government Printing Office.

Nelson, R. and S. Winter (1982) *An Evolutionary Theory of Economic Change.* Cambridge, Mass., Harvard University Press.

Newbould, G., B. P., *et al.* (1978) *Going International: The Experience of Smaller Companies Overseas.* New York, John Wiley and Sons.

Nicholas, S. (1982) 'British Multinational Investment Before 1939'. *Journal of European Economic History* (11): 605–30.

——(1983) 'Agency Contracts, Institutional Modes, and the Transition to Foreign Direct Investment by British Manufacturing Multinationals Before 1939'. *The Journal of Economic History* (XLIII): 675–86.

——(1991) 'The Expansion of British Multinational Companies: Testing for Managerial Failure'. *New Perspectives on the Late Victorian Economy: Essays in Quantitative Economic History 1860–1914.* J. Foreman-Peck (ed.). Cambridge, Cambridge University Press: 125–45.

Nicholas, S. and E. Maitland (1997) 'The Dynamics of Multinational Enterprise Growth: Theory, History and Empirical Evidence', *Business, Public Policy and Performance*: Proceedings of the Economic History Society of Australia and New Zealand. Carberra, ANU Economic History Department.

Nicholas, S., D. Merrett, *et al.* (1996) 'Japanese FDI in Australia in the 1990s: Manufacturing, Financial Services and Tourism'. *Pacific Economic Papers* No. 256 (June 1996).

North, D. (1990) *Institutions, Institutional Change and Economic Performance.* Cambridge, Cambridge University Press.

Penrose, E. T. (1959) *The Theory of the Growth of the Firm.* London, Basil Blackwell.

Peteraf, M. A. (1993) 'The Cornerstones of Competitive Advantage: A Resource-Based View'. *Strategic Management Journal* (14): 179–91.

Porter, M. (1980) *Competitive Strategy: Techniques for Analysing Industries and Competitors*. New York, Free Press.

——(1990) *The Competitive Advantage of Nations*. New York, Free Press.

Prahalad, C. K. and Y. Doz (1987) *The Multinational Mission: Balancing Local Demands and Global Vision*. New York, Free Press.

Reed, R. and R. DeFillippe (1990) 'Causal Ambiguity, Barriers to Imitation and Sustainable Competitive Advantages'. *Academy of Management Review* (15): 88–102.

Rose, E. and K. Ito (1998) 'Interactions: The International Investment Patterns of Japanese Automobile Manufacturers'. *Global Competition and Market Entry Strategies*. J.-F. Hennart (ed.). Amsterdam, Elsevier Science.

Rose, E. L. and K. Ito (1996) *Competitive Interactions: The International Investment Patterns of Japanese Automobile Manufacturers*. Los Angeles, University of Southern California.

Rugman, A. M. (1981) *Inside the Multinationals: The Economics of Internal Markets*. London, Croom Helm.

——(1982) 'Internalisation and Non-equity Forms of International Involvement'. *New Theories of the Multinational Enterprise*. A. M. Rugman (ed.). Bechenham, Kent, Croom Helm.

Stopford, J. M. and L.T. Wells (1972) *Managing the Multinational Enterprise*. New York, Basic Books.

Teece, D. J. (1980) 'Economies of Scope and the Scope of the Enterprise'. *Journal of Economic Behavior and Organization* (1): 223–47.

——(1981) 'The Market for Know-How and the Efficient International Transfer of Technology'. *Annals of the Academy of Political and Social Science* (458): 81–96.

——(1982) 'Towards an Economic Theory of Multiproduct Firm'. *Journal of Economic Behaviour and Organization* (3): 39–63.

——(1985) 'Multinational Enterprise, Internal Governance, and Industrial Organization'. *AEA Papers and Proceedings* (May 1985): 232–9.

——(1986) 'Transaction Cost Economics and the Multinational Enterprise'. *Journal of Economic Behaviour and Organization* (7): 21–45.

Teece, D. J., G. Pisano, *et al.* (1997) 'Dynamic Capabilities and Strategic Management'. *Strategic Management Journal* 18(7): 509–33.

Turnbull, P. (1987) 'A Challenge to the Stages Theory of the Internationalization Process'. *Managing Export Entry and Expansion*. P. R. a. S. Reid. New York, Praeger.

Welch, L. and R. Luostarinen (1988) 'Internationalization: Evolution of a Concept'. *Journal of General Management* (Winter): 34–57.

Wernerfelt, B. (1984) 'A Resource-Based View of the Firm'. *Strategic Management Journal* (5): 171–80.

Wernerfelt, B. and C. A. Montgomery (1988) 'Tobin's q and the Importance of Focus in Firm Performance'. *American Economic Review* (78): 246–50.

Wilkins, M. (1988) 'The Free-Standing Company, 1870–1914: An Important Type of British Foreign Direct Investment'. *Economic History Review* XLI(2): 259–82.

Williamson, O. (1975) *Markets and Hierarchies: Analysis and Antitrust Implications*. New York, Free Press.

——(1979) 'Transaction-Cost Economics: The Governance of Contractual Relations'. *Journal of Law and Economics* (22): 233–61.

——(1985) The Economic Institutions of Capitalism. New York, Free Press.

——(1999) 'Strategic Research: Governance and Corporate Perspectives'. *Strategic Management Journal* (20): 1087–108.

Willig, R. (1979) 'Multiproduct Technology and Market Structure'. *American Economic Review* (69): 177–83.

Wilson, B. D. (1980) 'The Propensity of Multinational Companies to Expand Through Acquisitions'. *Journal of International Buisness Studies* 11(1980): 59–65.

Woodcock, C. P., P. W. Beamish *et al.* (1994) 'Ownership-based Entry Mode Strategies and International Performance'. *Journal of International Buisness Studies* (1994): 253–73.

Yan, A. and M. Zeng (1999) 'International Joint Venture Instability: A Critique of Previous Research, a Reconceptualization, and Directions for Future Research'. *Journal of International Business Studies* (30): 397–414.

Zander, U. and B. Kogut (1995) 'Knowledge and the Speed of the Transfer and Imitation of Organizational Capabilities: An Empirical Test'. *Organization Science* 6(1): 76–92.

Zejan, M. C. (1990) 'New Ventures or Acquisitions. The Choice of Swedish Multinational Enterprises'. *Journal of Industrial Economics* 38(3): 349–55.

3 FDI

Strategic issues

Ron Edwards

Introduction

The purpose of this paper is to explore the strategic issues associated with foreign direct investment (FDI). The literature review is based on an extensive reading of works categorised as international business research. The review aims to identify the central themes in the international business literature in relation to the establishment of foreign value adding activities. Since this chapter cannot fairly review the whole field of international business it will limit discussion to three fields:

1. the link between strategy and structure of international firms;
2. stage models of internationalisation which seek to interpret the choices as part of a longer term, strategic process;
3. strategic aspects of location and entry mode choices for international businesses.

The section titled 'Literature review' will survey the relevant theoretical literature on the topics of internationalisation, international strategy and strategic aspects of mode choice and locational choice. The next section, 'Identification of a research agenda' identifies research issues of particular relevance to Australia and the last section 'Impediments to implementing the research agenda' discusses the factors which currently impede pursuit of these research issues.

Literature review

Different scholars have defined strategy and strategic management in different ways. A common element of most definitions is that it is a pattern or plan that integrates an organisation's major goals, structure, policies and sequences of actions into a cohesive whole. A firm's strategy supplies a sense of direction for the enterprise. It assists in coordinating the geographic, functional and product bases of the firm, minimises intra-organisational conflict and serves as a guide for decision making (Quinn, 1980; Hill, 1997; John *et al.*, 1997).

Internationalisation has been defined as the process of increasing involvement in international operations (Welch and Luostarinen, 1988). A strategic interpretation of this process focuses upon the systematic, ongoing development and change in the international firm in terms of scope of business activities across different countries, choices of entry mode including exporting, licensing and foreign production and, in the case of the latter, ownership arrangements and systems to coordinate these activities. The financing arrangements firms put in place to support their foreign operations is just one part of the broader picture.

The chapter is restricted to research themes which address the process and strategic dimension of the international firm's formation and development. It therefore gives scant attention to the dominating theories on foreign investments, Dunning's (1980) eclectic paradigm and the internalisation theory. Neither of these theories elucidate the process of internationalisation. Common to both these approaches is the assumption that each foreign market entry and mode choice is made in isolation (Eriksson *et al.*, 1997). Instead, two models which have sought to focus on the long term, sequential nature of internationalisation will be examined here: Vernon's (1966) product life cycle model and the (Uppsala) internationalisation process model (Johanson and Vahlne, 1977; Eriksson *et al.*, 1997). These models satisfy two criteria of a strategic interpretation internationalisation, that is, that it is a long-term process and that the different aspects of internationalisation are interrelated with each other and with the firm's strategy.

The product life cycle model seeks to bridge international trade theory and the individual firm's perspective of investment in product development. Vernon emphasised the role of product innovation and the standardisation of production methodologies over time as well as the gain and loss of comparative advantage of particular countries in the product as the maturation process takes place. He identified different stages in the life cycle of a product, each with different implications for the internationalisation of the innovative company. The first stage is domestic in nature, the home country being the major market. Exports to other industrial countries support the emerging goal of achieving economies of scale in production. As the production process comes to be better understood and documented the firm moves to the second stage. Production is transferred to other countries where wages are lower and technically skilled workers are available, the production process no longer requiring the highly skilled and innovative personnel involved in the original product development. Later again, in the mature stage, the production process becomes fully standardised and the market very competitive, the consequence of the production technology diffusing to rival firms, manufacturing is transferred to countries with low labour costs.

This model is of interest because it brings exporting and foreign production into a single explanation of foreign market entry. It also offers a developmental view on relocation of production activities, with locational changes being driven by various national characteristics such as technological know-how, demand and labour costs. However, the descriptive value of the model is weak for products with short lives, a circumstance which applies to more and more products (McKiernan, 1992). The applicability of this model is also limited if products are developed in companies that already have considerable operations in other countries (Vernon, 1979).

A number of theories, mainly inspired by Johanson, Wiedersheim-Paul and Vahlne, and dubbed the *internationalisation process* or *Uppsala* model, explain modal choice on the basis of a firm's knowledge gained through experience in international markets. This model posits that internationalisation occurs in stages, commencing with irregular export activity (Johanson and Wiedersheim-Paul, 1975; Cavusgil, 1984; Johanson and Vahlne, 1990). Businesses move from irregular exporting, through exporting via an independent agent, the use of a sales subsidiary, to, eventually, full production in foreign markets. Progression through the stages is driven by experiential knowledge accumulation. Each stage calls for more commitment to international markets and enables firms to gain in knowledge, skill and confidence. Because the knowledge relates to the existing mode of operation, firms tend to move gradually, adopting new modes which make most use of past experience.

The Uppsala model has a second strand which asserts that the locational pattern of FDI is determined by 'psychic distance', defined as the costs of acquiring and internalising relevant information about business conditions in other countries, the perception of risk and uncertainty involved in foreign operations, and the resources required to gain access to foreign networks (Johanson and Vahlne, 1977). The model asserts that the costs involved in overcoming psychic distance decline over time as a function of the experience gained by the firm in each market. Firms are thus expected to enter familiar, probably neighbouring markets first because of their historical familiarity and then to fan out into progressively more remote territory.

There are three exceptions to this incremental process (Johanson and Vahlne, 1990; Andersen, 1993). First, large firms can take bigger internationalisation steps. Second, when market conditions are stable, knowledge can be gained in ways other than through experience. Third, experience in similar markets may allow a firm to generalise this experience. These exceptions allow firms to jump stages.

In contrast to Dunning's eclectic paradigm and the internalisation model the Upsalla model explains internationalisation as a pattern of growth. It is based on behavioural theories, with assumptions about lack of information and the importance of perceived risk and uncertainty (Cavusgil, 1984). In this view, the internationalisation process is not seen as a sequence of deliberately planned steps founded on rational analysis. Instead, it is the incremental nature of successive learning through stages of increasing foreign commitment to foreign markets, that is, the main characteristic of the internationalisation process, which according to Johanson and Vahlne (1990), will proceed along the presented stages whether strategic decisions are made in this direction or not.

The Uppsala model and the literature it spawned have been subject to criticism. These shortcomings, which have been accepted by Johanson and Vahlne (1990), include failing to explain how or why internationalisation starts and for emphasising the characteristics of firms in each stage but giving insufficient attention to the causes of modal change. Critics have argued that the model does not fully explain multi-step mode changes or disinvestment (McKiernan, 1992), is limited in applicability to the early stages of internationalisation and is highly deterministic in nature (Melin, 1992; Anderson, 1993; Calof and Beamish, 1995). The model tells us little about the internationalisation process of experienced companies having the benefit of many years of international activities in many countries. Furthermore, the model does not pay enough attention to acquisition, joint venture and strategic alliances as pathways to internationalisation, options that alter the model's experiential knowledge imperative.

Forsgren (1989) has argued that the psychic distance theory is only valid in the early stages of internationalisation when lack of market knowledge and market resources are constraining forces. These cease to be as important when the firm has activities in a lot of countries. A study by Nordstrom (1991), for example, found that, while psychic distance played a role, market potential was the most important explanatory factor in locational choice. Nevertheless, the Uppsala model's staging and psychic distance constructs retain wide acceptance (Melin, 1992; Anderson, 1993; Calof and Beamish, 1995).

Both stage models discussed suffer from distinct limitations. They pose a unitary progression where each stage must occur in an ordered progression. Each stage is a necessary precursor of succeeding stages (Van de Ven, 1992). Each stage is the result of predetermined factors with unforeseen environmental developments playing no role. They disregard individual differences between large and small firms, service providers and manufacturers, and their deterministic nature offers little scope for managers to make voluntary strategic choices beyond the initial decision to expand into foreign markets.

The internationalisation process school, for all its weaknesses, retains considerable influence based mainly on the very large number of empirical studies which have identified a sequential pattern of entry mode choices by MNCs. Hence it is somewhat surprising that McKinsey and Company (1993) observed a growing incidence of 'born global' firms, those which began exporting within two years of commencement of operation, among the population of Australian manufacturing exporters. This development may reflect the late entry of Australian firms into the internationalisation process, giving these firms the opportunity to shorten or skip the initial 'domestic only', or primary stage in the Uppsala model. If so, it belies Johanson and Vahlne's contention that corporate strategy has no opportunity to circumvent the core role of experiential knowledge in entry mode choice. 'Born global' behaviour has been observed in other countries Madsen and Servais (1997). Welch and Luostarinen (1988), for example, found small English, Australian and Swedish firms skipped various stages and had FDIs unexpectedly quickly. Similarly, Edwards and Buckley (1998) found the majority of Australian manufacturing firms which had invested in facilities in Britain had not passed through an export stage.

Madsen and Servais (1997) attribute this behaviour to new market conditions, technological developments and changes in the capabilities of entrepreneurs. First, the trend to specialisation and the development of niche markets, especially in high-tech products, may force firms to look for export markets very early in their history to secure economies of scale. Second, new production technology has meant that internationally competitive levels of costs can be achieved at lower levels of production than applied in the past. Efficiencies in transportation of goods and people mean that this barrier to international trade has been reduced. Third, entrepreneurs have more international skills than in the past based on changes in education, travel and the fact that many start new businesses having the advantage of experience and networks stemming from working with large, international firms previously. The uncertainty which the Uppsala model asserts determines that slow evolution of internationalisation is therefore less significant than in the past.

A third area of the literature which identifies and seeks to explain internationalisation decisions in a long-term and integrated manner is that which focuses on the organisational arrangements firms must put in place to coordinate and control their overseas operations. This literature argues that the coordination and integration of the firm's activities will influence choices on the ownership arrangements (wholly owned subsidiaries or joint venture) and on the locational settings of the subsidiaries. In the first major study of organisational structures of international firms, Stopford and Wells (1972) found that managers in MNCs had followed similar strategies and had developed similar organisational structures in quite different industries. Based on a survey of 187 large, US manufacturing firms each having manufacturing facilities in at least six foreign countries, Stopford and Wells (1972) observed epochs of internationalisation. In their first forays into the international market place firms established relatively autonomous foreign subsidiaries. They called this the *international* stage. It was followed by a stage in which the MNC established an *international business division*, separate from domestic operations, intended to increase control and coordination of the expanding international activities. This division was responsible for all foreign activities of the firm and became its locus of international expertise (Egelhoff, 1988).

In time, as the proportion of foreign sales to home market sales grew, the autonomous international division came to constrain the internationalisation process since only the manager of the international division had responsibility beyond the home market. In the third stage, two new types of global structures replaced the international division: *worldwide product division* and *geographic area division*. In the former, the domestic product division assumed worldwide responsibility for its particular line of products. It centralised and integrated strategic decision making for a product line. This structure is especially suited to realising economies of scale in R&D, manufacturing and marketing (Martinez and Jarillo, 1991). A worldwide product division was more common for firms with great product diversity but which were less sensitive to local political and economic conditions since it emphasised optimising performance on a global basis.

For firms with less product diversity but considerable geographic spread, a regional division was created which would be responsible for sales of all products in the region. Each region would have a headquarters which was responsible for all the company's products within its geographic area. Consequently, this structure tend to coordinate around and optimise performance within a geographic area. Coordination between areas might be poor (Egelhoff, 1988). To the extent that political and economic conditions within an area were more similar than they were between areas, this structure led to strategies that were more responsive to local conditions than those of a worldwide product division.

Stopford and Wells (1972) also identified a matrix model which was a combination of these two structures. Subsidiaries report along two different channels, to both regional headquarters and the product division. This may provide a strategic compromise that is both locally responsive and achieves economies of scale in product development and marketing but is likely to be costly in terms of numbers of management personnel and in conflict resolution (Egelhoff, 1988; Hill, 1997). In other cases hybrid models were used with some products sold on a worldwide basis and others through regional divisions (Stopford and Wells, 1972; Egelhoff, 1988).

Franko's (1976) study of eighty-five large European industrial firms, found a different pattern of internationalisation. More firms retained the initial parent–subsidiary form with direct ties between the parent and each subsidiary than had been observed by Stopford and Wells (1972). In this study, as firms expanded their international activities, most firms did not use an international division but went directly to a worldwide product structure. Studies of Scandinavian firms have shown that they have followed the European pattern, retaining the parent subsidiary pattern until the 1970s when most firms adopted the global product division structure (Hedlund, 1984).

The studies by Stopford and Wells (1972) and Franko (1976) gave valuable insights into the historic development of international strategies and structures and identify *which* particular structures and strategies emerged. However, their contributions are far more modest in regard to *why* these changed over time and *how* the changes were carried out. Although they take a longitudinal approach, they present steady states of structural forms rather than describing the processes of formation and implementation related to these structures (Melin, 1992).

Egelhoff (1988) found that the Stopford and Wells (1972) model was limited in that it did not address the impact of foreign manufacturing on the choice of structure and this factor. He argued that this was important in explaining the choice between area division and worldwide product division. When a parent achieves foreign sales primarily through exports the primary interdependency is between foreign entities and the parent. A worldwide product division structure provides the kind of information processing and integration necessary to coordinate this kind of dependency. However, when foreign sales are supported with extensive foreign manufacturing, important interdependencies usually develop between foreign subsidiaries in a region as the MNC tries to replace the economies of scale lost through central production with regionally rationalised production. The area division structure provides the kind of information processing and integration required to coordinate this kind of interdependency.

Emerging in the mid-1980s, the 'process school' of research in international management criticised the Stopford and Wells and Franko interpretation of organisational structure and strategy as being too *architectural* (Doz and Prahalad,

1984). Instead, they saw managers constantly facing the competing imperatives of cost reduction, achieved through economies of scale in rationalisation of global operations, controlled at the centre, and the need to accommodate the differing needs of governments and customers in individual national markets. No unique structure provides the solution to this dilemma. They argued that senior management develop *multifocal* strategies where responsiveness and integration needs are weighed against each other separately for each decision. MNCs are therefore not symmetrical. Different subsidiaries adopt a different stance on the integration versus localisation dilemma (Doz, 1986). This school emphasises the functioning and capabilities of the MNC rather than its structural form. Informal coordination mechanisms such as normative values and patterns of communication replace hierarchical control. The main driving forces for change are environmental, with strategy adapting to opportunity (Martinez and Jarillo, 1991; Birkinshaw and Morrison, 1995).

From this perspective, Bartlett and Ghoshal (1991) see the European model described earlier as a *decentralised federation* of assets and responsibilities which allow foreign units to respond to local differences. The US model, by contrast, is a *coordinated federation* where the subsidiaries are more dependent on the parent company, being subject to more formal control in pursuit of economies of scale. They also identified a third model, dubbed the global organisation model, which they believed fits the managerial norms of Japanese MNCs. This can be characterised as a *centralised hub* in which most assets and decisions are centralised and foreign operations are used as pipelines to a generic global market. The subsidiaries are tightly controlled and highly dependent on the parent. Others in this school identify a trend to heterarchial MNCs with many centres, in which traditional headquarter functions are dispersed, subsidiaries have responsibility for strategy and where each part of the company shares information (Hedlund, 1984; Birkinshaw and Morrison, 1995).

However, the school has been criticised as lacking theoretical underpinnings and relying unrealistically on corporate culture to coordinate managerial decisions. On the other hand, the school has identified new organisational patterns of MNCs and, usefully, they have emphasised the need for multidimensional approaches to interpreting international strategy (Melin, 1992).

Hill *et al.* (1990) in seeking to develop an all-encompassing theory, link the organisational structures, as described by Franko, Stopford and Wells and Bartlett and Ghoshal to mode choice. They argue that this choice will be determined by a strategic assessment of three variables: the degree of control offered by the mode; the resource commitment the mode requires and the risk the firm must bear. *Control* refers to authority over operational and strategic decision making. The least level of control is offered by licensing and the highest by a wholly owned subsidiary. In the case of licensing, control is given to the licensee in return for monetary payments and a commitment to abide by any terms set out in the licensing contract. In the case of the wholly owned subsidiary, control over day-to-day operations and certain strategic decisions *may* be delegated to the foreign subsidiary but ultimate control always remains with the parent. In the case of joint venture, the level of control is dependent on the ownership split. Control is shared. Thus the level of control of a joint venture falls between that associated with licensing and that of a wholly owned subsidiary.

Resource commitment refers to the extent to which the mode requires dedicated assets, tangible or intangible, that cannot be redeployed to alternative uses without cost. In the case of licensing the licensee bears most of the cost of opening up and serving the foreign market. The resource commitment is therefore low. By contrast, a wholly owned subsidiary requires that the MNC bear all the resource cost. Once again, the level of resource commitment of a joint venture falls between these extremes, depending on the resource sharing between the venture partners.

Dissemination risk refers to the risk that firm-specific advantages in know-how will be expropriated. Technological and marketing know-how constitutes the basis of the competitive advantage of many MNCs (Casson, 1982; Caves, 1982). The MNC will not want to see firm-specific know-how disseminated as this reduces the future income flow.

Strategy influences the choice of entry mode, and thus the level of FDI required, primarily through the control requirements that the strategies entail. Different strategies require different degrees of control over the operating and strategic decisions of foreign affiliates and thus different entry modes. A central strategic decision of the MNC is whether to adopt a 'multidomestic' or 'global' strategy (being refinements of the structures identified by Stopford and Well, Franko and Bartlett and Ghoshal). In the former, subsidiaries may have their own marketing function, autonomous manufacturing facilities, products may vary with local consumer preferences and local strategy may vary depending on differences in competitive conditions. Assuming dissemination risk is not a particular concern, this implies that only a low degree of control is required. Thus, MNCs adopting a multidomestic strategy may prefer to choose joint venture or licensing entry mode as they represent a low-cost option, that is, they require less resource commitments.

However, where there is a potential for developing standardised products for the global market place, realising considerable economies of scale, firms may prefer a global strategy. This involves forgoing some of the benefits of a multidomestic strategy, preferring the cost savings of scale economies to any demand advantages of product differentiation. Global strategy may involve dispersing elements of the production process around the world on the basis of cost minimisation, with subsidiaries exchanging parts and products with other subsidiaries in the MNC's global system. Coordination of such an interdependent global production system necessarily involves a high degree of control over the operations of subsidiaries (Egelhoff, 1988; Martinez and Jarillo, 1991). The various production units must accept the parent's instructions on what they should produce, how much they should produce and how the output should be priced for transfer between units. Licensees and joint venture partners are unlikely to accept such a subservient role (Hill *et al.*, 1990). Thus, firms pursuing a global strategy are likely to favour a high-control entry mode, that is, wholly owned subsidiaries.

Where a firm is part of an international industry with a limited number of competitors who confront each other in many different national markets, oligopolistic interdependence may influence the strategic choices of the firms involved. For example, when they enter markets they may have strategic objectives that go beyond the standard assessment of cost and revenue. They may enter the home market of a rival, even though that market may not be viable on strictly economic grounds, simply to check their rival's ability to compete elsewhere. Such strategies must be controlled by the parent. Pricing, marketing and transfer pricing decisions must support the overall strategy. A foreign operation may even be required to operate at a loss, at least for a period of time. Such a strategy might be designed to check the rival's activities in third country markets, advantaging the profit of the group but disadvantaging profitability in the particular market concerned. Licensees and joint venture partners are unlikely to accept such conditions. Thus, when there is a need for global strategic coordination, a wholly owned subsidiary will be the favoured entry mode (Hill *et al.*, 1990).

Some writers have identified a trend for MNCs, under increasing pressure to reduce costs, to move away from multidomestic toward global structures (Levitt, 1983). Birkinshaw (1996) for example, argues that increasing liberalisation of trade has made the multidomestic structure uncompetitive. In his assessment, many subsidiary operations of firms with multidomestic structures have been closed and others have taken on specialised roles involving greater integration of the MNC's global operations. Two main types of specialisation are available: *rationalisation-integration* and *world product mandate*. Rationalisation-integration occurs when a subsidiary produces a component to be used by the MNC elsewhere in the production chain. The parent company retains control of all associated activities, notably the design and development of the product. The world product mandate, by contrast, gives the subsidiary responsibility for product development and export marketing. This arrangement ensures that high-value adding activities are undertaken in the subunit as well as providing its management with the opportunity to develop and grow the mandate over time.

Both rationalisation-integration and world product mandate versions of global structures imply a greater degree of interaction between and integration of the various units that comprise a global firm. In this light, MNCs may be seen as interoganisational networks in which, instead of all strategic decisions being made by the parent and handed down the hierarchy to each subsidiary, multiple centres of expertise around the world share products, expertise and initiatives (Ghoshal and Bartlett, 1990). Such organisational structures make the participation of separately owned licensees or joint venture partners problematic. Each transfer of product, knowledge, strategic initiatives will need to be tracked and accounted for in the division of profit. The more complex, the more integrated the group, the more likely wholly-owned subsidiaries will be preferred to licensing and joint venture arrangements, with the consequence that FDI will be that much greater than if shared ownership arrangements.

Market liberalisation in a regional context will also influence the strategies of international firms, providing incentive for more interdependency and integration within the MNC's regional network. It also encourages firms to commit FDI to establish 'insider status' within the regional trade area. Hirsh (1992) studied the competitive position of firms outside regional trade areas (RTAs) as against insiders, and the position of insider firms relative to each other, and this may lead to increased FDI to the region. He concluded that outsider firms exporting to an RTA are disadvantaged by comparison with insider firms exporting to fellow members. The 'inside' exporter enjoys reduced costs from the removal of tariffs or reduced border costs, whereas the foreign firm exporting to the RTA experiences no cost savings. Additional export opportunities are created for 'insider' firms as a result of this advantage. Hence, Australian firms have the opportunity to capitalise on the trade creation effects available to members by establishing subsidiaries in member countries. Such a strategy allows firms to minimise the trade diversion effect that would apply should they remain exclusively domiciled outside the group. It allows them better access to the expanded market. Consequently, regional trade liberalisation will induce firms to reconsider their entry strategies, with many replacing export strategies with local production.

Firms with existing operations in the trade area are likely to reorganise in two ways. First firms will adapt to the changed pattern of regional comparative advantage and will pursue economies of large-scale production made possible by the larger market (Doz, 1986; Cantwell, 1992). Rather than a multiplicity of relatively small, protected industries spread across the region, economic integration will see those regions with a comparative advantage in a particular industry expand that industry. Second, firms may reorganise the geographic location of their production facilities. Horizontal integration within multinational firms can be expected to decrease and vertical integration to increase. Where firms have a number of plants across the region, each serving a geographic segment of the market and having a similar production process, they may seek to achieve economies of scale by rationalising production, concentrating their operations in one location and thereby avoiding the cost of duplication. Alternatively, the possibility of promoting the internal division of labour within multiplant firms can be expected to lead to increased vertical integration. That is, firms will separate activities spatially in order to reduce costs. This may result in plants becoming more specialised and the number of plants may increase. Production will be sited where the input used most intensively in a particular process can be acquired at least cost. In time, this may lead to a divorce of locations for assembly and research and development (Cantwell, 1992). Such a situation calls for a high degree of control over each of the subunits that make up the regional MNC network. Control is strongest in the wholly-owned subsidiary structure. Hence, regional trade liberalisation may lead to an increase in FDI by firms to strengthen their control over their subsidiaries.

Many environmental factors such as country risk, location familiarity and demand conditions have been identified in the literature as being significant in determining the choice of entry mode. Hill *et al.* (1990) argue that these factors can be interpreted as impacting on strategic decision making through their implications for resource commitment, control and strategic flexibility. FDI creates sunk costs, establishing a physical and personal link in the foreign country which will remain even if the original market conditions which attracted the firm cease to apply (Buckley and Casson, 1981). Hence, firms may not be willing to commit resources to high-risk countries, preferring entry through exporting (Agarwal and Ramaswami, 1992). Firms may seek to limit their exposure to country risk by minimising their resource commitment and increasing their ability to exit high-risk markets without taking a substantial loss should the environment worsen (Hill *et al.*, 1992). The appeal of this strategy is enhanced if, as found by Bradley (1977), joint ventures with local partners are less likely to be expropriated than wholly-owned subsidiaries.

A strategic perspective on locational choice emphasises the potential role of any one location in relation to the whole of the MNC. Rather than interpreting the locational choice for any one subsidiary in isolation, this strand looks to the role of the subsidiary within the interdependent network of subsidiaries belonging to the MNC (Kogut, 1985; Kim and Hwang, 1992). Some locations may be viable for the MNC even if they have no potential to earn a profit in their market. For example, a subsidiary may be established to act as a competitive scanning post in an otherwise unprofitable market or to check the cash flow of a potential global competitor (Kim and Hwang, 1992).

A global strategy approach to market penetration involves building significant market share in globally strategic markets. Such countries are important beyond their stand-alone attractiveness. They may be a source of volume to meet economies of scale, the home of global competitors, or they may be a major source of industry innovation. Failure to compete in strategic markets can undermine competitiveness elsewhere (Lovelock and Yip, 1996). This is especially true for network firms such as airlines, financial services and logistics firms. For example, no service firm with global ambitions can afford not to have a presence in New York, London and Tokyo.

In summary, a strategic interpretation of FDI looks to the manner in which the investment contributes to the achievement of the firm's long-term objectives. The internationalisation process model, Vernon's product life cycle model and various theories of corporate control and coordination have been examined to ascertain what insights they offer to understanding the relationship between FDI and strategy. The mechanistic nature of the product life cycle and internationalisation process models meant they did not offer a role for strategic decision making either in mode choice or locational choice. The literature addressing corporate governance systems, on the other hand, suggests that FDI, especially that funding wholly-owned subsidiaries, is likely in MNCs that have adopted integrated global structures of governance because of the control this mode offers, control being essential in highly integrated MNCs to ensure that the interdependent subunits behave in a mutually supportive manner.

Identification of a research agenda

Research examining the internationalisation of the Australian economy has focussed primarily on macroeconomic aggregates such as the levels of imports and exports and the growing importance of these in the Australian GDP (e.g. see Snape *et al.*, 1993; Athukorala, 1995; Pomfret, 1995). Relatively little attention has been given to the internationalisation of the economy through offshore production by Australian firms or through production within Australia by foreign multinationals, the exceptions being the McKinsey and Company (1993), Yetton Davis and Swan (1991), Department of Industry, Science and Technology (1994) and Bureau of Industry Economics (1995). This section will propose a range of research questions which might give some direction for scholarly activity in this area.

The dynamic nature of internationalisation, and associated financing methods such as FDI, calls for research that is responsive to the longitudinal character of internationalisation as a development process through time. While it is valuable to study individual events, a more complete picture is supplied when the whole development of a firm from the time of its founding to the present time is examined (Melin, 1992). Hence, a rich, broadly focussed study that results from careful examination of a few organisations over a long period of time may be superior to statistically rigorous but narrowly focussed studies (Huff and Reger, 1987).

Stages model of internationalisation, including those of Vahlne and Johanson, Vernon, and evolutionary models of international structure, including those of Stopford and Wells, Franko and Bartlett and Goshal, are based on surveys of manufacturing firms. The internationalisation of service firms and firms that combine goods and services needs more attention (Lovelock and Yip, 1996). This observation is highly relevant for Australian scholars as the majority of Australian FDI abroad has been directed to service firms (ABS, 1997).

Research should give attention to new patterns of internationalisation, including that of 'born global' firms. Have McKinsey's 'born global' firms performed as well as those Australian firms that have pursued more traditional, sequential entry methods? Have services firms followed the same pattern? Do Australian firms move more quickly through the exporting stage, or even skip the exporting stage, more rapidly than firms from other countries? If so, do geographic, structural or historical factors explain the difference?

Research should give more attention to the acquisition mode. Firms with what organisational patterns are more likely to acquire existing firms? In what stage of internationalisation is acquisition more likely? Such research should not assume that such decisions are always rational. It may be that irrational factors are important at times. For example, it might be that the rush to acquire businesses in Europe prior to 1992 and to acquire companies in Asia in the mid-1990s reflected a bandwagon effect with firms developing strategies to legitimise their investments after the decision has been made (Hellgren and Melin, 1991).

Research might also give attention to a broader range of entry modes beyond exporting, licensing and FDI. Strategic alliances with local or other foreign firms may involve no transfer of funds. Alliances are another entry mode option which deliver similar strategic advantages to joint ventures but have received little attention in the literature beyond those firms whose home country is either the US or Japan (Yoon *et al.*, 1996; Tse *et al.*, 1997).

Studies of structure and coordination of MNCs have been characterised by cross-sectoral approaches and findings expressed in static models (Melin, 1992). How and why do control and coordination mechanisms change over time and how do these changes interplay with strategic actions? Have Australian firms altered their international organisational structures over time? If so, have they followed the US pattern incorporating international divisions, the European pattern that does so to a lesser degree, some other pattern, or none at all?

Changes in the structures of MNCs might have policy implications for Australian governments. Does Australia have less to offer MNCs which have moved to a global strategy than it does to MNCs in the 'multidomestic' stage? Do the foreign firms bring fewer benefits to the Australian economy? All subsidiaries require marketing, local R&D, accounting and other services. In a global strategy more of these services are provided in a uniform manner from the parent or from regional centres, possibly by subsidiaries of other multinational corporations which enjoy a global relationship with the MNC. This may imply a reduction in linkages with purely local Australian firms. A stronger central role by the parent might diminish the capacity for Australia to benefit from the establishment of regional headquarters, a priority for the government in the past (Department of Industry, Science and Technology, 1994). Further, if the organisational structure of MNCs reflects their region of origin, and different structures leave host countries with differing levels of externalities, then government policies designed to benefit from FDI inflow would be strengthened if they were attuned to this fact.

Finally, a central issue for Australian researchers is: how 'internationalised' have Australian firms become? The lack of a systematic measure of internationalisation has meant that researchers have not been able to develop a widely accepted measure of internationalisation. It is therefore difficult to assess the extent of internationalisation of firms or to get accurate pictures of how internationalisation takes place (Makhija *et al.*, 1997). Researchers have used various definitions of internationalisation. At the level of the firm various scholars have focussed on single variables to measure degree of internationalisation (Sullivan, 1994). These include foreign subsidiaries' sales as a percentage of total sales (Stopford and Dunning, 1983), foreign assets as a percentage of total assets (Daniels and Bracker, 1989) and the number of foreign subsidiaries (Stopford and Wells, 1972). More recent works have used composite measures. Morrison and Roth (1992), for example, used the level of international trade, intensity of international competition, worldwide product standardisation and the presence of competitors in all key international markets as their 'dimensions' of globalisation.

Reference to internationalisation theories suggests that the degree of internationalisation might be seen from three perspectives: *performance* (what goes on overseas, Vernon, [1971]), *structural* (what resources are overseas, Stopford and Wells, [1972]) and *attitudinal* (what is top management's international orientation, Perlmutter, [1969]). Sullivan (1994) uses a composite measure which operationalises all three perspectives. His measure included the single measures quoted above plus others reflecting behavioural models of internationalisation: the total duration of top managers' foreign assignments and 'psychic dispersion', measured as the spread of subsidiaries across various psychic zones around the world.

In summary, the range of issues examined in the international business literature and reported on in European and US based journals remains largley unexplored in the Australian context. Research into the locational choices for FDI, the reasons FDI has been preferred to other entry modes and the nature of organisational structures would complement macroeconomic studies of imports and exports. This offers fertile ground for academics whose work might give great insights for use by both international managers and government policy makers.

Impediments to implementing the research agenda

The primary impediment is the lack of an Australian community of scholars who are committed to the issues of interest to this conference. Very few papers are presented by Australian academics at regional gatherings of the Academy of International Business (AIB). Three factors might be important in explaining this situation. First, no network of scholars is in place. The Australian chapter of the AIB has been effectively dissolved and is now administered as part of the South East Asian chapter. This means that researchers tend to work in isolation. Second, research into many aspects of MNC activities is typically conducted using survey data. This can be tedious and expensive and may give unreliable results if firms choose not to respond, a likely result where they fear that the information may become available to competitors. Third, there are very few journals based in Australia that are prepared to consider international business submissions.

The problem of access to data may also explain why very few economists in Australia pursue research in this field. A count of articles published in Economic Papers and the Economic Record since 1983 revealed only four articles that, judging by titles, dealt with FDI. Anecdotal evidence, supported by an examination of the departmental allegiances of academics that have presented papers at AIB and European International Business Academy conferences, suggests that research into MNCs and FDI is conducted mainly by personnel in departments of management and marketing. How can we get more economists involved?

One useful step to overcome these problems is to establish a central data base of Australian firms with operations abroad and foreign firms with operations in Australia. To provide a comprehensive data source it should include organisational as well as financial data. A data base operated by Harvard University has been the source of many seminal papers on MNCs in the US. This would need to be maintained over time because a comprehensive understanding of the internationalisation process of Australian firms needs to capture long periods of time and even histories of the whole development of the firm. Such a data base would facilitate this kind of research.

In conclusion, research into FDI must recognise that the foreign operations it funds will be one aspect of internationalisation, a dynamic process which reflects the strategic directions of the firm. An understanding of FDI must presuppose an understanding of internationalisation as a strategic process. While it is entirely appropriate to study FDI at a macroeconomic level, it is also worthwhile examining it at the level of the firm. In doing so, scholars should consider the strategic imperatives of firms as these will be reflected in management decisions which lead to FDI.

References

Agarwal, S. and Ramaswami, S. (1992) 'Choice of Foreign Entry Mode: Impact of Ownership, Location and Internalisation Factors', *Journal of International Business Studies*, 23(1): 1–27.

Anderson, E. and Gatignon, H. (1986) 'Modes of Entry: A Transactions Cost Analysis and Propositions', *Journal of International Business Studies*, (Fall): 1–26.

Anderson, O. (1993) 'On the Internationalisation Process of Firms: A Critical Analysis', *Journal of International Business Studies*, 24(2): 209–33.

Athukorala, P. (1995) 'Internationalisation and Structural Adaptation', *Economic Papers*, 14(1): 1–11.

Australian Bureau of Statistics (ABS) (1997) *Balance of Payments and International Investment Position*, Catalogue Number 5363, ABS, Canberra.

Bartlett, C. and Ghoshal, S. (1991) 'Global Strategic Management: Impact on the New Frontiers of Strategy Research', *Strategic Management Journal*, 12: 5–16.

Benito, G. R. and Gripsrud, G. (1992) 'The Expansion of Foreign Direct Investments: Discrete Rational Location Choices or a Cultural Learning Process?', *Journal of International Business Studies*, 23(3): 461–76.

Birkinshaw, J. (1996) 'How Multinational Subsidiary Mandates are Gained and Lost', *Journal of International Business Studies*, 27(3): 467–96.

Birkinshaw, J. and Morrison, A. (1995) 'Configurations of Strategy and Structure in Subsidiaries of Multinational Corporations', *Journal of International Business Studies*, 26(4): 729–54.

Bower, J. L. (1970) *Managing the Resource Allocation Process: A Study of Corporate Planning and Investment*. Harvard University Press: Boston, MA.

Bradley, D. G. (1977) 'Managing Against Expropriation', *Harvard Business Review* July–August: 75–83.

Buckley, P. J. (1983) 'New Theories of International Business', in M. Casson (ed.). *The Growth of International Business*. London: Allen and Unwin.

Buckley P. J. and Casson M. (1976) *The Future of the Multinational Enterprise*. London: Macmillan.

—— (1981) 'The Optimal Timing of a Foreign Direct Investment', *The Economic Journal*, 91: 75–87.

Buckley, P. J., Newbould, G. D. and Thurwell, J. C. (1988) *Foreign Direct Investment by Smaller UK Firms*. London: Macmillan.

Bureau of Industry Economics (1984) *Australian Direct Investment Abroad*, Canberra: Australian Government Publishing Service.

Bureau of Industry Economics (1995) *Australian Direct Investment Abroad A Statistical Overview*, Canberra: Australian Government Publishing Service.

Calof, J. L. and Beamish, P. W. (1995) 'Adapting to Foreign Markets: Explaining Internationalisation', *International Business Review*, 4(2): 115–31.

Cantwell, J. (1992) 'The Effects of Integration on the Structure of Multinational Corporation Activity in the EC', in M. W. Klein and P. J. Welfens (eds). *Multinationals in the New Europe and Global Trade*. Berlin and New York: Springer–Verlag.

Casson, M. C. (1982) 'Transaction Costs and the Theory of the Multinational Enterprise' in A. Rugman, A. M. (ed.). *New Theories of the Multinational Enterprise*. New York: St. Martin's Press.

Caves R. (1982) *Multinational Enterprise and Economic Analysis*. New York: Cambridge University Press.

Cavusgil, S. T. (1984) 'Differences Among Exporting Firms Based on the Degree of Internationalisation', *Journal of Business Science Research*, 12: 195–208.

Chandler, A. D. (1962) *Strategy and Structure*. Cambridge MA: MIT Press.

Crookell, H. H. (1986) Specialisation and International Competitiveness, in H. Etemad and L. S. Dulude (eds). *Managing the Multinational Subsidiary*. London: Croom Helm.

Dalli, D. (1994) 'The "Exporting" Process: The Evolution of Small and Medium Sized Firms Toward Internationalisation', in S. T. Cavusgil and C. A. Axinn (eds). *Advances in International Marketing*. London: JAI Press.

Daniels J. D. and Bracker J. (1989) 'Profit Performance: Do Foreign Operations Make a Difference?', *Management International Review*, 29(1): 46–56.

Davidson, W. H. (1982) *Global Strategic Management*. New York: John Wiley and Sons.

Department of Industry, Science and Technology (1994) *The Benefits of Regional Headquarters and Factors Influencing their Location in Australia*. Melbourne: Allen Consulting Group.

Doz, Y. C. (1986) *Strategic Management in Multinational Companies*. Oxford: Pergamon.

Doz, Y. and Prahalad, C. K. (1984) 'Patterns of Strategic Control within Multinational Corporations', *Journal of International Business Studies*, 15: 55–72.

Dunning, J. (1980) 'Toward an Eclectic theory of International Production: Some Empirical Tests', *Journal of International Business Studies*, 11(1): 9–31.

—— (1988) *Trade, Location and Economic Activity*. London: Allen and Unwin.

—— (1992) *Multinational Corporations and the Global Economy*. Wokingham: Addison-Wesley.

Edwards, R. W. and Buckley, P. J. (1998) 'The Choice of Location and Mode: The Case of Australian Investors in the UK', *International Business Review*, 7(4): 503–20.

Egelhoff, W. G. (1988) 'Strategy and Structure in Multinational Corporations: A Revision of the Stopford and Wells Model', *Strategic Management Journal*, 9: 1–14.

Eriksson, K., Johanson, J., Majkgard, A. and Sharma, D. D. (1997) 'Experiential Knowledge and Cost in the Internationalisation Process', *Journal of International Business Studies*, 28: 337–60.

Erramilli, M. K. and Rao, C. P. (1990) 'Choice of Foreign Market Entry Modes by Service Firms: Role of Market Knowledge', *Management International Review*, 30(2): 135–50.

Fouraker, L. E. and Stopford, J. M. (1968) 'Organisation Structure and Multinational Strategy', *Administrative Science Quarterly*, 13(1): 47–64.

Forsgren, M. (1989) *Managing the Internationalisation Process – The Swedish Case*. London: Routledge.

Franko, L. G. (1976) *The European Multinationals: A Renewed Challenge to American and British Big Business*. Stamford, CT: Greylock.

Ghoshal, S. and Bartlett, C. (1990) 'The Multinational Corporation as an Interorganisational Network', *Academy of Management Review*, 15(4): 603–25.

Hedlund, G. (1984) 'Organisation in-between: The Evolution of the Mother-Daughter Structure of Managing Foreign Subsidiaries in Swedish MNCs', *Journal of International Business Studies*, 15(2): 109–23.

Hellgren, B. and Melin, L. (1991) 'Corporate Strategies in Nordic Firms Facing Europe-Acquisitions and Other Cooperative Strategies', in L. G. Mattsson and B. Stymne (eds). *Corporate and Industry Strategies for Europe*. Amsterdam: Elsevier: 327–51.

Hill, C. (1997) *International Business: Competing in the Global Marketplace*, Chicago: Irwin.

Hill, C., Hwang, P. and Kim, W. C. (1990) 'An Eclectic Theory of the Choice of International Entry Mode', *Strategic Management Journal*, 11: 117–28.

Hill, C. and Kim, W. (1988) 'Searching for a Dynamic Theory of the Multinational Enterprise: A Transaction Cost Model', *Strategic Management Journal*, 9 (Special Issue): 93–194.

Hirsh, S. (1992) *Outsiders' Response to Europe 1992: Theoretical Considerations and Empirical Evidence.* European International Business Academy Conference Proceedings, Reading.

Huff, T. and Reger, R. (1987) 'A Review of the Strategic Process', *Journal of Management*, 13(2): 211–36.

Johanson, J. and Vahlne, J. (1977) 'The Internationalisation Process of the Firm: A Model of Knowledge Development and Increasing Foreign Commitments', *Journal of International Business Studies*, (Spring–Summer): 23–32.

—— (1977) 'The Internationalisation Process of the Firm – A Model of Knowledge Development and Increasing Foreign Market Commitments' *Journal of International Business Studies*, 8: 23–32.

—— (1990) 'The Mechanism of Internationalisation', *International Marketing Review*, 7(4): 11–24.

Johanson, J. and Wiedersheim-Paul, F. (1975) 'The Internationalisation of the Firm – Four Swedish Cases', *Journal of Management Studies*, 12(3): 305–22.

John, R., Ietto-Gillies, G., Cox, H. and Grimwade, N. (1997) *Global Business Strategy.* London: Thomson.

Kim, C. W. and Hwang, P. (1992) 'Global Strategy and Multinationals' Entry Mode Choice, *Journal of International Business Studies*, 3: 29–53.

Kogut, B. (1985) 'Designing Global Strategies: Comparative and Competitive Value Added Chains', *Sloan Management Review*, (Fall): 15–28.

Kogut, B. and Singh, H. (1988) 'The Effect of National Culture on the Choice of Entry Mode', *Journal of International Business Studies*, (Fall): 411–32.

Levitt, T. (1983) 'The Globalisation of Markets', *Harvard Business Review*, (May–June): 92–102.

Lovelock, C. and Yip, G. (1996) 'Developing Global Strategies for Service Businesses', *California Management Review*, 38(2): 64–86.

Madsen, T. K. and Servais, P. (1997) 'The Internationalisation of Born Globals: an Evolutionary Process?', *International Business Review*, 6(6): 561–83.

Makhija, M. V., Kim, K. and Williamson, S. D. (1997) 'Measuring Globalisation of Industries Using a National Industry Approach: Empirical Evidence Across Five Countries and Over Time', *Journal of International Business Studies*, 28(4): 679–710.

Martinez, J. and Jarillo, J. (1991) 'Coordination Demands of International Strategies', *Journal of International Business Studies*, 3: 429–44.

McKiernan, P. (1992) *Strategies of Growth: Maturity, Recovery and Internationalisation.* London: Routledge.

McKinsey and Company (1993) *Emerging Exporters: Australia's High Value Added Manufacturing Exporters.* Melbourne: Australian Manufacturing Council.

Melin, L. (1992) 'Internationalisation as a Strategy Process', *Strategic Management Journal*, 13: 99–118.

Millington, A. and Bayliss, B. (1990) 'The Process of Internationalisation: UK Companies in the EC', *Management International Review*, 30(2): 151–61.

Morrison, A. and Roth, K. (1992) 'A Taxonomy of Business-Level Strategies in Global Industries', *Strategic Management Journal*, 13(6): 319–418.

Nordstrom, K. A. (1991) *The Internationalisation of the Firm Searching for New Patterns and Explanations*, IIB, Stockholm.

Perlmutter, H. V. (1969) The Tortuous Evolution of the Multinational Corporation, *Colombia Journal of World Business*, 4 (January–February): 9–18.

Pomfret, R. (1995) *Australia's Trade Policies*. Melbourne: Oxford University Press.

Porter, M. (1990) *The Competitive Advantage of Nations*. New York: Free Press.

Quinn, J. B. (1980) *Strategies for Change: Logical Incrementalism*. New York: Irwin.

Root, F. (1987) *Foreign Market Entry Strategies*. New York AMACOM.

Snape, R., Adams, J. and Morgan, D. (1993) *Regional Trade Agreements: Implications and Options for Australia*. Canberra: Australian Government Publishing Service.

Stopford J. M. (1977) 'Changing Perspectives on Investment by British Manufacturing Multinationals', *Journal of International Business Studies*, (Fall–Winter): 15–27.

Stopford J. and Dunning, J. (1983) *The World Directory of Multinational Enterprises 1982–83*. Detroit: Gale Research Company.

Stopford, J. M. and Wells, L. T. (1972) *Managing the Multinational Enterprise*. New York: Basic Books.

Sullivan, D. (1994) 'Measuring the Degree of Internationalisation of the Firm', *Journal of International Business Studies*, 25(2): 325–42.

Tallman, S., Geringer, J. M. and Olsen, D. M. (1997) 'Performance Effects of Diversification Strategies among Japanese Manufacturing Multinational Firms: A Simultaneous Equation Model from a Resource-Based Perspective', in K. Macharzina, M. Oesterle, and J. Wolf, (eds). *Global Business in the Information Age*. Stuttgart: Proceedings of the EIBA Conference.

Terpstra, V. and Yu, C. (1988) 'Determinants of Foreign Investment of US Advertising Agencies', *Journal of International Business Studies*, 19(1): 33–46.

Tse, D. K., Pan, Y. and Au, K. Y. (1997) 'How MNCs Choose Entry Modes and Form Alliances: The China Experience', *Journal of International Business Studies*, 28(4): 779–806.

Van de Ven, A. (1992) 'Suggestions for Studying Strategy Process: A Research Note', *Strategic Management Journal*, 13 (Summer): 169–88.

Vernon, R. (1966) 'International Investment and International Trade in the Product Cycle', *Quarterly Journal of Economics*, (May), 190–207.

—— (1971) *Sovereignty at Bay: The Multinational Spread of US Enterprises*. New York: Basic Books.

—— (1979) 'The Product Life Cycle Hypothesisin a New International Environment', *Oxford Bulletin of Economics and Statistics*, 41(4): 34–55.

Welch, L. and Luostarinen, R. (1988) Internationalisation: Evolution of a Concept, *Journal of General Management*, 14(2): 34–55.

Yetton, P., Davis J. and Swan, P. (1991) *Going International: Export Myths and Strategic Realities*. Melbourne: Australian Manufacturing Council.

Yoon, H. D., Morash, E. A. and Cooper, M. and Clinton, S. (1996) 'Global Comparisons of Channel Integration Strategies and Strategic Alliances', in Taylor, C. and Cavusgil, T. (eds). *Advances in International Marketing: Marketing in Asia Pacific and Beyond*. Greenwich, Connecticut: JAI Press.

4 The international distribution of multinational production

Bijit Bora

Introduction

The scope of international transactions has changed considerably in the past thirty years with international trade in services and foreign direct investment (FDI) becoming increasingly important. As a result, the research effort into these two areas has intensified, especially in FDI.

While FDI has traditionally been the domain of academics in the international business community, international trade theorists have recently moved into this area. As Markusen (1995) points out many of these developments are relatively new and general insights are limited.[1]

The lack of a general model of FDI has resulted in a wide variety of approaches to answering the question of why firms would seek to locate production facilities in another country. These approaches vary in terms of their choice of independent and dependent variables. The types of studies also vary from econometric with time-series data to firm level surveys.

The difficulty facing those who are doing empirical work in this area is to aggregate firm level determinants of location so that they interact at the national level in order to determine cross-border flows. Too much reliance on firm level determinants would ignore the economic significance of national boundaries. Alternatively, too much focus on aggregate variables would ignore the contribution and behaviour of affiliates.

This paper canvasses and reviews the work that has been done on the reasons why firms choose a cross-border commercial presence. Its focus will be on methodologies, as well as on insights. It concludes with some suggestions for future research and impediments facing researchers.[2]

The basic model

Before examining the empirical work we present a basic model of the multinational corporation. The purpose of the model will be to better understand the different methodologies adopted by researchers. It is useful to distinguish between two types of multinational corporations. A horizontally integrated multinational corporation (MNC) is one where a similar stage of production is replicated in a foreign country. In this case the decision is usually one of exporting or investing since the identical product is being produced in both the home and the foreign country. The second type is the vertically integrated MNC. Successive stages of production are physically separated and located in different countries. Trade between affiliates is then a necessary outcome as intermediate goods are transferred from one stage of production to the next across national boundaries.

The dichotomy between horizontally and vertically integrated multinationals is useful to analyse the structure and composition of the international transactions internationally and within the firm. Each type of MNC has a different objective for expanding beyond national borders; hence their role in the global economic system will be slightly different.

The motivation for the horizontally integrated firm is market access. It has the final product that it wishes to sell, but needs to overcome barriers into the foreign market. In this case the establishment of a foreign affiliate could be to bypass tariffs, transport costs or administrative barriers. These costs would usually be sufficient enough to offset the benefits of scale economies from producing in one location.

Once established the firm exports headquarter services, or intermediate products to the affiliate, which uses them as inputs to make the final product. In the host economy, the establishment of the affiliate will increase employment, technology transfer and experience growth effects from the injection of capital (Markusen, 1995).

Another possible strategy for the horizontally integrated MNC could be to deter entry by other firms, or for strategic considerations. In this case, the standard industrial organisation issues about strategic entry come into play, with the only exception that one player is a foreign company. Nevertheless, the net effect on the host economy remains the same.[3]

The vertically integrated multinational on the other hand is usually motivated by efficiency seeking behaviour,[4] such as access to cheaper inputs, or location specific inputs such as natural resources. In this case, the footloose nature and site specific nature of the investment would lead to the simultaneous import and export of goods and services to the host economy. A formal model of multinational corporations by Markusen (1995) can be used to illustrate these points.

Let us assume there are two countries, home (h) and foreign (F), with two factors of production capital (K) and labour (L) producing two homogenous goods (X and Y).[5] The production technology is such that good X is produced under increasing returns to scale and good Y is produced with constant returns to scale.

The cost function for good X is given as:

$$C_x(w,r) = F(w,r) + G(w,r,h) + m(w,r,h) + t \tag{1}$$

where F is the fixed costs associated with producing the good, G is the plant level cost, C is the variable cost and t is the transport cost of exporting a good to the foreign market. Firms in the X industry are assumed to behave in Cournot fashion and the home and foreign markets are segmented.

With this model and variants of the model, a number of authors have shown that a variety of equilibria with multinational corporations can emerge Markusen (1995). The most important element of these models is that equilibria are not as simple as national versus multinational corporations. Under certain assumptions about the characteristics of countries such as size, distance and relative factor endowments mixed equilibria can emerge with both national and multinational firms.

There is a tension, on the one hand, to take advantage of the scale economies from producing for both markets in one location and the cost of delivering the good to the market.[6] Locational theorists in economics such as Curtis Eaton and Richard Lipsey focussed their attention on this issue at the same time (Eaton *et al.*, 1994a,b). They discuss these forces as agglomeration and disagglomeration.

To obtain further insights from these models consider a case in which the two countries are identical and transport costs are set to zero. Markusen (1995) points out that in this situation a firm has no incentive to locate in the foreign country. The nature of 'globalisation' *per se* is simply merchandise trade. National firms have an advantage in production over multinational production.

Now, suppose that transport costs are extremely high, so that servicing the foreign markets with exports becomes expensive. Or, the cost of establishing a new plant in the foreign country (G), relative to exporting, becomes cheaper. In this case, the only equilibrium would be one where there are multinational corporations displacing national firms. Globalisation in this case is not only the consumption of foreign goods, but also the domestic production of foreign goods. International trade consists of bilateral trade in headquarter services, or the services derived from F. The decision to locate offshore then depends upon the ratio of plant fixed costs relative to trade costs.

A similar result can be obtained, if instead of varying transport costs, we varied factor endowments assuming transport costs are zero. In this case, the cost of producing a given quantity of a good is lower in the country with the abundant factor that is used intensively at the plant level. That is the fixed costs of establishing the plant can be offset by lower fixed and marginal costs in the foreign location.

If we move now to the case of vertically integrated multinationals, we have a different notion of the globalisation of production. In this case, the multinational seeks to locate in areas where costs are minimised, and not for market access reasons. Accordingly, a greater share of total output would be destined for export. Or, in the language used above where the cost advantages outweigh any location disadvantages. The pattern of international production and international trade differs from that of a world with only horizontally integrated multinationals.

In order to isolate this difference let us assume that there are no transport costs and two stages of production for the good so that the new cost function facing the firm is:

$$C_x(w,r) = F(w,r) + G_1(w,r,h) + G_2(w,r,h) + m(w,r) + t_1 + t_2 \tag{2}$$

The first stage of production produces inputs into the subsequent stages. This input is called h. Each of the stages of production requires a plant and these are designated as plant 1 and plant 2. For simplicity let us assume that the second stage is the most labour intensive, although as Dixit and Grossman (1982) have shown the sequencing of the stages of production is not the issue. It is the factor intensity of each stage that is important. Let us also assume that the foreign country is labour abundant.

Since there is an intermediate and a final product transports costs may differ between the two. Hence, t_1 in equation (2) represents the costs of transporting the intermediate good produced to plant 2 and t, as in equation (1) is the cost of transporting the final good.

Now, assume that transport costs are zero and that factor endowments are outside the diversification cone. In this case, as both Dixit and Grossman (1982) and also Helpman (1985) have shown, the home country will have an incentive to shift its labour-intensive production to the labour abundant country. Factor endowments have a role to play again by producing the stage that uses a factor intensively in the country that is abundantly endowed with the factor.

If transport costs are included in the model, the decision to locate production in the foreign country will depend, not only on the cost of exporting the final good relative to the establishment of the plant, but also on the effect of a positive transport cost on shipping the intermediate good. Nevertheless, for sufficient factor endowment differences it will always be cost effective to shift plants based on factor intensity.

Factor endowments, therefore, have an important role to play in determining international production. This, of course, is hardly an insight for trade theorists, given the longevity of the Heckscher–Ohlin theorem. In the context of multinational production, however, the issue is the extent to which this factor is mitigated against, by technology (firm level), such as the cost of establishing a plant and the role played by transport costs.

The key determinants, therefore, which define a multinational equilibrium are then:

- The level of plant fixed costs, which are required to set up a new facility.
- Country characteristics, such as factor endowments and size.
- Trade costs involved in the alternative mode of entry. These can include both tariffs and transport costs.

Various combinations of these parameters will determine whether or not an equilibrium is either one with just national firms, just multinational firms, or both national and multinational firms. There has been little dispute about these determinants at a theoretical level. When it comes to converting theoretical insights into empirical work the precise form and specification of the empirical work is up for some debate.

Measuring location: the left-hand side

There are a variety of methodologies available to researchers to examine the international distribution of FDI. Some range from simple ratios and others to sophisticated econometric analysis. In the first category descriptive approaches such as that used by Bora (1996a,b) can yield particular insights into the pattern of FDI, but are limited in their scope.

Case studies have always proven to be a popular methodology, especially amongst the international business fraternity. This approach exploits the access to detailed information, but for only one company. Results are then generalised to other firms. The focus here will be on econometric types of analysis and not on descriptive aggregate pictures, nor on case studies.

Dependent variables to proxy the location or emergence of multinationals adopted by empirical studies vary with the particular unit of analysis. If the unit of analysis is national government policy, then the studies have usually involved time-series, cross-section or a panel approach at a fairly aggregated level. Some studies have examined locational determinants at an intra-national level by taking the first stage of a decision to invest in a particular country as given, and then focussing on the second stage which is location within the country.

If the point of view is from the home country then the dependent variable is usually foreign production over total production (for a given firm). On the other hand if it is from the point of view of the host country it is host production over total production. The difference, of course, is that it will affect the choice of dependent variables. In the first case characteristics of the parent company and the home country are important. In the second case it is a combination of the ownership advantages and the host country location advantages.

Table 4.1 provides an overview of the different specifications of the dependent variable used by researchers and their methodology. These range from the use of firm level data to time-series balance of payment data on FDI.

Those employing firm level data have used a combination of different specifications. Some have modelled location choice as a discrete problem and then used a conditional or multinomial logit procedure based on McFadden (1974). In this case, for example, the paper by Woodward and Rolfe (1992) which examines the choice of location in the Caribbean, if the investment was in a particular country it was given a one, and zero otherwise. The advantages to this approach are that a particular location choice is modelled against an alternative.

The polychotomous-dependent variable approach works well with discrete choice situations such as for particular regions where competition amongst alternatives would be intense, such as amongst states within a Federation. It has been employed by a number of researchers including Coughlin *et al.* (1991) for the United States. Hines (1996) in a study on the effects of taxation chose not employ this approach, but instead chose the ratio of plant, property and equipment, which raises a question on the advantages of this type of approach over the use of qualitative variables.

When you move up one level of aggregation beyond firm specific data to the industry level the dependent variable changes. In this case the most usual specification is one of the share of value added in a particular industry, or the share of turnover (Saunders, 1982). As such, the variable indicates the contribution of foreign firms to a particular industry, and how well that can be explained by using

Table 4.1 Specification of the dependent variable

Type of study	*Dependent variable*	*Reference*
Firm cross-section	Limited dependent variable indicating state	Ondrich and Wasylenko (1993)
	Limited dependent – 0 if domestic, 1 if foreign	Coughlin *et al.* (1991)
	Overseas production ratio – foreign production to total production	Pearce (1993)
	Relative affiliate and parent assets, property and sales	Blomstrom and Lipsey (1991)
State cross-section	State share of plant, property and equipment	Hines (1996)
Industry cross-section	Overseas market sourcing – proportion of firm's total foreign sales accounted for by foreign production	Brainard (1997)
Country cross-section	Value of Korean firms FDI in manufacturing	Jeon, Y. D.
	Value of Norweigan FDI by 93 companies (203 cases)	Benito and Gripsrud (1992)
	Foreign affiliates of country *i* in country *j* as a per cent of total affiliates, OECD countries 1980	Veugelers (1991), Culem (1988)
Industry/Country panel	Sourcing ratio	Brainard (1993a)
	Capital expenditure of US affiliates	Mody and Wheeler (1992)
Time-series country cross-section	Limited dependent variable indicating location: 187 observations over 1984–1987	Woodward and Rolfe (1993)
	Bilateral FDI flows between US, Germany, France, UK, Netherlands and Belgium. Thirty country pairs over fourteen years	Culem (1988)
Time-series	Total US FDI in EEC, 1953–1977	Scaperlanda and Balough (1983), Lunn (1983)
	Stock of FDI using quarterly data	Barrel and Pain (1996)

independent variables allowing for firm and industry characteristics. This approach uses the standard linear regression analysis and is heavily contingent on the detail of the data. In most countries the data is only available at the two and sometimes three digit standard industry classification, hence presenting problems with sample size.

While there is a distinct difference in this approach since it uses quantitative data on the 'impact' or role played by foreign firms it is heavily reliant on industry characteristics to explain the variation. Most of the papers using this methodology are heavily influenced by the Structure-Conduct-Performance paradigm and are heavily dependent on market structure variables such as concentration indexes.[7]

This could be considered a drawback since the dependent variable is not constructed from any particular model. The share acts a proxy for location and delivers some insight into the inter-industry distribution of FDI, but not necessarily why a particular country was chosen in the first place.

Caves (1996) illustrates this point by distinguishing between the role of multinationals in a particular industry as measured by its contribution to industry activity $p(i)$ and the importance of that industry to country *j*'s GDP $v_j(i)$. In his terminology the issue is whether or not there is a link between $p(i)$ and $v_j(i)$. The latter would be determined by classical comparative advantage factors such as factor endowments, but the former could influence this.[8]

Aside from the obvious point that this issue has escaped the literature, there is also a separate issue of data availability. Brainard (1997) was able to combines both the intellectual input needed to make the connection with a robust dataset. In that paper, which we shall discuss in more detail later, Brainard uses a specification which is developed from a clear underlying model – she uses the share of sales in country *j* attributable to affiliates from country *i* over the sum of affiliate sales and exports. This comes directly from the basic model outlined earlier.

An added contribution from the Brainard (1997) paper is the use of panel data with a cross-section of countries and industries. This allows her to combine many of the industry characteristics associated with the cross-industry studies with the locational advantages associated with international borders.

Wheeler and Mody (1992) use a similar data structure, but include a time element by examining data between 1982 and 1989. Their dependent variable is capital expenditure by foreign affiliates, which they fit as a translog expenditure function. They clearly have a focus on the financial aspects of FDI. Their equation does not come out of a clearly specified model.

At another level of aggregation we find that studies ignore industry characteristics completely and focus on country characteristics. In this case the choice of dependent variable shifts from being derived from an underlying model to balance of payments data on FDI, or in the case of Veugelers (1991) the share of affiliates in country *j* from country *i*. Other examples of the use of aggregate data are Culum (1988) and most recently Barrel and Pain (1996). The latter paper uses quarterly data to construct FDI stocks.

Independent variables

The right-hand side specification is of course the one of most interest to theoreticians, empirical researchers and policy makers. There are a large number of candidates that would qualify for inclusions in any specification, and similarly a large number of proxies for specific variables. As with the case of the specification of dependent variables, the specification of independent variables, in many cases, lacks any theoretical foundation. Researchers, preferring instead, to use the 'kitchen sink' approach.

One common feature throughout the studies that we have examined is the poor quality of the data. In some cases, the research appears to have been done back to front with researchers fitting models to the data, as opposed to developing and testing models, or in fact testing specific models.

Theory does gives us some guidance about the appropriate specification. The most common specification is of the following form:

$$Y_i = \alpha_i + \beta_1 X_1 + \beta_2 X_2 + \beta_3 X_3 + \varepsilon$$

where X_1 is a vector variables which indicate market characteristics; X_2 a vector of production cost characteristics and X_3 a vector of government policy variables.

There are a number of different specifications of market characteristics and researchers have managed to pretty well include each and every one of them. Table 4.2 provides an overview of the different variables used as X_1. One way to think of these variables is to distinguish those that are demand side variables and

Table 4.2 Specification of market characteristics

Country characteristics	*Variable*	*Effect*	*Reference*
Size	GDP	Positive	Veuglers (1991), Culem (1988), Scaperlanda and Balough (1983), Lunn (1983)
Market potential	Change in GDP	Not significant	Scaperlanda and Mauer (1969)
		Positive	Culem (1988)
	Acceleration in GNP	Positive	Lunn (1983)
Language/Cultural similarity	Cultural index	Insignificant	Benito and Gripsrud (1992)
Neighbour	Dummy variable	Positive	Veugelers (1991), Brainard (1997)
Transport cost	Physical distance	Positive	Veugelers (1991)
	Total transport and insurance costs as a proportion of free alongside value	Negative	Woodward and Rolfe (1993)

those that are associated with the cost of servicing the market through markets. The most common variable in all the empirical studies using industry or national data is country size. In this case gross domestic product, or GDP, is used as a proxy. The rationale for this is obvious, given the inclusion of fixed cost in the cost function. Larger markets allow for returns to scale and the ability to offset export costs.

While the size variable is always significant in most of the studies, variables which proxy the growth rate of the market are not significant. This would suggest that market size is a long-term factor, not short-term factor. This would be consistent with the notion that the establishment of a foreign production facility requires both a fixed and variable cost component. A one-period change in GDP may not be sufficient to change expectations about the long-term viability of the investment.

Relative size is also a common variable. This is used to proxy similarity in market. In this case, there is something similar to the Linder effect, where varieties that are in demand in another market could be sourced from similar countries. American firms are more likely to find consumers for their products in countries that have similar per capita levels of income.[9]

In addition to income per capita, cultural similarity may also enter into demand side considerations. Different cultures not only make it difficult to operate subsidiaries, they also can have an impact on the demand structure. Benito and Gripsrud (1992) argue that FDI is a sequential and learning process. Initially, only culturally 'close' markets are potential location. As experience is developed in these markets, this makes it easier to penetrate more difficult or less culturally 'close' markets.

Measuring cultural distance has always proven to be a challenge. Benito and Gripsrud (1992) use a proxy which is the arithmetic mean of squared deviations between countries based on four criteria: uncertainty avoidance, individuality, power distance and masculinity–femininity. Despite such a unique initiative, the authors were not able to find any significant relationship between their cultural variables and the first FDI.

Veugelers (1991) and Brainard (1997) uses a simpler approach to measuring cultural similarity by using a dummy to proxy for language. He also has a dummy variable to proxy for a common boarder, but does not interact this variable with language. This would have had interesting effects for Canada and the United States. Of course, given the general use of English as a language of commerce within the OECD, it is unclear whether or not the variable would capture the desired effect.

Wheeler and Mody (1992) use a measure of relationship with the west in their study. This was combined with a variable to measure relations with neighbouring countries. Although it is not clear from their paper, whether or not the variable is meant to approximate a demand side effect, or political stability both were still positive. Other key characteristics of markets are their distance. A common characteristic of the models of multinationals is the dichotomous choice between exporting and investing. Transport costs bias this decision heavily in favour of investing. Theoretically, this variable is typically lumped in together with other trade costs such as tariffs and non-tariff barriers. In this paper, we consider these as specific government policy variables.[10] For example, Australia suffers geographically from being distant from major markets and sources of capital, but that is separate and distinct from a specific policy of tariff induced foreign investment to supplement the cost disadvantage associated with exporting to Australia.

In general, X_1 contains those variables that are distinct from specific cost of production advantages and specific government policy variables. Large isolated markets that are culturally similar are good candidates for commercial presence.

The X_2 type variables include various proxies for cost advantage, depending on the level of aggregation. An overview of some of the variables used is given in Table 4.3. The more interesting studies are those which attempt to combine either key aspects of country characteristics to reflect cost advantages, such as factor endowments, or specific measurements of cost advantages with firm specific advantages.

The ability to use more precise measures of cost at the disaggregated variable has been exploited in a number of studies. Carlton (1983), for example, in his study of geographic regions in the United States uses industry classified electricity and natural gas prices with the wages. These can also be combined with other factor endowment data such as land area, insurance rates, road miles, construction costs and population density as was done in Bartik (1985).

At the aggregate level location studies are plagued by data problems, although it should be pointed out that these data problems, although prevalent, have not proven to be as significant for factor endowment studies of trade patterns. Brainard (1997) probably goes to the most extreme level of aggregation by only using per capita GDP differences and nothing else more detailed, or broader.[11] Veugelers (1991) uses hourly wages in the United States divided by labour productivity, or a measure of efficiency wages. Culem (1988) uses per unit labour costs. Wheeler and Mody (1992) use average hourly wage in manufacturing and convert it into an index between 1 and 10.

The UNCTC (1992) survey of FDI reviewed the role of factor costs in a number of studies other than in the United States and found them to be insignificant. Paradoxically, when they reviewed studies that had measures of factor intensity, they concluded that the studies seemed to predominantly support this hypothesis. This may not seem to be much of a puzzle for labour economists since

Table 4.3 Specification of cost characteristics

Variable	*Sign*	*Study*
Factor endowments	Negative	Brainard (1997)
Labour cost variables	Negative	Woodward and Rolfe (1993), Wheeler and Mody (1992), Bartik (1985)
Other input costs, energy costs	Negative	Ondrich and Wasylenko (1983), Bartik (1985), Carlton (1983)
Manufacturing density	Positive	Coughlin *et al.* (1991)
Land	Positive	Woodward and Rolfe (1993)
State infrastructure	Positive	Bartik (1985), Coughlin *et al.* (1991)
Agglomeration effects		Ondrich and Wasylenko (1993), Woodward and Rolfe (1993), Coughlin *et al.* (1991), Bartik (1985)

institutional factors of wage determination maybe playing a role. Nevertheless, even detailed studies of transport costs and firm-specific advantages like Brainard (1997) 'cannot rule out country effects'.

One aspect of these studies which is disappointing is their assumption that the multinational firm is a homogenous entity. Only a few studies such as Kravis and Lipsey (1992) have accounted for the difference between horizontal and vertical FDI. Part of the difficulty is the bias towards industrialised countries, and in particular, the United States and Europe. In these cases, market structure issues and market access are critical. Yet, given the fact that there are some regions, such as east Asia, where high growth rates and low factor prices would yield a convenient test tube, good quality research is difficult to find.

Until recently, one of the least researched areas is the role of government policy in determining investment location. These variables make up X_3. There are numerous instruments available to governments, which when combined together will determine the aggregate 'investment climate' of country. Some of these are measurable and tangible such as the level of equity restriction in certain sectors, or prohibition of foreign investors. Others, however, are extremely difficult, such as access to dispute resolution, or transparency of laws policies and procedures.

In the area of tangible and specific government policies border measures for goods, taxation and the use of incentives are the one which seem to attract the most attention. Again, here aggregation becomes an issue as well as the quality of data. The state level types of studies and ones using multinomial logit analysis with firm data are able to use detailed tax data. Once the level of aggregation moves up to the issue of national borders the data becomes less difficult to find.

Table 4.4 summarises the key results and types of government policies that have been measured. Tariffs, for the obvious reasons enter into the analysis of almost every study except those, which look at the intra-national distribution issue. The results indicate that tariffs, like the measure of distance in Table 4.2, seem to have the desired effect.

Taxation and investment issues also pose similar problems. Brainard (1997) uses tax data in her industry-country panel data and Hines (1996) uses tax data for states. Hines (1996) is able to find strong effects for taxation indicating that a 1 per cent reduction in tax could yield a return of 11 per cent in foreign investment.

An important area of empirical work is investigating the effects of policy competition for FDI. There is no doubt that the market for foreign capital is competitive. When this fact is combined with a new sense of acceptance of the benefits of FDI there is a tendency for countries to compete for FDI by offering fiscal incentives. There has been considerable research on whether or not incentives actually have an effect on the locational decision. Most of this research has been through case studies. It is summarised nicely in UNCTAD (1996) where they conclude that 'there is overwhelming evidence to suggest that incentives are a relatively minor factor in the locational decisions of TNCs relative to other locational advantages'. This emphatic conclusion is tempered by the limited nature of the studies. None of the studies are able to fully account for fiscal incentives, preferring instead to examine tax holidays and infrastructure expenditure.

Table 4.4 Specification of government policy

Policy	*Effect*	*Reference*
Tariffs	Negative	Culem (1988)
	Negative	Scaperlanda and Balough (1983)
	Negative	Lunn (1983)
	Negative	Brainard (1997)
Political stability	Positive	Brainard (1997)
	Positive	Woodward and Rolfe (1993)
	Positive	Wheeler and Mody (1992)
Investment barriers	Negative	Brainard (1997)
	Uncertain	Wheeler and Mody (1992)
	Negative	Koechlin (1992)

Difficulty in developing cardinal, or even ordinal measures of investment protection maybe the reason for their omission from studies, but this is clearly an area that cannot be ignored. As Bora (1997) points out, there is a thirst for information on the effects of investment liberalisation by policy makers, yet the academic community has yet to deliver robust estimates. Wheeler and Mody (1992), Brainard (1997), Koechlin (1992) use survey measures of openness and are able to obtain estimates with the correct sign. Wei (1997) includes a measure of corruption in his FDI equation and finds that it has some impact. The limitation of their work, of course, is the fact that it is cross-sectional and does not capture any of the dynamic effects of investment policy changes.[12]

Avenues for further research

The results of the studies, in general, seem to correspond closely to the accepted theories as to why multinational production arises. Inter-industry studies find a strong correlation with firm specific advantages or knowledge based such as advertising, research and development and skill intensity. When compared with an alternative such as exporting, variables such as tariffs and distance seem to have the desired effect of encouraging more foreign investment. Government policy variables also have some effect, especially tariffs. Other variables have yet to be tested rigorously on a cross-country basis, although intra-national studies on taxation and incentives have found them to be significant.

From the above review we can see that the applied literature on the international distribution of multinational production has developed significantly in the past ten years. Most of the growth is due to the shift in interest in the international policies of countries and the developments in theory and the provision of data. Despite these well-document contributions, there is still significant scope for further work. Some of these are highlighted below.

First, and foremost, is the distinction between horizontal and vertically integrated multinationals. With the exception of Kravis and Lipsey (1982) and Woodward and Rolfe (1993), none of the studies cited here stratify their data to examine the impact of national variables on types of firms. In particular, even a distinction between these two types within a dataset, or the development of criteria to distinguish between the two types of firms is lacking. In the vertically integrated case, factor endowments, or traditional Heckscher–Ohlin type variables would prove to be more significant and less dominated by transport costs.

The explanatory power of the empirical studies has been fairly low, leaving most of the variance, regardless of the specification unexplained.[13] In addition to country size, national policy variables seem to perform fairly well. Given the policy debate on the lack of multilateral investment rules and investment liberalisation, there is a need to examine either for individual countries, or on a time-series and cross-section basis the impact of government policies toward, FDI. Preliminary work on the measurement of these barriers by Hardin and Holmes (1997) for the service sectors is promising and could substitute for the *ad hoc* approach taken by Bora and Guisinger (1997) and Petri (1997).

A third area is the concept of relative analysis. Selecting a commercial presence over exporting, by definition, requires a comparison of each choice. Empirical work has focussed on the characteristics of the home country, except in some cases such as Blomstrom and Lipsey (1991), which examined the characteristics of the parent. Data on the production structure of the parent relative to the affiliate is required for more robust analysis. Current collections of data, such as the US Department of Commerce Data survey parent companies for information, but this is the organisation, not the production unit. As a result, the comparison is not on a foreign production plant, relative to its domestic production plant. Some of this difficulty is circumscribed by firm case studies, but these results are difficult to generalise.

Perhaps the most significant area for research is the core of international trade and that is the role played by national borders. Krugman (1994) has focussed on trade and geography and essentially questions the process by which national borders are designated. Accidents and history determine the international division of ownership of resources, but globalisation in the form of trade and investment diminishes their economic significance. The theoretical and empirical work has focussed on a very 2×2 analysis of two modes of entry and two countries. Some foreign investment decisions, such as in the Asia Pacific region are focussed on regional issues and regional agglomeration effects. The empirical work needs to account for the possibility of bias in their estimates by not accounting for third countries, either in the specification of their equations, or in the collection of their data.

Impediments to research

The obvious impediment is data collection. Statistics on the operations on multinationals have been lacking relative to the rich international trade data. There are obvious statistical issues involved such as the ownership criteria and aggregation problems. Countries that collect good quality data such as the United States, Sweden and Canada have dominated the empirical research. Organisations such as the Organisation for Economic Cooperation and Development and the United Nations Conference on Trade and Development are making inroads in this area. However, their focus is limited to balance of payments type data collection such as the dollar values of the investment.

Even if the data is published, accessibility is another key issue. One can not help getting the feeling that some of the empirical work in this area is done 'back to front', where researchers with access to a dataset and then use a flexible approach to specification to suit their data. Accessibility means not only access to published information in a useable form, but also accessibility in terms of pricing. Some datasets are horribly expensive and in some cases, such as the United States a non-tariff barrier in the form of a citizenship content requirement is imposed.[14] A good model is the Penn World Database. Since its publication it has been instrumental in driving most of the applied macro growth literature and some of the trade literature. It is available for free from the National Bureau of Economic Research website so that undergraduate and graduate students, as well as academic staff without large grants can access the data, either for specific research programs or for exploratory research.

Data difficulties are also amplified by the recent trend towards panel data estimation techniques. For example, Bora and Wooden (1998) use a first stage wage equation with employee data that includes a fixed effect for a particular establishment. The fixed effect coefficients are then used as a dependent variable in an establishment equation with foreign ownership. This technique would be suitable for examining the international distribution of foreign ownership by accounting for country fixed effects in an industry equation and then regressing these against the country characteristics (Brainard, 1997). This can be done on a cross-section basis, or over time. The latter, of course, would require a longitudinal dataset.

Conclusions

This paper has reviewed the empirical work on the international distribution of foreign investment. The literature, although fragmented, provides some clear insights into the determinants of foreign investment. Some concern does arise due to the wide range of methodologies and datasets that have been employed. Without some international collection or initiative to collect data, such as the case of commodity trade data the literature will continue to evolve in this manner.

The main area of concern is the dominance of the United States and industrialised countries as the unit of analysis. Empirical work in other regions of the world has been less rigorous and focussed on case studies or anecdotal evidence. Initiatives to develop a comprehensive database on a regional level could make considerable inroads in empirical work, especially when they are combined with the recent developments in econometric analysis.

Notes

1 The existing models are divided into three categories: factor endowment differences (Helpman, 1984a,b; Ethier, 1986); industry and firm level characteristics such as plant level costs versus firm level costs (Brainard, 1997; Horstmann and Markusen, 1992; Markusen, 1995), and strategic models of entry and location (Horstmann and Markusen, 1987).

2 Caves (1996) and UNCTC (1992) provide recent reviews on the determinants of foreign investment. Their focus has been on the results, as opposed to the different methodologies available for use.

3 One crucial difference in these types of models, however, is the role of imperfect competition. In the perfectly competitive models, or the imperfectly competitive models with free entry the issue can be simplified to one of cost structures. In the strategic entry models, however, the issue maybe one of cost structures, as well as monopolistic behaviour, in which case the distribution of rents needs to be accounted.
4 This does not imply that horizontally integrated multinationals are not efficiency seekers. In fact, this has been a key to the shift in the policy debate, that multinationals may not necessarily be after market dominance, but efficiency seeking.
5 Markusen (1995) points out that Brainard (1993a) has applied the identical model to the case of differentiated products in the increasing returns to scale industry and developed the same results.
6 Although not explicitly acknowledged the role played by transport costs has had considerable attention from geographers (Weber, 1929; Chapman and Walker, 1991). Location theorists in economics such as Curtis Eaton and Richard Lipsey focussed their attention on this issue at the same time (Eaton *et al.*, 1994a,b).
7 Typically industry variables such as concentration indexes and advertising ratios are used.
8 Ramstetter (1991) includes a collection of papers, which examines the role of FDI and structural change in East Asia. Or, the influence of $p(i)$ on $v_j(i)$. The thesis in the book is that the increasing levels of FDI to the region has played a role in increasing the importance of manufacturing in some of the countries, although none of the papers develop or test that particular hypothesis.
9 For an analysis of this issue see Hunter and Markusen (1988).
10 Tariffs were a popular policy tool throughout the post-Second World War period to attract foreign investment. Bora (1995) discusses this with respect to the Australian economy. Developing countries used tariffs as part of an import-substitution program.
11 With a cross-section of twenty-seven countries there was significant scope to use more detailed data such as skilled labour composites or even land.
12 That is the fact that the share of overseas production of US firms in Australia is high in 1998 may have little to do with Australian investment policy in 1998, but a lot to do with investment policy in the 1970s and 1980s.
13 Brainard's (1997) R^2 values ranged from 0.04 to 0.18 in most of the regressions. In two cases, where fixed effects are accounted for, the R^2 value jumped to 0.449 and 0.480.
14 This is not to suggest that their policy is unfair, or unjust. It is imposed as a security policy, but it nevertheless changes the production structure of research – either forego a specific study or include US researchers.

References

Barrell, R. and N. Pain (1996), 'Econometric Analysis of US Foreign Direct Investment', *Review of Economics and Statistics*, 78: 200–7.

Bartik, T. (1985), 'Business Location Decisions in the United States: Estimates of the Effects of Unionisation, Taxes, and other Characteristics of States', *Journal of Business and Economic Statistics*, 3: 14–22.

Benito, G.R.G. and G. Gripsrud (1992), 'The Expansion of Foreign Direct Investments: Discrete Rational Location Choices or Cultural Learning Process', *Journal of International Business Studies*, 23: 461–76.

Blomstrom, M. and R. Lipsey (1991), 'Firm Size and Foreign Operations of Multinationals', *Scandanavian Journal of Economics*, 93(1): 101–7.

Bora, B. (1995), 'International Factor Flows', in R. Pomfret (ed.), *Australia's Trade Policies*, Melbourne: Oxford University Press.

Bora, B. (1996a), 'Foreign Direct Investment' in B. Bora and C. Findlay (eds), *Regional Integration and the Asia Pacific*, Melbourne: Oxford University Press.

Bora, B. (1996b), 'Trade and Investment Developments in APEC: 1980–1993', in P. Lloyd and L. Williams (eds), *Trade and Migration in the APEC Region*, Melbourne: Oxford University Press.

Bora, B. (1997), 'What do we Mean by Investment Liberalisation?', paper presented to the Economic Modeling Bureau of Australia Conference, Sydney, August 25–27.

Bora, B. and S. Guisinger (1997), 'The Impact of Investment Liberalisation in APEC', Mimeo, Flinders University.

Bora, B. and M. Wooden (1998), 'Human Capital, Foreign Ownership and Wages', Mimeo, Flinders University.

Brainard, L. (1993a), 'A Simple Theory of Multinational Corporations and Trade with a Trade-off Between Proximity and Concentration', National Bureau of Economic Research Working Paper No. 4269, Cambridge MA: NBER.

Brainard, L. (1993b), 'An Empirical Assessment of the Factor Proportions Explanation of Multinational Sales', National Bureau of Economic Research Working Paper No. 4580, December.

Brainard, L. (1997), 'An empirical Assessment of the Proximity-Concentration Trade-off between Multinational Sales and Trade', *American Economic Review*, 87: 520–44.

Carlton, D. (1983), 'The Location and Employment Choices of New Firms: An Econometric Model with Discrete and Continuous Endogenous Variables', *Review of Economics and Statistics*, 65: 440–9.

Caves, R. (1996), *Multinational Enterprise and Economic Analysis*, Cambridge, UK: Cambridge University Press.

Chapman, K. and Walker, D. (1991), *Industrial Location*, Oxford: Blackwell Publishers.

Coughlin, C.C., J. Terza and V. Arromdee (1991), 'State Characteristics and the Location of FDI within the United States', *Review of Economics and Statistics*, 73: 675–83.

Culem, C.G. (1988), 'The Locational Determinants of Direct Investments among Industrialised countries', *European Economic Review*, 32: 885–904.

Davidson, W. (1980), 'The Location of Foreign Direct Investment Activity: Country Characteristics and Experience Effects', *Journal of International Business Studies*, 12, 9–22.

Dixit, A. and G. Grossman (1982), 'Trade and Protection in a Multistage Production Model', *Review of Economic Studies*, 43: 583–94.

Eaton, C., R. Lipsey and E. Safarian (1994a), 'The Theory of Multinational Plant Location in a Regional Trading Area', in L. Eden (ed.), *Multinationals in North America*, Calgary: University of Calgary Press.

Eaton, C., R. Lipsey and E. Safarian (1994b), 'The Theory of Multinational Plant Location in a Regional Trading Area: Agglomeration and Dissaglomeration', in L. Eden (ed.), *Multinationals in North America*, Calgary: University of Calgary Press.

Ethier, W. (1986), 'The Multinational Firm', *Quarterly Journal of Economics*, 101: 85–133.

Hardin, A. and L. Holmes (1997), *Services Trade and Foreign Direct Investment*, Industry Commission Staff Research Paper, AGPS, Canberra.

Helpman, E. (1984), 'A Simple Theory of the Multinational Corporation', *Journal of Political Economy*, 92: 451–71.

Helpman, E. (1985), 'The Multinational Firm and the Structure of Trade', *Review of Economic Studies*, 52: 443–57.

Helpman, E. and P. Krugman (1985), *Market Structure and Foreign Trade*, Cambridge: MIT Press.

Hines, J. (1996), 'Altered States: Taxes and the Location of Foreign Direct Investment in America', *American Economic Review*, 86: 1076–94.

Horstman, I. and Markusen, J.R. (1987), 'Strategic Investments and the Development of Multinationals', *International Economic Review*, 28: 109–21.

Horstman, I. and Markusen, J.R. (1992), 'Endogenous Market Structures in International Trade', *Journal of International Economics*, 32: 109–29.

Hunter, L. and J. Markusen (1988), 'Per Capita Income as a Determinant of Trade', in Robert Feenstra (ed.), *Empirical Methods for International Economics*, Cambridge: MIT Press.

Koechlin, T. (1992), 'The Determinants of the Location of USA Direct Foreign Investment', *International Review of Applied Economics*, 6: 203–16.

Kravis, I.B. and R.E. Lipsey (1982), 'Location of Overseas Production and Production for Export by U.S. Multinational Firms', *Journal of International Economics*, 12: 201–23.

Krugman, P. (1994), *Re-thinking International Trade*, Cambridge Mass: MIT Press.

Lunn, J.L. (1983), 'Determinants of US Direct Investment in the EEC, Revisited Again', *European Economic Review*, 13: 93–101.

Markusen, J. (1995), 'The Boundaries of the Multinational Firm and International Trade', *Journal of Economic Perspectives*, Spring, 9(2): 169–89.

Markusen, J. and A. Venables (1998), 'Multinationals and the New Trade Theory', *Journal of International Economics*, 46: 193–203.

Markusen, J., A. Venables, D. Konan and K. Zhang (1996), 'A Unified Treatment of Horizontal Direct Investment, Vertical Direct Investment, and the Pattern of Trade in Goods and Services', Working Paper 5696, Cambridge: NBER.

McFadden (1974), 'Conditional Logit Analysis of Qualitative Choice Behaviour', in P. Zarembka (ed.), *Frontiers in Econometrics*, New York: Academic Press.

Ondrich, J. and M. Wasylenko (1993), *Foreign Direct Investment in the United States: Issues and Magnitude and Location Choice of New Manufacturing Plants*, Kalamazoo, Michigan: W.E. Upjohn Institute for Employment Research.

Pearce, R.D. (1993), *The Growth and Evolution of Multinational Enterprise: Patterns of Geographic and Industrial Diversification*, Cambridge: Cambridge University Press.

Petri, P. (1997), 'Foreign Direct Investment in a Computable General Equilibrium Framework', presented at *Making APEC Work: Economic Challenges and Policy Alternatives*, March 13–14, Tokyo: Keio University.

Ramstetter, E. (1991), *Direct Foreign Investment in Asia's Developing Economies and Structural Change*, Boulder: Westview Press.

Ray, E.J. (1989), 'The Determinants of FDI in the United States', in R. Feenstra (ed.), *Trade Policies for International Competitiveness*, Chicago: University of Chicago Press.

Saunders, R.S. (1982), 'The Determinants of Inter-industry Variation of Foreign Ownership in Canadian Manufacturing', *Canadian Journal of Economics*, 15: 77–84.

Scaperlanda, A. and R. Balough (1983), 'Determinants of U.S. Direct Investment in the EEC: Revisited', *European Economic Review*, 21: 381–90.

Scaperlanda, A. and L. Mauer (1969), 'The Determinants of US Direct Investment in the EEC', *American Economic Review*, 59: 558–68.

UNCTC (1992), *The Determinants of Foreign Direct Investment: A Survey of the Evidence*, New York: United Nations.

UNCTAD (1996), *Incentives and Foreign Direct Investment*, Geneva: United Nations.

Veugelers, R. (1991), 'Locational Determinants and Ranking of Host Countries: An Empirical Assessment', *Kyklos*, 44, 363–82.

Weber, A. (1929), *Theory of Location of Industries*, trans. C.J. Friedrich, Chicago: University of Chicago Press.

Wei, S.J. (1996), 'How Taxing is Corruption on Foreign Investors', Mimeo, Harvard University.

Wheeler, D. and A. Mody (1992), 'International Investment Location Decisions: The Case of U.S. firms', *Journal of International Economics*, 3: 57–76.

Woodward, D.P. and R.J. Rolfe (1993), The Location of Export-oriented Direct Investment in the Caribbean Basin', *Journal of International Business Studies*, 24: 121–44.

5 A method for improved international and intertemporal comparisons of US MNCs' overseas gross product in manufacturing

Raymond J. Mataloni, Jr.

Introduction

Interest in the effects of globalized production on national economies has been heightened in recent years by the rapid growth in direct investment. Research directed at assessing these effects is, however, often limited by the scarcity of relevant data. While most home and host countries maintain data on direct-investment-related capital and income flows, which show the amount invested and the returns on that investment, relatively few countries provide information on the operations of direct investment enterprises. Statistical agencies in a growing number of countries are trying to fill the data gap by collecting data on the scale and activity of multinational corporations (MNCs) – such as MNC assets, production, and employment – in addition to the data needed to construct the international economic accounts. The Bureau of Economic Analysis (BEA) of the US Department of Commerce is a pioneer in this area. BEA collected its first data on the foreign operations of US-based MNCs for the year 1950 and on the US operations of foreign-based MNCs for the year 1974.

These data are the basis for BEA estimates of the gross product, or value added, of foreign affiliates of US-based MNCs and of US affiliates of foreign-based MNCs.[1] Gross product measures a firm's production, exclusive of inputs received from outside suppliers. Affiliate gross product estimates provide insight into the significance of affiliates within their MNCs and within their host economies. For example, the ratio of gross product by foreign affiliates to host-country gross domestic product (GDP) measures the percentage of host-country GDP originating in the affiliates.

The gross product estimates for foreign affiliates of US MNCs are based on data collected in BEA surveys. BEA asks survey respondents to report the data for foreign affiliates in US dollars even though the company records containing the data are often denominated in foreign host-country currency. Survey respondents are asked to translate foreign-currency-denominated values to US dollars at market exchange rates. BEA's current dollar data on the operations of foreign affiliates (including the estimates of the gross product of foreign affiliates) are based on the dollar-denominated values reported by the survey respondents.

Until recently, comparisons of the estimates of gross product of foreign affiliates of US MNCs, across countries or over time, have been subject to valuation effects. The estimates could not always be accurately compared across countries because market exchange rates do not ensure that the values of a given bundle of goods and services in any two foreign countries will yield an equal value when translated from those countries' respective currencies into a common base currency (in this case, the US dollar). Nor could the foreign-affiliate gross product estimates always be accurately compared across time because they were not adjusted for price changes.

This chapter presents a method developed by BEA to remove the valuation effects from its gross product estimates for foreign affiliates of US MNCs. The methodology draws on the advancements in sources and methods for international GDP comparisons that have occurred over the last forty-five years. These advancements include the development of purchasing-power-parity (PPP) exchange rates, which are exchange rates that reflect the actual purchasing power of currencies.[2]

The remainder of the chapter is divided into four sections. The first section describes the available statistics of the foreign activities of US MNCs and explains why gross product is a preferred summary measure for many purposes. The second section describes BEA's method for estimating the gross product of US companies' majority-owned foreign affiliates (MOFA) in terms of current US dollars. The third section describes BEA's method for estimating the real gross product of US companies' MOFAs in manufacturing. The final section assesses the accuracy of the real gross product estimates.

Statistics on the foreign activities of MNCs

Traditional balance-of-payments and international investment measures of US direct investment abroad – such as direct investment capital flows and positions – track transactions between US companies and their foreign affiliates and the cumulative value of US companies' investment in their affiliates. These data are essential inputs to the major US economic accounts: The balance of payments accounts, the US international investment position, the national income and product accounts, and the input–output accounts. They are, however, at best only rough indicators of the scale of the foreign operations of US MNCs. Direct investment capital flows, for example, may not fully reflect all of the growth in the operations of foreign affiliates because they cover only financing provided by the parent company in the home country; they exclude financing obtained from unaffiliated parties in the home country or from host-country and third-country sources. In addition, international conventions require that direct investment capital flows be classified in the foreign country of immediate destination, which may or may not be the ultimate destination of the funds. For example, if a US company sends funds to a manufacturing affiliate in Hungary through a holding company the Netherlands, the associated direct investment capital flow would be attributed to the Netherlands even though the funds were to be ultimately used in Hungary.

Except for the small group of countries that tend to serve as locations for offshore financial centers or regional headquarters, however, a host country's level of affiliate activity can usually be at least roughly determined by direct investment capital flows and positions.

In addition to the traditional balance-of-payments and international investment data on US direct investment abroad, BEA also collects a variety of indicators of the scale and activities of the domestic and foreign operations of US MNCs. These data are collected to evaluate questions about US MNCs that cannot be fully addressed by the traditional data alone, such as the effects of US MNCs on the US economy and on foreign host economies. The items collected include balance sheets, income statements, employment, trade in goods, capital expenditures, sales of goods and services, taxes paid, and expenditures for research and development. These data on US-MNC operations are also used by the US BEA to develop estimates of US-MNC gross product.

Current dollar gross product estimates

BEA produces estimates of the gross product, or value added, of foreign affiliates in order to provide a summary measure of foreign affiliates' economic activity. Unlike sales, gross product is a nonduplicative measure that excludes the value of purchases from outside suppliers. Also, unlike assets or employment, it reflects the use by affiliates of both labor and capital. BEA's gross product estimates for foreign affiliates are based on data collected in its annual survey of the domestic and foreign operations of US MNCs. The estimates are limited to MOFAs because the necessary data items are not collected for other foreign affiliates.[3]

Survey respondents are asked to report data for foreign affiliates in US dollars, which, in most cases, requires the respondents to translate data that are denominated in a foreign affiliate's host-country currency to US dollars. Income and expense items are translated using average market exchange rates for the year.[4]

The method for computing the gross product estimates reflects the information available to survey respondents. There are two possible ways to compute the gross product of a firm – from the perspective of the products produced and purchased by the firm (the product side) or from the perspective of the income generated by a firm's value added in production (the income side). On the product side, gross product is measured as the firm's total output (sales plus inventory change) less its purchased inputs. On the income side gross product is measured as the sum of the income generated by the firm's value added in production. As noted in Stone and Stone (1977), "Most of [the income] in the form of wages, salaries, profits, interest, and rent, goes to the factors of production as a reward for their primary inputs; a smaller part goes to the government in indirect taxes; and the remainder goes to provide for depreciation." BEA computes gross product of foreign affiliates on the income side because the survey respondents can readily obtain the necessary data from their accounting records (Table 5.1).

The gross product estimates have been used to provide insights to the role of MNCs in the global economy that would not have been possible with other

Table 5.1 Components of the gross product of MOFAs, 1994

Component	*Millions of US dollars*
Total gross product	403,696
Employee compensation	183,591
Wages and salaries	146,616
Plus: Supplements to wages and salaries	36,975
Profit-type return	84,900
Net income	81,095
Plus: Income taxes	29,277
Plus: Depletion	1,715
Less: Capital gains and losses	90
Less: Income from equity investments	27,097
Net interest paid	−5,033
Monetary interest paid	33,335
Plus: Imputed interest paid	2,419
Less: Monetary interest received	35,047
Less: Imputed interest received	5,740
Indirect business taxes	102,540
Taxes other than income and payroll taxes	101,629
Plus: Production royalty payments to governments	2,363
Less: Subsidies received	1,451
Capital consumption allowances	37,698

Source: US Department of Commerce 1998.

measures. Lipsey *et al.* (1998), for example, used the gross product estimates with data for other countries to show that MNCs have increased their share of world output since the 1970s. Mataloni and Goldberg (1994) used the gross product estimates with sales data to show that foreign affiliates (especially those in manufacturing) have been producing less of their output internally and increasing their reliance on outside suppliers.

The current dollar gross product estimates are, however, of limited use for comparisons of foreign-affiliate production across time or across countries. Changes in the current dollar estimates across time can reflect price changes, as well as changes in the volume of production. Differences in the current dollar estimates across countries can reflect relative exchange rate valuations as well as differences in the volume of production. Ideally, the host-country-currency denominated value of affiliate production of a unit of a particular good or service in different countries would translate to the same US dollar value. In practice, this rarely happens because market exchange rates often do not reflect the true relative purchasing power of currencies. The current dollar estimates for a particular country will be understated at times when a given amount of that country's currency purchases less in the United States (when exchanged for dollars) than it does at home. Likewise, the current dollar estimates for a particular country will be overstated at times when a given amount of that country's currency purchases more in the United States than it does at home.

The effects of exchange rates on the current dollar gross product estimates can be seen by comparing changes in the current dollar estimates with changes in the estimates denominated in host-country currency and with changes in exchange rates. The case of German manufacturing affiliates in 1982–88 offers a typical example for the period (Figure 5.1). The current dollar estimates declined slightly when the dollar rose sharply relative to the German mark (1982–85) even though the estimates in current marks grew at a 2-percent annual rate;[5] thus, increases in the host-country-currency value of affiliate production were fully offset by dollar appreciation. Likewise, the current dollar estimates grew at a 19-percent rate when the dollar fell sharply relative to the German mark (1985–88) even though the estimates in current marks were essentially flat; thus, stability in the host-country-currency value of affiliate production was masked by dollar depreciation. The disparity in the patterns of the current dollar and current mark estimates cannot be fully explained by differences in price inflation because annual price inflation in the two countries, measured in producer prices, did not differ by more

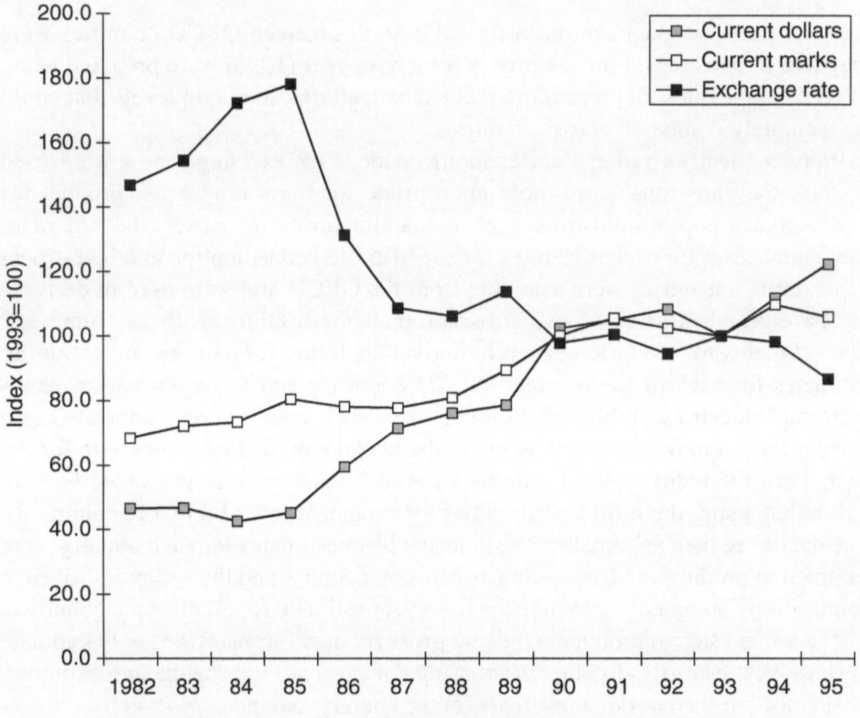

Figure 5.1 Gross product of majority-owned German affiliates in manufacturing in current dollars and in current marks and the dollar–mark exchange rate.

than a few percentage points in 1982–88 and was generally higher in the United States.

Real gross product estimates

In an initial attempt to produce a measure of the foreign manufacturing activities of US MNCs that is roughly comparable across time and across countries, BEA recently developed experimental estimates of the real gross product of MOFAs in manufacturing. The methodology for producing these estimates draws heavily from the tools and techniques for international GDP comparisons that have been developed over the last forty-five years.[6]

Two procedures were used to prepare the estimates of real gross product. A preferred procedure was used for the estimates for nineteen major Organisation for Economic Co-Operation and Development (OECD) host countries that account for over three-quarters of the total gross product of MOFAs in manufacturing. A cruder procedure was used for the estimates for other host countries, because the data needed for the preferred procedure were unavailable.

Nineteen OECD countries

The real gross product estimates for MOFAs in nineteen OECD countries were prepared in two steps. First, estimates for a base year (1993) were prepared using PPP exchange rates, in place of market exchange rates, to obtain levels that could be accurately compared across countries.

Product-specific, rather than economy wide, PPP exchange rates were used because they are considered more appropriate for translating gross product for a particular group of industries, such as manufacturing industries.[7] For the nineteen countries, PPP exchange rates for specific final consumption and investment expenditure categories were available from the OECD and were used in deriving the base-year estimates of real gross product for MOFAs in these countries.[8] The estimates for the base year were derived as follows. First, the current-dollar estimates for each of the nineteen OECD countries and for seven major manufacturing industries (Table 5.2, column 1) in each country were translated into current host-country currency by using the average market exchange rate for the year. Then the industry-level estimates for each country were translated back to US dollars using the most appropriate PPP exchange rate (Table 5.2, column 3). The data were then aggregated; the industry-level estimates for each country were summed to produce the base-year estimates by country, and the estimates for each country were summed to produce the base-year estimate for all nineteen countries.

The second step in producing the real gross product estimates was to extrapolate the base-year estimates to other years using a measure of the change in real output. To do this, the current-dollar estimates at the country and industry level were translated into host-country currency using the average market exchange rate for the year. The resulting estimates by industry were then used, along with country- and

Table 5.2 Categories used for price deflation and currency translation of the gross product estimates

Gross product category	*Foreign-country producer price index category*	*PPP exchange rate category*
Food and kindred products	Food and beverages	Food consumption
Chemicals and allied products	Chemicals	Total GDP
Primary and fabricated metals	Primary and fabricated metals	Total GDP
Industrial machinery and equipment	Nonelectrical machinery	Nonelectrical equipment investment
Electronic and other electric equipment	Electrical machinery	Electrical equipment investment
Transportation equipment	Motor vehicles	Personal transportation equipment consumption
Other manufacturing	Manufacturing except petroleum	Total GDP

industry-specific producer price indexes[9] (Table 5.2, column 2) to produce a Fisher quantity index.

The Fisher quantity index (Q) measures the year-to-year change in real gross product for MOFAs in each country. The formula uses producer price indexes to deflate the current-host-country-currency-denominated estimates, and computes the year-to-year change in the deflated estimates, using a chain-weighted index.

$$Q = \sqrt{\frac{\sum p_{i1}q_{i2}}{\sum p_{i1}q_{i1}} \times \frac{\sum p_{i2}q_{i2}}{\sum p_{i2}q_{i1}}}$$

where the p's are prices in local currency, the q's are quantities, the i's are industries, and 1 and 2 are adjacent years. Because the variables that represent the composites of prices in one period and the quantities in another (such as $p_{i1}q_{i2}$) are not directly observable, the quantity indexes were actually computed using an algebraically equivalent formula consisting of combinations of prices and quantities of the same period (the current-local-currency estimates) and indexes of relative prices in the two periods (the ratios of producer price indexes).[10]

The Fisher quantity indexes were used as the bases for extrapolating the dollar-denominated PPP-based estimates for the base year (1993) to other years covered (1982–92 and 1995). The estimate for all nineteen countries for each year was derived by extrapolating the base-year estimate using a Fisher quantity index that aggregated across countries as well as across industries.[11]

All other countries

Real gross product estimates for all other countries were derived using a cruder method because of the limited availability of data. The estimates were prepared based on the assumption that market exchange rates tend to maintain PPP between these countries' currencies and the US dollar. Therefore, the real gross product estimates were derived by simply deflating the current-dollar gross product estimates with the US implicit price deflator for GDP originating in manufacturing.

The assumption that market exchange rates maintain PPP between currencies is clearly naive, but certain factors precluded the use of the method followed for the nineteen OECD countries. First, some of the most important host countries in this group experienced hyperinflation during much of the period being examined, and the use of the available average annual market exchange rates could not be relied upon to produce estimates that approximated the actual local-currency-denominated values.[12] Second, although economy-wide PPP exchange rates were available for many (if not all) of these countries, PPP exchange rates can be very imprecise and difficult to interpret for pairs of countries – such as the United States and many lower income non-OECD countries – for which the patterns of consumption and production differ so sharply as almost to preclude the construction of a common representative market basket of goods and services. Because of these methodological limitations, real gross product estimates were not produced for these countries individually.

Despite the widespread divergences of market exchange rates from PPP exchange rates, there is reason to believe that the cruder methodology provides reasonable estimates at a highly aggregated level. Market exchange rates and PPP exchange rates may tend to converge over the long term, particularly for groups of countries (because the overvaluation of some currencies, in a PPP sense, may tend to be offset by the undervaluation of others).[13] In addition, the real gross product estimates tend to track long-term changes in MOFA employment with (as would be expected) a lead.

A Fisher quantity index for extrapolating the base-year estimates of all countries combined was derived using the same data and procedure used to create the index for the nineteen OECD countries, except that the estimates for all other countries combined were included in the computation as an additional observation.

Accuracy of the real gross product estimates

The goal of the real gross product estimates is to accurately depict the level of production by foreign affiliates across time and across countries. The success of the estimates in meeting this goal can be roughly gauged by comparing changes in the real and current dollar gross product estimates with changes in market exchange rates. For example, when the exchange value of the US dollar fell sharply in 1985–88, growth in the current dollar estimates abruptly accelerated (Figure 5.2). In contrast, growth in the real gross product estimates was moderate throughout the period. The accuracy of the real gross product estimates for individual countries is most evident in the case of Japan. From 1982 to 1995, when the US-dollar price of the yen increased by a factor of 2, the current dollar gross product

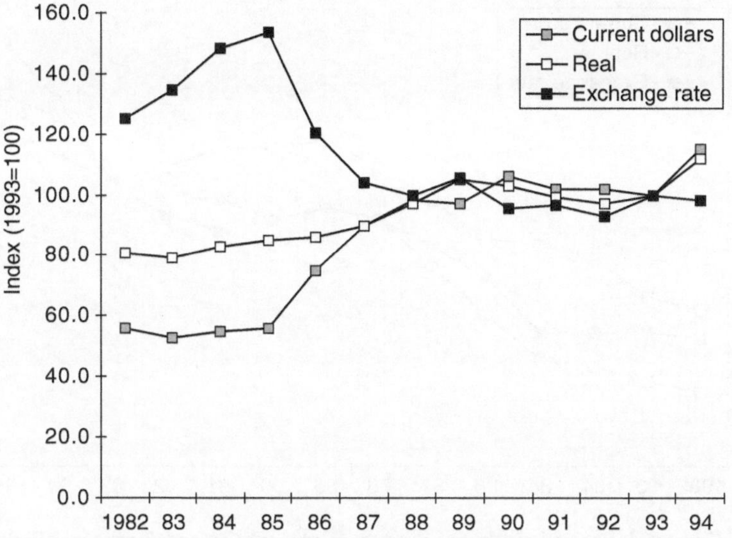

Figure 5.2 Current dollar and real gross product of MOFAs in manufacturing and foreign currency price of the US dollar, 1982–94.

estimates for Japanese affiliates grew by a factor of 6 and year-to-year changes closely tracked changes in the exchange rate (Figure 5.3). Although the real gross product estimates also grew strongly over this period, the changes were more gradual and were more consistent with the pattern one would expect given changes in business conditions and the increase in direct investment flows. Moreover, the changes in real gross product were more in line with another broad indicator of real growth in production – changes in employment by Japanese affiliates.

Areas for future research

Although the real gross product estimates have clear advantages over the current dollar estimates and over other measures of the operations of foreign affiliates, there is much room for improvement. The most obvious limitation of the estimates is their country and industry coverage. Estimates for individual countries are limited to nineteen member countries of the OECD because those are the only countries for which data are available for the preferred methodology. Because the OECD has added several new member countries in recent years, however, the data may soon be available to derive separate real gross product estimates for affiliates in some of these countries. It may also be possible to develop

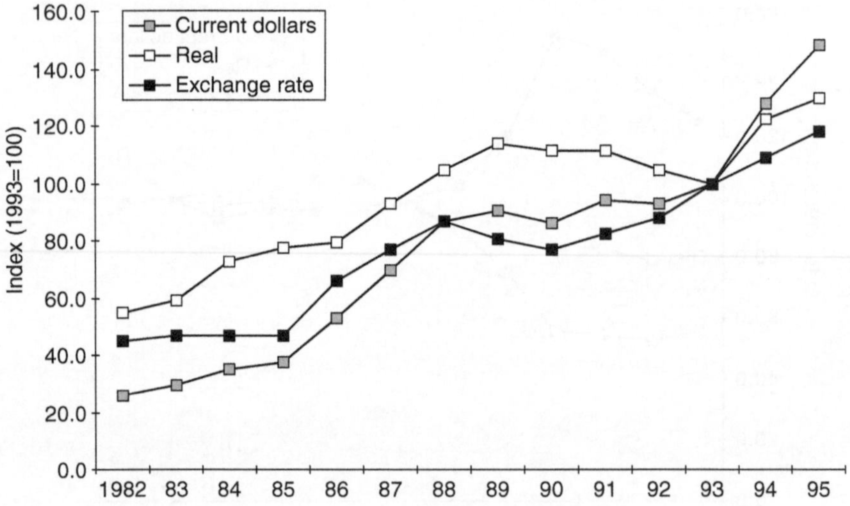

Figure 5.3 Current dollar and real gross product of majority-owned Japanese affiliates in manufacturing and dollar price of Yen, 1982–95.

country-level estimates for selected non-OECD countries by adapting the preferred methodology to reflect the limited price and PPP exchange rate data for these countries.

Expansion of the estimates to non-manufacturing industries, however, appears to be a more remote possibility. Not only are the price and PPP exchange rate data needed to revalue the current dollar estimates unavailable for most non-manufacturing industries, but the method used to derive the current dollar estimates may be less than ideal for some non-manufacturing industries. Nevertheless, although BEA hopes to be able to refine the methodologies used to derive the real gross product estimates and to extend the estimates to new countries, a great deal has already been achieved; the initial estimates have resolved the major valuation problems and have improved our understanding of the country distribution of, and growth in, overseas manufacturing production by US MNCs.

Acknowledgment

This chapter draws upon Raymond J. Mataloni, Jr., "Real Gross Product of U.S. Companies' MOFAs in Manufacturing," *Survey of Current Business* 77 (April 1997): 8–17. The views expressed in this chapter are those of the author and not necessarily those of the Bureau of Economic Analysis.

Notes

1 An affiliate is a business enterprise in which there is direct investment. It is a foreign (US) business enterprise in which a single US (foreign) owner actually, or effectively, has at least a 10 percent equity interest.

2 PPP exchange rates approximate the number of foreign currency units required in a country to buy goods and services that are equivalent to those that can be bought in a base country with one unit of base-country currency. They are derived by comparing the domestic prices of goods and services in different countries. For example, in a hypothetical one-good, two-country world economy, the PPP exchange rate would equal the ratio of the price of the good in one country to the price in the other country; if the good sold for 10 currency units in country A and 1 currency unit in country B, the PPP exchange rate would be 10 units of country A's currency to 1 unit of country B's currency. However, in practice, the derivation of PPP exchange rates is much more complex because of the multitude of goods and services produced and because of the differences among economies in the relative importance of those goods and services. International organizations, primarily the United Nations and the OECD, provide regular estimates of PPP exchange rates.

3 A MOFA is a foreign affiliate in which the combined equity interests of all US direct investors exceeds 50 percent.

4 In accordance with generally accepted accounting principles, however, the income and expenses of affiliates operating in hyperinflationary economies are translated daily at the prevailing market exchange rate. Thus, the accounts for these affiliates are, in effect, kept in dollars.

5 The estimates denominated in German marks were derived by translating the dollar-denominated estimates using an average annual market exchange rate.

6 A 1954 study by Gilbert and Kravis, comparing the GDPs of the members of the former Organisation for European Economic Co-Operation, was a turning point for international gross product comparisons because it made the comparisons based on PPPs. Kravis *et al.* (1975), extended this type of analysis to other geographical regions and founded the first organized effort to conduct these comparisons on a regular basis – the United Nations' International Comparison Project. This early research, and most of the subsequent research, focused on cross-country comparisons of total GDP. Increasingly, however, research in this area has focused on cross-country comparisons of gross product originating in selected groups of firms. The methodology developed by BEA is part of this newer branch of research.

7 See, for example, Hooper (1996).

8 The PPP exchange rates used in this study are from the OECD (1995).

9 The country- and industry-specific producer price indexes are from the OECD's quarterly *Indicators of Industrial Activities*.

10 The rewritten Fisher quantity index is as follows:

$$Q = \sqrt{\frac{\sum (p_{i1}/p_{i2}) \cdot p_{i2}q_{i2}}{\sum p_{i1}q_{i1}} \times \frac{\sum p_{i2}q_{i2}}{\sum (p_{i2}/p_{i1}) \cdot p_{i1}q_{i1}}}$$

11 In contrast to the computation of the index for each country, the current-local-currency estimates (such as $p_{i1}q_{i1}$) for each country had to be translated to a common currency before they could be used in computing the index for the nineteen countries combined. The current-local-currency estimates for all years (1982–94) were translated to US dollars using the PPP exchange rates for 1993, yielding dollar-denominated series that reflected host-country price conditions. Though not true PPP-based current-dollar series (because they reflected foreign rather than US price conditions), these dollar-denominated series had to be constructed as an intermediate step in deriving an extrapolator for the base-year aggregate.

12 As noted earlier, the data underlying the estimates for such countries typically would have been translated into on a daily basis.

13 Hakkio (1992) and Lothian and Taylor (1996) identify a tendency for market exchange rates to converge with PPP exchange rates over the long term.

References

Gilbert, Milton and Irving Kravis (1954), *An International Comparison of National Products and the Purchasing Power of Currencies*, Paris: OECD.

Hakkio, Craig S. (1992), "Is Purchasing Power Parity a Useful Guide to the Dollar?" *Economic Review*, 3: 37–51.

Hooper, Peter (1996), "Comparing Manufacturing Output Levels Among the Major Industrial Countries," in *Industry Productivity: International Comparison and Measurement Issues*, Paris: OECD.

Kravis, Irving, Zoltan Kenessey, Alan Heston, and Robert Summers (1975), *A System of International Comparisons of Gross Product and Purchasing Power*, Baltimore: Johns Hopkins University Press.

Lipsey, Robert E., Magnus Blomström, and Eric Ramstetter (1998), "Multinational Firms in World Production," in *Geography and Ownership as Bases for Economic Accounting*, Chicago: University of Chicago Press.

Lothian, James R. and Mark P. Taylor (1996), "Exchange Rate Behavior: The Recent Float from the Perspective of the Past Two Centuries," *Journal of Political Economy*, 104(3): 488–509.

Mataloni, Raymond John, Jr., and Lee Goldberg (1994), "Gross Product of US Multinational Companies, 1977–91," *Survey of Current Business*, 74: 42–63.

Organisation for Economic Co-Operation and Development (1995), *Purchasing Power Parities and Real Expenditures 1993, EKS Results*, Vol. 1, Paris: OECD.

——, *Indicators of Industrial Activities*, Paris: OECD.

Stone, Richard and Giovanna (1977), *National Income and Expenditure*, London: Bowes & Bowes.

6 Research issues in Japanese FDI

Roger Farrell

Introduction

Since the mid-1980s Japan has been one of the major sources of direct investment to the rest of the world, as many Japanese firms in the manufacturing and service sectors internationalised their operations and established a global network of subsidiaries. This important phenomenon had a significant impact on both Japan and host countries and an extensive literature developed to explain both the industrial and geographical distribution of investment. Generally, discussion has been in terms of the firm-specific, industry-specific and locational factors which influenced the pattern of investment. Nevertheless, examination of motivations and determinants of Japanese foreign direct investment (FDI) has been held back by the limitations of the available statistical database.

Understanding which firms and industries are more likely to pursue FDI, which is characterised by an extension of strategic control over corporate activities in other countries, is central to the study of its causes.[1] The leading paradigm used to explain FDI, the industrial organisation model, argues that direct investors require a firm-specific proprietary advantage to motivate the expansion of their operations into other countries, where they are assumed to be less familiar with local conditions than domestic competitors (Hymer, 1976; Dunning, 1993). This type II form of investment typically involves both ownership and active management of foreign subsidiaries over the longer term.[2]

An alternative approach is to emphasise general determinants, such as exchange rates, asset values or variations in international yields in the short term, particularly for categories of FDI which involve passive, or type I foreign investors (Hymer, 1976). In such cases nominal control may exceed the definitional ownership requirement of 10 per cent, but investment is essentially portfolio in nature, so that the firm-specific factors may be relatively unimportant (Caves, 1993; Froot and Stein, 1989). For industries such as real estate and finance and insurance, indirect determinants may be more important (Farrell, 1997).

The dichotomy implies that various industrial categories of Japanese FDI will have different levels of explanation. For direct investment by mining, energy and manufacturing industry, the more traditional types of resource-seeking, market-access or factor-cost motivations for FDI will dominate, although broader factors may be influential. On the other hand, FDI by Japanese real estate and finance industries may be dominated by non-strategic factors, such as low returns in the home country, rising asset prices and an appreciating exchange rate.[3] A comprehensive FDI database is necessary to test the relative importance of such factors.

This paper provides an overview of the pattern and theoretical explanations for Japanese FDI in recent decades and then considers the impediments to further research, such as the limitations of available FDI statistics from the Ministry of Finance (MOF), the Ministry of International Trade and Industry (MITI) and other sources. An outline is then given of an expanded version of the MOF database and its usefulness in overcoming a number of research impediments, together with the identification of a future research agenda for the study of Japanese FDI using this framework.

The pattern of investment

In recent years Japan has been one of the largest sources of FDI in the world, in a period when total global flows of FDI have increased sharply, from US$63 billion in 1985 to US$360 billion in 1996. In the same period Japanese outflows rose from US$10 billion to about US$50 billion, after peaking at US$68 billion in 1989. There have been a number of waves of investment, triggered by a variety of factors, including deregulation in Japan, the increasing international competitiveness of many Japanese corporations and the steady appreciation of the yen after it began to appreciate from 1971.

In the prewar period Japanese FDI occurred typically as an adjunct to international trade and trading companies were major investors (Wilkins, 1990). In the 1950s and 1960s, Japanese FDI was relatively small scale, but began to move upwards in the following decade with faster economic growth, the emergence of a current account surplus and some deregulation of outward capital controls in Japan. For the previous two decades much of FDI was directed to the acquisition of secure supplies of mineral resources, such as coal and iron ore, to the establishment of a marketing network and by labour-intensive manufacturing industries (Komiya and Wakasugi, 1990).

By 1970 direct investment was only significant for the mining, lumber and pulp and textiles industries. A decade later, the chemicals, steel and electrical equipment had become active investors, with FDI over 1 per cent of industry GDP, but manufacturing FDI overall accounted for only 0.5 per cent of industry GDP. The revision of the *Foreign Exchange Law* in 1980 removed an administrative obstacle to investment, since investors no longer required prior approval but were merely required to notify the MOF of intended investment.[4] The industrial and geographical distribution of Japanese FDI is shown in Figures 6.1 and 6.2.

Following the 1980 regulatory change, which narrowed the definition of FDI from 25 to 10 per cent of ownership, a number of other industries became more active in the establishment of overseas subsidiaries and operations, including the

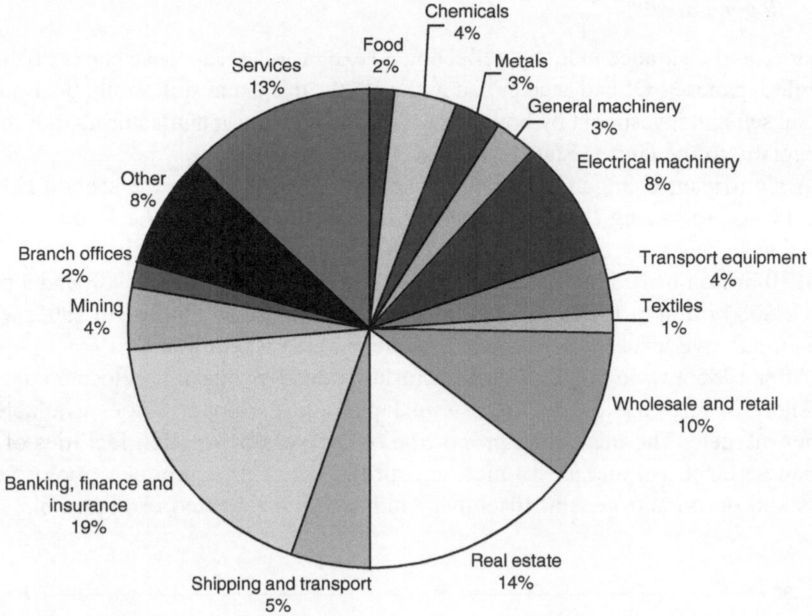

Figure 6.1 Japanese cumulative FDI by industry, March 1998.

Source: MOF, *Ministry of Finance Statistics Monthly*, Tokyo.

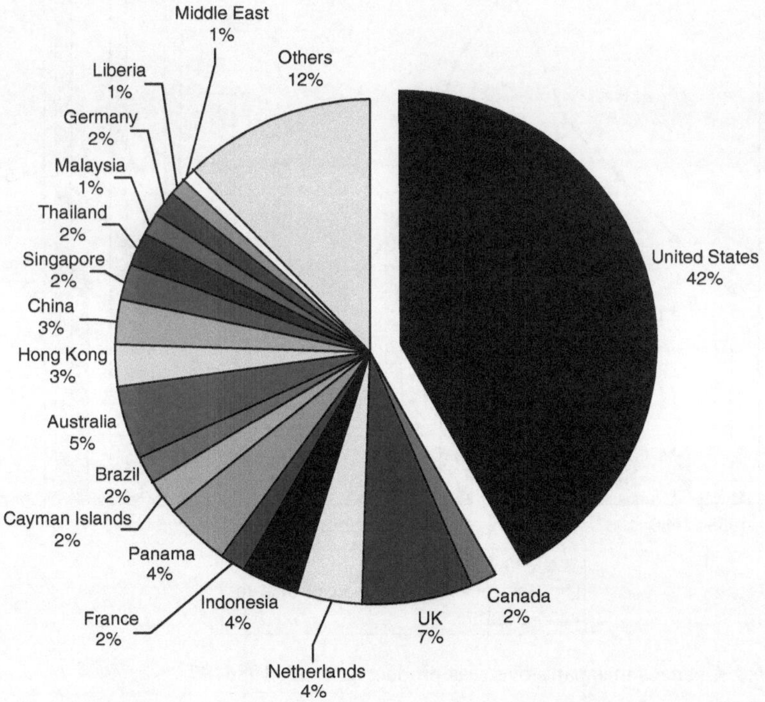

Figure 6.2 Japanese cumulative FDI by country, March 1998.

Source: MOF, *Ministry of Finance Statistics Monthly*, Tokyo.

finance and insurance industry, reflecting an expansion of Japanese banks offshore. While Japanese FDI had accelerated in the 1970s, this expansion would be dwarfed by subsequent investment by both manufacturing and non-manufacturing industries, especially to the United States and East Asian countries.

A significant change to postwar Japanese FDI occurred in the second half of the 1980s, following the sharp appreciation in the yen after the Plaza Accord. Outflows grew very quickly in the 1980s – from under US$5 billion in 1980 to US$10 billion in 1984, US$22 billion in 1986, US$47 billion in 1988 and a peak of US$68 billion in 1989, falling somewhat to about US$50 billion in 1995, when the cumulative level of investment approached US$800 billion.

After 1985 a wide range of manufacturing industries began to relocate industry offshore in response to higher costs in Japan and the opportunities available in other markets. The increasing proportion of overseas production facilities of the Japanese electrical and electronics, chemicals, transport equipment (motor vehicles and parts) and general machinery industries is reflected in Figure 6.3. The

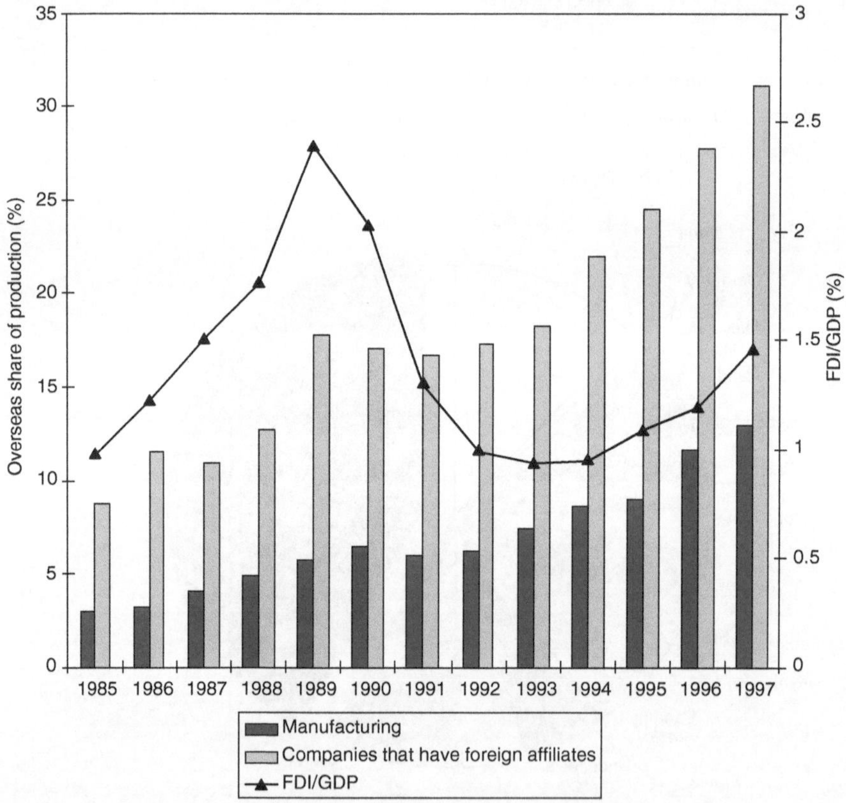

Figure 6.3 Changes in Japan's overseas production ratio, 1985–97.

Sources: MITI, Sixth *Basic Survey of Overseas Business Activities of Japanese Companies, 1998* and author's database of Japanese FDI.

propensity for Japanese industry to establish operations offshore has been less evident for industries that are less internationally competitive.

Manufacturing operations were predominantly established in 'Asia' and 'North America' according to MOF statistics, but no details are readily available of the host countries or changes in the scale of investment over time. In FY 1995 the overseas production ratio of the Japanese manufacturing industry was 9.0 per cent, up 0.4 points over the previous fiscal year. In FY 1996 it is expected to reach 9.6 per cent (see Figure 6.3). In recent years, Japanese manufacturing FDI has shifted from North America and Europe to Asia, with the number of companies

Table 6.1 Distribution of Japanese FDI in manufacturing, by country, 1951–95

Share of total Japanese Manufacturing FDI (%)						
Host country	*1951–79*	*1980–83*	*1984–87*	*1988–91*	*1992–95*	*1951–95*
North and Central America						
United States	32.6	35.1	53.7	51.2	36.4	41.0
Canada	5.6	1.9	3.9	3.1	1.8	2.7
Mexico	3.9	4.4	2.0	0.7	1.4	1.6
Europe						
United Kingdom	1.7	1.5	3.4	7.6	4.2	4.7
Netherlands	0.6	1.3	0.6	5.2	3.3	3.1
Germany	1.1	1.4	1.3	2.3	2.0	1.8
France	1.0	1.3	1.4	2.0	1.4	1.5
Asia						
Indonesia	22.6	11.3	2.9	2.7	4.3	5.5
Thailand	5.1	1.8	2.4	4.7	4.2	3.7
Malaysia	6.1	5.6	2.2	3.5	4.1	3.4
Philippines	3.5	1.2	0.8	1.0	2.1	1.4
Singapore	10.9	8.0	3.3	2.2	2.1	3.3
Hong Kong	3.1	0.7	1.1	0.8	1.6	1.1
Taiwan	5.7	2.5	4.2	1.8	1.5	2.3
South Korea	14.2	1.3	2.8	1.4	0.8	2.2
ASEAN-4	37.3	19.9	8.3	11.9	14.7	14.0
ASEAN-5	48.2	27.9	11.6	14.1	16.8	17.3
NIEs	23.0	4.5	8.1	4.0	3.9	5.6
Oceania						
Australia	9.6	2.9	2.5	1.9	4.4	3.0
South America						
Brazil	33.8	9.5	4.2	1.5	2.0	5.0
World ($USm)	5314 (100)	8675 (100)	16495 (100)	57886 (100)	53209 (100)	219533 (100)

Sources: Calculated from MOF, *Annual Report of the International Finance Bureau* (*Okurasho Kokusai Kinyu Kyoku Nenpo*), various years.

Notes
FDI approvals recorded up to 1980 and notifications thereafter. Figures in US$ values and for Japanese financial years (e.g. FY1997 refers to the period from April 1997 to March 1998). ASEAN-4 = Association of Southeast Asian Nations (Indonesia, Malaysia, Philippines, Thailand); ASEAN-5 includes Singapore; and NIEs refer to South Korea, Taiwan and Hong Kong.

reaching 10,416 at the end of FY 1995 (MITI, 1997).[5] Changes in the postwar geographical distribution of foreign affiliates of Japanese manufacturing firms are given in Table 6.1.

Movements in Japanese FDI and trade flows are closely linked (Petri, 1994). The establishment of overseas subsidiaries affects flows of Japanese exports and imports by particular industries, such as the electrical and electronics industry and the motor vehicle industry. These industries typically export to third countries or to Japan, while the host countries for such investment often import capital equipment and components from Japan (EXIM, 1995). The electrical, transport and precision machinery industries averaged 55 per cent in intra-firm exports in 1992 (Yoshimatsu, 1996).

The changing industrial distribution of Japanese FDI is shown by the decline in natural resources development, such as oil exploration and mining, compared to manufacturing – which in turn has become less important relative to services (Table 6.2). Within the manufacturing sector the relative composition of the major industries has changed over time with the rate of transfer of operations offshore. This transfer occurred rapidly for the electrical and electronics industry, particularly to ASEAN and China.

The concurrent expansion of Japanese FDI in non-manufacturing sectors such as finance, insurance, real estate and services since the mid-1980s has changed the composition of investment (Figure 6.2). The share of real estate FDI of total FDI outflows, for example, jumped from 1.9 per cent in 1980 to a peak of over 21 per cent in 1991 and 12.5 per cent in 1994. The cumulative stock of real estate FDI in 1995 exceeded US$75 billion – an annual average increase of over 40 per cent for the decade.

A similar expansion occurred for the finance and insurance industries, boosted by the bubble economy in Japan, together with a significant increase in FDI by service industries. A considerable part of such investment went to North America, Europe and Oceania. The mode of investment also changed, particularly in the United States, where mergers and acquisitions accounted for 88 per cent of Japanese FDI in 1988 (Watanabe, 1993).

More recently, the pace of outflows of Japanese FDI has moderated due to the economic slowdown in Japan and the increased liquidity problems experienced in a number of industries due to the collapse of land and stock asset prices after 1990. Nevertheless, the recent Asian financial crisis does not appear to have affected Japanese FDI in manufacturing industry in the affected countries and despite the capital flight of short-term speculative capital from these countries, it appears likely that FDI inflows will increase, including from Japan (Krugman, 1998).

The limitations of current measures of Japanese FDI

Official statistics on FDI often vary significantly, definitions of FDI change over time and their collection methodologies, coverage and levels of disaggregation all differ (Vukmanic, 1985). There are four major sources of statistics on FDI published in Japan; notifications to the MOF, industry surveys by the MITI, balance of payments data by the Bank of Japan (BOJ) and industry surveys by the

Table 6.2 Waves of Japanese FDI 1966–97, by sector

Industry of investor	*Average share of Japanese FDI (%)*							
	1966–69	*1970–73*	*1974–77*	*1978–81*	*1982–85*	*1986–89*	*1990–93*	*1994–97*
Agriculture, Forestry and Fisheries	2.4	2.5	2.8	2.0	0.5	0.4	0.5	0.5
Mining	34.2	22.2	23.4	18.5	5.6	2.0	2.7	2.8
Manufacturing	21.1	32.9	33.5	33.3	24.9	24.5	29.0	37.2
Food and Beverages	1.0	1.9	1.6	1.6	0.9	1.3	1.7	1.9
Textiles	4.5	7.2	4.6	1.9	0.9	0.7	1.4	1.4
Lumber and Pulp	3.5	2.5	2.2	0.9	0.8	0.9	0.8	0.9
Chemicals	1.4	6.2	7.9	6.4	3.0	2.7	4.5	4.2
Steel and Non-ferrous	3.9	4.3	4.7	9.0	5.4	2.4	2.1	4.1
General Machinery	1.4	2.3	2.5	2.5	2.3	2.6	3.0	3.2
Electrical Machinery	2.4	4.2	4.4	5.2	4.4	6.4	7.4	10.9
Transport Equipment	1.9	1.6	2.7	3.6	5.2	3.3	3.6	5.6
Other Manufactures	1.1	2.7	2.9	2.2	2.0	4.2	4.5	5.0
Construction	0.9	0.8	1.2	1.2	0.8	0.8	0.9	0.8
Wholesale and Retail	14.0	14.1	14.8	15.6	15.9	7.3	12.0	10.3
Finance and Insurance	9.3	7.5	7.1	6.8	19.9	27.3	14.2	16.3
Real Estate	Na	2.1	0.7	2.0	6.2	18.9	18.5	12.3
Transport and Communication	Na	Na	Na	3.1	13.5	5.5	5.1	4.8
Services	Na	Na	2.0	5.6	7.0	11.0	15.9	13.5
Total (US$ million)	100 (1724)	100 (8510)	100 (11943)	100 (23217)	100 (38220)	100 (170246)	100 (168658)	100 (198146)

Sources: Calculated from MOF, *Annual Report of the International Finance Bureau (Okurasho Kokusai Kinyu Kyoku Nenpo)*, various years, Tokyo.

Note
FDI approvals recorded up to 1980 and notifications thereafter. Figures in US$ values and for Japanese financial years (e.g. FY1997 refers to the period from April 1997 to March 1998).

Export–Import (EXIM) BOJ. The MITI and EXIM industry surveys exclude major industries, such as real estate, finance and insurance and services, while the BOJ balance of payments data is based on actual capital flows and does not include industry or country detail.

There are constraints on the study of FDI outflows because of the considerable problems in accessing and using Japanese FDI statistics. There are several indicators that measure the internationalisation of Japanese industry, including MOF notifications of FDI, BOJ data on disbursed FDI and surveys by the EXIM Bank, the Toyo Keizai company and the MITI.

Each has a number of disadvantages – the MITI surveys have a low and varying coverage rate, even though they provide considerable detail of sales, employment and sales and export to GDP ratios (Ramstetter, 1996). BOJ FDI data has no industry breakdown and excludes reinvested earnings, as does the MOF series. The EXIM surveys focus on case studies of investment and surveys of motivations for investment by country and industry, but a consolidated database is unavailable. The major source for these statistics is the MOF which records notifications of direct investment by Japanese corporations on an annual basis, but there are few details of investment by country *and* industry in the widely disseminated summary surveys.

The MOF statistical series, on overseas investment notified to the Ministry, is recorded in the *Monthly Report of Fiscal and Monetary Statistics* and the *Annual Report of the International Finance Bureau of the MOF*. Under current legislation governing foreign investment, direct investment is notified before the date of implementation, whereas prior to 1980, direct investment was tightly regulated and all investment had to be approved by the MOF.

The MOF statistics are broken down into investor by industry of investor in Japan, but the definition of FDI has changed over time. Up to November 1980, the statistics refer to proposed investment approved by the Ministry, but from December 1980 they are on a notification basis, following the revision of the Foreign Exchange Law in Japan. The precise accuracy of the statistics may be questioned, as it is unlikely that either approved or notified FDI equates with actual investment and divestment is excluded (Stein, 1995).

One deficiency of the MOF FDI statistics is that only a limited range of FDI by industry and country data is available from published source, particularly in English. A close examination of the literature confirms that virtually all researchers use statistics on industry by region, even when the concept of regions such as 'Asia' is not meaningful. Industry-specific studies also often lack detailed statistics of MOF outflows data by country – even though a large part of the literature on Japanese FDI has focused on explaining direct investment in major industries such as electronics, motor vehicles, chemicals and industrial machinery.

An expanded MOF database

To overcome some of these limitations, a set of annual statistics of Japanese FDI by industry and country has been compiled. Annual notifications data is available from 1966 for outflows; from 1972 for outflows by country; and from 1980 for outflows by country and industry (Farrell, 2000). The attached tables illustrate the richness of the revised database. Table 6.3 gives data for Japanese FDI by industry over the period 1966 to 1997.

This database allows either cross-sectional or time series examination of notifications of investment in sixty-two countries by industry over a period of over thirty years. The clearer blueprint in the database of Japanese FDI allow the industry-specific and geographical determinants of investment to be examined more fully. Likewise, the time series and cross-sectional data of Japanese investment allows the testing of hypotheses of the determinants of FDI and the industry-specific and country-specific factors which affected the decisions of Japanese investors to expand their operations offshore.

Using the database, the relative importance or intensity of Japanese FDI in a particular industry in a particular country, or for the industrial distribution of FDI in a country can be estimated. In the same way, time series or cross-sectional data of Japanese investment by country or industry can be used to allow the testing of hypotheses of the determinants of FDI. Access to such data allows a separate examination of the industry-specific and country-specific factors that influenced the decisions of Japanese investors to expand their operations offshore.

The larger MOF database creates a number of new possibilities for research into the industry-specific and country-specific determinants of the pattern of investment in recent decades – for example, data problems for Japanese FDI have inhibited the calculation of intensity indexes, particularly as industry data for particular countries has been difficult to obtain (Bora, 1996). Some of the areas opened up for research are discussed below.

Comparative advantage and FDI

A number of studies, such as Leamer (1984) and Song (1996) examine the empirical hypothesis that international trade is determined by factor endowments. Leamer (1984) uses cross-country data to examine links between trade and resource endowments and the role of comparative advantage. However, the analogous hypothesis that FDI is similarly influenced or determined by the characteristics of host countries has not been similarly explored.

This research appears possible, using a cross-country study of sixty-two countries and the factor endowment data assembled for the trade studies. Further research into the links between Japanese FDI and trade could be pursued (Petri, 1994). The locational determinants of Japanese FDI by industry can be tested on a cross-sectional basis to ascertain the importance of country-specific determinants, such as exchange rate changes, resource endowments or trade links or on a time series basis for individual countries.

Internationalisation of Japanese industry

Using this approach, gravity coefficients for the share of Japanese FDI by industry for a particular host country could be compared to that country's share of total

Table 6.3 Japanese FDI by industry, 1966–97 (US$ million, current prices)

Major industry	*1966*	*1967*	*1968*	*1969*	*1970*	*1971*	*1972*	*1973*	*1974*	*1975*	*1976*	*1977*	*1978*	*1979*	*1980*	*1981*
Agriculture, Forestry and Fisheries	5	8	13	15	18	65	28	98	52	64	64	150	123	155	73	111
Mining	73	62	159	296	235	222	919	511	742	605	995	452	338	857	565	2534
Manufacturing	86	77	68	133	239	534	528	1499	879	1027	1025	1074	2038	1693	1706	2305
Food and Beverages	2	6	5	4	15	52	29	68	64	58	25	48	67	103	54	142
Textiles	11	17	15	34	49	74	163	326	176	98	112	158	172	89	91	91
Lumber and Pulp	36	2	17	5	79	33	35	64	61	89	63	52	23	33	78	65
Chemicals	9	3	5	7	25	42	66	394	97	253	270	325	705	238	314	228
Steel and Non-ferrous	6	20	4	38	9	60	53	245	149	148	171	99	498	578	493	521
General Machinery	3	7	5	9	16	50	40	86	90	98	53	61	119	160	102	207
Electrical Machinery	5	7	7	22	22	111	69	156	99	96	164	161	243	180	309	475
Transport Equipment	10	12	4	6	3	13	42	80	40	101	93	86	114	150	176	406
Other Manufactures	3	3	5	7	22	99	31	79	103	87	74	85	99	161	89	169
Construction	6	1	1	7	5	38	8	18	18	32	51	39	72	85	37	96
Wholesale and Retail	23	42	118	58	47	485	227	440	351	674	404	344	823	834	797	1174
Finance and Insurance	21	46	50	44	89	65	174	308	143	310	219	176	154	198	380	843
Real Estate	na	na	na	na	na	na	55	120	18	11	15	35	98	105	91	167
Transport and Communication	na	na	na	na	na	na	na	na	na	na	na	na	na	na	na	722
Services	na	na	na	na	na	na	na	na	na	na	124	109	192	244	251	623
Total	227	275	557	665	904	1774	2338	3494	2395	3280	3462	2806	4598	4995	4693	8931
¥/US$ rate	360	360	360	360	360	349.3	303.2	271.7	292.1	296.8	296.6	268.5	210.4	219.1	226.7	220.5

Major industry	*1982*	*1983*	*1984*	*1985*	*1986*	*1987*	*1988*	*1989*	*1990*	*1991*	*1992*	*1993*	*1994*	*1995*	*1996*	*1997*
Agriculture, Forestry and Fisheries	62	35	50	54	67	141	256	198	214	348	230	129	368	199	245	168
Mining	685	382	484	598	669	511	1013	1262	1328	1003	1270	946	475	1100	1622	2374
Manufacturing	2076	2588	2505	2352	3806	7832	13805	16284	15486	12311	1005	11132	13784	19400	20937	19612
Food and Beverages	78	77	118	90	127	328	419	1300	821	632	517	888	1260	863	754	972
Textiles	67	174	85	28	63	206	317	533	796	616	428	498	641	1072	626	356
Lumber and Pulp	76	91	115	15	57	317	604	555	314	312	431	346	140	373	640	580
Chemicals	322	450	223	133	355	910	1293	2109	2292	1602	2015	1742	2601	2212	2128	1433
Steel and Non-ferrous	468	479	718	385	328	786	1367	1591	1047	907	824	754	1038	1594	2528	2950
General Machinery	164	169	185	352	626	687	1432	1762	1454	1284	1104	1171	1622	1926	1486	1302
Electrical Machinery	267	502	409	513	987	2421	3041	4480	5684	2296	1817	2762	2634	5521	6731	6783
Transport Equipment	439	486	437	627	828	1473	1281	2053	1872	1996	1188	942	2021	2063	4003	3056
Other Manufactures	195	160	215	208	435	703	4051	1901	1207	2666	1732	2029	1826	3776	2040	2181
Construction	44	55	112	94	250	87	309	646	300	429	534	274	357	410	331	463
Wholesale and Retail	1899	1164	1482	1550	1861	2269	3204	5148	6156	5247	3705	5096	4391	5478	4942	5612
Finance and Insurance	533	1167	2085	3805	7240	10673	13104	15395	8047	4972	4579	6401	6499	5609	8037	12139
Real Estate	354	375	430	1207	3997	5428	8641	14143	11107	8899	5147	6070	5122	6184	6418	6570
Transport and Communication	924	1363	1651	1240	1925	2145	2372	2927	2169	2489	1725	2157	2603	2347	1860	2724
Services	702	622	681	665	1560	2780	3732	10616	11292	5413	6530	3543	7061	11011	4182	4436
Total	7703	8145	10155	12217	22320	33364	47022	67540	56911	41584	34138	36025	41051	52732	49628	54735
¥/US$ rate	249.1	237.5	237.5	238.5	168.5	144.6	128.2	138.0	144.8	134.7	126.7	111.2	102.2	0.94	109.0	121.0

Sources: Calculated from MOF, *Annual Report of the International Finance Bureau* (*Okurasho Kokusai Kinyu Kyoku Nenpo*), various years and Economic Planning Agency, *Annual Report on National Accounts*, Tokyo, various years. Figures for 1996 and 1997 GDP by industry estimated at same level as 1995.

Notes

a Figures for 1995, 1996 and 1997 in yen values (converted at ¥100 = US$), while those for previous years were in US$ values.

b Excludes FDI made for the purpose of establishing or expanding overseas branches of Japanese companies.

c An industry breakdown of FDI is unavailable before 1966. FDI approvals recorded up to 1980 and notifications thereafter.

d Figures in US$ values and for Japanese financial years (e.g. FY1997 refers to the period from April 1997 to March 1998).

Table 6.4 Internationalisation of Japanese industry, 1966–97 (FDI/GDP for each industry, per cent)

Major industry	*1966*	*1967*	*1968*	*1969*	*1970*	*1971*	*1972*	*1973*	*1974*	*1975*	*1976*	*1977*	*1978*	*1979*	*1980*	*1981*
Agriculture, Forestry and Fisheries	0.06	0.07	0.12	0.11	0.13	0.54	0.16	0.41	0.20	0.23	0.22	0.43	0.28	0.36	0.19	0.27
Mining	6.44	5.23	12.08	19.45	13.69	12.28	42.21	16.93	22.96	23.20	35.12	12.56	8.06	14.84	9.28	41.81
Manufacturing	0.25	0.18	0.13	0.22	0.33	0.66	0.50	1.03	0.57	0.69	0.60	0.52	0.71	0.56	0.54	0.66
Food and Beverages	0.06	0.10	0.08	0.04	0.18	0.58	0.29	0.50	0.47	0.35	0.12	0.19	0.20	0.32	0.15	0.37
Textiles	0.49	0.67	0.47	1.02	1.25	1.71	3.20	4.37	2.23	1.40	1.43	1.67	1.43	0.69	0.76	0.64
Lumber and Pulp	3.42	0.24	1.22	0.36	4.00	1.60	1.31	1.57	1.10	1.88	1.23	0.87	0.29	0.39	0.91	0.68
Chemicals	0.26	0.07	0.12	0.15	0.41	0.62	0.73	3.59	0.82	2.23	2.13	2.12	3.10	0.99	1.40	0.94
Steel and Non-ferrous	0.17	0.49	0.06	0.65	0.10	0.71	0.45	1.40	0.78	0.90	0.89	0.50	1.60	1.52	1.25	1.57
General Machinery	0.09	0.21	0.11	0.13	0.21	0.56	0.40	0.64	0.57	0.65	0.33	0.34	0.49	0.59	0.36	0.60
Electrical Machinery	0.19	0.20	0.16	0.34	0.28	1.34	0.60	1.01	0.63	0.69	0.92	0.75	0.79	0.53	0.82	1.10
Transport Equipment	0.30	0.24	0.05	0.09	0.04	0.16	0.35	0.47	0.22	0.52	0.41	0.31	0.31	0.39	0.42	0.85
Other Manufactures	0.06	0.05	0.08	0.10	0.24	0.95	0.20	0.37	0.44	0.34	0.29	0.28	0.23	0.36	0.20	0.33
Construction	0.08	0	0	0.07	0.04	0.20	0.02	0.05	0.04	0.06	0.10	0.06	0.08	0.09	0.04	0.09
Wholesale and Retail	0.15	0.25	0.56	0.24	0.16	1.50	0.53	0.75	0.50	0.91	0.49	0.36	0.64	0.65	0.62	0.81
Finance and Insurance	0.48	0.87	0.77	0.60	0.93	0.58	1.13	1.43	0.58	1.11	0.75	0.50	0.31	0.39	0.68	1.55
Real Estate	na	na	na	na	na	na	0.21	0.34	0.05	0.02	0.03	0.05	0.11	0.11	0.09	0.14
Transport and Communication	na	na	na	na	na	na	na	na	na	na	na	na	na	na	na	0.91
Services	na	na	na	na	na	na	na	na	na	na	na	0.14	0.21	0.21	0.20	0.46
Total	0.23	0.23	0.40	0.40	0.46	0.80	0.80	0.87	0.55	0.70	0.66	0.44	0.51	0.54	0.48	0.84
¥/US$ rate	360	360	360	360	360	349.33	303.17	271.70	292.08	296.79	296.55	268.51	210.44	219.14	226.74	220.5

Major industry	*1982*	*1983*	*1984*	*1985*	*1986*	*1987*	*1988*	*1989*	*1990*	*1991*	*1992*	*1993*	*1994*	*1995*	*1996*	*1997*
Agriculture, Forestry and Fisheries	0.16	0.09	0.12	0.13	0.12	0.21	0.35	0.25	0.28	0.44	0.28	0.15	0.36	0.20	0.29	0.22
Mining	13.95	7.45	9.52	11.80	8.82	6.04	9.50	18.1	17.47	11.89	14.15	10.03	4.74	10.10	17.27	28.06
Manufacturing	0.64	0.76	0.67	0.60	0.67	1.14	1.66	1.93	1.87	1.31	1.02	1.05	1.23	1.53	1.91	1.99
Food and Beverages	0.21	0.19	0.29	0.22	0.20	0.46	0.51	1.53	0.98	0.68	0.49	0.70	0.97	0.60	0.61	0.87
Textiles	0.54	1.45	0.70	0.24	0.39	1.04	1.38	2.95	4.61	3.41	2.16	2.38	3.18	5.26	3.56	2.25
Lumber and Pulp	0.89	0.94	1.08	0.15	0.37	1.62	2.50	2.16	1.34	1.25	1.65	1.19	0.45	1.01	2.01	2.02
Chemicals	1.36	1.68	0.76	0.46	0.74	1.54	1.83	3.01	3.58	2.27	2.55	2.07	2.82	2.09	2.33	1.74
Steel and Non-ferrous	1.60	1.67	1.90	0.99	0.61	1.16	1.54	2.21	1.62	1.25	1.11	1.03	1.31	1.75	3.22	4.17
General Machinery	0.50	0.45	0.46	0.77	0.99	0.99	1.60	1.69	1.35	1.00	0.86	0.95	1.28	1.28	1.15	1.11
Electrical Machinery	0.65	1.12	0.75	0.90	1.25	2.60	2.66	3.37	4.31	1.52	1.23	1.74	1.51	2.77	3.92	4.38
Transport Equipment	1.00	1.20	1.01	1.08	1.58	1.86	1.37	2.49	2.32	2.24	1.26	0.90	1.84	1.61	3.62	3.07
Other Manufactures	0.42	0.30	0.39	0.35	0.49	0.66	3.22	1.48	0.92	1.81	1.11	1.17	1.02	1.91	1.20	1.42
Construction	0.05	0.06	0.12	0.09	0.17	0.05	0.13	0.22	0.10	0.13	0.14	0.06	0.07	0.08	0.07	0.12
Wholesale and Retail	1.47	0.66	0.83	0.86	0.72	0.71	0.85	1.28	1.55	1.14	0.75	1.18	0.75	0.84	0.88	1.11
Finance and Insurance	0.94	1.74	2.99	5.08	6.65	7.75	7.77	8.02	4.62	2.67	2.41	3.14	2.77	2.25	3.74	6.27
Real Estate	0.31	0.33	0.35	0.93	2.05	2.21	2.90	4.32	3.46	2.42	1.23	1.21	0.89	0.93	1.12	1.27
Transport and Communication	0.95	0.86	0.87	0.81	1.61	1.92	2.18	1.42	1.11	1.13	0.74	0.83	0.89	0.70	0.64	1.05
Services	0.42	0.76	1.25	2.01	0.54	3.07	3.16	2.50	2.63	1.06	1.13	0.52	0.89	1.26	0.55	0.65
Total	0.78	0.74	0.73	0.98	1.22	1.50	1.76	2.39	2.03	1.30	0.99	0.93	0.95	1.09	1.19	1.46
¥/US$ rate	249.1	237.5	237.5	238.5	168.5	144.6	128.2	138.0	144.8	134.7	126.7	111.2	102.2	0.94	109.0	121.0

Sources: Calculated from MOF (*Okura-sho*), *Annual Report of the International Finance Bureau* (*Okurasho Kokusai Kinyu Kyoku Nenpo*), various years and Economic Planning Agency, *Annual Report on National Accounts*, Tokyo, various years. Figures for 1996 and 1997 GDP by industry estimated at same level as 1995.

Notes

a Figures published in US$ values and for Japanese financial years (FY 1997 refers to the period from April 1997 to March 1998).
b Excludes FDI made for the purpose of establishing or expanding overseas branches of Japanese companies.
c An industry breakdown of FDI is unavailable before 1966.
d Figures for 1995, 1996 and 1997 published in yen values (converted at ¥100 = US$), while those for previous years published in US$ values.
e FDI approvals recorded up to 1980 and notifications thereafter.

Japanese FDI outflows. The index could indicate the relative importance of industry FDI over the range of host countries, as is often calculated for trade (Drysdale and Garnaut, 1993). This could be compared to estimates of revealed comparative advantage for Japanese industries. The ratio of FDI/GDP could also be compared or regressed against these measures over time to ascertain the link between trade, FDI and perceived comparative advantage of host countries.

While Japanese FDI data is published in $US values (except from 1995 onwards), the yen equivalent of investment has been calculated and compared to National Accounts data on a 2-digit basis. This ratio is an industry-specific indicator of the internationalisation of Japanese industry and allows an assessment of the significance of FDI relative to domestic investment, profits, employment, taxes and GDP of the appropriate industry. The ratio of FDI to GDP is an indicator of the rate and extent of the internationalisation of Japanese industry over the period since 1966 (Table 6.4).

Given this indicator, the effect of variables, such as government policy, could be tested in a regression against the dependent variable of FDI/GDP by industry. The availability of this data would also allow testing of the responsiveness of Japanese industries to external changes, such as annual average yen/dollar rates, oil price shocks, trade and Official Development Assistance (ODA) flows and changes in the relative importance of mining, agriculture, manufacturing and service industries.

Conclusion

Japanese FDI has responded to a variety of motivations over the postwar period and these have differed by domestic industry and host country. The evolving nature of Japanese FDI over time has been difficult to evaluate because of data deficiencies in the published MOF statistics. While this series is the internationally accepted yardstick for studies of Japanese FDI, no consolidated version of FDI outflows has been available in either Japanese or English, so that the expanded MOF database discussed above provides a basis for further detailed research.

One future approach could include a more comprehensive testing of the determinants of Japanese FDI by industry and country to take into account characteristics of host countries, such as their changing stocks of human and natural resources – in the same way that comparative advantage motivations for trade have been explored (Song, 1996). Other factors of importance would be relative exchange rates, industry restructuring, liquidity, trade frictions and productivity changes across industry sectors. Hence, new perspectives are possible into the pattern and rationale for Japanese overseas investment.

Notes

1 FDI involves a significant level of ownership of assets, sufficient to constitute a 'lasting interest' and is generally considered to require an active involvement in the control and management of the acquisition. It is difficult to define 'control' precisely, but FDI implicitly refers to 'the extension of corporate control across national boundaries' (Froot, 1991: 3). In practice, official statistics usually define investment as FDI if the level of control exceeds 10 per cent of an entity's shares or assets, although this varies

by country. At this level of control the foreign investor is assumed to be an active participant in the management of the enterprise.

2 Dunning (1993: 275) states in his eclectic theory of FDI that 'a firm will engage in FDI if three conditions are satisfied: (1) It posses net ownership advantages *vis-à-vis* forms of other nationalities in serving particular markets. These ownership advantages largely take the form of the possession of intangible assets, which are, at least for a period of time, exclusive or specific to the firm possessing them; (2) Assuming condition (1) is satisfied, it must be more beneficial to the enterprise possessing these advantages to use them itself rather than to sell or lease them to foreign firms, that is, for it to internalise its advantages through an extension of its own activities rather than externalise them through licensing and similar contracts with independent firms; (3) Assuming conditions (1) and (2) are satisfied, it must be more profitable for the enterprise to utilise these advantages in conjunction with at least some factor inputs (including natural resources) outside its home country; otherwise foreign markets would be served entirely by exports, and domestic markets by domestic production.'

3 A distinction can be made between financial and strategic real estate FDI according to the motivation of investors and the organisation of investment. The land bubble in Japan in the late-1980s bolstered speculative development and the acquisition of foreign real estate by Japanese investors. Many investors speculated on rising prices and eschewed a strategic approach, involving active management, to real estate FDI (Farrell, 1997).

4 The MOF statistics are broken down into investor by industry in Japan and the host country of investment, but the definition of FDI has changed over time. Up to November 1980 the statistics refer to proposed investment approved by the Ministry, but from December 1980 they are on a notification basis, following the revision of the Foreign Exchange Law in Japan. The accuracy of the statistics may also be questioned to some extent, as it is unlikely that either approved or notified FDI equates with actual investment and divestment is also not included. Other classification and coverage problems also exist with the MOF series. The classification of direct and portfolio investment changed from December 1980, when the existing 25 per cent ownership benchmark was replaced by an ownership ratio of 10 per cent as the definition of FDI. Further, small amounts of direct investment (e.g. less than ¥3 million in 1980–84 and less than ¥10 million from April 1984 to 1989) do not have to be notified. Nevertheless, the exclusion of such small investments in MOF statistics is likely to be unimportant. The absence of data on direct investment from the retained earnings of Japanese companies may be a significant omission in some cases, despite the comparatively recent upsurge in Japanese FDI.

5 In the survey the term 'foreign affiliate' refers to foreign incorporated enterprises where the Japanese equity ownership ratio is greater than 10 per cent, as well as those foreign affiliates in which a Japanese owned subsidiary (having at least a majority of Japanese ownership interest) itself has more than 50 per cent equity share in a foreign affiliate.

References

Aggarwal, R. (1993), 'An overview of Japanese finance: uniqueness in an age of global integration', in Stansell S. (ed.), *International Financial Market Integration*, London: Blackwell.

Bora, B. (1996), 'Trade and investment in the APEC Region, 1980–1993', in P. Lloyd and L. Williams (eds), *Trade and Migration in the APEC Region*, Melbourne: Oxford University Press.

Caves, R. (1993), 'Japanese investment in the United States: lessons for the economic analysis of foreign investment', *Discussion Paper No. 1652*, Harvard Institute of Economic Research, Cambridge, MA: Harvard University.

Drake, T. and Caves, R. (1992), 'Changing determinants of Japanese foreign investment in the United States', *Journal of the Japanese and International Economies*, 6: 228–46.

Drysdale, P. (1993), 'Japanese direct foreign investment in Australia in comparative perspective', *Pacific Economic Papers No. 178*, Canberra: Australian National University.

Drysdale, P. and Garnaut, R. (1993), 'The Pacific: an application of a general theory of economic integration', in Fred Bergsten, C. and Noland, M. (eds), *Pacific Dynamism and the International Economic System*, Washington DC: Institute for International Economics, pp, 183–224.

Dunning, J. (1993), *Multinational Enterprises and the Global Economy*, New York: Addison–Wesley.

Farrell, R. (1997), 'Japanese foreign direct investment in real estate 1985–1994', *Pacific Economic Paper No. 272*, Canberra: Australian National University.

—— (2000), 'Japanese foreign direct investment in the world economy 1951–1997', *Pacific Economic Paper No. 299*, Canberra: Australian National University.

Frankel, J. (1991), 'The Japanese cost of finance: a survey', *Financial Management*, 20: 95–127.

Froot, K. (1991), 'Japanese foreign direct investment', *NBER Working Paper 3737*, Cambridge, Mass: NBER.

Froot, K. and Stein, J. (1989), 'Exchange rates and foreign direct investment: an imperfect capital markets approach', *NBER Working Party 2914*, Cambridge, Mass: NBER.

Graham, E. M. and Krugman, P. R. (1991), *Foreign Direct Investment in the United States*, Washington DC: Institute of International Economics.

Hymer, S. (1976), *The International Operation of National Firms: A Study of Direct Investment*, (1960 PhD Thesis), MIT Press.

Komiya, R. and Wakasugi, R. (1990), 'Japan's foreign direct investment', *MITI/RI Discussion Paper No. 90*, Tokyo, May.

Krugman, P. (1998), 'What happened to Asia?', http://www.mit.edu/krugman/dister.html

Leamer, Edward, (1984), *Sources of International Comparative Advantage: Theory and Evidence*, Cambridge Mass: MIT Press.

Petri, P. (1994), 'The interdependence of trade and investment in the Pacific', in Chen, E. and Drysdale, P. (eds), *Corporate Links and Foreign Direct Investment in Asia and the Pacific*, Sydney: Harper Collins.

Ramstetter, E. (1996), 'Estimating economic activities by Japanese transnational corporations: how to make sense of the data?', *Transnational Corporations*, Vol. 5, No. 2, August.

Schler, M. J. and Beechler, S. L. (1994), 'Japanese banking in the US – from transient advantage to strategic failure', *Mimeo.*

Seth, R. and Quijano, A. (1993) 'Growth in Japanese lending and direct investment in the United States: are they related?' *Japan and the World Economy*, 5: 363–72.

Song, L. (1996), *Changing Global Comparative Advantage: Evidence from Asia and the Pacific*, Sydney: Addison–Wesley.

Stein, L. (1995), 'Japan's direct foreign investment', Centre for Japanese Economic Studies, Macquarie University, *Working Paper 95-1*, April.

Vukmanic F. G., Czinkots, M. R. and Ricks, D. A. (1985), 'National and international data problems and solutions in the empirical analysis of intra-industry direct foreign investment', in Erdilek, A. (ed), *Multinationals as Mutual Invaders*, London: Croom Helm.

Yoshimatsu, H. (1996), 'The internationalisation of Japanese corporations and its impact on Japan's commercial policy', *Unpublished PhD Thesis*, Canberra: Australian National University.

Watanabe, S. (1993), 'Growth and structural changes of Japanese overseas direct investment: implications for labour and management in host countries', in Bailey, P., *et al.* (eds), *EXIM Review*, Vol. 7, No. 2, March.

Wilkins, M. (1990), *The History of Foreign Investment in the US*, Cambridge MA: Harvard University Press.

Part II

Structural issues related to the impact on FDI

7 FDI and trade

James R. Markusen

Introduction

Recent efforts by international trade economics have led to the integration of the theory of the multinational corporation (MNC) into the theory of international trade. This is both an exciting and an important development. Prior to the last decade or so, analysis of the MNC was largely distinct from trade theory. The former was partial equilibrium in nature, while trade theory maintained the assumptions of constant returns to scale and perfect competition, which generally precluded any discussion of multinational firms by definition. Beginning about 1980, the industrial-organization approach to trade began developing general-equilibrium models with increasing returns to scale and imperfect competition. Yet the multinational firm was generally missing, in spite of having precisely these characteristics.

The purpose of this chapter is to review recent work which builds on the industrial-organization approach to trade by incorporating the MNC into formal general-equilibrium models. Although empirical work is still limited, results to date are extremely encouraging in that they give strong support to the empirical predictions of the theory.

In the next section, I will briefly review a few stylized facts about the multinationals and the characteristics of countries which are the source and host to direct investment. In the section titled "A knowledge capital approach", I will present a general conceptual model which attempt to capture or reproduce these stylized facts. The following section outlines a formal model and the sections which follow present some theoretical results, many of which generate testable predictions. These include results on:

1 What types of firms exist in equilibrium, as a function of technology and country characteristics?
2 How do multinationals affect the direction of trade?
3 How do multinationals affect the volume of trade in goods and services?
4 How do multinationals affect factor prices and income distribution?
5 How do changes in trade costs affect multinational investment?

Although I will not discuss empirical results in detail in this chapter, the theoretical results receive good support in formal empirical work.

The chapter will conclude by summarizing the findings and with a few thoughts about future data collection efforts.

A few stylized facts

Before beginning, a few stylized facts are in order. These are discussed in much more detail in Markusen (1995; 1998). Two terms are used throughout the chapter to classify types of direct investment: horizontal multinationals are firms which produce the same goods and services in different locations; vertical multinationals are firms which geographically fragment the production process by stages. For the most part, what follows has been extensively documented and, in my opinion, not controversial.

1 Firm characteristics: multinationals are firms intensive in the use of knowledge capital. Physical capital intensity and plant-level scale economies do not explain multinationality.
2 Country characteristics: most direct investment occurs among the high-income developed countries. Outward direct investment is associated with a high level of human capital.
3 Most direct investment is horizontal, although it is admittedly hard to separate horizontal and vertical investments in the data.
4 Are trade and direct foreign investment (DFI) substitutes? At a superficial level they look like complements. More recent, formal empirical work suggests that they are indeed substitutes at a fine level of disaggregation, but DFI in a four-digit industry may be complementary to imports in a different four-digit industry.
5 There is only weak evidence that trade barriers and/or tax avoidance contribute to explaining direct investment.

Now we consider what sort of a model might explain these stylized facts, linking technology characteristics with country characteristics.

A knowledge capital approach

A typical point of departure for theory has been the logical premise that firms incur significant costs of doing business abroad relative to domestic firms in those countries. Therefore, for a firm to become a multinational, it must have offsetting advantages. A limited but very useful organizing framework for inquiring into the nature of these advantages was proposed by John Dunning (1977; 1981; 1993). Dunning proposed that there are three conditions needed for firms to have a strong incentive to undertake DFIs.

- Ownership advantage: the firm must have a product or a production process such that the firm enjoys some market power advantage in foreign markets.

- Location advantage: the firm must have a reason to want to locate production abroad rather than concentrate it in the home country, especially if there are scale economies at the plant level.
- Internalization advantage: the firm must have a reason to want to exploit its ownership advantage internally, rather than license or sell its product/process to a foreign firm.

An important task of theory is to connect these ideas with the firm and country characteristics in a consistent way. This is something that was undertaken in a number of papers including Markusen (1984), Ethier (1986; 1994), Helpman (1984; 1985), Horstmann and Markusen (1987a, b; 1992), Brainard (1993), Ethier and Markusen (1996), and Markusen and Venables (1998). I will refer to this as the "knowledge-capital" model, although I note that this is not a widely used term.

Consider first ownership advantages. Evidence indicates that multinationals are related to R&D, marketing, scientific and technical workers, product newness and complexity, and product differentiation. This suggests that multinationals are firms which are intensive in the use of knowledge capital. This is a broad term which includes the human capital of the employees; patents, blueprints, procedures, and other proprietary knowledge, and finally marketing assets such as trademarks, reputations, and brand names.

The crucial question then is, why should knowledge capital be associated with multinationals while physical capital is not? I have suggested that the answer lies in two features of knowledge capital. These will appear as assumptions in theoretical models. First, the services of knowledge capital can be easily transported to foreign production facilities, at least relative to the services of physical capital. Engineers and managers can visit multiple production facilities with some ease (although stationing them abroad is costly) and communicate with them in a low-cost fashion via telephone, fax, and electronic mail. This property of knowledge capital is important to firms making either horizontal or vertical investments.

The second property of knowledge capital that leads to the association of multinationals with knowledge capital is the fact that knowledge capital often has a joint-input or "public-good" property within the firm. Blueprints, chemical formula, or even reputation capital may be very costly to produce, but once they are they can be supplied at relatively low cost to foreign production facilities without reducing the value or productivity of those assets in existing facilities. The blueprint, for example, can yield a flow of services in multiple locations simultaneously. This property of knowledge capital, which does not characterize physical capital, is particularly important to horizontal multinationals. But it may be quite important to vertical multinationals as well insofar as the "blueprint" indicates exactly how the geographically fragmented activities, components, and products must fit and work together. In the knowledge-capital framework, multinationals are then exports of the services of knowledge-based assets: managerial and engineering services, financial services, reputations, and trademarks.

A third feature of knowledge capital is important in explaining the link between foreign direct investment (FDI) and country characteristics, particularly that skilled-labor-abundant countries are the major source countries for FDI. This is apparently obvious (but nevertheless important to note) assumption that knowledge-capital production is skilled-labor intensive relative to the final production of the MNCs goods and services. Such an assumption is indeed crucial for explaining vertical multinationals which fragment production by stages. Summarizing then, empirical evidence leads us to make three assumptions.

a *Transportability*: the services of knowledge-based assets are easily supplied to geographically separate facilities.
b *Jointness*: the services of knowledge-based assets are (at least partially) joint ("public") inputs into geographically separate production facilities.
c *Factor intensity*: Knowledge capital is skilled-labor intensive relative to final production.

The sources of location advantages are somewhat more ambiguous, primarily because they can differ between horizontal and vertical firms. Consider horizontal firms that produce the same goods and services in each of several locations. Given the existence of plant-level scale economies, there are two principal sources of location advantages in a particular market. The first is the existence of trade costs between that market and the MNCs home country, in the form of transport costs, tariffs and quotas, and more intangible "proximity" advantages. Indeed, if trade costs were truly zero, production would be concentrated in a single location (again, assuming plant-level scale economies) with the other location served by exports. That is, some sort of trade costs seem to be a necessary condition for horizontal multinationals to exist. The second source of location advantage, again following from the existence of plant-level scale economies, is a large market in the potential host country. If that market is very small, it will not pay a firm to establish a local production facility but the firm will instead service that market by exports.

The sources of location advantage for vertical multinationals are somewhat different. Suppose, for example, (as we will do in the next section) that an MNC exports the services of its knowledge capital and perhaps other intermediate inputs to a foreign production facility for final assembly and shipment back to the MNCs home country. This type of investment is likely to be encouraged by low trade costs rather than by high trade costs. Second, the most logical situation in which this type of fragmentation arises is when the stages of production have different factor intensities and the countries have different relative factor endowments. Then, for example, skilled-labor-intensive R&D and intermediate goods should be produced in the skilled-labor abundant country and less-skilled-labor final assembly should be done in a country with low-wage unskilled labor. Fragmentation arises to exploit factor-price differences across countries.

Internalization advantages are the most abstract of the three. The topic quickly gets into fundamental issues such as what is a firm, and why and how agency problems might be better solved within a firm than through an arm's-length arrangement with a licensee or contractor. Basically, it is my view that internalization advantages arise from the same joint-input, public-goods property of knowledge that create ownership advantages. The property of knowledge that makes it easily transferred to foreign locations makes it easily dissipated. Firms transfer knowledge internally in order to maintain the value of assets and prevent asset dissipation. Licensees can easily absorb the knowledge capital and then defect from the firm or ruin the firm's reputation for short-run profit. Internalization issues are largely peripheral to the themes of this special issue, so I will not deal with them in this chapter (again, see Markusen 1995; 1998).

We can summarize this section as follows:

Ownership advantages: Arise from knowledge capital, which (a) can be easily transported or transferred to foreign production facilities, and (b) has a joint-input property across the different production facilities.

Location advantages: For horizontal firms, location advantages arise when the host-country market is large, and (broadly defined) trade costs are moderate to high. For vertical firms, location advantages arise when trade costs are low, stages of production differ in factor intensities, and countries differ significantly in relative factor endowments.

Internalization advantages: Internalization advantages arise from the same joint-input characteristic of knowledge capital that creates ownership advantages. Transferring knowledge-based assets through arm's-length market mechanisms runs the risk of asset dissipation.

A model with endogenous multinationals

In this section, I will outline a model that permits both vertical and horizontal multinationals to arise endogenously in equilibrium. The model and a schematic representation of its results are drawn from Markusen *et al.* (1996) and Markusen (1998). Principal features of the model are as follows:

1 There are two homogeneous goods, X and Y;
There are two countries, *h* and *f*;
There are two factors, unskilled labor: L, skilled labor: S.

2 Y – competitive, constant returns to scale, L intensive.

3 X – imperfectly competitive, increasing returns to scale, S intensive overall.
'Headquarters' and 'plant' may be geographically separated.
A firm may have plants in one or both countries.

4 There are six firm types, with free entry and exit into and out of firm types.
Regime denotes a set of firm types active in equilibrium.

Type m_h – horizontal multinationals which maintain plants in both countries, headquarters is located in country *h*.

Type m_f – horizontal multinationals which maintain plants in both countries, headquarters is located in country *f*.

Type n_h – national firms that maintain a single plant and headquarters in country *h*. Type *h* firms may or may not export to country *f*.

Type n_f – national firms that maintain a single plant and headquarters in country *f*. Type *f* firms may or may not export to country *h*.
Type v_h – vertical multinationals that maintain a single plant in country *f*, headquarters in country *h*. Type v_h firms may or may not export to country *h*.
Type v_f – vertical multinationals that maintain a single plant in country *h*, headquarters in country *f*. Type v_f firms may or may not export to country *f*.

Note that if multinationals were suppressed (type-m and type-v firms) then the model would collapse to a standard oligopoly model of international trade. When we do introduce the multinationals, assumptions about the size, location, and factor composition of fixed costs are crucial to the results. First, with respect to the size of fixed costs, we assume that two-plant multinationals have higher fixed costs than those for a single plant, but not twice as high. This is to say that we assume that there are both firm- and plant-level scale economies. If there were no firm-level scale economies (two-plant multinationals have twice the fixed costs of a one-plant firm), then there would never exist two-plant type-m firms in equilibrium. If there were no plant-level scale economies (two- and one-plant firms have the same total fixed costs), then in general there will never exist one-plant firms in equilibrium.

Second, with respect to the location of fixed costs, we assume that one-plant type-n firms have all their fixed costs in the country where their integrated headquarters and plant are located. One-plant type-v firms are assumed to have the same total fixed costs as type-n firms, but incur these fixed costs in both the headquarters country and in the other country were the plant is located. Two-plant type-m firms have most of their fixed costs in their headquarters country but a significant amount in the other location as well.

Third, results depend very much on the factor composition of fixed costs. We assume that a headquarters uses only skilled labor. An integrated headquarters and plant (a type-n firm) uses a combination of skilled and unskilled labor. A branch plant of a type-m or a type-v firm is less skilled-labor intensive than an integrated headquarter plant, but still requires significant amounts of skilled labor. We make the assumption that a branch plant is indeed more skilled-labor intensive than Y, the composite "other" sector of the economy. The importance of this last assumption will become clear later. These assumption are summarized as follows:

skilled-labor intensity of activities

[headquarters only] > [integrated X] > [plant only] > [Y]

We indicated above that type-m firms have higher fixed costs than type-n or type-v firms. We also assume that type-m firms have a higher skilled-labor intensity than the other two. The idea is that type-m firms need additional managers and technicians for branch-plant operation, whereas type-v and type-n firms use only additional unskilled labor in the shipping costs incurred to serve the other market.

skilled-labor intensity of firm types

[type-m firms] > [type-v and type-n firms]

A few clarifying comments might be useful before showing some of the results produced by this type of model. (1) What is traded: X, Y, and headquarters' services, the latter produced with skilled labor. Factors are *not* directly tradable. Payments for headquarters' services will show up as the repatriation of markup revenues from foreign plants (since there is free entry, there are no pure profits and markup revenues cover firm- and plant-specific fixed costs). (2) What is Technology Transfer: Headquarters' services, "blueprints". They may be complements or substitutes for host-country skilled labor. This depends on whether branch plants draw skilled labor from the host-country Y sector or an existing X sector. (3) Why is Investment Liberalization different from Trade Liberalization: A skilled-labor scarce country is likely to import X under trade liberalization, but restricted investment. But it may be host to branch plants and export X when investment is liberalized, providing that trade costs are not too high.

Production regimes and the volume of multinational activity

Figures 7.1–7.3 show results derived from simulations of the model outlined in the previous section when trade costs are high. Each figure is the world Edgeworth box, with the total world endowment of skilled labor on the vertical axis and the total endowment of unskilled labor on the horizontal axis. Any point in the box thus represents a division of the total world endowment between the two countries, with the countries identical at the center of the box. The endowment of country *h* is measured from the southwest (SW) corner and that of country *f* from the northeast (NE) corner. Along the SW–NE diagonal of the box, the countries differ in size (except at the midpoint), but have identical relative endowments. Along the northwest (NW) to southeast (SE) diagonal, the countries have similar total incomes but differ in relative endowments. The diagram thus offers many different possibilities in which countries may differ in size and/or relative endowments.

Figure 7.1 gives a stylized summary of the production regime: the types of firms active in equilibrium when trade costs are moderate to high. When countries are relatively similar in both size and in relative endowments near the center of the box, type-m firms dominate. Similar countries interact through direct investment with type-m_h and type-m_f firms invading each others markets in what we might term intra-industry direct investment. This is an important finding, in that it seems closely consistent with extensive empirical evidence.

When the countries are similar in relative endowments but very different in size, type-n firms headquartered in the larger country dominate. This is especially true if the larger country is also skilled-labor abundant. For example, there are only type-n_h firms operating near the NE corner of the Edgeworth box, along the

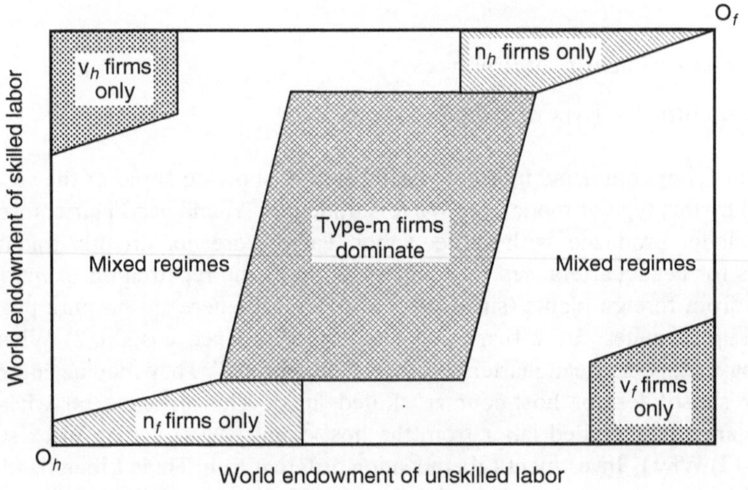

Figure 7.1 Equilibrium regime with high trade costs.

unskilled-labor axis (country *h* large and skilled-labor abundant). In such an area, the type-n_h firms have an advantage over type-n_f firms, and all type-m and type-v firms. Type-n_f firms are handicapped in that their low-cost (no transport costs) domestic market is small, and they need to bear transport costs to the large country *h* market. Type-m firms are handicapped in that they must make a fixed-cost investment in a country *f* plant to serve a very small market. Type-n_h firms simply pay the unit transport cost on a small amount of output shipped to the small country *f* market. Finally, there is no economic motive for type-v firms to enter. Country *h* is both large and skilled-labor abundant, indicating that both a firm's plant and its headquarters should be located in country *h*.

Now consider the region in the NW corner of Figure 7.1 where country *h* is very skilled-labor abundant relative to country *f* but not large relative to country *f*. In this region, only type-v_h firms are active. The intuition is that, in the absence of type-v_h firms, factor prices would be very unequal in this region. Type-n firms are handicapped in that they must by definition locate their plant and headquarters together. Type-m firms can partially exploit the factor-price difference by locating their headquarters in the country with the low wage for skilled labor, but must locate plants in both countries. Type-v_h firms are in the strongest position to exploit the factor-price differences, locating their headquarters in country *h* and their single plant in country *f*.

Summarizing the case for moderate to high trade costs in Figure 7.1, type-m firms are dominant when countries are similar in both size and in relative endowments. Type-n firms (located in the larger country) are dominant when the countries are very different in size, especially when the larger country is also skilled-labor abundant. Type-v firms (located in the skilled-labor-abundant country) are dominant when the countries are similar in size but very different in relative endowments.

Other areas of Figure 7.1 consist of complicated and varying mixed regimes, and it is not very important for the purposes of this chapter to examine those areas in detail. One exception is the area below the NW corner where country *h* is skilled-labor abundant but small. This might be relevant to countries such as Sweden, Switzerland, and the Netherlands. In this region, type-v_h firms are the dominant type of multinationals, but there are also significant numbers of type-n_f firms by virtue of the large size of country *f*. Headquarters of firms tend to be concentrated in country *h*, but due to the difference in market size, plants tend to be concentrated in country *f*. This type of fragmentation, which has been of some concern in the smaller, skilled-labor-abundant countries just mentioned, is nicely captured by the model.

Figure 7.2 presents stylized results on the trade pattern for the moderate-high trade-cost case. Perhaps the most important conceptual point is that there are two determinants of the direction of trade, with or without multinationals. One is relative factor endowments, with the skilled-labor-abundant country having the advantage in X sector production. The other is country size, due to scale economies at the plant level, with the large country having the advantage in X sector production. When one country is both large and skilled-labor abundant, these two determinants of comparative advantage work in the same direction. Thus we see an area in the NE corner of Figure 7.2 along the top of the box where country *h* exports X. When country *h* is skilled-labor abundant but smaller, the two determinants of comparative advantage pull in opposite directions. The large size of country *f* in the NW region of the box tends to pull production to country *f*. But

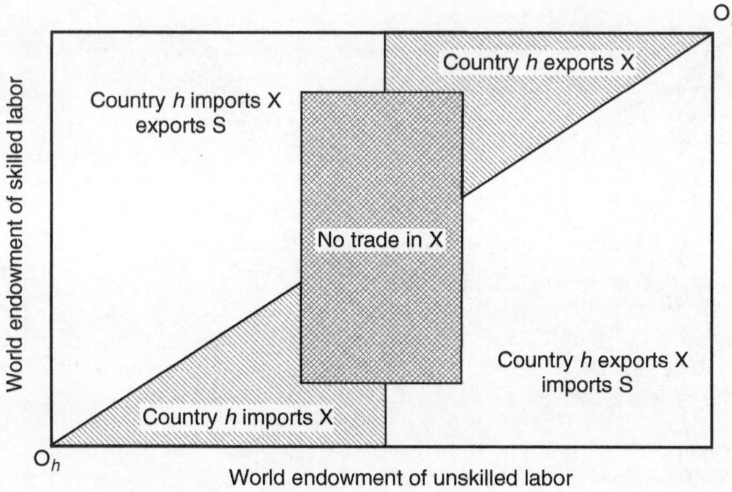

Figure 7.2 Trade regime with high trade costs.

that in turn has factor-market effects in the absence of multinationals, lowering the skilled-labor wage in country *h*. Type-v_h firms enter to exploit this difference, locating their headquarters in country *h* and their single plant in country *f*. Headquarters are concentrated (out of proportion to size) according to factor-price differences in country *h*. Since headquarters services are costlessly transported by assumption, country size plays no role in their location. Plant location, on the other hand, is concentrated more according to country size because of the transport costs needed to serve the other market. Thus in the NW–SW region of Figure 7.2, country *h* imports X, but exports headquarters services, denoted by S.

Finally, note that in the center region of Figure 7.2 there is no trade at all in X. With most production done by type-m firms (some may be done by non-trading type-n firms when the countries differ), interaction by direct investment completely dominates. While this is clearly counter empirical to any real-world situation, it is true, for example, that North Atlantic trade has been largely stagnant for fifteen years, while North Atlantic direct investment has grown dramatically.

Figure 7.3 presents the results of an actual computer run of the model for quite high-trade costs. The vertical axis measures the volume of affiliate production in the "world" economy: production by branch plants of country *h* firms in country *f* an vice versa. Along the SW–NE diagonal, where countries differ in size, the surface has an inverted-U shape. Affiliate production is highest when the countries are identical, and indeed in the center exactly half of all world production is affiliate production. But the highest level of affiliate production occurs when one country is relatively small (but not too small) and skilled-labor abundant. Then most or even all firms are headquartered in that country and most or even

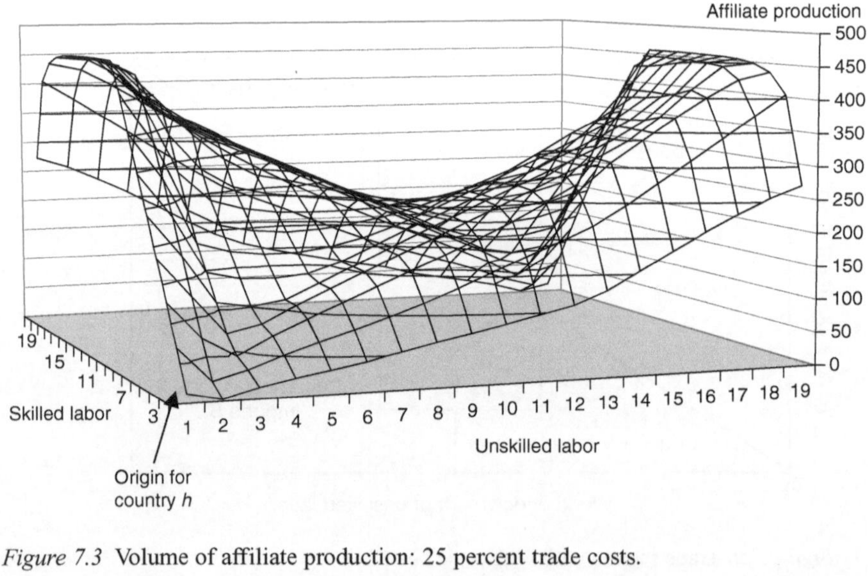

Figure 7.3 Volume of affiliate production: 25 percent trade costs.

all plants are located in the large, skilled-labor-scarce country. It is possible that 100 percent of all world production can then be classified as affiliate production.

Figures 7.4 and 7.5 presents corresponding results for the case of very low or zero trade costs. The most important difference between Figure 7.4 and Figure 7.1 is that there are no type-m firms active in Figure 7.4 as trade costs go to zero. Given plant-level scale economies, no firm will build a second plant when trade is completely costless. In the center region of Figure 7.4, only type-n firms are

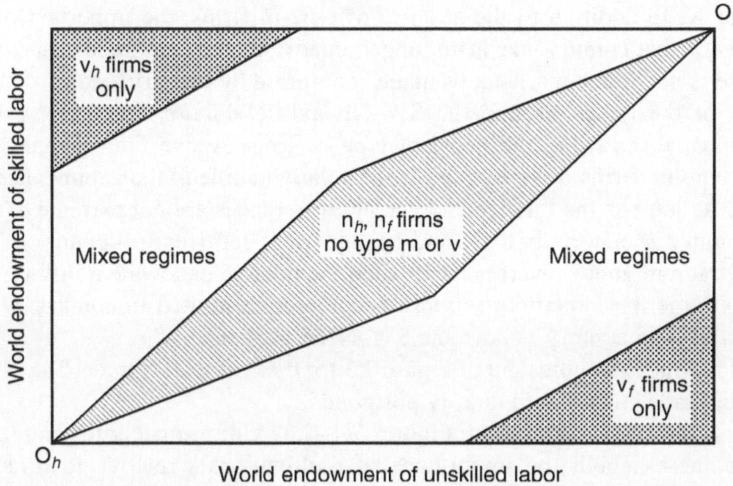

Figure 7.4 Equilibrium regime with low trade costs.

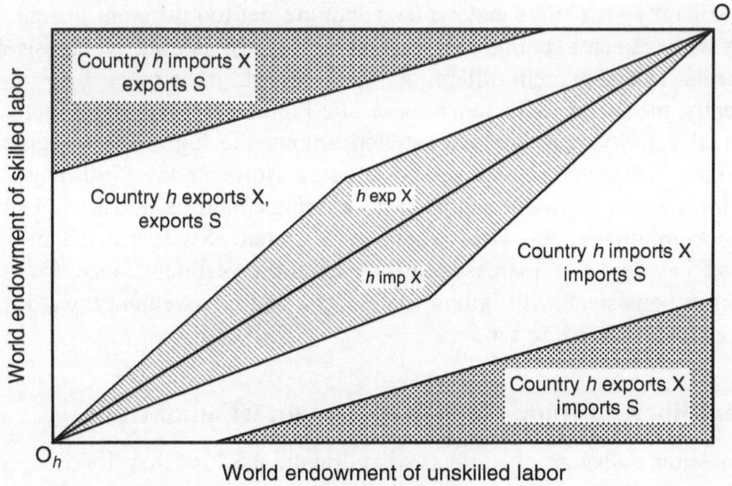

Figure 7.5 Trade regime with low trade costs.

active, reminiscent of many papers in the so-called "new trade theory". Factor prices are equalized in this region, giving no motive for type-v firms to enter. The NW and SE corners of Figure 7.4 are dominated by type-v firms headquartered in the skilled-labor abundant country much like Figure 7.1. These firms draw their advantage from exploiting or arbitraging factor-price differences as we noted above.

Figure 7.5 presents corresponding results on the direction of trade for the low-zero trade-cost case. Intra-industry trade in X occurs when countries are similar in relative endowments, with the skilled-labor abundant country being the net exporter of X. In addition to the absence of type-m firms, the important point to note here is that country size is no longer an advantage when trade costs go to zero. There is no "home market advantage" conferred by country size.

Outside of the region around the SW–NE axis of Figure 7.5, factor prices become unequal, allowing the entry of type-v firms. Above the diagonal, for example, type-n_h firms arise to exploit the relative skilled-labor abundance of country *h*. As long as the relative endowment differences are not extreme in this region, country *h* exports both X and headquarters services to country *f*. The pattern of trade in goods reverses itself when the relative endowment differences become extreme. Headquarters services become concentrated in country *h* and production of X in country *f* above the SW–NE diagonal.

I do not produce an equivalent of Figure 7.3 for the case of low trade. The effect of changing trade costs is temporarily postponed.

What lessons can we draw from Figures 7.1–7.5? Unfortunately for empirical work, hypotheses about the importance of multinationals relative to trade in a bilateral framework depends on the level of trade costs. For moderate to high trade costs, multinationals are most important between countries that are similar in both size and in relative endowments (often proxied by per-capita income). For low to zero trade costs, multinationals are most important between countries that differ significantly in relative endowments, but are not too different in size. The hypothesis with respect to country size is relatively sharp, but the hypothesis with respect to relative endowment differences interacts with trade costs.

Empirically, the world looks much more like Figures 7.1 than like Figure 7.4. Multinational activity remains concentrated among the high-income countries that are similar in size and in relative endowments. However, the 1990s have seen an increasing amount of investment go to developing countries, and several small, skilled-labor-abundant countries such as Sweden, Switzerland, and the Netherlands have greatly increased their outward investment since the early 1980s. This is consistent with falling trade costs, and a movement toward more type-v investment relative to type-m.

Investment liberalization, the volume and direction of trade

The old question, "what are the effects of multinationals" is often ill posed, since it requires a well-defined counterfactual, "as opposed to what", in order to be meaningful. The model outlined above provides a natural counterfactual, obtained by running the model with type-m and type-v firms suppressed. The resulting model is then the well-known free-entry oligopoly model of international trade theory.

Figures 7.6 and 7.7 present results on the direction and volume of trade in good X, comparing the results with multinationals permitted to results with multinationals suppressed. These figures are formed as composite of cases using different levels of trade costs from Markusen *et al.* (1996), and hence they do not correspond exactly to either Figures 7.1 and 7.2 or 7.3 and 7.4.

Figure 7.6 shows that the liberalization of investment leads to a reversal in the direction of trade when countries differ significantly in relative endowments, but

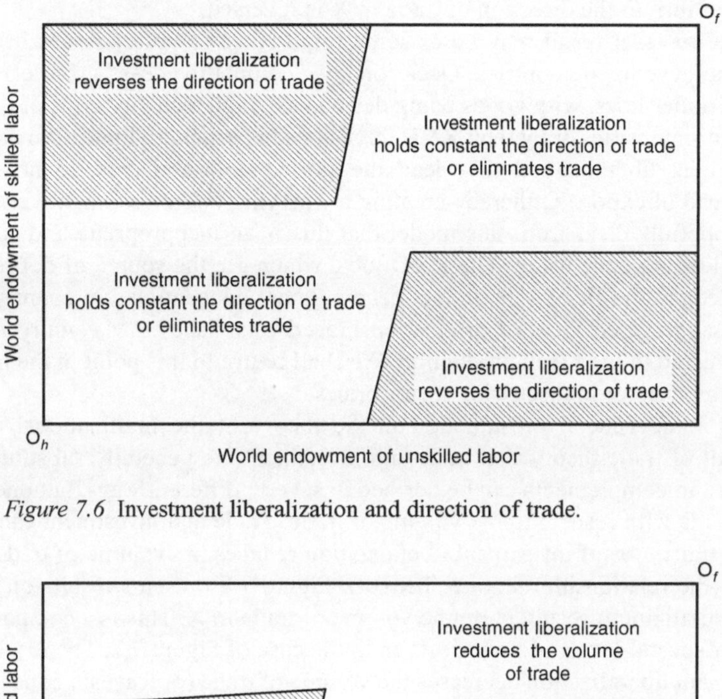

Figure 7.6 Investment liberalization and direction of trade.

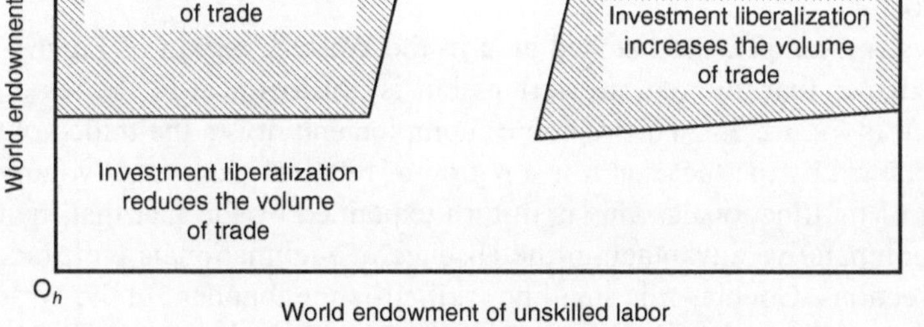

Figure 7.7 Investment liberalization and the volume of trade.

are not extremely different in size. Referring back to Figures 7.2 and 7.4, it is clear that in these areas, the skilled-labor-abundant country is importing X with investment unrestricted and therefore exporting X when multinationals are suppressed. Consider the region in the NW corner of Figure 7.6, for example. The exclusion of multinationals in this region means that production is primarily by type-n_h firms, headquartered and producing in the skilled-labor-abundant country *h*. Relative endowments are sufficiently unequal that the price of skilled labor is significantly less in country *h* and the price of unskilled labor is significantly less in country *f*. Liberalization of investment leads to a regime shift from primarily type-n_h firms to primarily type-v_h firms. Headquarters are concentrated almost entirely in country *h*, but enough production is shifted to country *f* that in the new equilibrium the direction of trade in X is reversed.

The trade-reversal result may be of some importance to policy issues in the high-income developed countries. Occasionally, “competitiveness” gets defined in terms of trade flows, with goods being defined as “high tech” in terms of their overall factor intensities or by their R&D intensities in particular. Figure 7.6 notes that investment liberalization may lead the skilled-labor-abundant country to import instead of export X, thereby creating a worrying loss of competitiveness. But it is hopefully clear from this model that this is an inappropriate and completely misleading conclusion. The R&D jobs, which are the source of defining X as high tech in the first place, in fact become more concentrated in country *h*. A more disaggregated view of production indeed establishes that country *h* is more specialized in high tech production. We shall return to this point in the next section of the chapter in discussing factor prices.

There is some general presumption in the theory of the multinational and indeed in all of trade theory that trade and investment are generally substitutes. Substitutes and complements can be defined in several different ways, but one of interest here is with respect to the volume of trade. Trade and investment can be defined as substitutes if investment liberalization reduces the volume of trade or vice versa (the relationship is not reflexive!). Figure 7.8 presents results on the effect of liberalizing investment on the volume of trade in X. This is a composite diagram for several levels of trade costs as in the case of Figure 7.7. The result is that investment liberalization decreases the volume of trade (or leaves it constant) over much of parameter space. However, trade and investment are complements when the skilled-labor-abundant country is also the small country, but not extremely so.

Consider, for example, the hatched area in the Western region of Figure 7.7. Note in particular that this region overlaps but is not identical to the region of trade reversal in Figure 7.6. This region of complementarity in the trade-volume sense is explained by the fact that it is a region of relatively low-trade volume in the absence of multinationals. This is in turn explained by the fact that the two sources of comparative advantage in the absence of multinationals pull trade in opposite directions. Country *h* is small but skilled-labor abundant in the Western hatched region of Figure 7.7, and we noted earlier that both size and skilled-labor abundance are sources of comparative advantage in X. In the hatched region, country *h* has a source of comparative advantage in X from its relative factor endowment, but a source of comparative disadvantage in X from its small size. Indeed, there is a locus of points in both hatched regions (not shown) where the volume of trade in X and Y is zero in the absence of multinationals: the size and relative endowment differences exactly cancel one another (Markusen *et al.*, 1996).

The hatched regions in Figures 7.6 and 7.7 may have some relevance to small, skilled-labor abundant countries such as Sweden. In particular, investment liberalization (generally in the rest of the world and not necessarily, for example, in Sweden) may reverse the direction of trade in some supposedly "high-tech" goods, and may increase the volume of trade. Neither phenomenon is by itself any cause for concern and they represent only a geographic rearrangement of activities by comparative advantage due to the fragmentation permitted by liberalization.

Investment liberalization and factor prices

Another important question, both from the point of view of positive theory and the point of view of policy analysis, is the effect of investment liberalization on factor prices. Factor prices, of course, in turn determine the distribution of income.

Figure 7.8 presents some simulation results, focusing on the real wage of skilled labor in country *h* (*h* is again measured from the SW corner of the world Edgeworth box). The hatched areas are areas in which the real wage of skilled labor rises in both countries following investment liberalization from an initial situation in which multinationals are initially banned. When country *h* is skilled-labor abundant (above the SW–NE diagonal), liberalization results in the

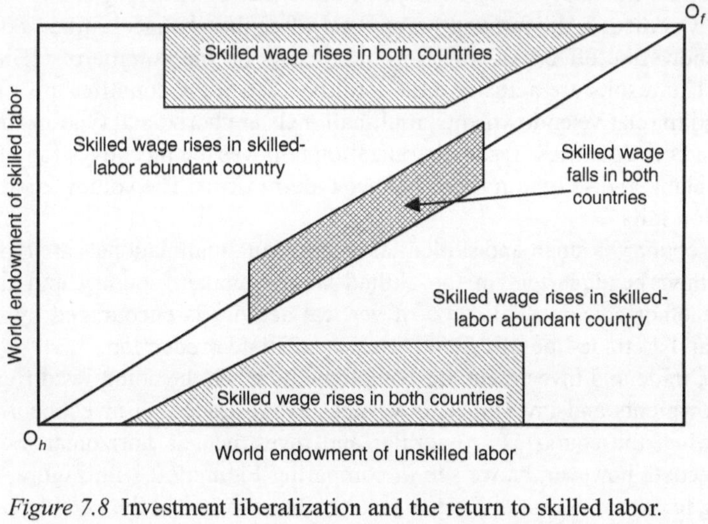

Figure 7.8 Investment liberalization and the return to skilled labor.

concentration of corporate headquarters in country *h*, the entry of type-v_h and/or type-m_h firms. This raises the real wage of skilled labor in equilibrium. But the interesting thing to note is that the skilled-labor also benefits if country *h* is relatively small and skilled-labor scarce (along part of the horizontal axis). In this area, country *h* produces little or no X with MNCs banned by assumption. Investment liberalization results in country *h* getting branch plants of type-v_f firms, with resources drawn from country *h*'s Y sector, not from local X producers. Since plants are more skilled-labor intensive than the composite Y sector by assumption, this results in an equilibrium increase in the real wage of skilled labor in country *h*.

Figure 7.8 shows the combined results for both countries, with the hatched areas being regions in which the skilled-labor wage rises in both countries. This tends to occur when one country is large and skilled-labor abundant and the other is small and skilled-labor scarce. What is happening here is that investment liberalization results in the transfer of plants from country *h* to country *f* as just noted above. These plants are skilled-labor intensive from the small country's point of view (resources are drawn from the Y sector), but not from the large country's point of view (which becomes more specialized in headquarters' services). Thus resources are being shifted toward skilled-labor-intensive activities in both countries, something that cannot occur in the Heckscher–Ohlin model for example.

Figure 7.8 is interesting in light of evidence that the gap between skilled and unskilled wages has been rising in both the developed and many developing countries. To date, multinationals and world investment liberalization has not been viewed as playing a possible role. Almost all of the debate has centered on whether it is due to technological change or to trade liberalization.

Changes in trade costs

We can conclude the analysis by looking at the effect of changing trade costs, given that investment is liberalized before and after the change in trade costs. Figure 7.9 shows the effects of lowering trade costs on the volume of affiliate production. The results are actually quite intuitive. When the countries are similar in size and in relative endowments, multinationals are horizontal type-m firms with plants in both countries. Trade liberalization removes the incentives for a foreign branch plant, and so type-n firms replace type-m firms. The volume of affiliate production falls.

When one country is small and skilled-labor abundant, multinationals are type-v firms with their headquarters in the skilled-labor-abundant country and their plants in the other country. This type of vertical activity is encouraged by low trade costs, and so trade liberalization increases affiliate production.

In a sense, trade and investment are complements when the countries differ in relative endowments and investment is vertical, while trade and investment are substitutes when the countries are similar and investment is horizontal. Some caution is needed, however, as we see in comparing Figure 7.7 with Figure 7.9. We are going to get somewhat difference results when we look at the liberalization

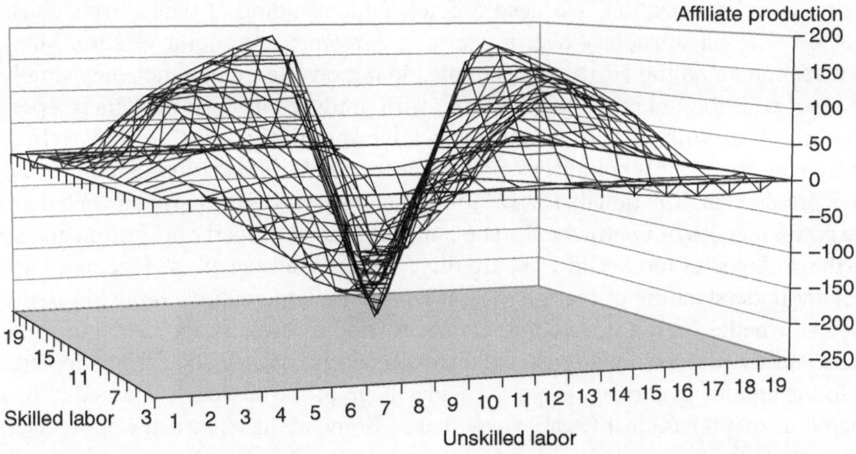

Figure 7.9 Effect of trade liberalization on the volume of affiliate production.

of investment holding trade costs constant (Figure 7.7) than when we look at the liberalization of trade costs holding investment barriers at zero (Figure 7.9).

Conclusions, directors for further data collection

Principal conclusions of the analysis can be summarized as follows:

1. Countries will tend to interact by direct investment when (A) they are relatively similar in size and in relative endowments (horizontal investment), or (B) when one country is smaller but skilled-labor abundant (vertical investment).
2. Investment liberalization can reverse the direction of trade when one country is small and skilled-labor abundant. Such a country substitutes the export of services for the export of X.
3. Investment liberalization can decrease the volume of trade in X if trade barriers are relatively high and countries are similar (horizontal investment), but can increase the volume of trade if trade barriers are low and the countries differ in relative endowments (vertical investment).
4. Trade liberalization (in the presence of relatively liberal investment) will tend to reduce investment for relatively similar countries (horizontal investment) but tend to increase investment for relatively dissimilar countries (vertical investments).
5. Investment liberalization has a skilled-labor bias for source countries, but may also have a skilled-labor bias for host countries. The latter occurs when branch plants of foreign multinationals draw factors from less skilled-labor intensive sectors rather than from competing, skilled-labor intensive local firms.

What is the way forward? In the area of theory, much needs to be done endogenizing firm organization. We need a better understanding of when firms chose a wholly owned subsidiary over a licensing agreement or a joint venture. Many footwear and clothing firms, for example, do not own foreign plants, they simply contract with foreign producers once the firm produces its designs. This is a positive question with closely related normative questions: what are the welfare consequences for host countries of different forms of organization. Should countries pressure multinationals toward joint ventures with local partners? What are the consequences of contract enforcement, intellectual property protection and so forth on choice of mode and what are their welfare consequences? Once we have a better understanding of these issues, it will be easier to approach the big issues such as whether or not developing countries should commit to a code on investment and whether or not an international competition policy should be adopted.

In the area of empirical analysis, an advantage of the approach outlined in this chapter is that it has clear testable hypotheses. Some of the empirical work to date, particularly the Brainard (1997) and Ekholm (1995; 1997; 1998) papers along with Carr *et al.* (2000) give good support to the theory. But much remains to be done, including firm-level studies and analyses that can clearly differentiate between horizontal and vertical investments. Policy analysis could benefit greatly from empirical analyses of what sort of policies are most encouraging (e.g. infrastructure) and discouraging (e.g. taxes, political instability, weak legal institutions) to inward investment.

Finally, I will conclude with a few brief comments about data collection. From my perspective as a microeconomic international trade economist, data collection on multinationals is dominated by financial data, such as stock and flows of investment. What we would like to have, in order to examine the ideas in this chapter more fully, are more "real" data on production and intra-firm trade in goods, and especially intra-firm trade in the services of intangible assets.

1. What do foreign affiliates of domestic firms produce abroad?
2. What is the pattern of intra-firm trade in goods (e.g. final and intermediate)?
3. What is the pattern of intra-firm trade in services, particularly the exports of managerial, technical, engineering, financial, and marketing services from the home firm to the affiliate?
4. What is factor intensity of domestic versus foreign operations (e.g. employment of skilled versus less skilled works, engineers and technicians etc. in home versus affiliate operations)?

This type of information would give us a much better understanding of multinationals, and a much better ability to predict the effects of trade and investment liberalization on the location of production and employment, and on trade flows and factor prices.

Acknowledgments

I express my gratitude to several of my co-authors who have worked with me over the years on the theory of multinationals, including Ignatius Horstmann, Anthony

Venables, and Wilfred Ethier. Finally, I wish to thank the National Science Foundation for financial support, and the Universitat Pompeu Fabra, Barcelona for providing such an excellent research environment during my sabbatical year, 1996–7.

References

Brainard, S. Lael (1993), "A Simple Theory of Multinational Corporations and Trade with a Trade-off between Proximity and Concentration," NBER Working Paper No. 4269, Cambridge MA: NBER.

Brainard, S. Lael (1997), "An Empirical Assessment of the Proximity-Concentration Tradeoff between Multinational Sales and Trade," *American Economic Review*, 87: 520–44.

Buckley, Peter J. and Mark Casson (1989), *The Future of the Multinational Enterprise*. London: Macmillan.

Carr, David L., James R. Markusen and Keith E. Maskus (2001), "Estimating the Knowledge-Capital Model of the Multinational Enterprise," *American Economic Review*, 91: 693–708.

Dunning, John H. (1977), "Trade, Location of Economic Activity and MNE: A Search for an Eclectic Approach," In Ohlin, B., P.O. Hesselborn, and P.M. Wijkman (eds), *The International Allocation of Economic Activity*. London: Macmillan.

Dunning, John H. (1981), *International Production and the Multinational Enterprise*. London: George Allen and Unwin.

Dunning, John H. (1993), *The Globalization of Business*. London: Routledge.

Ekhlom, Karolina (1995), *Multinational Production and Trade in Technological Knowledge*, Lund Economic Studies, number 58.

Ekholm, Karolina (1997), "Factor Endowments and the Pattern of Affiliate Production by Multinational Enterprises," CREDIT Working Paper No. 97/19, University of Nottingham.

Ekholm, Karolina (1998), "Headquarter Services and Revealed Factor Abundance," *Review of International Economics* 6: 545–53.

Ethier, Wilfred J. (1986), "The Multinational Firm," *Quarterly Journal of Economics*, 101: 805–33.

Ethier, Wilfred J. (1994), "Multinational Firms in the Theory of International Trade," in Bacha, E. (ed.), *Economics in a Changing World, Vol. 4: Development, Trade and the Environment*. London: Macmillan.

Ethier, Wilfred J. and James R. Markusen (1996), "Multinational Firms, Technology Diffusion and Trade," *Journal of International Economics*, 41: 1–28.

Helpman, Elhanan (1984), "A Simple Theory of Trade with Multinational Corporations," *Journal of Political Economy*, 92: 451–71.

Helpman, Elhanan (1985), "Multinational Corporations and Trade Structure," *Review of Economic Studies*, 52: 443–58.

Horstmann, Ignatius J. and James R. Markusen (1987a), "Strategic Investments and the Development of Multinationals," *International Economic Review*, 28: 109–21.

Horstmann, Ignatius J. and James R. Markusen (1987b), "Licensing Versus Direct Investment: A Model of Internalization by the Multinational Enterprise," *Canadian Journal of Economics*, 20: 464–81.

Horstmann, Ignatius J. and James R. Markusen (1992), "Endogenous Market Structures in International Trade," *Journal of International Economics*, 32: 109–29.

Horstmann, Ignatius J. and James R. Markusen (1996), "Exploring New Markets: Direct Investment, Contractual Relations, and the Multinational Enterprise," *International Economic Review*, 37: 1–19.

Markusen, James R. (1984), "Multinationals, Multi-Plant Economies, and the Gains from Trade," *Journal of International Economics*, 16: 205–26.

Markusen, James R., Thomas F. Rutherford, and Linda Hunter (1996), "Trade Liberalization in a Multinational-Dominated Industry," *Journal of International Economics*, 38: 95–118.

Markusen, James R. (1995), "The Boundaries of Multinational Firms and the Theory of International Trade," *Journal of Economic Perspectives*, 9: 169–89.

Markusen, James R. (1998), "Trade versus Investment Liberalization," NBER Working Paper 6231, Cambridge MA: NBER.

Markusen, James R. and Anthony J. Venables (1998), "Multinational Firms and the New Trade Theory," *Journal of International Economics*, 46: 183–203.

Markusen, James R., Anthony J. Venables, Denise Eby Konan, and Kevin Zhang (1996), "A Unified Treatment of Horizontal Direct Investment, Vertical Direct Investment, and the Pattern of Trade in Goods and Services," NBER Working Paper 5696, Cambridge Mass: NBER.

8 Cross-border investment and effects on competition in the telecommunications sector

Edward M. Graham[1]

Introduction and motivation

Telecommunications long was a sector where sellers of services operated in protected local markets, where law and government regulation created and enforced barriers to entry, especially by foreign firms.[2] In many nations, in fact, the provision of telecommunications services was reserved for state-owned monopoly suppliers. During the late 1980s and through the 1990s, however, many of these barriers have been removed while formerly state-owned firms have been partially or wholly privatized.[3] This has in turn engendered some cross entry by telecom service providers; firms that once were purely domestic in the scope of their operations thus have become multinational.

During the summer of 2000, however, US Senator Ernest Hollings, with co-sponsorship of twenty-nine other US Senators, introduced a bill (S.2793) into the US Congress that would have effectively blocked non-US telecommunications service providers from acquiring US telecoms firms if the former were state-owned, or even only partly state-owned. The bill was aimed specifically at the proposed acquisition of US mobile telecommunications service provider Voice Stream by the German firm Deutsche Telekom (DT), but the language of the bill would have served to block virtually any non-US state-owned firm in the telecoms sector from buying a US firm. While the bill did not come into law, it reflected a long history of efforts in Congress to prevent US firms from being acquired by state-owned non-US firms (e.g. a legislative bill to do this had been introduced by Senator Frank Murkowski during the late 1980s, and while this bill also failed to be passed into law, some provisions from the bill were incorporated into the Exon–Florio legislation that was first enacted as a temporary measure in 1988 but subsequently made part of US permanent law in 1992).

The Hollings bill was doubtlessly motivated in part by xenophobia (Senator Hollings is himself of the American generation that fought Germany during the Second World War). But it was also motivated, as was the Murkowski bill a decade earlier, by fears that subsidies and/or monopoly profits accruing to state-owned firms in their home markets might be used to affect operations in the US market to the detriment of locally-owned competitors. The extreme case of such behavior would be predatory pricing by the state-owned firm aimed at bankrupting its competitors, where temporary losses created by below-cost pricing in the

US market would be offset by subsidies or monopoly profits in the home market. The ultimate goal of the predatory firm would be to establish a monopoly in the United States. In fact, the Hollings bill was shelved in part because DT was able to establish that it was neither recipient of significant subsidies in Germany nor a monopoly service provider in the German market (although the firm once held a statutory monopoly there, the market has been opened to competition and some new entry has occurred).[4] Also figuring in the shelving of the bill was argumentation that competition in the US market for wireless telecom services would be enhanced by the entry of DT.[5] However, fears about the possibly deleterious effects of subsidies or monopoly profits garnered by a firm in its home market on competition in a geographically separate market in which that firm (or a subsidiary of that firm) is a seller have persisted. Indeed, the issues raised by the Hollings bill pertain to numerous sectors in which multinational firms compete. Accordingly, the US Council of Economic Advisors was ordered by the US President following the introduction of the Hollings bill to advise on what might be the effects of such competition.

Even with deregulation, markets for telecommunications services are oligopolistic in nature, as indeed are most markets in which multinational firms operate, a fact long-recognized in the literature on multinational firms. In spite of the latter, however, surprisingly little research on these firms, or on foreign direct investment (FDI) in general, accounts for the oligopolistic nature of competition in the markets in which they operate. This chapter thus is an attempt to apply models of oligopoly competition to address some of the issues raised in the context of the Hollings bill.

Specifically, the chapter thus looks at these issues in the following context: there exist two separate markets for identical goods. The markets are separate in the sense that sellers in one market do not, initially at least, sell in the other market and, in fact, there exist barriers to entry that deter them from doing so. The sellers operate with cost structures typical of telecommunications, that is, much of the cost of providing the relevant services is fixed in nature (i.e. does not vary directly with the volume of service provided or at least not in the short run). The barriers can be naturally occurring or governmentally imposed. Given this, we ask in the sections following what are the effects on competition in each market that result from entry into one market by a firm that has not previously been a seller in that market but has been a seller in the second market, and how these effects are themselves affected by subsidies and/or closure of a market.

The analytic aspects of the model developed in the following section to explore these issues are based on standard oligopoly theory, and in particular, upon results shown by Kreps and Scheinkman (1983). The model as used here is deliberately kept simple – it is at heart simply a standard Cournot model but with some non-standard twists to it – for reasons of tractability. Even so, as will be seen, some of the conclusions that can be drawn are not those normally accepted as "common wisdom".

The next section develops the basic model, and this section can be by-passed by readers familiar with Cournot oligopoly models. The section titled "Applying the model to competition in the telecoms sector" modifies the standard model to try to fit the circumstances of the telecoms industry. The following section – "Cross-border investment" then uses the modified model to examine issues specific to cross-border investment in telecoms markets. The final section examines what directions for future research are suggested by all of this.

A simple but suitable model

Any appropriate model for examining rivalry among firms where at least one of these firms operates in two distinct markets (and thus is a multinational firm) must be one that embodies oligopolistic competition. Indeed, that markets (or sectors) characterized by the presence of multinational firms are typically oligopolistic in nature is one of the important threads in the literature on multinationals dating at least to Stephen Hymer's influential 1958 doctoral dissertation (published as Hymer 1976). However, the dynamics of oligopolistic competition are notoriously difficult to model. The key aspect of such competition that differentiates it from competition in monopoly or competitive markets is that, in making profit-maximizing decisions regarding price or output, an oligopolist must take into account not only the relationship between supply and demand but also the expected responses of rival firms to its own price or output decision.

To formalize this last aspect somewhat, let us assume that a firm sells a single undifferentiated product and must decide what quantity of this product to offer in order to maximize profits. If price is given by p and the quantity offered is q such that total costs are $TC(q)$, then the problem is simply to maximize profits π where

$$\pi = pq - TC(q).$$

The term pq is, of course, revenue. In a competitive industry, p can be taken as exogenous and constant, so that profit maximization is achieved under standard regularity conditions at the point where price, which identically equals marginal revenue (the first derivative of revenue with respect to q), also equals marginal cost (the first derivative of total cost with respect to q). This follows immediately from the first order conditions for maximization of π. If, by contrast, the firm is a monopoly seller in the market unworried about the possibility of entry by new sellers if realized price rises above the competitive price, price can still be taken as exogenous, but not constant. Rather, it is a function of q, so that profit maximization still occurs where marginal revenue equals marginal cost, where marginal revenue now is a function of q but still is deterministic.

In the case of an oligopoly, however, things are not as straightforward. Price will in general be a function of the total quantity offered by all sellers, and this quantity will in turn be a function of the quantity offered by any one seller where that quantity is, *inter alia*, a function of expected reactions (quantities offered) of other sellers to this quantity. Thus, if Q is total quantity offered, then $p = p(Q)$ where $Q = Q(q)$ and is now most appropriately considered not to be a deterministic function but rather a random variable (the seller is not certain what the reactions of other sellers might be). Thus, p also is a random variable. First order conditions for profit maximization for the firm are given by:

$$\frac{\mathrm{d}\pi}{\mathrm{d}q} = 0 = p + q\frac{\mathrm{d}p}{\mathrm{d}Q}\frac{\mathrm{d}Q}{\mathrm{d}q} - \frac{\mathrm{d}TC(q)}{\mathrm{d}q}. \tag{1}$$

Because Q is a random variable, the term $\mathrm{d}Q/\mathrm{d}q$ is not a known quantity and, indeed, necessarily involves a conjecture by the firm as to how rivals will react to a change in quantity offered by the firm (e.g. the term is an expected value given some conjecture about rivals' behavior). A naïve conjecture is that the rivals do not react at all but rather hold quantity constant. This conjecture, known as the Cournot conjecture after French economist Augustin Cournot, is naïve because not to change quantity in response to quantity changes by a rival firm is not itself, in general, a profit-maximizing strategy by a firm. (In the parlance of modern game theory, for firm j to respond to a quantity change by firm k by holding its own quantity offered constant is not a best response to the move of the latter by the former). Nonetheless, employment of the Cournot conjecture often leads to a tractable result, because the conjecture implies very simply that $\mathrm{d}Q = \mathrm{d}q$, such that $\mathrm{d}Q/\mathrm{d}q = 1$ (or, if one prefers, $E(\mathrm{d}Q/\mathrm{d}q) = 1$, where E indicates expected value).

The fact that it tends to lead to tractable results is certainly one main reason why the Cournot conjecture has in fact become a standard facet of oligopoly theory. Plainly put, it keeps things simple, while many other conjectures lead one down paths to non-tractable results. But, fortunately, a body of literature has developed showing that at least some other plausible conjectures or strategies of oligopolists can, under certain assumptions, lead to the same equilibrium (see just below) as do strategies based on the Cournot conjecture.

For example, in the telecommunications services sector, firms generally are not price takers, but price setters. That is, they offer telecoms service at a specified price, and then meet the demand for the service at that price, subject to constraints imposed by capacity (the firm cannot, for example, switch more calls than it has capacity to do, as any telephone user who has received a trunk-line "busy" signal can attest). Under these circumstances, a Cournot conjecture would not seem appropriate to modeling a telecommunication firm's behavior. If anything, the appropriate conjecture would seem be a so-called "Bertrand" conjecture, where the firm sets prices rather than outputs under a conjecture that rivals make no price response to any change of it own price at which it offers the relevant services. However, even so, use of Cournot equilibria can be appropriate. In particular, if oligopolists must first create capacity, then compete on the basis of setting prices following a Bertrand conjecture subject to the constraint imposed by the capacity they have created, these oligopolists arrive at a Cournot equilibrium (Kreps and Scheinkman 1983).

To derive the equilibrium mentioned just above, let us return to a world in which firms compete by setting quantities offered rather than prices and note that in a Cournot model of oligopolistic competition, not just one, but rather all firms selling in a given market must follow the Cournot conjecture. This implies, of course, that exactly none of these firms conjectures correctly about its rivals' quantity adjustments and thus, when it becomes apparent exactly what these adjustments actually are, each firm realizes that it initially got it wrong and therefore must reset output. But, in doing so, each firm again uses the Cournot assumption (or, in other words, no firm learns from its mistake but, rather, all firms keep repeating the same mistake!). Eventually, under normal conditions of demand, however, repeated adjustments of output by each firm leads to an equilibrium where no firm can improve its profits via further quantity adjustment, such that the best response of each firm to the given price/quantity configuration then is to do nothing further.[6] This equilibrium is given in the case of n firms by solving simultaneously n equations of form (1) above, subject to a market clearing condition, where of course the variables π, q, and TC are specific to each firm. Thus, the ith equation (remembering that dQ/dq_i is unity) becomes

$$\frac{d\pi}{dq} = 0 = p + q\frac{dp}{dQ} - \frac{dTC(q)}{dq}.$$

This equation is often termed the "reaction function" for the ith firm. The market clearing condition is simply $\Sigma q_i(p) = D(p)$, where $D(p)$ is quantity of the product demanded at price p. This condition is needed in a technical sense; the reaction functions yield n equations but in $(n+1)$ variables (these variables are the n, q_i's and p), and an $(n+1)$th equation is necessary (but not sufficient) to solve all variables simultaneously.[7] Obviously, for this to be the case, there must be an explicit relationship between p and $D(p)$, that is, a demand function must exist.

Although the Cournot conjecture is implausible, the equilibrium to which it leads has some ring of plausibility to it and, as noted above, this same equilibrium is attained in certain models where oligopolists follow other, and arguably more plausible, conjectures. Thus, in what follows, the assumption will be that telecoms firms behave *as per* Cournot conjectures.

As noted in Note 4, for a solution to the n reaction functions and the market clearing condition to exist and be unique, it is sufficient (albeit not necessary) that the $n+1$ equations be linear and independent of one another. For the market clearing function to be linear, it is necessary and sufficient that the underlying demand function also be linear. Fortunately, this latter can be assumed to be the case, as demand in almost all economic theory is treated as a linear function of price, or sufficiently nearly so that a linear approximation is close to the true demand function. If demand for telecommunications services is indeed linear and if Q is quantity of this service demanded, then $Q = A - Bp$, where A and B are constants. Then also $dQ/dp = -B$, where B is the magnitude of the slope of the demand function. The reaction function for the ith firm then becomes

$$p = \frac{1}{B}q_i + \frac{dTC_i(q_i)}{dq_i}. \tag{1a}$$

To go further than this, we need to know something about $TC_i(q_i)$, the cost structure of the typical firm. In the telecommunications sector, the cost structure for a typical seller is such that there is a recurring fixed cost and a marginal cost where the latter is, for all practical purposes, constant. Thus, $TC_i = F + q_i c_i$, where F and c are both constants but where F is per unit of time, for example, \$X per month. However, as is well understood, no cost is truly fixed in the long run and, in particular, F depends upon capacity $\sup(q_i)$, where the latter indicates the maximum output of the ith firm (i.e. its capacity). We can assume that capacity is fixed in the short to middle run and hence that F is constant in this time frame, but we have to recognize that, in the long run, capacity can be adjusted.

If the costs of each firm are the same as for any other firm, the solution for the equilibrium is then quite easy. If there are n firms selling the service at a constant marginal cost c (where each firm also incurs a recurring fixed cost F), then for all firms $\mathrm{d}TC_i(q_i)/\mathrm{d}q_i = c$, so that (1a) simply becomes

$$p = \frac{1}{B}q_i + c$$

and the market clearing condition is simply

$$Q = \sum_{i=1}^{n} q_i = A - Bp.$$

It is obvious that if for all i and j, $c_i = c_j$, then also $q_i = q_j = q$, so that $Q = nq$. Hence, the unique solution for the equilibrium is

$$p = \frac{A + Bcn}{B(n+1)} \qquad q = \frac{A - cB}{n+1}.$$

If this result does not seem familiar to persons who have some familiarity with Cournot equilibria, the likely reason is that the result is usually expressed in terms of an "inverse" demand function $p = f^{-1}(Q)$ rather than a demand function $Q = f(p)$. A linear function is invertible, of course (mathematically, linear functions with finite, non-zero slope belong to the class of one to one, differentiable functions from $\Re^1$ onto $\Re^1$ and hence are invertible) and hence the inverse of a linear demand function exists and, for the function $Q = A - Bp$, is easily seen to be

$$p = \frac{A}{B} - \frac{1}{B}Q.$$

If we let $A_{\text{new}} = (A/B)_{\text{old}}$ and $B_{\text{new}} = (1/B)_{\text{old}}$, then the equilibrium relationships above become

$$p = \frac{A_{\text{new}} + cn}{n+1}, \tag{2a}$$

$$q = \frac{A_{\text{new}} - c}{B_{\text{new}}(n+1)}. \tag{2b}$$

Then, for example, dropping the "new" subscripts and letting $n = 2$, the familiar Cournot duopoly solutions appear:

$$p = \frac{A + 2c}{3} \qquad q = \frac{A - c}{3B}.$$

Likewise, if $n = 1$, the familiar solutions for monopoly price and quantity appear. However, although these are all familiar results, they are not especially useful ones, because we will be largely interested in cases where $c_i \neq c_j$. Even so, these familiar results do illustrate one point, which is that it is algebraically easier to use inverse demand functions than demand functions, when considering Cournot oligopolies (and so we shall do so henceforth). Also, before we go further into the case where firms do not have equal costs, let us note two further things that follow from developments thus far.

First, it is necessary for the *i*th firm to be profitable that it covers its fixed costs, that is, in the case where costs for all firms are the same, that $(p-c)q > F$ for each firm. Because

$$(p - c)q = \frac{A^2 - 2Ac + c^2}{B(n + 1)^2}$$

and letting *NR* (for net revenue, i.e. revenue minus variable costs) $= (p-c)q$, it is clear that $d(NR)/dn < 0$ for $2Ac < (A^2 + c^2)$, this latter being a condition that must hold because, otherwise, no firm can participate in the market without incurring a loss. Also, for all finite *n*, it is clear that $NR > 0$ and that $NR \to 0$ as $n \to \infty$. Given this, and assuming that at least one firm can profitably operate in this market, that is, that $F < (A^2-2Ac+c^2)/4B$, it follows that there is some value of *n*, call this value *N*, such that if $n > N$, no firm can operate profitably. If *N* is the lowest integer such that firms can operate profitably, this would be the expected number of firms in the market:[8] if there were more firms than *N*, some of these would exit, whereas if there were less than *N*, there would be excess profits to be had for new entrants and these would be expected to enter the sector until further excess profit had been bid away.

A second point is that if there are significant barriers to entry (or, equivalently, there are incumbency advantages) such that *F* for a new entrant is significantly higher than for an incumbent, then firms can do better than achieve the profits implied by (2a) and (2b) above. Instead of competing, firms could act collusively to charge the monopoly price and agree to split profits among them. To do so would Pareto-dominate the Cournot equilibrium, that is, every firm would be better off to collude rather than to engage in oligopolistic competition. As is widely noted, however, for firms to collude and share profits does not achieve a Nash equilibrium, because there is an incentive for each firm to cheat on the collusion by undercutting the monopoly price and taking market share away from rival firms. (To cheat is a best response of firm *i* to the expectation that other firms will collude.) Such a "market share" strategy, if played by each firm, leads to the Cournot equilibrium (Rickard and Murray 1978). However, if firms explicitly realize that collusion creates an incentive to cheat and that this leads to a Pareto-inferior outcome, they might then agree to "punish" any price-cutter by, for example, moving immediately to the Cournot price if cheating is detected, so that the price cut is ineffective for any firm as a means of capturing market share. If such an agreement to punish is credible (see just below), the conditions of the "folk theorem" for repeated non-cooperative games are met, such that collusion does become a Nash equilibrium, or at least so if firms expect to remain in the market in perpetuity (Friedman 1971). The credibility of the agreement to punish deviant firms depends upon whether the agreement is "sub-game perfect" or, more rigorously, "ε-perfect" (Selten 1965), that is, whether those firms that must implement the agreement stand to gain or lose from doing so in the event of a deviation by a rival firm. (Otherwise put, to punish must be, for non-cheating firms, a best response to a rival firm's cheating.)

Friedman (1971) argues that an agreement to move to the Cournot equilibrium in the event of a price cut is sub-game perfect because, if a deviant firm cuts price, that deviant will gain 100 percent market share and all other firms will be left with nothing, or at least so until they adjust their prices. Thus, it is better for each firm, in the event of price cutting by a deviant, to move immediately to the Nash equilibrium rather than to suffer being shut out of the market, even if this shut-out might be short lived (because customers would switch back once non-price cutting firms responded to the price cut by the deviant firm).

But for Friedman's reasoning to hold, it must be assumed that short-run price elasticity of demand is very high (indeed, infinitely high, implying that consumers care only about price and not at all about other attributes of the product or service in question) so that customers will switch from one supplier to another even in response to small and possibly short-lived price differences. In practice, some such switching does seem to occur in response to price cuts by telecoms services providers (otherwise, why else would every residence in North America be subject to telephone solicitations from telecoms firms seeking to get that residence to switch its service provider?). But available evidence does not suggest that short-run price cutting in practice leads to massive shifts by consumers or to volatility of market share among telecoms services providers. Thus, whether the Friedman approach to a punishment strategy is, in proactive, sub-game perfect remains an open issue.

In practice, there is some evidence that in telecoms markets, the presence of five or six sellers tends to be associated with something like competitive pricing (or at least a Cournot equilibrium), whereas the presence in the market of fewer sellers tends to be associated with non-competitive pricing (the firms agree even if only implicitly to price monopolistically and share monopoly rents).[9] One possible reason why a small number of sellers in this sector is able to sustain monopoly pricing is that they can keep track easily of capacity of each of their rivals, and additions to capacity are necessary for a price cutting strategy to be implemented (if a firm cuts price in the expectation of gaining market share, it must have the capacity to service the additional demand). Thus, there is in effect an advance warning of any firm's intent to change strategy, and given a signal that a rival might be about to do so, a firm can take countermeasures (e.g. increase its own capacity, thus signaling a willingness to match price cuts). Exactly why this signaling should work if there were, say, five sellers in the market but not if there were six or more is not, however, quite clear.

It should go without saying that outcomes wherein monopoly prices are sustained are not in the interests of consumers or, indeed, in the interests of economic efficiency. The goal of public policy thus is to prevent such outcomes and, rather, to promote competitive outcomes, even if in this case "competitive outcome" means, other than one that would prevail under perfect competition (hard to achieve when fixed costs place an upper bound on the number of sellers that can participate in a market!), a Cournot equilibrium. As just stated, these points should go without saying, but they are points that sometimes are missed in places like the US Senate.

Applying the model to competition in the telecoms sector

Thus far, about all that has been accomplished is presentation of more or less standard ideas regarding the dynamics of competition in oligopoly markets under Cournot conjectures, with some reference to why these ideas can be applied to telecoms markets. In this section, the goal is to extend this application to include more about the dynamics of competition in these markets. Then, building upon developments in this section, the section following discusses specific issues surrounding cross-border investment when the investor might be recipient of a subsidy or monopoly rights in its home market.

To begin, the following assumption is made: in the provision of telecoms services, marginal cost c_i can be reduced by increasing total capacity. However, to do so raises the recurring fixed cost F_i. Marginal cost, holding capacity constant, is itself constant. Thus, c_i is a function of $\sup(q_i)$ but not of q_i. This would imply that there is some scale economy associated with total capacity beyond that which is implied by the presence of a fixed cost. The presence of a fixed cost implies, of course, that average cost declines or that there is a scale economy even if marginal cost is constant with respect to capacity. This additional scale economy might be the result of organization scale economies (it might be possible, say, to add automated capacity without adding additional staff, or at least to add capacity without an equi-proportional increase in staff). In the case of telecommunications, it plausibly could originate from an ability to increase capacity by adding capital to an existing network (e.g. cables, switching equipment) while holding constant the land over (or under) which the cables pass or the buildings housing the equipment stand.

At this point, an admission must be forthcoming: the above considerations would suggest not that marginal costs decline with increased capacity as claimed, but rather that fixed costs per unit of capacity decline. This is because it is the marginal cost of additional capacity, not the marginal cost of providing additional units of service, that would seem to fall as a function of total capacity. The consequence of this, however, is that the industry would be expected to evolve towards a single seller and, indeed, historically telecoms has been often been cited as an example of a "natural monopoly" for exactly these reasons. However, experience in modern times has been that evolution of the industry has been in the exact opposite direction, that is, in almost every major national market worldwide, the number of sellers has increased rather than decreased.

One possible reason for this is that firms' cost structures are, in some sense, path-dependent. This could be the result of rival firms possession of somewhat different technologies, at least some of which have evolved from each firm's own *sui generis* experience (such that firms, in essence, do things somewhat differently but such that the techniques of one firm might simply not fit into the *modus operandi* of another firm). Thus, cost structures of different firms could be different, but such that a less efficient firm cannot readily replicate those attributes of a more efficient rival that give rise to the efficiencies.[10] Also, capacity additions might be associated with technological advances, where the advance does reduce the cost of actually operating the network over which telecoms services pass. Otherwise expressed, the realization of technological advances that reduce marginal costs might require capacity augmentation.

This latter does not necessarily imply, nor even guarantee, that those firms that make the heaviest investments in capacity necessarily would have the higher operating efficiencies than rivals that make lower such investments. This is because of the path-dependency of individual firm's technologies. Rather, there might be no predictable relationship between total investment in capacity and operating efficiency; it could even happen that the firm with the highest fixed cost per unit of capacity also had the highest marginal cost of all firms selling in a market. What is claimed is only that, to reduce marginal costs, the firm must increase total capacity and hence total fixed cost.

A second assumption, and one that is important in what follows, is that the total costs of the firm are dominated by the fixed cost component, which is to say that at equilibria that are reached, $F_i >> c_i q_i$ for each firm. This assumption is in accord with reality. In the telecoms sector, fixed costs indeed are significantly greater than variable costs.

Further, in what follows, there is an implicit assumption that firms behave according to some precept of "bounded rationality" in the sense of Herbert Simon. That is to say, no firm holds perfect information regarding rival's costs and capacities, but all firms are able to make reasonably good estimates as to what currently are these costs and capacities. Also, firms have reasonably accurate expectations regarding equilibrium prices and outputs given, albeit again not perfect information. Were information perfect, firms might be able to calculate the long-term equilibrium that would be attained in the market and move immediately to install capacity that is compatible with this equilibrium.[11] But, in what follows, we assume that this does not happen. This would lead to an unrealistic, static, and not very interesting outcome. Rather, we assume that, by whatever means, the market has evolved to some equilibrium. We then examine circumstances under which this equilibrium might change when firms move somewhat cautiously.

The main analytic task then is to examine equilbria where marginal costs of sellers are not all the same and then to explore how these equilibria change in response to changes in cost structure. Alas, the algebra of Cournot equilibria where different firms have different marginal costs becomes increasingly unwieldy as the number of firms increases, even if the marginal cost of the individual firm is assumed to be constant and demand linear. Price in this general case is given by

$$p = \frac{A + \sum_{i=1}^{n} c_i}{n+1}$$

and quantity for the ith firm by

$$q_i = \frac{A + \sum_{i=1}^{n} c_i - (n+1)c_i}{B(n+1)}$$

such that considerable unwieldness is created by the multiplicity of cross-product terms that are implied by the above (e.g. the cross terms become unwieldy if one wishes to consider net revenue, $(p - c_i)q_i$). Fortunately, without loss of much generality, we can look at the case of $n = 2$ (duopoly) without becoming too overwhelmed by unwieldiness.

If demand is as before (the inverse demand function is $p = A - BQ$), and there are two sellers in the market with marginal costs c_1 and c_2, equilibrium price and quantities are:

$$p = \frac{A + c_1 + c_2}{3}, \tag{3a}$$

$$q_1 = \frac{A - 2c_1 + c_2}{3B}, \tag{3b}$$

$$q_2 = \frac{A - 2c_2 + c_1}{3B}. \tag{3c}$$

Adopting a convention that π = net revenue (i.e. π henceforth is not profit), then

$$\pi_1 = \frac{A^2 - 4Ac_1 + 2Ac_2 + 4c_1^2 + c_2^2 - 4c_1c_2}{9B}. \tag{4}$$

Noting that the conditions that each firm participate in the market remain $\pi_1 > F_1$ and $\pi_2 > F_2$, taking first and second partial derivatives of π_1 with respect to "own" marginal cost, we observe that

$$\frac{\partial \pi_1}{\partial c_1} = \frac{-4A + 8c_1 - 4c_2}{9B}. \tag{5}$$

This implies that a decrease in marginal cost creates an increase in net revenues if $2c_1 < (A - c_2)$, where this last condition is necessary if the firm is to have positive net revenue with $q_1 > 0$, that is, the firm's output is feasible. Thus, the firm can, as one might expect, increase its net revenue by lowering its marginal costs. But, to do so, the firm must increase its capacity or, in terms of our model, increase its recurring fixed cost. Obviously, the firm will do so only if the increase in net revenue per period exceeds the additional fixed cost required to achieve this increase. But also

$$\frac{\partial^2 \pi_1}{\partial c_1^2} = \frac{8}{9B}$$

which is unambiguously positive so that as marginal costs decline, net revenue increases at an increasing rate in the range of feasible output, but the total additional revenue is bounded (the maximum is reached where c_1 is zero, because negative marginal costs are of course not feasible). If fixed costs per unit of additional capacity are constant, there does exist an optimum capacity for firm 1 for a given c_2. Because analogous results hold for firm 2, there likewise does exist an optimum capacity for this firm given any given c_1. Thus, as noted previously, under circumstances of perfect information, the two firms might each independently be able to calculate by induction a long-run equilibrium. Again, however, we assume this away, and rather assume that each firm, perhaps because of some uncertainty about the cost structure of the other firm, makes capacity decisions somewhat cautiously, but moving in a direction in which it believes it can increase net revenues.

However, we shall assume that each firm understands the following: because

$$\frac{\partial q_1}{\partial c_1} = -\frac{2}{3B},$$

$$\frac{\partial q_2}{\partial c_1} = \frac{1}{3B},$$

$$\frac{\partial Q}{\partial c_1} = \frac{\partial (q_1 + q_2)}{\partial c_1} = -\frac{1}{3B},$$

a lowering of firm 1's marginal cost results in an increase in total quantity demanded at the equilibrium (and hence a drop in price, which can easily be shown analytically) but a loss in the total quantity serviced by firm 2. Absent some response on its part, firm 2 thus suffers an absolute loss and not simply a relative loss. Firm 2 loses net revenue. Correspondingly, and obviously, firm 1 gains market share as well as net revenue, a result of course consistent with its increase in capacity. Analogous results follow if firm 2 lowers marginal cost by increasing capacity.

It follows that it is possible that capacity expansion/marginal cost reduction by one firm, in the absence of a corresponding move by the other, could force the other out of the market. This would happen if, at the new equilibrium, the non-expanding firm could not meet its fixed cost (and recall that fixed costs dominate total costs). If a firm loses market share, its revenue is reduced, but this to some extent is offset by reductions in variable costs. But the fixed cost, by definition, remains fixed. Average costs (total costs divided by quantity) necessarily go up and, indeed, because average fixed cost is hyperbolic in q, the more q falls, the faster these costs rise.

However, this firm can recapture market share, and increase its net revenue, by itself expanding capacity and reducing marginal cost in order to regain market share. If, by expanding capacity, this firm can increase net revenue in excess of the required increase in recurring fixed cost, so as to put itself back into the black, it would of course be expected to do so. But otherwise, it would exit from the market.

This suggests that, starting from one equilibrium, it is possible that capacity expansions resulting in marginal cost reductions by both firms could benefit both. Such moves would (clearly) also benefit consumers because price would fall. A best response of either firm to a capacity increase of the other can be to increase its own capacity.[12] However, each firm might be reluctant to be the first mover to increase capacity if each is uncertain about the consequences of such a move in terms of the response of the other.

This would especially be so if, rather than competing in the market, the two firms were to be cooperating to achieve a monopoly price and to split monopoly profit. As noted earlier in the previous section, to maintain this strategy as a (repeated game) Nash equilibrium, it is necessary that both firms be able to detect and respond to cheating by the other (i.e. to be able to implement punishment strategies). In such a case, addition of capacity might be seen as a signal by one firm of the other's intent to cheat. In this case, both firms would have an incentive not to add capacity, for fear of transforming a monopolistic equilibrium into a Cournot equilibrium, with attendant loss of rent to both firms.

If firm 1 were to receive an operating subsidy, this would be equivalent to a lowering of marginal cost without a corresponding increase in recurring fixed cost. This would enable the firm to capture market share from its rival, but it could only realize this additional share if it were to increase its capacity. But, in this case, the increase net revenue enabled by a capacity increase is augmented by the subsidy. The opportunity cost associated with the reduction of marginal cost rather is borne elsewhere in the economy (or, in the event that firm 1 is foreign-owned, perhaps in some other economy). Under most circumstances, this latter would be undesirable, because there would be created a wedge between prices and the opportunity costs associated with meeting demand at those prices. This would in turn result in a misallocation of resources; excess resources would flow into telecoms, at the expense of better opportunities elsewhere in the economy. However, it is possible by the above reasoning that, a recipient of a subsidy might be less adverse than an unsubsidized firm to investing in a capacity increase because it can be more certain of a positive outcome, that is, increased market share and increased profit. This in turn could drive a positive outcome if the result were to be that rivals also would make such an investment such that all firms (and consumers) were to be better off than before. But, as already suggested, the outcome could also be bad, if the non-subsidized firm would be driven from the market that would otherwise, in the absence of subsidies, be viable participants in the market. Exactly what outcome would prevail, or would likely prevail, depends upon specific circumstances, for example, the exact cost structures of firms including the relationship between marginal cost and capacity.

More consideration of subsidization is provided in the following section.

Cross-border investment

Now, consider the following: there are two geographically separated markets for our stylized telecoms services, and each market is initially structured as a government-enforced monopoly. We adopt the following convention: for market-specific variables or parameters, a single subscript will be used to denote the market to which that variable or parameter applies: thus, we write, for example, inverse demand functions as $p_i = A_i - B_iQ_i$ where the subscript i ($i = 1$ or 2) indicates that the relevant variable or parameter is for market i. However, for variables that are specific to firms, we use two subscripts to indicate both the identity of the firm (first subscript) and the identity of the market in which it operates (second subscript). Thus, for example, q_{12} would indicate quantity offered by firm 1 in market 2. This second convention is to take account of the possibility that each firm sells in both markets.

If at the outset, both markets 1 and 2 are monopolies, and assuming that firm 1 is the monopoly seller in market 1 and firm 2 is the monopoly seller in market 2, then, in the absence of government regulation, each firm would be expected to price monopolistically in the market in which it operates. In the case of telecommunications, the assumption of no government regulation would not be wholly realistic, or at least not in all markets. However, in many national markets, for example, France, historically telecoms service providers have been state-owned firms whose role has been seen by the government as net revenue generators. Such firms indeed have tended to act as unregulated monopolists.[13] In other markets, for example, the United States, a privately-owned monopoly supplier has existed, but subject to price regulation such that the firm was unable to practice monopoly pricing. In order to keep things somewhat simple, in this section we assume that, at the outset at least, the two national markets are more like France than the United States.

In this case, each firm will price to achieve maximum profit in each market, so that price, quantity, and net revenue will be

$$p_i = \frac{A_i + c_{ii}}{2},$$

$$q_{ii} = \frac{A_i - c_{ii}}{2B_i}.$$

Now, consider what might happen if both countries were to end the government monopoly and open these markets to new entry. Suppose that each firm calculates that it can create capacity in the foreign market such that both fixed costs per unit of capacity and marginal cost of production are as in its home market. (This is tantamount to saying that each firm believes that it can transfer technology to the foreign market costlessly, or nearly so.) In that case, $c_{11} = c_{12}$, and also $c_{21} = c_{22}$, so that we can continue to write cost to firm 1 as c_1 and marginal cost of firm 2 as c_2 irrespective of the market which this relevant cost applies.

From firm 1's perspective, if it enters into market 2, price will fall to the duopoly Cournot level, so that it will increase its net revenues by

$$\pi_{12} = \frac{A_1^2 - 4A_1c_1 + 2A_1c_2 + 4c_1^2 + c_2^2 - 4c_1c_2}{9B_1}$$

and, of course, if $\pi_{12} < F_{12}$, this firm will not enter this market. Note of course that F_{12} must create enough capacity for firm 1 to be able to service q_{12} of demand, where q_{12} is the demand at the Cournot equilibrium. For the moment, let us abandon the assumption of the previous section that marginal cost declines as capacity is increased, but retain an assumption that the recurring fixed cost per unit of capacity is constant. We can see from above that

$$\frac{\partial \pi_{12}}{\partial A_1} = 2A_1 - 4c_1 + 2c_2.$$

So, subject once again to a feasible operation condition $2c_1 < (A_1 + c_2)$, the net revenue realizable from entry into market 2 rises as the size of market 2 increases. Also,

$$\frac{\partial^2 \pi_{12}}{\partial A_1^2} = 2 > 0,$$

so this net revenue increases without bound and at an increasing rate. If unit fixed cost of capacity is constant, there is some size of market for which firm 1 would want to enter market 2, that is, there exists some K for which $\pi_{12} > F_{12}$ if $A_1 > K$.

However, it is also true that firm 1 faces the possibility of entry of firm 2 into its home market. If this were to occur, firm 1 would lose net revenue in the home market equal to the difference between net revenue at the monopoly position minus net revenue at the duopoly position. This firm might however be able to recoup part of its loss by shutting what now would be redundant capacity and reducing the recurring fixed cost. Net lost profit in market 1 for firm 1 would be

$$\delta_{11} = \frac{5A_1^2 - 2A_1c_1 - 7c_1^2 - 8A_1c_2 - 4c_2^2 + 16c_1c_2}{36B_1} - \Delta F_{11},$$

where the last term is any recovery of fixed costs in market 1.

The situation for firm 2 is, of course, analogous. Each firm might thus contemplate whether or not it might make more sense to come to an agreement to stay out of each other's market than mutually to enter these markets, in the event that both markets become open to new entry. Such an agreement would be desirable if, for each firm,

$$\pi_{ij} > F_{ij} \quad \text{but } (\pi_{ij} - F_{ij}) < \delta_{ij}. \tag{6}$$

In this situation, a strategy for each firm to agree to stay out of each other's markets, with a punishment strategy of "if you enter my market, I will enter your market", Pareto-dominates the strategy "I'll enter your market, and you can make up your own mind whether to enter my market". Importantly, the punishment strategy is clearly sub-game perfect.

What is interesting to contemplate at this point is the situation where only one market is open, but the other remains a governmentally-enforced monopoly. In this case, the firm whose home market is closed has an incentive to enter the other market. The punishment strategy is moot, because entry by the other firm is not possible. Hence, the following rather provocative (and, to most observers, counter-intuitive) possibility opens itself: if a government seeks to achieve more competition in its home telecoms market, its best strategy might be unilaterally to open this market, without insistence that there be any reciprocation on the part of governments of countries in which potential new entrants currently act as suppliers. Indeed, reciprocal opening could retard entry.

Is there a downside to a government doing this? One downside is that the foreign entrant will garner some rent from the home market, creating a claim by foreigners on national resources.[14] Another downside occurs if the new entrant believes that it can force the incumbent firm out of the market so as to establish itself (the new entrant) as the monopoly supplier. This, as touched upon in the previous section, requires that the new entrant prices so that the incumbent is unable to earn enough net revenue to cover fixed costs.[15] But, also, it requires that the new entrant be able to raise prices to monopoly levels after the exit of the incumbent and to do so without risk that the incumbent will re-enter the market.

Under these circumstance, does it pay for the new entrant to use monopoly rents garnered in its home market to subsidize its operation in the foreign market in order to drive out the incumbent? Perhaps the first thing to be said is that subsidization of the foreign operation is not, in general, a profit maximizing strategy, and hence the only reason that the strategy would be rationally pursued is to attempt to drive out the incumbent to establish a monopoly. To show that the strategy is not profit-maximizing, suppose that marginal cost is again c_1, but that the firm prices below the Cournot price implied by c_1, where this price p is given by (3a). Call the subsidized price p_S, where $p_S = (1-k)p$, $0 \leq k < 1$. Note that

$$p_S = (1-k)p = (1-k)\frac{A_2 + c_1 + c_2}{3} = \frac{A_2 + (c_1 - s) + c_2}{3},$$

where $s = k(A_2 + c_1 + c_2)$, such that a new Cournot equilibrium is reached where firm 1 behaves as though marginal cost is $(c_1 - s)$ where s is a subsidy component. At this new equilibrium, total revenue, using (3a) and (3b), is

$$p_S q_{12S} = \frac{A_2 + (c_1 - s) + c_2}{3} \times \frac{A_2 - 2(c_1 - s) + c_2}{3B_2},$$

where the subscript S indicates that these are at the subsidized price. The net gain or loss in revenue from subsidization is just the terms involving s, or

$$\Delta\text{revenue} = \frac{A_2 s + 4c_1 s + c_2 s - 2s^2}{9B_2}.$$

This term is unambiguously positive for small k because, given the definition of s, $2s < (A_2 + 4c_1 + c_2)$ if $k < 0.5$. The change in variable costs (i.e. not counting any increase in recurring fixed costs required to meet the additional demand created by the subsidized price) is $c_1(q_{12S} - q_{12})$, where q_{12S} is given, using (3b), by

$$q_{12S} = \frac{A_2 - 2(c_1 - s) + c_2}{3B_2}.$$

Thus, the change in cost is

$$\Delta\text{cost} = \frac{2c_1 s}{3B_2}.$$

The change in net revenue thus is

$$\Delta NR = \frac{A_2 s - 2c_1 s + c_2 s - 2s^2}{9B_2}.$$

But is ΔNR positive or negative? A condition for it to be negative is that $2(c_1 + s) > (A_2 + c_2)$. But again, $s = k(A_2 + c_1 + c_2)$, so this condition is equivalent to

$$c_1 > \frac{(A_2 + c_2)}{2} \times \frac{(1 - 2k)}{(1 + k)},$$

in fact, however, for small k this condition is likely not to be fulfilled, because the dominance of fixed costs in the total cost structure of the firm implies that, in order to be in business, $c_1 \ll A_2$. However, this reminds us that a condition for the subsidy to be warranted (in the absence of the possibility that the subsidy will serve to put a rival out of business) is not simply that it result in an increase in net revenue, but that increase in total costs be covered. In other words, it is not sufficient that $\Delta NR > 0$, but that $\Delta NR > \Delta F$, where the latter is the increase in recurring fixed costs associated with the increase in capacity necessary to service the additional demand place on firm 1 by virtue of the subsidy. Without specifying what the exact cost of capacity is, we cannot explicitly evaluate whether this condition is met or not. What we argue is, it is likely not met.

Let us now return to the case where both markets have opened. We have argued that mutual market opening might not lead to each firm electing to enter the other's market, a desirable outcome from the perspective of public policy. However, the conditions for mutual non-entry to be a sub-game perfect repeated non-cooperative Nash equilibrium (6) might not hold. It in fact might be optimal for one firm to enter the other's market even if to do so would almost surely mean that the move would be reciprocated, that is, that the second firm would enter the home market of the first. However, this situation will always be asymmetric. That is, if one firm prefers cross entry of both firms into each other's home markets to each firm staying at home, the other firm will prefer that both firms stay at home. If the cost structures of the two firms are not too different from each other, the firm from the smaller market will be the "aggressor" (again, assuming that (6) does not hold), but if the cost structures do vary, the aggressor could be the low cost firm. In other words, FDI could be driven by either "market pull" or considerations of relative efficiency.[16]

Conclusions and an agenda for research

As noted in the introduction, issues addressed in this chapter go beyond the specific circumstances of the telecommunications sector. Issues such as under what circumstances will a firm cross-national boundaries to invest in markets in which other firms already participate, where these latter incumbent firms might react to this move by themselves investing in the home market, obviously are ones that are raised in virtually all sectors. Indeed, the sector specifically considered in this chapter, telecommunications, is one in which cross-border direct investment until relatively recently did not generally take place. If nothing else, this chapter strives to show that the oligopolistic nature of this, and many other sectors, complicates the answer to this issue. It is not, for example, necessarily true that cross-border entry can be expected whenever the would-be investor can expect to garner satisfactory returns in the new market by investing there. Rather, the investor has to take into account the possibility of lost profits in its home market.

Alas, the modeling of the dynamics of competition in an oligopolistic market remain difficult. The Cournot conjecture used in this chapter is not wholly satisfactory in terms of a "reality test" (i.e. does it capture anything like real firm behavior?) and, accordingly, one does not have full faith in the equilibria that are derived from employment of this conjecture. This remains true in spite of work that suggests that Cournot equilibria might be more robust than the conjecture from which they are derived.

This type of objection notwithstanding, amazingly little research on multinational firms takes into explicit account the fact that these firms participate in oligopolistic markets, whereby the strategic moves of any one firm must always be conditioned upon the expected response of rival firms. Indeed, given the lack of accounting for this important but difficult-to-model aspect of the dynamics of competition among these firms, one can legitimately question whether many of the conclusions arrived at regarding the benefits of multinational investment are wholly correct. It is therefore hoped that this chapter both makes a little headway in addressing this lack and, at the same time, points the way for future research.

Notes

1 Senior Fellow, Institute for International Economics, Washington, DC.
2 See, for example, Sidak 1997 for a history of US law and policy that effectively blocked foreign entry in telecoms; the United States was one of the less overtly protected of the world's major markets.
3 See, for example, Ergas 1997 and Wilson 1997.
4 Nonetheless, because of incumbency advantages that are strong in the telecommunications sector, DT has remained the dominant supplier of telecoms services in Germany.
5 Both these arguments favoring the acquisition of Voice Stream by DT are elaborated in Hufbauer and Graham 2000. See also Sidak 2000.
6 Specifically, this is a Nash equilibrium. In the context of oligopoly, firms are in a Nash equilibrium if the best response of each firm to the current quantities offered by rival firms is to continue to offer that quantity that currently is offered.
7 In fact, at this point, of course no solution is guaranteed and, if a solution does exist, it is not necessarily unique. A sufficient condition for a solution to exist and be unique is that the $n+1$ equations be linear in the $n+1$ variables and be linearly independent of one another. See below.
8 Otherwise, this number would be $N-1$.
9 For evidence, see Atje and Hufbauer (1996).
10 The possibility of such path-dependency is explored by Cantwell (1991), who finds it a plausible reason for variance in cost structures among firms that compete in end-markets.
11 The possibility that technological change that alters firms cost structures in fact largely rules out such an outcome.
12 Indeed, in the situation as posed, it would be in either firm's interest to increase capacity even in the absence of an initiating move on the part of the other firm.
13 (reference).
14 This possibility has been one of the major concerns of the "new trade theory", which is of course no longer so very new; see Brander and Spencer (1985) for a full treatment of this issue.

15 If there are costs to exit, the incumbent might not exit even if net revenue fails to cover recurring fixed costs, especially if the incumbent believes that the adverse situation will not be sustained. This reluctance to exit will be reinforced if there are costs associated with re-entry. On this, see Dixit *et al.* (1999).

16 In an earlier article (Graham 1998), I have shown that in an oligopoly context, and contrary to much of the literature on FDI, it is not necessarily the most efficient firm that becomes a foreign direct investor.

References

Atje, Raymond and Gary C. Hufbauer (1996) "The Market Structure Benefits of Trade and Investment Liberalization", Institute for International Economics, Working Paper No. 96-7, Washington, DC: Institute for International Economics.

Brander, James A. and Barbara J. Spencer (1985) "Export Subsidies and Market Share Rivalry", *Journal of International Economics* 18(1/2), 83–100.

Cantwell, John A. (1991) "The International Agglomeration of Technological Activity", in Mark C. Casson (ed.), *Global Research Strategy and International Competitiveness*, Oxford: Basil Blackwell.

Dixit, Avinash, Robert S. Pindyck, and Sigbjorn Sodal (1999) "A Markup Interpretation of Optimal Investment Rules", *Economic Journal* 109, 179–189.

Ergas, Henry (1997) "International Trade in Telecommunications Services: An Economic Perspective", in G. Hufbauer and E. Wada (eds), *Unfinished Business: Telecommunications After the Uruguay Round*, Washington, DC: Institute for International Economics.

Friedman, James W. (1971) "A Noncooperative Equilibrium for Supergames", *Review of Economic Studies* 38(1), 1–12.

Graham, Edward M. (1998) "Market Structure and the Multinational Enterprise: A Game Theoretic Approach", *Journal of International Business Studies* 29(1), 67–83.

Hufbauer, Gary C. and Graham, Edward M. (2000) "No to Foreign Telecoms Equals 'No' to the New Economy", *Institute for International Economics*, Policy Brief 00-7.

Hymer, Stephen H. (1976) *The International Operations of National Firms*, Cambridge, MA: The MIT Press.

Kreps, David and J. Scheinkman (1983) "Quantity Precommitment and Bertrand Competition Yield Cournot Outcomes", *Bell Journal of Economics* 14, 326–37.

Rickard, J. A. and I. W. Murray (1978) "The Dynamics of Some Duopoly Games Involving the Market Share and Nichol Strategies", *Journal of Economic Theory* 17, 51–65.

Selten, R. (1965) "Spieltheoretische Behandlung eines Oligolmodells mit Nachfrageträgheit", *Zeitschrifte für die gesamte Staatswissenschaft* 121, 667–689.

Sidak, J. (1997) *Foreign Investment in American Telecommunications*, Chicago: University of Chicago Press.

Sidak, J. (2000) *Declaration before the US Federal Communications Commission*, Docket No. 00-187.

Wilson, John S. (1997) "Telecommunications Liberalization: The Goods and Services Connection", in G. Hufbauer and E. Wada (eds), *Unfinished Business: Telecommunications After the Uruguay Round*, Washington, DC: Institute for International Economics.

9 Outsourcing jobs and enterprise-level bargaining

'Cheshire cat' unions revisited?

Noel Gaston

> '... the bargaining power of employers has increased *vis-à-vis* that of employees because employers can increasingly say in a global economy that they will pack their bags and leave.'
>
> Bhagwati (1995: 46)

> '... large corporations ... can build, expand, or acquire facilities outside the [United States] altogether. In fact, all the strategic innovations devised by multiplant companies for playing off one group of workers against another ... have become standard operating procedure in the global economy.'
>
> Bluestone and Harrison (1982: 170)

Introduction

Much attention has understandably been focused on the relationship between commodity trade and labour market outcomes. Gaston and Nelson (1998) survey the state of play on that controversial issue and conclude that trade liberalisation may very well have contributed to the increasing wage dispersion observed during the 1980s, particularly in countries such as the United States and the United Kingdom. The increased globalisation may have also contributed to the unemployment problems experienced by some West European economies during the same time period. Overall, Gaston and Nelson (1998) conclude that the 'facts' are consistent with the predictions of short- and medium-run models of labour market adjustment, for example, models in which labour markets fail to clear instantaneously, models of union-firm bargaining, models of imperfect product market competition, and political economy models of lobbying on trade legislation by self-interested parties.

Foreign direct investment (FDI) is similarly controversial. FDI has grown more rapidly than trade over the past decade (Lawrence, 1996). In addition, FDI may have labour market effects that, at least in the short- and medium-run, may well dwarf the effects of trade. Unfortunately, the effects of FDI on labour markets are hard to gauge.[1] The analysis of FDI has all the same problems that plague attempts to relate trade flows to labour market effects. FDI involves additional difficulties. For instance, FDI generally involves changes in competitive conditions in commodity markets as well as endowment effects. Conventional models of FDI treat multinational corporations as firms with some kind of competitive advantage that permits them to enter foreign markets. The growing global nature of firms in particular sectors of the domestic economy surely must also have non-trivial labour market effects.

The attention of this chapter is directed at one piece of the FDI and labour market effects puzzle. The main catalyst is related to the wide-ranging debate concerning the effects of globalisation on labour markets. The opening quotations are pointed references to a prominent concern and popularly held view regarding the effects of multinational corporations on labour markets. The widespread fear of jobs being outsourced or firms 'delocalising' is often allied to a concern that increasing import penetration, particularly from low-wage countries, has adverse labour market consequences for domestic workers.

The debate surrounding trade and wages has highlighted various candidate explanations for the labour market performances in advanced economies. Related to the themes developed in this chapter is the recent research that has emphasised the role played by different types of labour market institutions and the way in which demand shocks translate into very different wage inequality outcomes (e.g. Blau and Kahn, 1996; Fortin and Lemieux, 1997). The present chapter develops a model that investigates the optimal union response to the 'new' global environment. In particular, I examine the effect of the outsourcing of production facilities overseas, or at least the threat by firms to outsource, on domestic wage and employment bargains. It is shown that the global environment may lead union workers to prefer more wage-oriented forms of bargaining with their employers.

Lindbeck and Snower (1996) provide a model with a similar punch-line to my own. They show that in the age of the new global firm, which stresses multi-tasking activities by employees, that centralised wage bargaining is inefficient. Efficiency necessitates the eventual switch to less-centralised forms of wage bargaining and a greater reliance on individual contracts.[2] The relevance, for the present purposes, is that models like Lindbeck and Snower's and the one developed further, may help to explain some of the 'stylised facts' that are now so ingrained in the conscientiousness of researchers working in the area of globalising labour markets. In particular, movements away from centralised wage bargaining would by themselves increase the dispersion of labour market earnings.[3]

In my view, the decentralisation of collective bargaining is an under-researched phenomenon associated with the tumultuous changes in the labour markets experienced since the early 1980s. It should be mentioned, however, that some authors have explicitly linked increased international competition and trade as a reason for a move towards more decentralised wage bargaining. For example, Marginson and Sisson (1988) have noted that British multinational corporations are less likely to engage in multi-employer bargaining (see also Katz, 1993; Ehrenberg, 1994).[4] Katz (1993: 16) argues that the '... increasing prevalence of multinational trade and multinational firms may ... help to explain the declines in multi-employer bargaining that have occurred in a number of countries.'[5] Standing (1997) argues that international trends towards increased labour market flexibility and deunionisation have been propelled by globalisation. In fact, the 'erosion' of labour security has been '*fuelled by the international division of labour*' (p. 12).

In this chapter, I show that the decentralisation of collective bargaining by unions would mitigate some of the adverse consequences for workers working for multinationals or global firms. In the next section, I explore what it is that we 'know' about multinationals and their labour market effects. It provides further grist for the mill before we move on to the Australian setting and the specific focus of my model (in sections titled 'Enterprise bargaining in Australia – why?' and 'Bargaining with an outsourcing threat'). The results of the model are shown to support the institutional developments as a political economy equilibrium. While no claims are made about having identified the sole determinant of increasing wage dispersion, it is noted that wage inequality in Australia has accelerated since wage determination and collective bargaining became more decentralised.[6] The last two sections of the chapter contain a discussion and concluding comments.

Concordant and dicordant themes in recent findings relating FDI and multinationals to labour market outcomes

As usual, most of the high profile and cross-referenced research is for the United States. Hence, the focus is generally either on the behaviour of affiliates of foreign-owned firms in the United States, or on the behaviour of US-owned affiliates in foreign countries. I am not foolhardy enough to attempt a comprehensive survey of this exponentially growing literature. However, in the penultimate section of the chapter, I provide a simplified taxonomy of models of FDI and labour markets and explain where my model fits into the overall scheme of things.

First, some questions. The usual motivation for research on FDI (read, multinationals) and associated labour market effects is actually quite straightforward. (Unlike the answers!) To wit, does FDI lead to jobs being outsourced? Does FDI magnify earned income inequality? Does FDI increase the relative demand for more skilled workers? More simply, given the well-documented surge of international capital flows during the past thirty-something years, does outward FDI or capital outflows place downward pressure on the wages of domestic production workers? That is, does FDI operate in a manner similar to the effect that increased import penetration from unskilled labour abundant countries is thought to have on the wages of workers in import-competing sectors of the economy? Does it matter whether FDI is driven by an inexorable 'slicing up of the value added chain' a la Krugman or whether it is purely strategic and horizontal in nature?

As for a direct labour market linkage with FDI note that if a feature of multinational behaviour is the exploitation of wage differentials across countries then this behaviour could have effects which may be observationally equivalent to shifts caused by skill-biased technological change. Rapid technological advancement has for many commentators been the leading candidate explanation for the increased earnings inequality experienced by many advanced and developing countries during the 1980s and early 1990s (see Baldwin, 1995; or alternatively, Gaston and Nelson, 1998 for a less sanguine view). An intra-industry shift in labour demand towards relatively more skilled and/or more highly educated workers would increase the skilled wage premium across all industries. FDI may also lead to relative increases in skilled labour demand and would have effects indistinguishable from those of skill-biased technical change on relative wages (see Slaughter, 1995; Lawrence, 1996; Markusen and Venables, 1997). Some of the 'new' trade models attempt to explicitly capture this feature (see Feenstra and Hanson, 1996a,b, 1997; Flam and Helpman, 1987).

Next, some answers, some facts, and yet more questions. First, on the wages front, average compensation per worker tends to be greater in foreign-owned than in domestically-owned establishments. In addition, there are wage spillover effects, that is, the presence of foreign firms raises average wages at domestic firms (Lipsey, 1994b; Aitken *et al.*, 1996). One explanation for the wage effect is that when domestic firms are taken over by foreign firms, average compensation rises and total employment falls, which suggests that low paid and low productivity employees are sloughed off. The wage differential, however, is strongly associated with firm size. That is, controlling for firm size, there is *no* effect of foreign ownership on wages (Lipsey, 1994b).

As for industry location, inwards FDI is often concentrated in high-wage and high-skill-intensity industries. Foreign ownership also tends to be heavily concentrated in manufacturing (Lipsey, 1994b). An interesting caveat, is that foreign-owned establishments tend to locate in lower-wage US states (Lipsey, 1994b). This is possibly due to right-to-work laws and the low rates of unionisation in these states. Wheeler and Mody (1992) present evidence supporting the importance of differential labour costs in multinational locational preferences. More recently, Cooke (1997) has presented extremely interesting evidence on the FDI decisions of US firms. Of most interest are Cooke's findings that FDI is negatively related to the presence of high levels of union penetration, centralised collective bargaining structures and governmental restrictions on layoffs. This seems to give credence to the two observations cited at the beginning of the chapter.

FDI is concentrated in industries in which US direct investment abroad is highest. Therefore, FDI is industry-specific. Specifically, it is intended to affect the state of competition in the strategic sense (Lipsey, 1994a,b). This seems to argue somewhat against the vertical slicing up view of FDI and multinationals adopted by some commentators (see Krugman, 1995; Katz and Murphy, 1992; Brainard, 1997). It seems that much FDI is horizontal in nature, designed with explicit competition-affecting or strategic considerations in mind (see Markusen, 1995).

Outsourcing? First, more than 80 per cent of FDI is directed to industrialised countries (see Graham and Krugman, 1991; Markusen, 1995). Thus, taken by itself this suggests that the substitution of low-wage labour in developing countries for domestic unskilled labour is unlikely to be an empirically important factor behind FDI growth.[7] In addition, the support for the view that US multinationals outsource employment to non-OECD countries is extremely weak (see Baldwin, 1995). Blomström *et al.* (1997) find that Swedish firms are even less likely to outsource low-skill jobs to affiliates in developing countries. Home and foreign production workers are at best weak substitutes. In fact, domestic industry employment and overseas affiliate employment may be complements (Slaughter, 1995). Hence, the effect is not substitution between workers at foreign affiliates and domestic workers, but substitution between other low-wage locations (Brainard and Riker, 1997). Employment at affiliates is also very wage sensitive (see Lipsey *et al.*, 1982; Brainard and Riker, 1997; Riker and Brainard, 1997). In addition, US total manufacturing employment shrank 10 per cent between 1979 and 1989, and total overseas affiliate employment shrank 14 per cent (see Lawrence, 1994; Slaughter, 1995). Once again, this implies that domestic and foreign affiliate employment are not negatively correlated.[8].

Where are we now? My interpretation of the recent evidence is that the 'direct' impact of FDI on domestic wage and employment outcomes is marginal at best. The behaviour of multinational corporations, however, is very much affected by unions, both at home and abroad. However, it is unreasonable to assume that labour market institutions do not evolve in response to the rise of the multinational corporation. In my opinion, the evolution of different schemes of compensating workers and changes in collective bargaining practices, specifically, the move towards more firm-level and efficiency-based bargaining is under-researched. Empirically, we should *not* expect to find dramatic negative effects on workers, particularly, those workers with substantial bargaining power. It is working assumption of the model developed below, that outsourcing only occurs in the event of a bargaining breakdown. This does not, however, imply that the *threat* of outsourcing has no effects on organised workers.

Enterprise bargaining in Australia – why?

The *Industrial Relations Reform Act* of 1993 formalised the process of enterprise bargaining (EB).[9] EB essentially involves the devolution of negotiation of wages and employment to the level of the enterprise or workplace. Employees are generally represented by their unions. When approved by the Industrial Relations Commission, enterprise bargains (EB's) supersede Federal award provisions. Historically, wages and employment have been negotiated and administered at the industry-level in Australia.[10] Awards are the principal legal provision in industrial law in Australia and stipulate work conditions and rates of pay. In the event that EB's are not negotiated, the Federal award conditions act as the 'safety net'. Interestingly, EB's cover all workers – both union and non-union.

There is a debate about the merits of EB for unions, in particular. On one hand, the widespread support for EB by employers was seen to be driven by the increasing international competition engendered by globalisation and Australia's policy of tariff reductions (see Gaston, 1998). In addition, the sentiment that EB would eventually attenuate the influence of unions was also significant. Evidence from New Zealand, for instance, reveals dramatic declines in union membership since more decentralised collective bargaining was introduced in that country with the passage of the *Employment Contracts Act* of 1991 (see Whitfield and Ross, 1996: 193). The idea behind a 'divide and conquer' strategy entails an undercutting of wages by competing unions in order to capture market share from one another (recall the Bluestone and Harrison quote; see also Dowrick, 1993). On the other hand, globalisation of the world economy may actually enhance the bargaining power of unions. The cost of potential disruptions is greater for firms with vertically organised production which tilts bargaining power in favour of unions. This, however, is likely to be a short-run phenomenon. In the long run, global firms may re-organise production and delocalise.

While the bargaining power of certain unions may be enhanced, it is difficult to rationalise the political adoption of EB and the support for more wage-oriented bargaining by unions. For example, Davis and Lansbury (1993) note that the position of low-paid workers may be under increasing threat and how this may be at odds with the 'traditional' objectives of the union movement.[11]

EB is thought to be associated with more wage-oriented bargaining.[12] In turn, this benefits the more senior members of stronger unions. Senior workers face a lower risk of layoff and prefer that union bargaining power be directed towards increasing their wages. However, increasing wage-oriented behaviour by unions may lead to what is sometimes referred to as the 'Cheshire cat' phenomenon (see Burda, 1990), in which the median union member may support a wage policy that is inimical to the long-run survival of the union. This phenomenon requires a significant degree of 'irrational' myopia on the part of the union.

Another aspect of more wage-oriented or decentralised bargaining by the stronger unions is that wage inequality might be exacerbated.[13] That is, the members of strong unions are able to negotiate higher wages, the members of weak unions and workers in non-unionised sectors of the economy are not. The wage gap between high income earners and low income earners, as measured by the 90–10 real wage differential for full-time, non-managerial employees, for example, has widened since the transition towards EB's in the Australian workplace. It is clear that some workers have fared progressively better and some progressively worse during the 1990s. In addition, since the wage negotiated in EB's extends to non-unionised workers in the same sector it could be argued that 'inside' or union workers can shift the consequences of their higher wages onto the shoulders of non-union workers in the same industry.

The next section examines a rationale for union preference for EB. In particular, I investigate whether EB or wage-oriented bargaining may be preferable for unions in a more globalised economy. That is, do workers prefer EB or firm-level bargaining to industry-level bargaining when firms can outsource their jobs to foreign affiliates.

Bargaining with an outsourcing threat

Consider an industry in which there are no strategic interactions between firms. A critical assumption is that the industry market structure generates rents that are shared between firms and domestic unions. I focus on the impact of a more globalised economy and the ability of the firm to outsource employment overseas, rather than the impact of globalisation on product market rents.

Wage and employment bargains. Attention is focused on a representative firm facing a union. The firm's profits are given by $\pi(w, l; p) = R(l, p) - wl$, where $R(l, p)$ is the revenue function when employment is l and w is the wage. Higher values of p are associated with higher total and marginal revenue, that is, $R_p > 0$ and $R_{lp} > 0$. Hence, higher p unambiguously indexes good times. Further, we assume $R_l > 0$ and $R_{ll} < 0$.

The firm bargains with the union over wage-employment contracts (w, l). We assume that bargaining over wages and employment is efficient and that the choice from the set of efficient contracts is the one that maximises the symmetric Nash product, that is,

$$S(w, l) = \left[U(w, l; r) - \overline{U}\right]\left[\pi(w, l; p) - \overline{\pi}\right], \tag{1}$$

where $U(\cdot)$ is the union's utility function and r denotes the reservation alternative for workers. Differences in bargaining power are incorporated into the disagreement point, $(\overline{\pi}, \overline{U})$, which is discussed further below.

We assume that the Nash solution lies in the interior of the choice set and that S is strictly concave so that the solution is unique and may be characterised by the following first-order conditions. We suppress arguments where no ambiguity exists and use subscripts to denote partial derivatives.

$$S_w(\cdot) = U_w\Delta^{-1} - \pi_w\Pi^{-1} = 0, \tag{2a}$$

$$S_l(\cdot) = U_l\Delta^{-1} - \pi_l\Pi^{-1} = 0, \tag{2b}$$

where $\Pi = [\pi(w, l; p) - \overline{\pi}]$ and $\Delta = [U(w, l; r) - \overline{U}]$, the economic rent for firms and employed workers, respectively. Substituting (2a) into (2b), gives the equation for the contract curve, which equates the slope of the union's indifference curve and the firm's iso-profit curve,

$$-\frac{U_l}{U_w} = -\frac{\pi_l}{\pi_w}. \tag{3}$$

Further headway is made by investigating the implications of some commonly-considered functional forms for union preferences.

Union preferences. Consider the popular specification used by McDonald and Solow (1981). Here the union comprises m workers, each endowed with one unit of labour time. Prior to actual wage and employment negotiations, a worker's expected utility is given by

$$EU = \frac{l}{m}U(w) + \frac{(m-l)}{m}U(r), \tag{4}$$

where $U(\cdot)$ is increasing and concave, w is the wage rate if employed and the reservation alternative, or benefit when unemployed, is denoted by r.[14]

Alternatively, ignoring the issue of union membership, the union is assumed to maximise

$$EU(w, l) = lU(w) + (1 - l)U(r), \tag{5}$$

where l is normalised to denote the probability of employment.[15] The union's disagreement payoff is $\overline{U} = U(r)$.

Equation (3) yields the set of efficient contracts

$$\frac{U(w) - U(r)}{U_w} = w - R_l. \tag{6}$$

With union risk neutrality, $R_l = r$ so that labour is hired until its marginal revenue product equals the reservation wage.

It is straightforward to conduct comparative statics on equations (2a) and (2b). For complete transparency, Proposition 1 summarises the results for the risk-neutral union case.[16] The exogenous variables are the reservation wage, the price and the firm's disagreement outcome.

Proposition 1 (*Risk neutral union*)

(a) $w = w(r, p, \overline{\pi})$: $w_r > 0$; w_p *has indeterminate sign; and* $w_{\overline{\pi}} < 0$;

(b) $l = l(r, p, \overline{\pi})$: $l_r < 0$; $l_p > 0$; *and* $l_{\overline{\pi}} = 0$;

(c) $\pi = \pi(r, p, \overline{\pi})$: $\pi_r < 0$; $\pi_p > 0$; *and* $\pi_{\overline{\pi}} > 0$;

(d) $U = U(r, p, \overline{\pi})$: $U_r > 0$; $U_p > 0$; *and* $U_{\overline{\pi}} < 0$.

Proof See Appendix.

There are no real surprises here. The impact on wages of higher reservation wages shifts the threat point in the union's favour, raising their total welfare. The impact of higher product prices is to raise employment. The wage indeterminacy with respect to higher product prices is well-known and is explored in detail by Gaston and Trefler (1995). However, note that higher prices unambiguously benefit both the union and firm.

Most importantly, Proposition 1 also states that the domestic union is adversely affected by a higher value of the firm's disagreement outcome. Mezzetti and Dinopoulos (1991) interpret $\overline{\pi}$ as the value of the option to switch production abroad. That is, $\overline{\pi}$ varies positively with a credible outsourcing alternative for the firm.[17] It is credible threat in the case of a multinational corporation because of the lack of coordination between domestic and foreign unions or workers. As Caves (1996: 125) notes multinational corporations enjoy bargaining ploys that the national firms do not possess.

The ability to outsource shifts the domestic collective bargaining outcome in favour of the firm. That is, when it bargains with a domestic union, the firm can threaten to close the domestic plant and switch production to the foreign country.

During any dispute, the domestic firm supplies the market from abroad. The threat point of the firm is therefore its reservation profit when its production facilities are moved off-shore.[18]

A pertinent issue is how unions might respond to the possibility of outsourcing production and employment by firms. If FDI and outsourcing production facilities overseas by firms are features of the new global environment, then it is simply unrealistic to assume that unions and workers sit idly by. Unions adapt to the new global environment or risk extinction. Labour market institutions evolve.

Choosing the stance of bargaining: For transparency, the risk-neutrality assumption is retained, that is, the union's underlying preferences are given by $U(w, l) = (w - r)l$. However, we now suppose that the union leadership is free to choose the weight, λ, in the symmetric Nash product

$$S(w, l) = [(w - r)^{\lambda} l^{1-\lambda}][\pi(w, l; p) - \overline{\pi}], \tag{1'}$$

where $\lambda \in [0, 1]$ is the intra-union bargaining weight when the median union's membership is secure. Pemberton (1988) interprets low values of λ as reflecting a relatively greater weight being placed on the desire for high membership on the part of union leadership *vis-à-vis* the desire for high wages on the part of the median union member. In the following, we treat λ as a variable that can be strategically chosen by the union.[19] Note that neither $\overline{U}$ nor $\overline{\pi}$ are treated as strategic variables.

Once again, equation (3) yields an expression for the contract curve

$$\frac{(1-\lambda)}{\lambda}(w - r) = w - R_l. \tag{7}$$

As $\lambda \rightarrow 0$, $w \rightarrow r$ and employment is maximised, that is, the union is completely employment-oriented. As $\lambda \rightarrow 1$, $w \rightarrow R_l$ and worker's receive the entire marginal revenue product. With complete wage-oriented bargaining, employment and wage outcomes occur along the demand for labour schedule. The symmetric case considered in the previous section is represented by $\lambda = 1/2$ (so that $R_l = r$).

Rearranging equation (2b) and suppressing arguments, yields the Nash bargaining condition or 'equity locus'

$$w = \theta\left(\frac{R}{l} - \frac{\pi}{l}\right) + (1 - \theta)R_l. \tag{8}$$

where $\theta = (1 - \lambda)/(2 - \lambda)$. Thus, the negotiated wage is simply the weighted mean of the marginal and the (net) average revenue products of labour. It is also apparent from equation (8) that, for a given level of employment, the threat to move production overseas ($\overline{\pi} > 0$), results in a lower negotiated wage.

The ability to credibly choose the wage-orientation or bargaining posture has a number of obvious advantages for the union, but the one I focus on below is the union's response to the firm's threat to outsource. Specifically, the union's optimal choice of λ increases in $\overline{\pi}$. We prove this in two steps. First, Proposition 2 states that the union chooses a *more* wage-oriented posture if it has the option to do so. Second, Corollary 1 states that the union chooses a more wage-oriented posture in bargaining in order to maximise the welfare of its members, when the firm's outsourcing threat is greater.

Proposition 2

Suppose that wages and employment are chosen to maximise the symmetric Nash product $[(w-r)^{\lambda}l^{1-\lambda}][\pi(w,l)-\overline{\pi}]$, $\lambda \in [0, 1]$. *Suppose also that a risk-neutral union can choose the degree of wage-orientation when it bargains with the domestic firm. That is, it can choose* λ^* *in its bargaining objective* $U(w, l; \lambda) = (w-r)^{\lambda}l^{1-\lambda}$, $\lambda \in [0,1]$. *Then the union will optimally choose a more wage-oriented bargaining posture, that is,* $\lambda^* > 0.5$.

Proof See Appendix.

Corollary 1

The union chooses a more wage-oriented bargaining posture the greater is the firm's threat to outsource employment and production, that is, $d\lambda^*/d\overline{\pi} > 0$.

Proof See Appendix.

The finding in Proposition 2 is not novel and is closely related to the literature on strategic delegation. For example, Jones (1989) noted that a preferred outcome for the union could be achieved if a credible institutional mechanism existed that increased wages, even though its members were exposed to a greater risk of unemployment. Consequently, a preferred contract for the union would involve higher wages with greater employment risk.[20] On the other hand, the firm would prefer that contracts stipulate low wages and high employment. The real issue, of course, is how either the firm or union can credibly commit to adopt bargaining postures different from that implied by their 'true' underlying preferences.

It is the argument of this chapter that the political support and ratification of EB achieves exactly this outcome. In fact, EB can be rationalised as the outcome of a political economic equilibrium. The possibility that firms bargaining with unions may actually outsource to mitigate the power of unions, is countered by institutional changes in the way in which unions bargain. In addition, the political support for EB is the optimal response to the globalised world economy and the possibilities of capital flight. This is the case for members of a strong union at least.

Corollary 1 *is* novel and states that by setting a higher λ^* the union can ameliorate the effect of a growing $\overline{\pi}$ on worker welfare. That is, the union can offset the firm's increased ability to be able to locate overseas. A growing threat to locate production overseas, or a *higher* $\overline{\pi}$ results in a *larger* λ^* or even greater wage-oriented bargaining posture on the part of the union.[21] The higher value of λ means that the interests of the median union worker are pursued more aggressively by the union leadership. Consequently, unions become more aggressive in wage-bargaining with firms that threaten to outsource employment overseas in the event of a bargaining breakdown. The support for EB is optimal from the viewpoint of the union's membership. Doing so, however, may jeopardise the union's marginal workers. When demand fails to grow it may thus imply falling levels of union membership. In addition, this implies that wage and employment bargains are struck 'closer' to the demand for labour curve. Some recent and consistent evidence for this is presented by Haskel *et al.* (1997) who show that increasing labour market flexibility in the United Kingdom has resulted in labour input being more closely aligned to the business cycle.

Implications for further research

There are essentially two broad types of models that investigate the relationship between FDI and labour markets – general equilibrium or trade models and partial equilibrium or labour models. Both types of models have their advantages, depending on the precise questions posed. In addition, trade models are of two basic types – the conventional or HOS model and the 'new' trade or industrial organisation models.

Predictions about changing factor prices from the standard HOS trade model are inevitably bound up with the Stolper–Samuelson Theorem. Much of the focus in developed countries has been on the effects of outsourcing unskilled, blue collar jobs to developing countries. For example, in the United States a prominent concern of the labour movement is the loss of jobs to Mexico's *maquiladoras*. Lawrence (1996) argues that the evidence for a large globalisation effect, via either increased trade or capital flows, on labour markets is fairly weak. In particular, it should be expected that if outsourcing unskilled jobs to developing countries is empirically important, that the skilled wage premium should rise in the developed countries and fall in the developing countries. Attendant with this should be falls in the proportion of skilled workers employed in developed countries. This has simply not happened. Lawrence (1996), like a number of other trade economists, has opted for the skill-biased technological change explanation for the increased wage inequality experienced in a number of countries – both developed and developing – since the early 1980s.

Since conventional trade theory has little to say about direct investment (see Ethier, 1994), most recent attention has been devoted to the new trade models. In general, economists working with these models do not reach such optimistic conclusions as the HOS devotees. Also, much of the empirical evidence presented is more in keeping with the partial equilibrium models presented by labour economists. In accord with stylised facts, many of these economists work with models of product differentiation.

For example, Feenstra and Hanson (1996a,b; 1997) argue that FDI has increased the relative demand (and therefore, wages) for skilled workers in both the North and the South. The North produces ever increasingly high quality goods, reducing the demand for unskilled workers. However, as the relatively unskilled activities (from the North's perspective) head South, the demand for skilled labour in the South increases (since the activities are relatively skilled from the South's perspective). Hence, it is possible for FDI to have effects on labour markets similar to the effects engendered by skill-biased technological change.

In a similar fashion, Markusen and Venables (1997) show that anything that liberalises investment, relative to international trade, will lead to an increased formation of multinational corporations since exporting and producing overseas for the host country's market are substitutes. If multinational corporations use relatively more skilled labour than 'national' firms, then the skilled wage premium increases with greater investment liberalisation. In fact, in a similar fashion to the Feenstra and Hanson model, the skilled–unskilled wage gap widens world-wide.

Much of the new trade literature is devoted to understanding the growth and formation of multinationals. They address the ownership, location and internalisation motives for FDI. For example, why ownership and control is important; why and where multinationals locate abroad; and why activities need to take place within the boundaries of the firm (particularly, when subcontracting or licensing are obvious alternatives). In his survey of multinationals and trade, Markusen (1995) points out that the internalisation motive is the most abstract and difficult to rationalise. The bargaining models may provide some insight into why firms may choose FDI over licensing activities or 'arm's length' contracting – investing overseas, which may entail substantial investment in plant and equipment, provides a credible threat to outsource employment; licensing in all likelihood will not.[22] In addition, strategic considerations involving unions in developed countries are consistent with two-way FDI within the same industry – which is a prominent feature of modern FDI (Ethier, 1994).

In contrast, labour economists take the existence of FDI and global firms as their point of departure when examining labour market effects. A typical inquiry is how the existence of production facilities overseas may affect the domestic wage and employment bargains that are struck between global firms and organised workers. There has been a proliferation of models that deal with every possible bargaining scenario. For example, bargaining could be between a national employers' association and a large national union, a single firm dealing with multiple unions, a single union dealing with many firms.[23] In addition, an important distinction that must also be drawn is that between horizontally-integrated global firms ('cross-hauling' FDI) versus vertically-integrated global firms ('slicing up the value-added chain'). The union's and firm's welfare not only depend crucially on the structure of bargaining, but also the type of firm integration under consideration.

A basic issue is whether any union can potentially 'hold-up' a vertically-integrated firm or whether workers will be pressured to reduce wages by dint of the increased competition from workers at foreign affiliates and outsourcing threats. In the latter case, it may seem obvious that unions can be played off against one another, but it depends crucially on whether the workers in separate unions (or 'bargaining units') are complements or substitutes for one another (Horn and Wolinsky, 1988; Dowrick, 1993). If the two groups of workers are complements (substitutes) in production, then both groups can do better by bargaining separately (jointly).

The industrial relations benefits of 'going global' for firms are particularly obvious when they integrate horizontally rather than vertically (see Mezzetti and Dinopoulos, 1991; Zhao, 1995; 1998). This is the case modelled in the present paper. Of course, these are similar to the tensions associated with vertically integrated firms. While it may pay for unions to band together to push up the wage bargain (see Davidson, 1988; Dowrick, 1989; 1993), it is not always possible for unions to credibly increase their threat payoff. Alternatively, the same objectives may be achieved by unions adopting a more wage-oriented bargaining posture. They can institutionalise this through their political support for enterprise bargaining. This avenue is particularly attractive, when it may be difficult for unions to integrate across national boundaries (see Caves, 1996).

Conclusion

This chapter sought to increase our understanding of one dimension of the relationship between multinational corporations and labour markets. In particular, we investigated the evolution of less centralised wage bargaining in an era characterised by a growing number of global firms. In Australia, enterprise bargaining has introduced radical changes to the way in which wages are determined. It was argued that the changes in the manner in which bargaining is conducted in Australia may best be viewed as an endogenous institutional or political economic response by unions to the growing internationalisation of the firms they work for.

The increased importance of multinational firms and the greater exposure to international competition has brought with it many changes. One such change is the demise of centralised wage bargaining. The model presented in this chapter shows that unions prefer a greater degree of wage-orientation in their bargaining posture when dealing with firms that threaten to outsource their jobs. The relevance of the model for recent labour market developments is that the model's findings help to explain the increased dispersion of labour market earnings. Less directly, another feature of the model is that large flows of outsourcing to foreign countries should not be a prominent feature of actual labour markets. Overall, it should not be terribly surprising that changes in labour market institutions have accompanied the growing internationalisation of labour markets.

Acknowledgments

I would like to thank the participants of the Conference on Research Issues in Foreign Direct Investment held at Flinders University of South Australia, 14–15 May 1998, where an earlier version was first presented. This version of the chapter also benefitted from the comments received by seminar participants at Keio University and the Institute of Economic and Social Research at Osaka University. In particular, I am grateful to Bill Ethier, Keith Hancock, Daniel Léonard, Hajime Miyazaki, Doug Nelson, Yoshio Okunishi and Mark Wooden for their insightful comments. The usual disclaimers naturally apply.

Notes

1 Caves (1996) surveys earlier research, while Graham and Krugman (1991), Lipsey (1994a,b), Slaughter (1995), Brainard (1993a,b), Brainard and Riker (1997) and Riker and Brainard (1997) are more recent references.

2 Freeman and Gibbons (1995) provide a model of the breakdown of centralised bargaining, which they apply to the case of Sweden. They attribute the decline in Sweden's peak-level wage bargaining system to wages drift and the increasing need for flexibility. In turn, these latter features were affected by economic forces, that increased the dispersion of wages for Sweden's increasingly heterogeneous work-force, as well as falling inflation, which increased wage discipline.

3 In a similar vein, some authors have pointed to the growth of profit-sharing plans and contingent-pay schemes as being a potentially significant factor behind the growing wage inequality witnessed in the United States during the 1980s (see Bell and Neumark, 1991; Ehrenberg and Smith, 1994). With the increasing prevalence of such pay schemes, volatility in output and income implies greater dispersion in the distribution of earned income. A possible reason for the proliferation of these more flexible forms of employee compensation and the reduced reliance on 'pattern bargaining' is globalisation. (See the discussants' comments after the Bell and Neumark, 1991 article.)

4 Edwards and Podgursky (1986: 46) argue that '*[u]nions now find themselves negotiating with increasingly centralized corporations at an increasingly decentralized level*'.

5 Katz lists Sweden, Australia, the former West Germany, Italy, the United Kingdom, and the United States as having bargaining structures that have to varying degrees experienced decentralisation of their collective bargaining structures. At the beginning of the 1980s, Sweden and Australia had 'extremely centralised' collective bargaining.

6 A recent study notes that countries with higher unionisation and more coordinated bargaining experience less earnings inequality (OECD, 1997). Rowthorn (1992) shows that wage inequality increases as the degree of coordination among national unions falls. Zweimüller and Barth (1994) show that countries with more decentralised regimes display greater dispersion in their inter-industry wage structure as well.

7 In fact, it is difficult to see how any other conclusion is warranted. Multinationals employ about 70 million workers worldwide, about three-quarters of whom are employed in their home countries. In addition, the remainder were predominantly employed in industrialised countries. FDI is a '*First World business directed largely at First World locations*'. In 1990, the United States, Canada, Germany, the United Kingdom, the Netherlands, France, Italy, Switzerland and Japan were the source of more than 90 per cent of the world's outwards stock of FDI and the host to more than two-thirds of the inwards stock. The quotation and figures are from Renshaw (1993). See also Lawrence (1996), Chapter 5.

8 There is indirect evidence that marginal differences in operating costs are unlikely to drive 'delocalisation' decisions. For example, Wheeler and Mody (1992) indicate that tax avoidance is rarely a motive. Also, there appears to be little evidence to support the 'pollution haven' hypothesis, that is, firms locating their 'dirty' operations in developing countries with low labour costs and slack environmental standards (Eskeland and Harrison, 1997).

9 The move towards of enterprise bargaining in Australia was actually initiated much earlier than 1993. The national wage case decisions of 1988 and 1989 foreshadowed 'award restructuring' at the firm-level and a move towards 'managed decentralism' and the eventual shift to more comprehensive enterprise bargaining (see Katz, 1993). The Industrial Relations Commission outlined the Enterprise Bargaining Principle in 1991, which promulgated bargaining at the firm level (or plant level where appropriate).

10 Davis and Lansbury (1993) provide an accessible industrial relations perspective of the legal, political and economic framework of wage determination in Australia. Hawke

and Wooden (1998) provide a nice discussion of the rise of enterprise bargaining and decline in trade union membership.

11 *The Australian* newspaper (6 June 1998) reported that the membership of some branches of the Australian Workers Union (AWU) were in 'freefall', in deep financial crisis and were fighting for their survival. The AWU is one of Australia's oldest and largest unions. The percentage of the total workforce that is unionised has been slowly, but steadily, declining in Australia. In 1986 the figure stood at 45.6 per cent; 41.6 per cent in 1988; 40.5 per cent in 1990; 39.6 per cent in 1992; 35.0 per cent in 1994; and 33.5 per cent in 1996 (source: Trade Union Members, Australia [ABS catalogue no. 6325.0, various issues]).

12 For example, Calmfors (1993) notes that centralisation of collective bargaining leads to 'negative wage externalities' being internalised. Decentralised bargaining results in less wage restraint by those who have the bargaining power to increase their own wages. Hawke and Wooden (1998) argue that the uniform wages generated by centralised bargaining in Australia involved rents being transferred from efficient competitive industries to less efficient protected sectors.

13 Declines in collective bargaining coverage or the retreat from centralised negotiations have produced wider earnings distributions in the United States, United Kingdom, Sweden and Italy. See Freeman (1998) for references. Countries with more centralised/coordinated systems of bargaining also show some tendency to have lower unemployment and higher employment rates as well (see OECD, 1997).

14 In line with the discussion in the last section, r may be interpreted as the Federal award wage. Hence, $(w - r)$ represents the amount of 'wages drift' (see Freeman and Gibbons, 1995).

15 A union representing workers is assumed to treat its employed and unemployed members equally. Workers are homogeneous and all face the same risk of unemployment, $(1 - l)$.

16 See Gaston and Trefler (1995) for the risk averse case. Risk aversion, however, is not central for the results that follow.

17 It is helpful to think of $\overline{\pi}$ as being inversely related to barriers or restrictions to FDI. FDI liberalisation is therefore associated with a higher $\overline{\pi}$. As in Mezzetti and Dinopoulos (1991), I focus on the case in which the firm produces in the home country in equilibrium, despite its option to shift production abroad. The analysis is easily extended to the case in which the firm produces both at home and overseas.

18 Presumably, if foreign and domestic workers are equally productive and the foreign wage is less than the domestic wage (due to the absence of unions in the foreign country), there are some additional fixed costs of moving overseas or taxes on overseas production, otherwise production would never occur at home.

19 Drawing on the literature on strategic delegation (e.g. Vickers, 1985; Sklivas, 1987), Jones (1989) investigated the desirability of entrenching a union leadership that was sufficiently bloody-minded to pursue a more 'wage-oriented' strategy. However, firms also have a similar incentive to be bloody-minded in pursuing low wage-high employment outcomes. Consequently, an increase in industrial disputes may result. Institutionalising EB in the political economic sense, may therefore be a less costly way of credibly committing to a more wage-oriented bargaining posture. Political economy models that endogenise labour market institutions seem to be more readily embraced by economists these days. Wright (1986) uses a dynamic voting model to show how workers with heterogeneous employment opportunities help to entrench a public unemployment insurance system that may prescribe sub-optimal levels of benefits. Saint-Paul (1996) and Fredriksson and Gaston (1999) use political economy models to show that incumbent workers or 'insiders' may 'vote' for labour market policies that exclude 'outsiders'.

20 The same conclusion pertains for efficient bargains constrained to lie on the labour demand curve (i.e. a 'right-to-manage' model). See Jones (1989).

21 This result holds as long as R_l is not 'too' convex. See Proof of Corollary 1. Mezzetti and Dinopoulos (1991) have a similar restriction in their strategic trade model.

22 The issues are far from clear-cut, however. While multinational firms may find it beneficial to make capital investments in production facilities overseas to tilt the bargaining outcome in their favour, Grout (1984) showed that firms may *under*-invest in capital in order to avoid expropriation by strong unions. More recently, Ulph (1989) has shown that unions may be better off by weakening their bargaining position, so that firms increase their investment whereby, although getting a smaller slice, the larger pie more than compensates. However, Ulph shows that firms may *over*-invest in capital in order to make credible a threat to use other workers.

23 Ulph and Ulph (1990) provide an accessible survey of the structure of union bargaining.

References

Aitken, B., A. Harrison and R. E. Lipsey (1996). 'Wages and Foreign Ownership: A Comparative Study of Mexico, Venezuela, and the United States'. *Journal of International Economics* 40: 345–71.

Baldwin, R. E. (1995). 'The Effects of Trade and Foreign Direct Investment on Employment and Relative Wages'. *OECD Economic Studies* 23: 7–54.

Bell, L. and D. Neumark (1991). 'Lump-Sum Payments and Wage Moderation in the Union Sector'. In R. W. Eberts and E. L. Groshen (eds) *Structural Changes in U.S. Labor Markets: Causes and Consequences*. New York: M. E. Sharpe.

Bhagwati, J. (1995). 'Trade and Wages: Choosing Among Alternative Explanations'. *Economic Policy Review* 1(1): 42–7.

Blau, F. D. and L. M. Kahn (1996). 'International Differences in Male Wage Inequality: Institutions versus Market Forces'. *Journal of Political Economy* 104(4): 791–837.

Blomström, M., G. Fors and R. E. Lipsey (1997). 'Foreign Direct Investment and Employment: Home Country Experience in the United States and Sweden'. *Economic Journal* 107: 1787–97.

Bluestone, B. and B. Harrison (1982). *The Deindustrialization of America: Plant Closings, Community Abandonment, and the Dismantling of Industry*. New York: Basic Books.

Brainard, S. L. (1993a). 'A Simple Theory of Multinational Corporations and Trade With a Trade-off Between Proximity and Concentration'. *NBER Working Paper* #4269, Cambridge, Mass.: NBER.

—— (1993b). 'An Empirical Assessment of the Factor Proportions Explanation of Multinational Sales'. *NBER Working Paper* #4583.

—— (1997). 'An Empirical Assessment of the Proximity-Concentration Tradeoff Between Multinational Sales and Trade'. *American Economic Review* 87(4): 520–44.

—— and D. A. Riker (1997). 'Are U.S. Multinationals Exporting U.S. Jobs?' *NBER Working Paper* #5958.

Burda, M. C. (1990). 'Membership, Seniority and Wage-setting in Democratic Labour Unions'. *Economica* 57: 455–66.

Calmfors, L. (1993). 'Centralisation of Wage Bargaining and Macroeconomic Performance – A Survey'. OECD Economic Studies 21: 161–91.

Caves, R. E. (1996). *Multinational Enterprise and Economic Analysis*, 2nd edn. New York: Cambridge University Press.

Cooke, W. N. (1997). 'The Influence of Industrial Relations Factors on U.S. Foreign Direct Investment Abroad'. *Industrial and Labor Relations Review* 51(1): 3–17.

Davidson, C. (1988). 'Multiunit Bargaining in Oligopolistic Industries'. *Journal of Labor Economics* 6(3), 397–422.

Davis, E. M. and R. D. Lansbury (1993). 'Industrial Relations in Australia'. In G. J. Bamber and R. D. Lansbury (eds) *International and Comparative Industrial Relations*, 2nd edn. Sydney: Allen and Unwin.

Dowrick, S. (1989). 'Union-Oligopoly Bargaining'. *Economic Journal* 99: 1123–42.

—— (1993). 'Enterprise Bargaining, Union Structure and Wages'. *Economic Record* 69: 393–404.

Edwards, R. and M. Podgursky (1986). 'The Unraveling Accord: American Unions in Crisis'. In R. Edwards (ed.) *Unions in Crisis and Beyond*. Dover, Mass.: Auburn House.

Ehrenberg, R. G. (1994). *Labor Markets and Integrating National Economies*. Washington, DC: The Brookings Institution.

—— and R. S. Smith (1994). *Modern Labor Economics*, 5th edn. New York: Harper-Collins.

Eskeland, G. S. and A. E. Harrison (1997). 'Moving to Greener Pastures? Multinationals and the Pollution-haven Hypothesis'. *World Bank Policy Research Working Paper* #1744.

Ethier, W. J. (1994). 'Multinational Firms in the Theory of International Trade'. In E. L. Bacha (ed.) *Economics in a Changing World: Proceedings of the Tenth World Congress of the International Economic Association, Moscow*. Volume 4. Development, Trade and the Environment. IEA Conference Volume, no. 110, New York: St. Martin's Press, 3–33.

Feenstra, R. and G. Hanson (1996a). 'Foreign Investment, Outsourcing and Relative Wages'. In R. Feenstra, G. Grossman and D. Irwin (eds) *The Political Economic of Trade Policy*. Cambridge, Mass.: MIT Press.

—— (1996b). 'Globalization, Outsourcing, and Wage Inequality'. *American Economic Review* 86(2): 240–5.

—— (1997). 'Foreign Direct Investment and Relative Wages: Evidence from Mexico's Maquiladoras'. *Journal of International Economics* 42(3/4): 371–93.

Flam, H. and E. Helpman (1987). 'Vertical Product Differentiation and North-South Trade'. *American Economic Review* 77(5): 810–22.

Fortin, N. M. and T. Lemieux (1997). 'Institutional Changes and Rising Wage Inequality: Is There a Linkage?' *Journal of Economic Perspectives* 11(2): 75–96.

Fredriksson, P. G. and N. Gaston (1999). 'The 'Greening' of Trade Unions and the Demand for Eco-Taxes'. *European Journal of Political Economy* 15(4): 663–86.

Freeman, R. B. (1998). 'War of the Models: Which Labour Market Institutions for the 21st Century?' *Labour Economics* 5(1): 1–24.

—— and R. S. Gibbons (1995). 'Getting Together and Breaking Apart: The Decline of Centralized Collective Bargaining'. In R. B. Freeman and L. H. Katz (eds) *Differences and Changes in Wage Structures*. Chicago: University of Chicago Press, 345–70.

Gaston, N. (1998). 'The Impact of International Trade and Protection on Australian Manufacturing Employment'. *Australian Economic Papers* 37(2): 119–36.

—— and D. Nelson (1998). 'Globalisation and Wages in OECD Economies: Linking Theory and Evidence'. Forthcoming in J. Francois, D. Roland-Holst and D. van der Mensbrugghe (eds) *Globalisation and Employment Patterns: Policy, Theory and Evidence*. London: CEPR and OECD.

—— and D. Trefler (1995). 'Union Wage Sensitivity to Trade and Protection: Theory and Evidence'. *Journal of International Economics* 39(1/2): 1–25.

Graham, E. M. and P. R. Krugman (1991). *Foreign Direct Investment in the United States*, 2nd edn. Washington, DC: Institute for International Economics.

Grout, P. (1984). 'Investment and Wages in the Absence of Legally Binding Contracts: A Nash Bargaining Approach'. *Econometrica* 52: 449–60.

Haskel, J., B. Kersley and C. Martin (1997). 'Labour Market Flexibility and Employment Adjustment: Micro Evidence from UK Establishments'. *Oxford Economic Papers* 49(3): 362–79.

Hawke, A. and M. Wooden (1998). 'The Changing Face of Australian Industrial Relations'. *Economic Record* 74: 74–88.

Horn, H. and A. Wolinsky (1988). 'Worker Substitutability and Patterns of Unionisation'. *Economic Journal* 98: 484–97.

Jones, S. R. G. (1989). 'The Role of Negotiators in Union-Firm Bargaining'. *Canadian Journal of Economics* 22(3): 630–42.

Katz, H. C. (1993). 'The Decentralization of Collective Bargaining: A Literature Review and Comparative Analysis'. *Industrial and Labor Relations Review* 47(1): 3–22.

Katz, L. F. and K. M. Murphy (1992). 'Changes in Relative Wages 1963–1987: Supply and Demand Factors'. *Quarterly Journal of Economics* 107(1): 35–78.

Krugman, P. (1995). 'Growing World Trade: Causes and Consequences'. *Brookings Papers on Economic Activity* 1: 327–62.

Lawrence, R. Z. (1994). 'Trade, Multinationals, and Labor'. *NBER Working Paper* #4836, Cambridge Mass.: NBER.

—— (1996). *Single World, Divided Nations? International Trade and OECD Labor Markets*. Washington, DC: Brookings-OECD.

Lindbeck, A. and D. J. Snower (1996). 'Reorganization of Firms and Labor-Market Inequality'. *American Economic Review* 86(2): 315–21.

Lipsey, R. E. (1994a). 'Outward Direct Investment and the U.S. Economy'. *NBER Working Paper* #4691 Cambridge Mass.: NBER.

—— (1994b). 'Foreign-Owned Firms and U.S. Wages'. *NBER Working Paper* #4927 Cambridge Mass.: NBER.

——, I. B. Kravis and R. A. Roldan (1982). 'Do Multinational Firms Adapt Factor Proportions to Relative Factor Prices?' In A. O. Krueger (ed.) *Trade and Employment in Developing Countries: Factor Supply and Substitution*. Chicago: University of Chicago Press, 215–55.

McDonald, I. M. and R. M. Solow (1981). 'Wage Bargaining and Employment'. *American Economic Review* 71: 896–908.

Marginson, P. and K. Sisson (1988). 'The Enterprises in Profile'. In P. Marginson, P. K. Edwards, R. Martin, J. Purcell, and K. Sisson (eds) *Beyond the Workplace: Managing Industrial Relations in the Multi-establishment Enterprise*. Warwick Studies in Industrial Relations, Oxford: Blackwell.

Markusen, J. R. (1995). 'The Boundaries of Multinational Enterprises and the Theory of International Trade'. *Journal of Economic Perspectives* 9(2): 169–89.

—— and A. J. Venables (1997). 'The Role of Multinational Firms in the Wage-Gap Debate'. *Review of International Economics* 5(4): 435–51.

Mezzetti, C. and E. Dinopoulos (1991). 'Domestic Unionization and Import Competition'. *Journal of International Economics* 31(1/2): 79–100.

Organisation for Economic Co-operation and Development (OECD) (1997). *Employment Outlook*. Paris: OECD.

Pemberton, J. (1988). 'A 'Managerial' Model of the Trade Union'. *Economic Journal* 98: 755–71.

Renshaw, G. (1993). 'Overview and Conclusions'. In P. Bailey, A. Parisotto and, G. Renshaw (eds) *Multinationals and Employment: The Global Economy in the 1990s*. Geneva: International Labour Office, 293–325.

Riker, D. A. and S. L. Brainard (1997). 'U.S. Multinationals and Competition from Low Wage Countries'. *NBER Working Paper* #5959.

Rowthorn, R. E. (1992). 'Centralisation, Employment and Wage Dispersion'. *Economic Journal* 102: 506–23.

Saint-Paul, G. (1996). 'Exploring the Political Economy of Labour Market Institutions'. *Economic Policy* 23: 263–315.

Sklivas, S. D. (1987). 'The Strategic Choice of Managerial Incentives'. *Rand Journal of Economics* 18(3): 452–58.

Slaughter, M. J. (1995). 'Multinational Corporations, Outsourcing, and American Wage Divergence'. *NBER Working Paper* #5253, Cambridge Mass.: NBER.

Standing, G. (1997). 'Globalization, Labour Flexibility and Insecurity: The Era of Market Regulation'. *European Journal of Industrial Relations* 3: 7–37.

Ulph, A. (1989). 'The Incentives to Make Commitments in Wage Bargains'. *Review of Economic Studies* 56(3): 449–66.

—— and D. Ulph (1990). 'Union Bargaining: A Survey of Recent Work'. In D. Sapsford and Z. Tzannatos (eds) *Current Issues in Labour Economics*. London, UK: Macmillan.

Vickers, J. S. (1985). 'Delegation and the Theory of the Firm'. *Economic Journal* 95: 138–47.

Wheeler, D. and A. Mody (1992). 'International Investment Location Decisions'. *Journal of International Economics* 33(1): 57–76.

Whitfield, K. and R. Ross (1996). *The Australian Labour Market*, 2nd edn. Sydney: Harper-Collins.

Wright, R. D. (1986). 'The Redistributive Roles of Unemployment Insurance and the Dynamics of Voting'. *Journal of Public Economics* 31: 377–99.

Zhao, L. (1995). 'Cross-hauling Direct Foreign Investment and Unionized Oligopoly'. *European Economic Review* 39(6): 1237–53.

—— (1998). 'The Impact of Foreign Direct Investment on Wages and Employment'. *Oxford Economic Papers* 50(2): 284–301.

Zweimüller, J. and E. Barth (1994). 'Bargaining Structure, Wage Determination, and Wage Dispersion in 6 OECD Countries'. *Kyklos* 47(1): 81–93.

Appendix

Proof of Proposition 1 Totally differentiate equations (2a) and (6), using equation (2b) to simplify, to obtain

$$\begin{bmatrix} 2l & 2(w-r) \\ 0 & R_{ll} \end{bmatrix}\begin{bmatrix} \mathrm{d}w \\ \mathrm{d}l \end{bmatrix} = \begin{bmatrix} R_p & l & -1 \\ -R_{lp} & 1 & 0 \end{bmatrix}\begin{bmatrix} \mathrm{d}p \\ \mathrm{d}r \\ \mathrm{d}\overline{\pi} \end{bmatrix}. \tag{A.1}$$

The determinant is $2lR_{ll} < 0$, by concavity. Using Cramer's Rule the results follow. ■

Proof of Proposition 2 Totally differentiate the first-order conditions, using equation (7) to simplify, to obtain

$$\begin{bmatrix} (\lambda+1)l & (2-\lambda)(w-r) \\ (\lambda-2)l & \dfrac{(\lambda-2)(1-\lambda)(w-r)}{\lambda} + lR_{ll} \end{bmatrix}\begin{bmatrix} \mathrm{d}w \\ \mathrm{d}l \end{bmatrix} = \begin{bmatrix} -\lambda & (\pi-\overline{\pi}) \\ (1-\lambda) & (\pi-\overline{\pi}) \end{bmatrix}\begin{bmatrix} \mathrm{d}\overline{\pi} \\ \mathrm{d}\lambda \end{bmatrix}. \tag{A.2}$$

The determinant is

$$D = (\lambda - 2)(w - r)\left(\frac{1 - 2\lambda}{\lambda}\right)l + (\lambda + 1)l^2 R_{ll}.$$

$D < 0$ as long as

$$\frac{(\lambda - 2)(1 - 2\lambda)}{\lambda(\lambda + 1)} < \frac{-lR_{ll}}{(w - r)}.$$

The union chooses λ to maximise $U(w, l; \lambda) = (w(\lambda) - r)l(\lambda)$. It therefore solves $U_\lambda = (w - r)l_\lambda + lw_\lambda = 0$. Using Cramer's Rule on equation (A.2), we have $l_\lambda = 3l(\pi - \overline{\pi})/D < 0$ and

$$w_\lambda = \frac{(\pi - \overline{\pi})}{D}\left(\frac{(\lambda - 2)(w - r)}{\lambda} + lR_{ll}\right) > 0.$$

Substitution into U_λ yields

$$\frac{2(2\lambda - 1)}{\lambda} = -\frac{lR_{ll}}{(w - r)} > 0. \tag{A.3}$$

Clearly, $\lambda^* = \frac{1}{2}$. When evaluated at the λ^* defined by equation (A.3), also note that $D = \frac{3}{2}\lambda l^2 R_{ll} < 0$. ■

Proof of Corollary 1 First, we note that for the λ^* defined by equation (A.3) to maximise $U(\lambda)$, we require that the second-order condition,

$$U_{\lambda\lambda} = \frac{(\pi - \overline{\pi})U}{D}\left[\frac{2}{\lambda^2} + \frac{(2R_{ll} + lR_{lll})l_\lambda}{(w - r)}\right]$$

is negative. Sufficient is $2R_{ll} + lR_{lll} < 0$, which is satisfied as long as R_{lll} is not 'too' positive.

The effect on union welfare of higher $\overline{\pi}$ is $U_{\overline{\pi}} = (w - r)l_{\overline{\pi}} + lw_{\overline{\pi}}$. From equation (A.2), we have $l_{\overline{\pi}} = (1 - 2\lambda)l/D > 0$ (since $\lambda^* > \frac{1}{2}$) and $w_{\overline{\pi}} = -\lambda lR_{ll}/D < 0$. By substitution,

$$U_{\overline{\pi}} = \frac{(w - r)(1 - 2\lambda)l - \lambda l^2 R_{ll}}{D}. \tag{A.4}$$

Evaluated at the optimal λ^* we have $U_{\overline{\pi}} = -\frac{1}{3}$.
Note that $\lambda^* = 2U/(4U + l^2 R_{ll})$. Differentiating with respect to $\overline{\pi}$ gives:

$$\frac{d\lambda^*}{d\overline{\pi}} = \frac{2\lambda(1 - 2\lambda)U_{\overline{\pi}} - \lambda^2(2lR_{ll} + l^2 R_{lll})l_{\overline{\pi}}}{2U} > 0. \tag{A.5}$$

Equation (A.5) is positive since $U_{\overline{\pi}} < 0$, $l_{\overline{\pi}} > 0$ and $2R_{ll} + lR_{lll} < 0$. ■

10 FDI and the structure of home country production

Ari Kokko

Introduction

The effects of foreign direct investment (FDI) on the home countries of multinational corporations (MNCs) have been discussed for several decades, but the topic has attracted renewed attention in the international debate during the past few years. The global liberalisation of trade and investment flows agreed upon in GATT's Uruguay Round and the regional integration processes in Europe, the Americas, and the Asia-Pacific region are important reasons for this resurgence of interest. The reduction of trade and investment barriers at the global as well as regional level is creating new, large markets and removing restrictions on where plants can be located. One of the consequences is a marked increase in cross-border mergers and acquisitions as MNCs are adjusting to the new environment, particularly in the EU where formal integration has reached further than in other parts of the world. It is likely that these processes of globalisation and regionalisation will change the pattern of international investment, with consequences for both home and host countries.

The purpose of this chapter is to provide a selective survey of the literature on some of the home country effects of FDI, and to discuss a few questions that have rarely been addressed in detail in earlier research. The focus will be on production interactions between the foreign and domestic operations of multinational firms. These interactions occur because FDI typically affects the MNC's home country operations. The most common question in this context has concerned the impact of outward investment on home country exports: does the establishment of a foreign affiliate substitute for home exports or increase home exports of components and intermediate goods used by the foreign affiliates?[1]

Much of the discussion will draw on evidence from Sweden, for good reasons. Swedish MNCs are not only prominent on the international scene, but they also occupy a dominant position in the Swedish economy. Although over 60 per cent of their production is located outside Sweden, they account for about a third of Swedish employment, two-thirds of exports, and three-quarters of the economy's total R&D spending. This means that any effects of outward investment will inevitably be felt throughout the national economy. Moreover, the flows of outward investment have been much larger than flows of inward investment until the last few years. The sum of Swedish investment abroad between 1981 and 1990 was more than five times larger than inward FDI (OECD, 1993), and the stock of outward FDI was more than 2.5 times that of inward FDI in the mid-1990s (Braunerhjelm *et al.*, 1996).[2] Much work has therefore been invested in analyses of the effects of Swedish outward investment on the Swedish economy. Some of the findings regarding the impact of FDI on home country exports are reviewed in the section on production interactions and effects of outward FDI on home country exports. The following section turns to a discussion of some newer research issues, with emphasis on the structural effects of outward FDI and the last section concludes the chapter.

Production interactions: effects of outward FDI on home country exports

Questions regarding the impact of outward foreign investment on domestic exports, investment, and employment have been addressed by business-oriented analyses as well as econometric studies at different points in time in several countries, which means that there is quite some variation in methodology and generality of results. Typically, the more business oriented authors have attempted to examine what would have happened in specific cases if investment abroad had not been possible, whereas the econometric studies have tried to detect the overall relationship between FDI and home country exports in larger samples of firms or industries.

An example of a Swedish business-oriented analysis of FDI and home country exports is Jordan and Vahlne (1981). This study aims to compare the domestic employment effects of FDI with alternative ways to exploit the competitive advantages of a sample of Swedish firms. The alternatives considered are exports from Sweden, licensing, and minority joint ventures, and the analysis attempts to take into account several factors that may influence Swedish exports and employment in the medium term. These include estimates of the market shares that can be captured under the alternative strategies, differences in the ability to face and solve customer problems in the relevant markets, flows of royalties and license payments (which influences the possibilities to undertake R&D), and differences in related product sales under the alternative strategies.

Jordan and Vahlne's (1981) overall conclusion is that FDI has positive effects on Swedish exports and employment, because the establishment of foreign affiliates typically leads to large increases in the foreign market shares and in exports of intermediate products to affiliates. The driving force is the existence (or fear) of various types of trade barriers that would limit the market shares if export was the only available alternative. Moreover, FDI is connected with higher royalty and license payments (from affiliates) and higher exports of related products. Foreign production is judged, by Jordan and Vahlne, (1981) to be particularly beneficial for low-technology products with high transportation costs. However, the results rest on very specific assumptions about export survival rates, that is, the fractions of the affiliates' market share that could have been served by home exports. In some cases, for standardised products, the assumed survival rates are as low as 2 to 8 per cent. A related government research report (SOU, 1981: 33) examines a larger sample of firms and reaches similar results, with the summary conclusion that FDI has been a necessary strategy for the survival and international competitiveness of Swedish firms. FDI has been complementary to Swedish exports and employment, because the alternatives would have resulted in much lower foreign market shares for Swedish firms.

It is obvious that the assumptions about export survival rates are of central importance for the outcome, and it is therefore interesting to relate Jordan and Vahlne's (1981) estimates with data from other sources. Such a comparison reveals that many other business-oriented case studies have also been based on very low survival rates. For instance, Stobaugh *et al.* (1972), who studied nine US firms, concluded that their entire foreign markets would have been lost within five years in the absence of FDI. A problem with this kind of studies is that the estimates of survival rates are often based on surveys and interviews with company officials, who naturally are interested in 'portraying their foreign activities in as favourable a light as possible *vis-à-vis* their impact on the domestic economy' (Frank and Freeman, 1978: 9). A more careful approach would be to calculate survival rates from data on costs, revenues, and demand conditions. Unfortunately, we are not aware of any such studies for Sweden, but Frank and Freeman (1978) set up a related model for the US economy. Their exercise yields estimates of survival rates ranging between 20 and 40 per cent depending on industry, which imply a higher probability that FDI may substitute for home country exports.[3] They also calculate a short run 'break-even' survival rate for the US economy in 1970, that would lead to equally large export displacement and export stimulus from FDI. This break-even estimate is 11 per cent: FDI will stimulate domestic exports if the surviving market shares are smaller, but reduce exports if it is larger. Hence, their own estimates of survival rates in the region 20–40 per cent suggest that FDI substituted for US exports and that the effect of FDI on US net employment was negative.

The problem of assessing survival rates does not usually come up in econometric studies of the relation between FDI and exports. These studies typically employ regression analysis to determine the relation between exports and various firm, industry, and country characteristics. Controlling for as many other determinants as possible, the focus is on the partial effect of FDI (measured e.g. as the stock of foreign assets or the value of foreign production). A negative coefficient for FDI implies that foreign production substitutes for exports, whereas a positive sign suggests that complementarity – the stimulus to home exports of intermediate and other related products – is more important in aggregate. It can be noted that most international studies of this type, including Bajo-Rubio and Montero-Muñoz (1999), Buigues and Jacquemin (1994), Bergsten *et al.* (1978), Horst (1974), Australia (1994), Kravis and Lipsey (1988), Lipsey and Weiss (1981; 1984), Mucchielli and Saucier (1997), Pfaffermayr (1996), and Yamawaki (1991), conclude that the complementarities have tended to outweigh the substitution effects. Yet, there are probably differences between the competitive advantages of multinationals originating in different countries, and it may not be possible to generalise results across countries.

The most comprehensive econometric analysis of the Swedish FDI–trade relationship are presented in Swedenborg (1979; 1982; 2000), Blomström *et al.* (1988), and Svensson (1996). The studies are all based on a detailed data set on Swedish multinationals collected by the Industrial Institute for Economic and Social Research (IUI) in Stockholm, but there are significant differences in methodology and results.

The major innovation in both of Swedenborg's early studies (1979; 1982) is that she bases her analysis on 2SLS (two-stage least squares) estimations, in order to avoid the bias that comes about because both foreign production and exports may be affected by the same omitted variables. The first stage estimates the size of foreign production as a function of various firm, industry, and host country characteristics, and the second stage estimates exports from the Swedish parent company with the first-stage fitted values of foreign production as one of the independent variables. In Swedenborg (1979), the focus is on a sample of some 100 Swedish manufacturing MNCs with more than 300 foreign affiliates in 1974. Her findings suggest that there was no significant overall effect of foreign production on the exports of Swedish parents that year, but that the aggregate results hide two significant, but opposite effects. Foreign production seems to substitute for some exports to sales affiliates and non-affiliated customers in the host country, but there is a concurrent (larger) positive effect on the exports of goods to producing affiliates (both intermediates and finished products). Swedenborg (1982) adds observations for three more years (1965, 1970, and 1978), with very similar results. The effect on total export is still not statistically significant, but there is a clear pattern when complementary and substituting exports are examined separately. A one dollar increase in foreign production is found to result in a 12 cent increase in exports to producing affiliates, but only a 2 cent fall in exports to other customers in the host country, that is, a net export stimulus of 10 cents. Swedenborg (2000) largely confirms these results in a panel data analysis, covering the period 1965–94.

Blomström *et al.* (1988) argue that Swedenborg's results are uncertain because her first-stage estimations have low explanatory power, so that much of the relevant variation in the affiliates' production is neglected in the second stage. They examine Swedish exports and FDI for ten aggregate industry groups in 1978, as well as changes between 1970 and 1978, in a conventional OLS (ordinary least squares) framework. By focussing on changes in the variables, they hope to eliminate the impact of the omitted variables that simultaneously affect foreign production and exports, but not those that affect changes in production or exports. Moreover, they look at total Swedish exports in each industry, rather than only the parent corporations' exports. This means that they may capture some instances where the affiliates' activities have substituted for other firms' exports, but also cases where FDI has facilitated other Swedish firms' exports to the host market. The latter situation may occur if foreign production familiarises the host country with Swedish products, or if the affiliates transfer information about the host country's business environment back to Sweden.

Yet, the findings in Blomström *et al.* (1988) differ little from those presented by Swedenborg. There are no signs of substitution between Swedish exports and foreign production for any of the industries included – if anything, the authors find a larger complementary effect – and there is no evidence that affiliate production in a foreign country reduces the country's subsequent imports from Sweden.

A couple of more recent studies have challenged the earlier findings. Svensson (1996), using unpublished data from later surveys of Swedish direct investment abroad, argues that it is necessary to account for the foreign affiliates' exports to third countries, because they are likely to substitute directly for parent exports. Doing this, he finds that there now appears to be substitution between Swedish investment abroad and exports from Sweden. The increasing preference among Swedish MNCs for acquisitions rather than greenfield ventures is likely to strengthen this conclusion. Acquired affiliates have established linkages with suppliers and subcontractors, and are not necessarily dependent on imports of intermediates from their new Swedish parent company. Braunerhjelm and Oxelheim (1998) address the discrepancy between Svensson (1996) and earlier studies by suggesting that the impact of FDI may vary depending on industry characteristics.[4] They argue that FDI and exports should be complements in industries that rely on immobile natural resources (Heckscher–Ohlin industries), but that they may be substitutes in industries relying on technology, brand names, and other intangible assets that are not fixed to the home country (Schumpeter industries), in particular if the economic environment in the home country is less attractive than that in the host countries. They also find some empirical support for this hypothesis by examining the relationship between domestic and foreign investment in a regression framework. The conclusion is that industry differences are likely to be important, and that more disaggregated studies are needed to formulate efficient economic policies.

Although some of the recent studies have found signs of a substitutive relationship between FDI and home country operations, they all note that the quantitative impact remains relatively small. It is therefore not unfair to summarise the discussion on the FDI–export interactions by noting that the Swedish FDI does not appear to be detrimental to Swedish exports. Having said this, it must be noted that the discussion above has left out some important aspects of production interactions. For a more complete analysis, we must turn our attention to another set of issues that has been discussed less frequently, at least until recently: the structural effects that come about because FDI influences the composition of home country exports and production. It is possible that the impact of FDI on *what* we produce and export is more important than its effects on *how much* we produce and export.

Production interactions: effects on the economic structure in the home country

The structural effects of FDI on the home country have received relatively little attention in the international debate, and the few studies that are available have focussed on a limited set of issues. A number of studies have examined the relation between FDI and profits (or, more generally, market power) in the home country, and concluded that internationalisation typically strengthens the domestic market position and the firm characteristics that made it possible to undertake FDI in the first place (see e.g. Benvignati, 1983; Bergsten *et al.*, 1978; Cohen, 1972; Lipsey, 1995; Pagoulatos and Sorensen, 1976). The MNCs' profitability benefits from their ability to 'achieve greater vertical integration (utilising cheap labour and/or raw materials), spread joint costs across a larger base, diversify portfolios across different economies and markets and reduce tax liabilities' (UN, 1993: 73–4). Higher profits, in turn, stimulate investments in R&D and marketing and enhance the oligopolistic nature of the industries where MNCs typically operate. Other researchers have discussed the impact of FDI on the composition of domestic (mainly US) labour demand (see e.g. Brainard and Riker, 1997; Frank and Freeman, 1978; Gunderson and Verma, 1994; Hawkins, 1972; Blomström *et al.*, 1997; US Tariff Commission, 1973). The picture emerging from these studies is that although FDI may reduce home country employment at the margin, there is typically a shift in labour demand favouring 'white-collar' employees at the expense of 'blue-collar' workers, arguably because multinational firms tend to export labour-intensive production activities, while concentrating management, marketing, R&D, and other advanced activities at the home base.

This shift in labour demand is the result of structural changes in home country production. The establishment of a foreign affiliate is likely to substitute for exports of finished products from the home country to independent customers in the foreign country, but may boost exports of intermediates from the home country to the foreign affiliate. In the case of US MNCs, this is apparently a process where the home country specialises in relatively skill-intensive activities, whereas the foreign operations are more labour-intensive. However, in an increasingly internationalised world economy, we should probably not expect a pattern where the most qualified activities are always concentrated to the home country. A more likely development is instead one where the comparative advantages of home and host countries determine the international division of labour within the MNC. Hence, in most cases, FDI is likely to emphasise the pattern of specialisation that is brought about by international trade.

Only a few studies have explicitly examined this kind of structural impact of FDI, but there is a reasonable amount of circumstantial evidence to examine the impact on home countries like Sweden. The remainder of this section will first discuss what type of operations the Swedish MNCs are likely to retain at home, and then try to identify some possible consequences of this pattern of specialisation.

What type of production is located in Sweden?

To date, no detailed studies of the production structure or the international division of labour within Swedish MNCs have been published. There is no comprehensive information on what specific products the MNC parents and affiliates are manufacturing, nor are there readily available data on the factor contents in the MNCs' foreign and domestic production. Yet, there is evidence from trade data and unpublished information on Swedish MNCs to suggest that the division of labour between parents and affiliates is becoming more accentuated, and that the degree of specialisation in home production is increasing (see Andersson, 1993).

The intra-firm trade between parents and affiliates has always made up a large share of the Swedish parents' total exports, but the importance of these flows increased significantly during the late 1980s, particularly for affiliates from the EC. About a third of the parent exports to the six original EC members went to producing affiliates in 1986, but the share had increased to nearly half by 1990. The rates of increase in intra-firm exports to affiliates located in the other EC countries were equally large, although from lower initial levels. Concurrently, there were marked changes in the structure of these exports. Whereas intermediates and finished goods had accounted for roughly 50 per cent each in 1986, the share of intermediates had grown to nearly 75 per cent in 1990. The affiliates' exports back to Sweden have also increased much faster than their sales since the mid-1980s, to reach over 10 per cent of total output in 1994 (Braunerhjelm *et al.*, 1996). Hence, it appears clear that Swedish MNC parents are concentrating their efforts on production of intermediate inputs.

This specialisation and transformation is facilitated by a very significant flexibility in the structure of the Swedish MNCs. For instance, there are very large annual changes in the population of plants owned by MNCs. Fors and Kokko (2000) show that over half of the 229 domestic plants and over a third of the 304 foreign plants owned in 1986 by a sample of 17 leading Swedish MNCs had been closed or sold to other companies by 1990. Simultaneously, the same 17 MNCs had established 105 new plants in Sweden and 205 new foreign affiliates. The changes in the population of plants between 1990 and 1994 were of a similar magnitude. Hakkala and Kokko (2000) examine the turnover of employees in Sweden's 30 largest MNCs, between 1986 and 1994, and note that at least a fifth of their employees were affected by some kind of reorganisation each year, either because of changes in the number of workers in existing plants, or because of changes in the population of plants. Although the period 1986–90 was probably unusually turbulent (with the establishment of the European Single Market, a change in the Swedish attitude towards EU membership, and a serious financial crisis) it is clear that the Swedish MNCs are significantly more dynamic than what is revealed by data on net changes in employment and output.

Can we say anything about the characteristics of the intermediate products that are becoming more important in the MNCs' Swedish operations? There are arguments to suggest that the intra-firm trade of MNCs should coincide with the trade patterns of the countries where the affiliates are located. The factor requirements of different stages in the production process vary, and each separate stage should be located where the most intensively used inputs are most abundant. This benefits the MNCs, because production costs are minimised, and it typically also benefits the countries where production is located, because specialisation according to comparative advantages increases welfare. Historically, Swedish comparative advantages have been based on natural resources like timber, ore, and hydropower, and products developed from these assets continue to be important in Swedish exports. According to Blomström *et al.* (1990) and Hansson and Lundberg (1995), Sweden's comparative advantages *vis-à-vis* other OECD countries in the early 1990s were still concentrated to products with low R&D content, many of which are based on the indigenous natural resources. Raw material based industries (metals, wood products, and paper products) have been particularly prominent in Swedish exports to the EC, whereas imports from the EC are largely made up of engineering products (machinery, electronics, and transport equipment). Developments during the second half of the 1990s have changed this picture to some extent, with tremendous export increases in the telecommunications industry, which is dominated by one single company – Ericsson. Conventional trade theory therefore suggests that the production undertaken at home by most Swedish multinationals should also capitalise on Sweden's comparative advantages and focus on products with relatively high raw material content.

However, more modern trade theories suggest that other country characteristics than only factor abundance are needed to explain the comparative advantages and competitiveness of different economies. It is unclear to what extent these country characteristics also influence the production pattern of MNCs. Market size and market structure, agglomeration effects, technology gaps, and government policies aiming to secure national control over 'strategically important' industries are some of the new determinants of the pattern of international trade and the specialisation of individual countries (see Helpman and Krugman, 1985; Krugman, 1986; Porter, 1990). The problem is that the different skills and technologies that are treated as country-specific in the literature on international trade can often be transferred between the affiliates of a MNC. For instance, technology gap theories argue that new and advanced products should be manufactured in and exported from the most developed countries, because this is where innovations are made and where demand for new products is strongest. Yet, MNCs may find it profitable to transfer the technology for new product manufacturing to their foreign affiliates. Similarly, public support to R&D in a 'strategically important' sector does not guarantee R&D intensive production and exports, since the MNCs may decide to transfer the output from their R&D to foreign affiliates.

Due to lack of data on product categories and factor intensities, there are no detailed analyses of how Swedish MNCs have distributed their international production across countries. Some authors have therefore used information on other aspects of MNC operations to speculate about the pattern of specialisation. Andersson (1993) notes that the labour productivity of EC affiliates increased at an average annual rate of 5.5 per cent between 1986 and 1990, while the parents' productivity growth rates were negative. He posits that this was mainly caused by a shift in the location of the Swedish MNCs' various production stages. Earlier, most of the value added was produced in the parent company and many affiliates functioned as relatively simple assembly plants. After the mid-1980s, he argues, affiliates took over some of the more skill-intensive parts of the production process, and parents specialised in simpler, raw material based operations at lower stages in of the value added chain. Andersson also examines firm level data for the periods 1974–78 and 1986–90 in a regression analysis, and finds a significant negative relation between labour productivity growth in parents and increases in the share of intermediate goods in the parents' total exports to their EC affiliates. From this, he concludes that FDI contributed to an increasing specialisation of home country production in raw-material-based intermediates with relatively low value added between the mid-1970s and early 1990s.

Given the lack of direct evidence, it is necessary to interpret any conclusions with caution. Swedish productivity growth may have been low for reasons that have nothing to do with the division of labour between MNC parents and affiliates – for instance, the incentives to work hard were probably weak in Sweden during the period in question because of high income taxes and a very compressed wage structure. Yet, it is interesting to note that the few available studies of the employment structure in Swedish MNCs outlines a picture that is at least partly consistent with Andersson (1993). Increasing foreign production in Swedish MNCs was apparently accompanied by lower skill requirements in home-based production already in the early 1980s – the largest MNCs employed a lower share of qualified production workers than Swedish industry on average (SOU, 1983: 16, 172). More recently, Blomström *et al.* (1997) have noted that the expansion of Swedish outward investment has been related to an increase in Swedish employment of 'blue-collar' rather than 'white-collar' workers. This may reflect comparative advantages in skilled labour-intensive industries, rather than in R&D-intensive high-tech activities. Blomström (1999) has also pointed out that the average wage in the OECD affiliates of Swedish MNCs exceeded the average wage in the Swedish parent companies by the mid-1990s. This may reflect lower relative productivity in Swedish plants, but it is probably also related to the large depreciation of the Swedish currency after 1992.

In addition to the suspected specialisation in intermediates with relatively high labour and raw material content, Swedish MNCs have also retained most of their technology production at home. Over two-thirds of the MNCs' R&D expenditures are still undertaken in Sweden, although the affiliates' share of R&D has increased over the past decades (Braunerhjelm *et al.*, 1996; NUTEK, 1999). As a result of this concentration of research efforts, Sweden has exhibited the world's highest ratios of R&D expenditures to value added in manufacturing since the early 1980s, along with the United States (Hansson and Lundberg, 1995). However, there is a contradiction between this intensive research effort and the concerns regarding the relatively low export share of products with a high R&D content expressed above. Why had exports apparently not shifted towards more R&D intensive products before the mid-1990s? One possible answer could be that the resources spent on R&D were wasted, but this is inconsistent with the observation that the competitiveness of Swedish MNC has remained high over the past decades. An alternative explanation is that Swedish R&D was mainly directed towards rationalising techniques for the production of low-tech manufactures, such as pulp and paper. A third possible argument – that assumes an international division of labour within MNCs – is that the MNCs have not found Sweden to be the most suitable location for their high-tech production. Whereas Sweden has been a favoured location for R&D, it appears that much of the production of R&D intensive products has been located to the foreign affiliates of Swedish MNCs (see Blomström, 1990).

Thus, the limited evidence we have about what type of production is located in Sweden suggests a somewhat peculiar pattern. On the one hand, there appears to be a concentration to production of intermediates, which, according to some authors, were characterised by relatively low value added and high raw material content until the mid-1990s. On the other hand, there is also a focus on technology production, which is the area where Swedish MNCs have their firm specific competitive advantages. It is possible that this peculiar pattern may only arise in advanced countries with abundant natural resources, but not in advanced countries with comparative advantages in human capital or technology, where the country's and MNCs' advantages are likely to coincide. Hence, the pattern in Sweden (and perhaps also countries like Australia, Canada, and Finland) may differ from that in countries that are poor in natural resources, like Japan, the Netherlands, or Switzerland.

Some of the arguments above have been qualified with the restriction 'until the mid-1990s'. The reason is that there are some recent signs indicating changes in the pattern of comparative advantages and specialisation. It is possible that the period from the early 1980s to the early or mid-1990s was characterised by a business environment that discouraged the development of more advanced and R&D-intensive activities in Sweden, and that this bias has been reduced or eliminated since that time. For instance, the Swedish currency was fixed at an overvalued exchange rate for several years before 1992, when it was allowed to float and depreciated by about 40 per cent against the US dollar. Swedish income tax rates were the highest in the world until a large tax reform was introduced in 1991. Until 1991, Sweden also declared that it would stay outside the EU, which may have motivated Swedish MNCs to locate much of their new production capacity abroad, in the Single Market area. The financial crisis in 1991–2 opened the way for reforms in all these areas, and there is little doubt that the Swedish business climate has improved significantly since then. One indication of the stronger competitiveness of the Swedish economy is that the ratio of exports to GDP has increased from around 30 per cent in 1990 to about 45 per cent in 1999. A large share of the export growth since the early 1990s has been concentrated to electronics and telecommunications equipment, which now account for over a fifth of total exports. However, it is too early to tell whether these improvements have also made Sweden a favoured location for high-tech production.

Effects of increasing specialisation

The discussion above implies that Swedish multinationals are concentrating their home production in two areas: R&D and intermediate products. Since the MNCs' location choices are based on profit maximisation, it can be assumed that their decisions reveal that there are private gains to be made from specialisation. It is not equally obvious what the net effects are for Sweden. One reason is differences in market structure, which mean that some industries can charge higher prices and generate larger profits than others. Certain types of production may also be connected with positive external effects and spillovers. The aggregate impact of FDI on the home country may be beneficial if production processes with high profits and positive externalities are retained at home, but effects are likely to be less advantageous, or even negative, if these are among the activities that are moved to foreign affiliates. Another reason is that very few studies have examined the effects of FDI from this point of view. There is no generally accepted notion of what industries are most beneficial, what kinds of externalities are relevant, how important they are in quantitative terms, and how they compare with the gains from specialisation. The sole exception seems to be a consensus that FDI has allowed the Swedish MNCs to grow larger and to spend more resources on R&D than what would otherwise have been possible, and that this has had a positive impact on the scientific and technological capability of Sweden. The discussion of the possible long-term effects of increasing specialisation will therefore be rather speculative, and the ensuing paragraphs are perhaps best seen as an agenda for future research.

The view that the MNCs' decisions to concentrate R&D in the parent company are beneficial for Sweden is seldom questioned, as noted above, and there is no need to repeat the well-known arguments for why R&D may be connected with positive externalities. Instead, it is interesting to note that the recent debate has raised several questions about Sweden's ability to benefit from the potential R&D spillovers in the long run.

First, the debate has revealed worries that R&D is also moving abroad, and the foreign affiliates' share of the Swedish MNCs' total R&D expenditures have indeed increased significantly since the mid-1980s. It is not clear how far this trend will continue, but the recent changes call attention to questions about what has determined the location of R&D. More specifically, it has been argued that R&D has been cheap in Sweden because the salaries of scientists and engineers have been low compared to other OECD countries (Blomström, 1999). However, low salaries have also meant that the incentives to invest in higher education are weak, and skilled labour is becoming scarcer. Sweden has therefore lost its position among the countries with the highest education and skill levels in manufacturing, and it may be difficult to retain the comparative advantages in R&D if present trends continue.

A second cause of concern has been the lack of a shift in total Swedish exports towards more high-tech products during the past decades, in spite of the very high R&D expenditures. As discussed earlier, this may indicate that Swedish research results are not exploited at home, but rather exported to foreign affiliates where production takes place. The question is then which activities yield the most positive externalities: production of high technology (i.e. R&D) or high-technology production. A third point to note is that Sweden can only benefit from the potential R&D externalities if there is a population of local firms that are able to absorb spillovers (see Blomström and Kokko, 1998). However, if MNCs actually concentrate their Swedish operations to fewer and perhaps less advanced intermediates, this will have a profound impact on thousands of their non-multinational suppliers and subcontractors in Sweden. Overall, there has for a long time been a downward trend in the number of subcontractors, and the share of inputs purchased in Sweden has also been falling (Braunerhjelm, 1991). A further specialisation of the MNCs' Swedish operations would enhance this trend. This effect of FDI on industry structure therefore raises questions about the possibilities to absorb the spillovers from the MNCs' R&D efforts in the future.

The emergence of a more concentrated industry structure may also have other implications. When the parent companies specialise in the production of some of the intermediate inputs used in their final products, there are fewer components to be made in Sweden, and the motives to engage Swedish suppliers are reduced. The number of suppliers employed by Swedish MNCs has also been falling rapidly over the past years, as noted above. Moreover, few domestic (non-multinational) suppliers and subcontractors have been able to follow the MNCs abroad, as shown by Braunerhjelm (1991). Examining a sample of 140 Swedish subcontractors, he noted that only 4 per cent of their output was shipped to Swedish MNC affiliates abroad, while Swedish MNCs at home accounted for 43 per cent of their sales. This means that a continued division of labour along the lines discussed above – even one that is successful enough to increase the total employment in Swedish industry – may have a profound impact on Swedish industry structure. It is conceivable that the present structure of the manufacturing sector, which comprises a few large MNCs and thousands of smaller subcontractors and suppliers, may be replaced by a structure with an unchanged number of MNCs (that are perhaps even larger than today), but a significantly lower number of smaller firms.

We already noted that this kind of development might reduce the opportunities to benefit from R&D-spillovers, but there may be additional effects on, for example, growth rates. It is generally believed that small and medium sized firms were instrumental in generating economic growth in the US and the UK during the 1980s, and they have played major roles in the development of new high-tech industries all over the industrialised world. Empirical studies have also demonstrated that firm growth decreases with firm size and firm age (see. e.g. Evans, 1987; Hall, 1987; Dunne *et al.* 1989). The link between firm size and growth in Sweden may be different, but any significant relation provides a motive to think twice about the possible effects of FDI on the home country's economic structure.

Conclusion

This chapter has provided a selective survey of the literature on home country effects of FDI, and tried to point to some new questions regarding the impact of outward FDI on economic structure in the home country. Much of the existing literature on production interactions between the domestic and foreign operations of MNCs has examined what happens to home country exports and employment as a result of outward FDI. Although the results of earlier studies vary somewhat, there appears to be a consensus that the quantitative effects are not dramatic. The reduced exports of finished products from the home country to independent foreign customers are balanced by increases in exports of intermediate products to the foreign affiliates. However, the structural changes – the transformation that occurs when the parent company becomes increasingly specialised in the production of intermediate goods – have not been discussed in great detail. Drawing heavily on the example of Sweden, we have therefore outlined some of the changes that have occurred as a result of the increasing globalisation of Swedish industry, and discussed some possible consequences for the Swedish economy. Due to the lack of detailed data on factor intensities and other production characteristics, the discussion has largely been speculative. The number of unanswered questions and tentative conclusions in the previous section corroborates the need for future research in this area.

The main obstacle to research on the structural effects of FDI is undoubtedly the lack of detailed data on the domestic and foreign operations of MNCs. A careful analysis of the international division of labour within MNCs requires plant level data for several countries, as well as comparative data on the operations of non-multinational firms. Few countries collect information at this level of aggregation (although a promising data set for Swedish MNCs is under construction). Another serious problem is the lack of formal models to explain the determinants of the MNCs' location decisions. The production pattern that can be discerned at any given point in time reflects current conditions as well as past decisions, which means that empirical analysis is not likely to be sufficient for distinguishing the main determinants of MNC behaviour. Fortunately, an increasing amount of theoretical work is presently focused on research where international trade, investment, and location decisions are interconnected.

Notes

1 There are, of course, many other kinds of home country effects from FDI. Stevens and Lipsey (1992) point to financial interactions that come about because investments in different locations compete for scarce funds, Dunning (1997) focuses on the impact of FDI on economic policy, Blomström and Kokko (1998) discuss external effects on the home country, while Caves (1996), Dunning (1993), Hood and Young (1979), and IC (1996) provide an overview of a host of other issues, including the effects of FDI on taxation, income distribution, and environment.

2 This picture has recently begun to change. For instance, the inflow of FDI to Sweden exceeded the outflow by a wide margin in 1999, as a result of several foreign acquisitions of large Swedish firms (Volvo being the most notable example).

3 However, Frank and Freeman (1978) rule out shifts in market size that are 'occasioned by the establishment of a foreign subsidiary' (p. 35), which means that their figures are likely to be on the high side: the establishment of an affiliate is likely to lead to shifts in the demand curve as well as increases in foreign market shares.

4 More specifically, Braunerhjelm and Oxelheim (1998) focus on the question of investment substitution. Other studies in this field include Belderbos (1992), Feldstein (1994), and Stevens and Lipsey (1992).

References

Andersson, T. (1993) 'Utlandsinvesteringar och policyimplikationer'. Supplement 3 to SOU 1993: 16, *Nya villkor för ekonomi och politik*. Stockholm: Allmänna Förlaget.

Andersson, T. and T. Fredriksson (1993) *Sveriges val, EG och direktinvesteringar*. Supplement 7, EG-konsekvensutredningen, Samhällsekonomi (Fi 1993: 06), Stockholm: Allmänna Förlaget.

Australia (1996) *Implications for Australia of Firms Locating Offshore*. Belconnen: Industry Commission.

Bajo-Rubio, O. and M. Montero-Munoz (1999) 'Foreign Direct Investment and Trade: A Causality Analysis'. Estudios Sobre La Economia Española No. 6, FEDEA.

Belderbos, R.A. (1992) 'Large Multinational Enterprises Based in a Small Economy: Effects on Domestic Investment'. *Weltwirtschaftliches Archiv*, 128: 543–57.

Benvignati, A. (1983) *Domestic Profit Advantages of Multinationals*. Washington, DC: US Federal Trade Commission.

Bergsten, F., T. Horst, and T. Moran (1978) *American Multinationals and American Interests*. Washington, DC: Brookings Institution.

Blomström, M. (1980) 'Competitiveness of Firms and Countries'. In J. Dunning, B. Kogut, and M. Blomström (eds), *Globalization of Firms and the Competitiveness of Nations*. Crafoord Lectures 1989, Lund: Lund University Press.

Blomström, M. (1999) 'Internationalisering och tillväxt'. In L. Calmfors och M. Persson (eds), *Tillväxt och ekonomisk politik*. Lund: Studentlitteratur.

Blomström, M., G. Fors, and R.E. Lipsey (1997) 'Foreign Direct Investment and Employment: Home Country Experience in the United States and Sweden'. *The Economic Journal*, 107: 1787–97.

Blomström, M. and A. Kokko (1998) 'Multinational Corporations and Spillovers'. *Journal of Economic Surveys*, 12: 247–77.

Blomström, M. and R.E. Lipsey (1989) 'The Export Performance of U.S. and Swedish Multinationals'. *Review of Income and Wealth*, Series 35: 245–64.

Blomström, M., R.E. Lipsey, and K. Kulchucky (1988) 'U.S. and Swedish Direct Investment and Exports'. In R. Baldwin (ed.), *Trade Policy Issues and Empirical Analysis*. Chicago: University of Chicago Press.

Blomström, M., R.E. Lipsey, and L. Ohlsson (1990) 'What Do Rich Countries Trade with Each Other? R&D and Composition of U.S. and Swedish Trade'. *Banca Nazionale del Lavoro Quarterly Review*, 173: 215–35.

Brainard, S.L. and D.A. Riker (1997) 'Are U.S. Multinationals Exporting U.S. Jobs?' NBER Working Paper No. 5958, Cambridge MA: NBER.

Braunerhjelm, P. (1991) *Svenska underleverantörer och småföretag i det nya Europa: Struktur, kompetens och internationalisering*. Research Report No. 38, Stockholm: Industrial Institute for Economic and Social Research.

Braunerhjelm, P., K. Ekholm, L. Grundberg, and P. Karpaty (1996) 'Swedish Multinational Corporations: Recent Trends in Foreign Activities'. IUI Working Paper No. 462, Stockholm: IUI.

Braunerhjelm, P. and L. Oxelheim (1998) 'Does Foreign Direct Investment Replace Home Country Investment?', Paper presented at *Symposium on New Issues in Trade and Location*, Lund, August 28–30.

Buigues, P. and A. Jacquemin (1994) 'Foreign Direct Investment and Exports to the European Community'. In M. Mason and D. Encarnation (eds), *Does Ownership Matter? Japanese Multinationals in Europe*. Oxford and New York: Oxford University Press.

Caves, R.E. (1996) *Multinational Enterprise and Economic Analysis 2nd edn*. Cambridge: Cambridge University Press.

Cohen, B.I. (1972) 'Foreign Investment by United States Corporations as a Way of Reducing Risk'. Discussion Paper No. 151, Economic Growth Center, Yale University.

Dunne, T., M. Roberts, and L. Samuelson (1989) 'The Growth and Failure of U.S. Manufacturing Plants'. *Quarterly Journal of Economics*, 104.

Dunning, J.H. (1993) *Multinational Enterprises and the Global Economy*. Wokingham: Addison-Wesley Publishing Company.

Dunning, J.H. (ed.) (1997) *Governments, Globalization, and International Business*. Oxford: Oxford University Press.

Evans, D.S. (1987) 'Tests of Alternative Theories of Firm Growth'. *Journal of Political Economy*, 95: 657–74.

Feldstein, M. (1994) 'The Effects of Outbound Foreign Direct Investment on the Domestic Capital Stock'. NBER Working Paper No, 4668, Cambridge MA: NBER.

Frank, R.H. and R.T. Freeman (1978) *Distributional Consequences of Direct Foreign Investment*. New York: Academic Press.

Fors, G. and A. Kokko (2000) 'Home Country Effects of Foreign Direct Investment'. In M. Blomström and L. Goldberg (eds), *Topics in Empirical International Research: A Festschrift in Honor of Robert E. Lipsey*. Chicago: University of Chicago Press.

Gunderson, M. and S. Verma (1994) 'Labour-Market Implications of Outward Foreign Direct Invesment'. In S. Globerman (ed.), *Canadian-Based Multinationals*. Calgary: University of Calgary Press.

Hakkala, K. and A. Kokko (2000) 'Sverige i en globaliserad ekonomi'. In B. Södersten (ed.), *Marknad och Politik*. Stockholm: SNS Förlag.

Hall, B.H. (1987) 'The Relationship Between Firm Size and Firm Growth in the U.S. Manufacturing Sector'. *Journal of Industrial Economics*, 35: 583–606.

Hansson, P. and L. Lundberg (1995) *Från basindustri till högteknologi*. Stockholm: SNS Förlag.

Hawkins, R.G. (1972) Job Displacement and the Multinational Firm: A Methodological Review. Occasional Paper No. 3, Washington, DC: Center for Multinational Studies.

Helpman, H. and P.R. Krugman (1985) *Market Structure and Foreign Trade*. Cambridge, Mass: MIT Press.

Hood, N. and S. Young (1979) *The Economics of Multinational Enterprise*. London and New York: Longman.

Horst, T. (1974) 'American Exports and Foreign Direct Investments'. Discussion Paper No. 362, Harvard Institute of Economic Research.

Jordan, J.L and J.E. Vahlne (1981) 'Domestic Employment Effects of Direct Investment Abroad by Two Swedish Multinationals'. Working Paper No. 13, Multinational Enterprises Programme, Geneva: International Labour Office.

Kravis, I. and R.E. Lipsey (1988) 'The Effect of Multinational Firms' Foreign Operations on Their Domestic Employment'. NBER Working Paper No. 2760.

Krugman, P.R. (1986) *Strategic Trade Policy and the New International Economics*. Cambridge, Mass: MIT Press.

Lipsey, R.E. (1995) 'Outward Direct Investment and the U.S. Economy'. In M. Feldstein, J. Hines, and R. Hubbard (eds), *The Effects of Taxation on Multinational Corporations*. Chicago: University of Chicago Press.

Lipsey, R.E. and M.Y. Weiss (1981) 'Foreign Production and Exports in Manufacturing Industries'. *Review of Economics and Statistics*, 63: 488–94.

—— (1984) 'Foreign Production and Exports of Individual Firms'. *Review of Economics and Statistics*, 66: 304–08.

Mucchielli, J.-L. and P. Saucier (1997) 'European Industrial Relocations in Low-Wage Countries: Policy and Theory Debates'. In P.J. Buckley and J.-L. Mucchielli (eds), *Multinational Firms and International Relocation*. Cheltenham: Edward Elgar.

NUTEK (1999) *Forskning och utveckling i internationella företag*. Nv 18 SM, Stockholm: NUTEK.

OECD (1993) *OECD Reviews on Foreign Direct Investment: Sweden*. Paris: OECD.

Pagoulatos, E. and R. Sorensen (1976) 'International Trade, International Investment and Industrial Profitability in U.S. Manufacturing'. *Southern Economic Journal*, 42: 425–34.

Pfaffermayr, M. (1996) 'Foreign Outward Direct Investment and Exports in Austrian Manufacturing: Substitutes or Complements?' *Weltwirtschaftliches Archiv*, Band 132: 501–22.

Porter, M.E. (1990) *The Competitive Advantage of Nations*. New York: The Free Press.

SOU 1981:33 (1981) *Effekter av investeringar utomlands*. Stockholm: Liber Förlag.

—— 1983:16 (1983) *Sysselsättningsstrukturen i industriella företag*. Stockholm: Liber Förlag.

Stevens, G.V.G. and R.E. Lipsey (1992) 'Interactions between Domestic and Foreign Investment'. *Journal of International Money and Finance*, 11: 40–62.

Stobaugh, R.B. *et al.* (1972) *U.S. Multinational Enterprises and the U.S. Economy*. Boston: Harvard Graduate School of Business Administration.

Svensson, R. (1996) 'Effects of Overseas Production on Home Country Exports: Evidence Based on Swedish Multinationals.' *Weltwirtschaftliches Archiv*, 132: 304–29.

Swedenborg, B. (1979) *The Multinational Operations of Swedish Firms*. Stockholm: Almqvist & Wicksell International.

—— (1982) *Svensk industri i utlandet. En analys av drivkrafter och effekter*. Stockholm: Industrial Institute for Economic and Social Research.

—— (2000) 'Determinants and Effects of MNC Growth: The Swedish Case Revisited'. In M. Blomström and L. Goldberg (eds), *Topics in Empirical International Research: A Festschrift in Honor of Robert E. Lipsey*. Chicago: University of Chicago Press.

UN (1993) *Transnational Corporations from Developing Countries*. Transnational Corporations and Management Division, New York: United Nations.

US Tariff Commission (1973) *Implications of Multinational Firms for World Trade and Investment and for U.S. Trade and Labor*. Report to the US Senate Committee on Finance.

Yamawaki, H. (1991) 'Exports and Foreign Distributional Activities: Evidence on Japanese Firms in the United States'. *Review of Economics and Statistics*, 73: 294–300.

11 Host-country impact of FDI in East Asia*

Prema-chandra Athukorala and Hal Hill

Introduction

Foreign direct investment (FDI) has played a key role in economic dynamism in East Asia. For over two decades up to the onset of the Asian financial crisis in mid-1997, at least three major trends were clearly evident in investment patterns. First, FDI flows were increasing rapidly, much more quickly than international trade flows, which in turn were increasing faster than world GDP. Second, although the 'OECD North' continued to be the dominant source of FDI, cross-border flows were everywhere apparent, with notable increases over time. The East Asian Newly industrialized economics (NIEs), which emerged as sizeable outward investors in the 1980s, became even more significant investors, in some cases eclipsing Japan, the USA and Europe. Third, there was a clear shift in investment flows away from traditional import-substituting activities and towards export-oriented production, particularly export-platform activities in vertically integrated high-tech industries. Contrary to some pessimistic predictions, the crisis has not introduced a major discontinuity into this story, apart from a modest decline in inflows in the immediate aftermath of the crisis, and sharp decline in inflows to Indonesia due mostly to non-economic factors. In fact the remarkable resilience of FDI flows to the crisis economies, compared to other forms of capital inflow, seems to have ushered in an era of firmer commitment to an open FDI regime in the region.

The purpose of this chapter is to survey trends and patterns of FDI in East Asia and to discuss its developmental implications with emphasis on two key themes – the transfer of technology and the investment-trade nexus. The chapter is organised as follows. We begin with an overview of key developments in foreign investment regimes of the countries in the region. This is followed by a survey of trends and patterns of FDI inflows flows. The next two sections examine in turn the links between trade regimes and foreign investment, the FDI-trade nexus and FDI and technology development. The major arguments are summarised, with suggestions for further research, in the concluding section.

Host-policy regimes

As an integral part of a palpable shift away from import-substitutions towards an export-oriented development strategy, FDI policy regimes in East Asian countries have become more liberal over the past two decades (ADB, 1997; Hill, 1990; Radelet and Sachs, 1997; Riedel, 1997). Not only have bureaucratic impediments to the entry of foreign business been reduced, but also the sectors open to FDI have been expanded. Since around 1990, if there is a concern about FDI it is more likely to have been that the host economy is attracting *insufficient* foreign capital, in contrast to earlier concerns about an excessive foreign presence.

Until the 1980s, the role of the investment regulatory agencies in East Asia, with some exceptions such as the Economic Development Board of Singapore, was generally to ration access to domestic markets characterised by protection, and fiscal, credit and other incentives (Hughes, 1993: 15). The pendulum has swung decisively, as governments recognise that FDI, in concert with appropriate domestic policies, is an effective means of acquiring new technologies and promoting exports. Nowadays, one rarely hears high-level support for the once popular Korean model (on which see e.g. Kim, 1997), which included a restrictive approach to FDI as a means of developing indigenous technological capability. The China factor – the need to compete with what is now, by a large margin, the developing world's largest recipient of FDI – has become an important additional element in the swing of the pendulum.

There has been some nationalist opposition to the inevitable increase in foreign ownership in the region during the post-crisis years, as financial institutions and firms re-capitalise their operations through injections of foreign equity. But, with the possible exception principally of Indonesia, where nationalist opposition to rising foreign ownership could re-surface, the principal policy issue now is whether host economies should adopt a neutral or pro-active strategy towards FDI. Singapore exemplifies the latter approach,[1] whereas Hong Kong is the best illustration of the former. Nevertheless, except Hong Kong, none of the countries in the region has made a complete departure from the conventional dualistic approach to FDI in the developing world characterised by favoured treatments for export-oriented ventures compared to still-significant restrictions on import-substitution projects.

One effective means of implementing a more liberal approach has been the adoption of a so-called 'negative list', which involves governments explicitly listing those activities closed to FDI, with the implication that any activity not so listed is open. This puts the onus on governments to enact a more transparent policy regime, as was found to be the case in Korea and Indonesia, which introduced such an initiative in 1984 and 1988, respectively. Thus, during the 1990s new sectors throughout the region have emerged as major recipients of FDI. These include notably finance, real estate, construction, retail trade, infrastructure and oil and gas exploration. These policy liberalisations, together with structural change in host countries, explain the significant increase in the share of FDI directed towards services. Investments in infrastructure have been particularly important, as they are complementary to investment in tradable goods sectors and often remove bottlenecks on further expansion. There are, however, new challenges for the policy regime, in managing FDI in the context of (potential or actual) natural monopolies, and in avoiding government exposure to large contingent liabilities in the event of project under performance.

The pros and cons of fiscal incentives continue to be debated. Professional opinion is generally skeptical of the merits of these incentives: most business surveys conclude that firms generally regard them as less important than economic conditions, competitiveness, and business regulations; the opportunity cost of these incentives can be very high, especially if it means less resources for much needed physical and social infrastructure investments; and they can become a tool of both inappropriate industry policy and corruption. However, incentives have re-emerged in different guises as a policy issue in the late 1990s. One example, in the context of the crisis economies, occurs where investors are likely to demand them as compensation for the risk premium associated with entering an uncertain business and political environment. Another, prominent in the late years of the Soeharto rule, saw incentives being awarded on quite blatant political grounds to crony projects, in part because trade reforms had closed off many of the traditional opportunities for rent-seeking via import protection. A third example concerns the growing trend towards subnational competition for investment projects, especially in countries with federal administrative and political structures, under which local authorities are permitted to offer fiscal incentives independently of the national government. China is the most prominent example in East Asia of such practices. Given that countries are going to maintain some sort of investment board – as much for political as economic reasons – the administrative form these boards take, and the balance between their regulatory and promotion functions, may have a significant influence over FDI flows.

Liberalisation of FDI policy regimes in developing East Asian economies has generally proceeded on a unilateral basis. However, there have been some discussions among the ASEAN countries about a proposed ASEAN Investment Area (AIA). The issue first formally surfaced at the 1995 Bangkok Summit and was examined subsequently by the heads of investment agencies and academics. It is probable that these agencies will engage in some joint extra-regional promotional efforts, and perhaps some effort to harmonise certain aspects of the FDI regulatory regime within the region. But it is difficult to envisage much more than this. For example, attempts to develop common FDI policy regimes (including not just regulatory but also fiscal provisions) would almost certainly flounder, as would the concept of offering preferential treatment to investors from other member countries. To illustrate the difficulties involved, in the last couple of years a number of quite serious intra-ASEAN investment disputes have broken out. For example, in early 1997 Indonesia banned Malaysian investments in palm oil plantations located in its western region. Several Malaysian and Singaporean investment projects have encountered major problems in the Philippines.

Another form of multilateral initiatives to promote FDI cross-border arrangements occurs where two or more governments accelerate the process of trade liberalisation and thus facilitate the emergence of so-called natural economic zones. These zones may embrace an entire economy, as in already free-trade Singapore and Hong Kong, or they may be a geographically defined district of an economy, as in China and Indonesia. The most successful of these zones, in southern coastal China and the Singapore-based Sijori, are built in proximity, exceptionally strong complementarity, cultural familiarity (more so in China than

Southeast Asia), and outward-oriented economic policies. These are market-driven subnational economic entities, in which the government's role is essentially confined to the provision of a supportive regulatory environment and cross-border infrastructure coordination. Zones which have been established without these key pre-conditions – such as the Greater Mekong and the Eastern ASEAN (BIMP-EAGA) initiatives – may be justified on broader political or regional development criteria, but they are unlikely to have significant effects on investment flows in the short to medium term.

Trends and patterns of FDI

Table 11.1 presents data on FDI flows to developing East Asian economies in a global context. Developing Asian countries (dominated by East Asia) received 6.1 per cent of global FDI over the period 1975–80. This share trebled to 18.1 per cent for 1990–5. In this latter period, inflows into this region were similar to that into the US, and were almost two-thirds of total developing country receipts. Six East Asian economies were among the eight largest developing country recipients of FDI in 1990–5.[2] China alone received 28 per cent of the developing country total, and it was the world's fourth largest recipient, behind the USA, the UK and France (the latter two only marginally so). Singapore ranked second among these economies, and was eighth globally, receiving more than such large economies as Germany and Canada. Developing Asian economies individually do not yet rank as major global investors, although collectively they accounted for 8.1 per cent of (imperfectly estimated) world outflows, 1990–4, a figure which was more than half that of the USA (15.3 per cent) and not far below the UK (10.2 per cent).

FDI inflows also need to be viewed in the context of overall trends in host-country investment and ownership patterns. It is frequently assumed that rising FDI flows and rising foreign ownership go hand-in-hand. However, this is not necessarily the case if domestic investment is increasing at an equally rapid rate (Ramstetter, 1999a). The analysis by Ramstetter also highlights large differences in the MNC presence within the region, differences which reflect current and past policy regimes, and economic structure (in particular, the share of sectors which are usually 'MNC-intensive'). Although domestic data sources are not always comparable, the inter-country variations are often so large that they do indicate significant differences. Consider, for example, Ramstetter's estimates of foreign firms' share of manufacturing value added in the early 1990s: Hong Kong 17 per cent, Indonesia 19 per cent, Korea 12 per cent (1986), Malaysia 44 per cent, Singapore 70 per cent, Taiwan 20 per cent and Thailand 15 per cent.

It is also important to place FDI flows in the broader context of recent trends in capital movements to East Asia. There was a remarkable broadening in the composition of private capital flows to the region in the 1990s. Three trends (which were common to all developing countries as a group) are particularly noteworthy (Table 11.2). First, official flows (grants) were falling, sharply, from 56 per cent of total net resource flows in 1970 to 7.5 per cent in 1990 and a mere 2 per cent at the onset of the Asian crisis). In some years there was even an absolute decline. Second, FDI has become the largest single component of

Table 11.1 FDI inflows: East Asia in the global context (1980–98)

	1980–84	*1985–89*	*1990*	*1991*	*1992*	*1993*	*1994*	*1995*	*1996*	*1997*	*1998*
Value of inflow ($ mn)											
World	246573	642471	203812	157773	168122	219421	253506	328862	358869	464341	643879
Developed Countries	187230	531189	169777	114001	114002	133850	146379	208372	211120	273276	460431
Developing Countries	59339	110998	33735	41324	50376	78813	101196	106224	135343	172533	165936
Asia	22854	53389	19803	20781	27024	44835	63844	68126	82035	95505	84880
East Asia	22040	51640	19339	20325	26400	47813	58844	63391	75832	83817	73785
Brunei	−9	1.8	3	1	4	14	6	13[a]	11[a]	5[a]	4[a]
Cambodia	—	—	0	0	33	54	69	151	294	204	140[a]
China	2324	12435	3487	4366	11156	27515	33787	35849	40180	44236	45460
China: Hong Kong	3298.3	7850.3	1728	538	2051	3657[a]	4131[a]	3279[a]	5521[a]	6000[a]	1600[a]
Indonesia	1052	2211	1093	1482	1777	2004	2109	4346	6194	6473	−356
Korea, Rep of	356	3442	788	1180	727	588	809	1776	2325	2844	5143
Lao, PDR	—	6	6	7	8	30	59	88	128	86	45
Malaysia	5655	3994	2333	3998	5183	5006	4342	4178	5078	5106	3727
Philippines	196	1945	530	544	228	1238	1591	1478	1517	1222	1713
Singapore	6934	12134	5575	4887	2204	4686	8550	7206	7884	8710	7218
Taiwan	771	3945	1330	1271	879	917	1375	1559	1864	2248	222
Thailand	1423	3659	2444	2014	2113	1804	1366	2068	2336	3733	6969
Vietnam	31	12	16	32	24	300	650	1400	2500	2950	1900
As a percentage of GDP											
Asia	0.6	0.9	1.3	1.3	1.5	2.4	2.6	2.5	2.6	2.4	2.5
East Asia	0.7	1.2	1.6	1.5	1.8	2.9	3.1	3.0	3.2	2.3	3.4
Brunei	—	—	0.1	0.0	0.1	0.3	0.1	0.1	0.1	0.1	0.0
Cambodia	—	—	0.0	0.0	1.7	2.4	2.9	5.4	4.7	3.7	—
China	0.2	0.8	1.0	1.2	2.7	6.4	6.2	5.1	6.0	5.8	5.6

China: Hong Kong	2.2	3.1	2.3	0.6	2.0	1.4	1.5	1.5	1.6	1.2	0.8
Indonesia	0.2	0.5	1.0	1.2	1.3	1.3	1.2	2.1	2.7	2.1	***
Korea, Rep of	0.1	0.5	0.3	0.4	0.2	0.2	0.2	0.4	0.6	0.7	0.8
Lao, PDR		0.1	0.7	0.7	0.7	2.3	3.9	5.0	5.2	3.7	3.3
Malaysia	4.0	2.4	5.5	8.5	9.0	8.0	6.1	6.8	6.7	6.4	6.7
Philippines	0.1	1.1	1.2	1.2	0.4	2.3	2.5	2.0	2.1	2.0	0.7
Singapore	9.0	11.1	15.3	11.6	4.5	8.2	12.0	8.4	7.9	9.6	7.6
Taiwan	0.3	0.8	0.8	0.7	0.4	0.4	0.6	0.6	0.6	0.5	0.7
Thailand	0.8	1.4	2.9	2.0	1.9	1.4	1.0	1.2	1.3	1.1	1.6
Vietnam			0.2	0.3	0.2	2.3	4.2	6.9	6.7	3.4	3.7
As a percentage of GDFC											
Asia	2.0	3.2	4.2	4.1	4.9	7.4	7.9	8.0	8.3	7.4	7.5
East Asia	2.4	4.0	5.0	4.7	5.5	8.3	8.8	8.8	9.1	7.2	8.1
Cambodia	—	—	0.0	0.0	17.1	17.0	15.0	16.5	17.1	12.3	—
China	0.6	2.2	2.8	3.3	7.4	14.7	15.7	12.7	17.2	17.2	16.3
China: Hong Kong	7.1	12.1	8.4	2.3	7.2	5.2	4.8	4.2	3.2	2.7	2.0
Indonesia	0.9	1.8	3.1	4.1	4.7	3.8	3.5	6.7	8.8	6.8	***
Korea, Rep. of	0.3	1.5	0.8	1.0	0.6	0.5	0.6	1.1	1.2	1.0	1.7
Lao, PDR	—	1.0	5.6	5.3							
Malaysia	11.5	9.3	16.3	23.7	25.6	22.7	24.7	27.9	29.4	30.4	33.1
Philippines	0.4	6.2	5.0	5.9	2.0	9.5	10.3	8.9	9.1	7.2	8.7
Singapore	18.9	29.3	38.7	30.4	12.3	23.1	36.1	25.4	23.1	25.8	24.6
Taiwan	1.2	3.6	3.6	3.0	1.7	1.6	2.4	2.5	2.1	1.7	1.6
Thailand	2.6	4.5	6.9	4.8	4.7	3.6	2.3	2.9	3.1	7.8	22.6
Vietnam	—	0.1	1.9	2.2	1.4	11.4	16.4	25.4	26.1	23.5	26.4

Source: FDI inflow: UNCTAD, *World Investment Reports* (annual), GDP and GDCF: IMF, *International Financial Statistics Yearbook 1998.*

Notes
GDFC Gross domestic fixed capital formation.
— Data not available or negligible.
*** Zero or negligible.
a Estimates.

capital flows, official or private. In 1997, FDI flows constituted $64.3 billion, or 52.4 per cent of the estimated $122.6 billion which flowed to these countries (up from 40 per cent in 1990). Third, notwithstanding the greatly increased importance of FDI, other forms of private capital flows have increased faster still. In some cases, the amounts involved were very small even as recently as 1990. The extremely rapid growth of these more short-term, volatile capital flows explains in part the crises in several East Asian economies in 1997–99 (Athukorala and Warr, 1999).

In assessing the size and impact of FDI, it always needs to be stressed that 'foreign influences' and equity investment are not the same thing. The former includes the latter, but it extends well beyond it, to include effects via trade, international buying groups, licensing agreements and independent movements of skilled labour. As always, the concept of 'foreign ownership' remains elusive, especially in countries where a large number of current or former citizens reside abroad, or where common ethnic groups straddle national boundaries. East Asia's 'overseas Chinese' business groups are the most prominent example of this phenomenon (see Mackie (1992) and the discussion below on regional economic zones). The overseas Vietnamese community (Viet Kieu) is another example, although it is less well documented and its commercial activities in Vietnam are viewed by the authorities with ambivalence (Nguyen, 1996).

Analyses of sources of FDI prior to the 1990s concentrated overwhelmingly on Japan, the US and Europe, not only because they were the major investors but also because there was some debate in the literature (much of it triggered by the work of Professor Kiyoshi Kojima)[3] about the relative merits of these different investment sources. There are still traces of this literature in the 1990s, both positive and normative, but it is now a much less frequently debated topic, principally because differences among OECD investors, once standardised by source country characteristics, are generally found not to be particularly important.

A notable development in East Asia is the emergence of high-performing economies in the region, especially the four NIEs, and to a lesser extent some other ASEAN countries and China, as significant investors, both within the region and globally. Since the NIEs have all been substantial investors abroad for at least a decade or more, it is now possible to discern some of the major patterns and effects. Some of these countries are now sizeable international investors: over the period 1991–3, for example, they are estimated to have invested abroad about $16.5 billion, not far short of the Japanese figure ($20.6 billion), although much smaller than the comparable flows from North America ($48.9 billion) and Europe ($108.6 billion). Hong Kong dominated these flows with $10.5 billion; while Taiwan, Korea and China topped the $1 billion mark; in the late 1980s Taiwan was by far the largest investor from the region (Wells, 1994).

At the risk of over simplification, two general models of outward FDI from the region are evident: one essentially market (and comparative advantage) driven, in which firms' commercial decisions are the primary driving factor, and another which involves much more government intervention (ranging from incentives and commands to strong moral exhortation). Hong Kong and Taiwan are closer to

Table 11.2 Net resource flows to East Asia and the Pacific, 1970–98 (selected years) ($ billion)

	1970	*1980*	*1990*	*1997*	*1998*
Long-term debt (ex. IMF lending)	1.2	10.6	12.2	46.7	24.1
Foreign direct investment	0.3	1.3	11.1	64.3	61.0
Portfolio equity flows	0.0	0.0	2.3	9.2	8.4
Grants (ex. technical cooperation)	0.8	1.2	2.1	2.4	2.2
Total net resource flows	2.2	13.1	27.8	122.6	95.6

Source: World Bank (1999).

the first model, and Korea and Malaysia to the second; Singapore sits somewhere in the middle. Of course, all countries' patterns exhibit both characteristics to some degree. Taiwan's earlier investments abroad were heavily political in nature, explaining in part projects in far-off parts of Africa and Central America. And investments in which governments have played a role are still generally expected to meet some sort of market test eventually, and so commercial considerations do of course intrude in these 'type II' investments.

In the aftermath of the onset of the Asian crisis in mid-1997, a major concern in the debate on the recovery process of 'crisis' countries was whether MNCs would continue to treat these countries as preferred locations for international production. Some observers, particularly those in the popular press, attempted to paint a gloomy picture by referring to massive capital outflows following the onset of the crisis. This view was, however, based on a false aggregation of FDI with portfolio investment and bank credits. Unlike financial flows in the latter categories, FDI flows are determined by long-term considerations governing international production decisions of MNCs, not by financial panics and related short-term economic changes.

Three years after the onset of the crisis we now have firm evidence that, in much of East Asia (except Indonesia where political unrest has scared investors away), FDI inflows have been much more resilient than other forms of private capital (World Bank, 1999; IMF, 2000; UNCTAD, 1998). Between 1997 and 1998 total net resource flows to developing countries in East Asia and the Pacific contracted by 22 per cent (from $122.6 to $95.6 billion). But net FDI contracted only by 5.1 per cent (from $64.3 to 61.0 billion). FDI flows to Thailand, Korea and the Philippines rose in 1998, despite the severity of the recession in these countries (particularly in the first two) (Table 11.3). Flows to Malaysia recorded a mild decline in 1998 by about 10 per cent as compared to 1996, but this shortfall emanated solely from domestic market oriented investment. Export-oriented investment remained by and large unchanged at pre-crisis levels. Moreover unlike in Thailand and Korea, Malaysia has not resorted to new legislation favouring acquisition of local business by foreign companies as part of its crisis management strategy. A comparison of FDI behaviour among the crisis countries based on Table 11.3 needs to be qualified for the fact that these data do not capture

Table 11.3 FDI[1] in Korea, Malaysia and Thailand, 1995–99 (US$ million)

	Indonesia	*Korea*	*Malaysia*	*Philippines*	*Thailand*
1995	4346	1776	7618	1478	2068
1996	6194	2326	8082	1517	2336
1997	4677	2844	6573	1222	3746
1998	−356	5416	5091	1752	7131
1999[2]	−2244	7774	6204	944	5823
1997-1	2342	624	1776	−565	645
1997-2	1267	791	3719	214	842
1997-3	1392	611	2134	295	1222
1997-4	−324	819	1521	148	1037
1998-1	−502	505	1181	251	2038
1998-2	367	1168	1081	247	2636
1998-3	−144	2162	680	218	1432
1998-4	−77	1582	2024	1036	1025
1999-1	−232	1407	1028	469	1004
1999-2	−890	1819	2013	154	2210
1999-3	—	2605	1612	85	1153

Sources: Asia Recovery Information Centre (ARIC), Asian Development Bank (http:aric.adb.org) and Bank Negara Malaysia, *Monthly Statistical Bulletin* (various issues).

Notes
1 Net flows.
2 Pro-rata estimates based on the figures for the first two quarters for Indonesia and the first three quarters for the other four countries.
— Data not available.

investment financed from retained earnings. This component of MNC investment is presumably much more important in Malaysia, given the much larger historical MNC presence in the domestic economy (Athukorala, 2000).

It is important to note that total FDI inflows to the crisis countries were resilient despite a significant decline in investment flows from several East Asian source countries. This implies that an analysis which distinguishes between inflows from non-crisis countries and regional inflows would yield even stronger support for the conventional wisdom – overlooked by many in the current debate on crisis management – that, in terms of underlying determinants of mobility, long-term investment (FDI) is quite different from 'hot money'. Mead (1951: 298) made such an observation almost fifty years ago. Another noteworthy aspect is that in Korea, Malaysia, Philippines and Thailand (and also in Singapore) the share of FDI in total domestic capital formation was higher in 1998 compared to the pre-crisis level (Table 11.1). In other words, FDI has weathered the crisis far better than domestic private investment. The important inference here, and one which deserves further scrutiny, is that depending on the nature of domestic FDI policy regime FDI can act as an effective cushion against the possible collapse in domestic investment during a crisis.

FDI's resilience during the crisis can be explained by at least three factors. First, large exchange-rate depreciations reduced domestic production costs and asset values, making foreign investment more profitable. Second, the cost of investment was also significantly reduced by falling asset prices resulting from the decline in investment profitability brought about by the contraction in domestic demand. Third, corporate restructuring in crisis affected countries (in Korea and Thailand in particular) opened up new opportunities for cross-border mergers and acquisitions. These three factors helped to offset the negative impact on FDI flows of the diminished market size (in foreign currency terms), lower immediate growth prospects, and policy uncertainty (Krugman, 1997; UNCTAD, 1998; World Bank, 1999: 47).

The FDI-trade nexus

Over the past decade, the relationship between international trade and international production (production by MNC affiliates) has been a major growth area in the literature on East Asia. The growing policy emphasis on regional economic integration and the perceived role of FDI in the process, and the improved availability of trade and investment data seem to have contributed to this renewed research emphasis. In this section we examine the FDI-trade nexus, focusing in turn on the role of FDI in regional economic integration through trade flows, and the contribution to export performance in individual countries.

FDI and intra-regional trade

By the late 1980s intra-regional trade in East Asia had grown beyond a level that would be expected on the basis of the relative size of their economies (Riedel, 1991; 143). By that time the share of intra-Asian trade in total exports from the region stood at 38 per cent, whereas Asia's share in world income was only 25 per cent. In the absence of any preferential trade arrangements to account for increased intra-regional trade intensity, the growing importance of intra-Asian FDI is one possible explanation for this development. For instance, there was a significant rise in Asia's share of Japanese FDI in the region, and a corresponding rise in the export orientation of Japanese investment in developing countries, from 33 per cent of total sales in 1980 to 42.3 per cent in 1988. However, increased export orientation of MNC affiliates does not necessarily imply that FDI leads to regional integration. This is because foreign firms may be involved in triangular trade: they may use the region to maintain export market share in countries outside the region.

Petri (1992) tests this possibility by using a new methodology based on international input–output analysis to examine the impact of Japanese investment on Thailand's trade. The results suggests that Japanese affiliated firms in Thailand are predominantly involved in 'triangular trade' that widens Thailand's trade deficit with Japan and enhances the former's surpluses with countries outside the region. Studies by Lee (1994) of Korean investment and Kapellas and Liu (1990) and Lin (1996) of Taiwanese investment in Southeast Asia, however, suggest that investment in the region by firms from these countries contributes more to trade between host and home countries (and thus intra-regional trade) than to triangular trade.

Dobson and Chia (1997) report the results of the first major multi-country research project on trade and investment activities of MNCs and their impact on regional integration in East Asia. The volume contains chapters of eight countries (Singapore, Taiwan, Hong Kong, Thailand, Malaysia, China (Guandong), Philippines and Indonesia) and a unique longitudinal comparative case study of eight large electronics multinationals operating in the region (chapter 10). The findings generally support the hypothesis that, on balance, regional integration is enhanced by MNCs. On the one hand, firms from East Asian countries who invest defensively in other regional locations, and MNCs (or their affiliates) investing in multi-plant operations encompassing two or more countries in the regions, contribute to intra-regional trade.

On the other hand, regional integration is reduced (and global integration is promoted) by the US and European firms whose trade is largely with their home countries, and Japanese firms who use the region as an export platform to maintain competitiveness in third countries. Although the relative magnitude of these offsetting effects is difficult to estimates, there is evidence, contra Hatch and Yamamura (1996) discussed above, that the positive influences have become far greater compared to negative influences in recent years. There is also evidence that the 'triangular trade bias' of Japanese investment has begun to diminish and that exports to Japan from the East Asian subsidiaries of Japanese firms are catching up with imports from Japan. As a byproduct of the inquiry into the FDI-regional integration relationship, the studies in the Dobson–Chia volume also have come up with interesting findings relating to a number of other facts of the trade–investment nexus. These will be incorporated in the discussion below where relevant.

A striking feature of MNC operations in East Asia is the emergence and growing importance of cross-border multi-plant operations (Dobson and Chia, 1997; Huff, 1994; Petri, 1993; Athukorala and Menon, 1997). Faced with intensifying competition emanating from deregulation, falling trade barriers and increasing capital mobility, international firms seek production efficiencies, and in consequence MNCs have begun to 'slice up' the value chain of their production according to a location's comparative advantage, and to relocate certain segments/processes of production activities, rather than entire industries (Krugman, 1995). This process has created a new regional division of labour, based on skill differences, differential factor prices (especially wages) and superior communication facilities. Under this process, MNCs move more sophisticated products and key components production from home-country plants to the more sophisticated offshore locations, such as Hong Kong, Singapore and Taiwan. Some segments of the production process are then relocated to neighbouring countries. Production is thus dispersed within the region, leading to intensified intra-regional trade in the context of a global industrial network.

One important implication of these cross-border production activities, which are primarily focused on the complementarity of national resource endowments, is that promoting FDI is a 'positive sum game' in which all players gain from trade in differentiated products (Dobson and Chia, 1997). Thus, governments should feel less pressure to use incentives to lure investment to one location over another; rather the policy emphasis should be on harnessing regional diversities. Huff (1994: 314) points to an important implication for the analysis of trade flows in the context of growing cross-broader trade based on slicing of product change activities – such practices 'render the [published] trade statistics an uncertain guide to activities actually undertaken in a given country'.[4]

Causes and consequences of intra-firm (or intra-affiliate) trade (IFT) of MNCs have been widely discussed in the MNC literature. It has both positive and negative effects on the host economy. On the positive side, it facilitates industry upgrading through participation in the value chain of vertically integrated global industries. On the negative side, a high degree of IFT means less policy sovereignty for the governments, particularly with respect to transfer pricing (Caves, 1996: 32–3). The growing importance of multi-plant operations is reflected in the increased share of IFT. For instance, the value of IFT, including both exports and imports, was estimated to be $83.9 billion in 1992, or 55.5 per cent of total electronics trade in Hong Kong, Indonesia, Malaysia, Philippines, Singapore and Thailand (Dobson and Chia, 1997: 263). Another interesting finding of the Dobson–Chia project is that the relative importance of IFT tends to diminish as the host economy becomes more developed and matures (Table 11.2, p. 254). Market channels are used more heavily in Taiwan than in the other two countries (Malaysia and Thailand). Both US and Japanese multinationals in Taiwan sell around 40 per cent their production in the local market in Taiwan, whereas such sales are negligible in Thailand and Malaysia. This is because, as the host economy matures, MNC affiliates involved in vertically integrated cross-border industries shift over to final stages of the value change and the country also attracts more FDI into industries producing sophisticated consumer durables.

FDI and export performance

Much of the existing literature on the effects of MNC operations on home-country exports has focused on the question of whether MNCs are more or less export oriented (measured in terms of export–sale ratios) than the operation of domestically oriented firms (Hill, 1990: 35). The relevance of this issue has waned in the light of the dramatic transformation in the patterns of international production and the dismantling of trade and investment restrictions in investment receiving countries. An important development in the pattern of international production has been the growing significance of efficiency-seeking investment in total FDI flows to developing countries. Efficiency-seeking MNC affiliates generally tend to be fully export oriented by their very nature. Aggregating data comparing foreign firms' export propensities with that of local firms may therefore be quite misleading with respect to the potential role of MNCs in export expansion. The relative attractiveness of a given country as a location for efficiency-seeking (export oriented) investment compared to market-seeking (or conventional tariff jumping) investment – which naturally tend to be less (or zero) export oriented – depends significantly on the nature of the host-country investment and trade regimes. In this context, an empirical analysis that attempts to capture relative export propensities may be in fact erroneously capturing the influences of the policy regime and industry effects. Studies contained in Dobson and Chia (1997) provide ample empirical evidence that in East Asian countries 'corporate nationality influences production, but location and industry effects dominate corporate nationality as determinants of trade patterns' (p. 253–60). For instance, US firms are more export oriented than their Japanese counterparts in Singapore and Thailand (export–sales ratios of 90 per cent versus 65 per cent, respectively). This is merely a reflection of the fact that US firms concentrate on industrial electronics, for which export–sales ratios are high. By comparison Japanese firms concentrate in consumer electronics for which export ratios are low, as investment decisions have been partly motivated by the objectives of exploiting host-country market opportunities. In automobiles, import-substitution policies still operate in most host countries in the region. Consequently, US and Japanese auto producers both sell and source locally, as domestic policies dictate. That industry effects, rather than nationality of ownership, are the key determinant of export propensity of firms is confirmed by a close scrutiny of the findings of studies by Ramstetter (1997) of export propensity of local and foreign firms in Thailand and Singapore. The overall Thai results point to greater export propensity for foreign firms, but this was mostly dictated by the heavy concentration of foreign firms in highly export oriented office and computing machinery, and electronic machinery. The analysis of Singapore finds a strong positive relationship between export propensities and the foreign ownership share. This result is not surprising because fully foreign-owned US firms dominate the highly export-oriented industrial electronics industry in that country.

In this context the more relevant issue for empirical testing is the relative contribution of foreign firms to export expansion in the host country. To the extent that MNCs bring with them tangible or intangible resources (including capital, research and development, technology and management practices) that increases the capacity of a country to produce better quality goods and services, the export performance of the country will be affected positively. Positive effects can also result from the expansion of market access that MNCs can bring about, directly or indirectly, as a consequence of intra-firm transactions, including their greater ability to reach national and international markets. The available economy-wide estimates of the contribution of MNC affiliates to manufactured export expansion are presented in Table 11.4. The estimates generally point to the important role of FDI in export expansion in 'second tier' exporting countries as against the conventional view, based on the early experience of Taiwan, Hong Kong and Korea that FDI is not important in determining export success (Helleiner, 1988: 130; Biggs and Levy, 1991).

Table 11.4 Share of foreign affiliates in total manufactured exports[1] from developing host countries in East Asia (per cent)

	Source	*Criterion of foreign ownership (FDI share in equity capital)*	*Year of estimate*	*Approximate share (%)*
China	Naughton (1996) and Pomfret (1997)[2]	All firms with FDI	1985	2.2
			1988	7.5
			1990	16.9
			1993	33.6
			1996	47.6
Hong Kong	Nayyar (1978)	All firms with FDI	1972	10.0
	UNTCMD (1992)	"	1984	16.5
South Korea	Nayyar (1978)	10 % or more	1971	15.0
	Koo (1985)	"	1974	23.6
	Ramstetter (1993)	"	1977	25.3
	Ramstetter (1993)	"	1986	26.1
Taiwan	Nayyar (1978)	10 % or more	1971	20.0
	Ranis and Schive (1985)	10 % or more	1974	23.7
	Schive and Tu (1991)	10 % or more	1976	31.3
	UNTCMD (1992)	na	1981	25.6
	Ramstetter (1993)	10 % or more	1989	18.0
Malaysia	UNTCMD (1992)	na	1980	41.0
	UNTCMD (1992)	na	1986	51.2
	Athukorala (1998, chapter 8)	49 % or more	1988	72.0
		"	1992	75.6
Singapore	Chia (1985)	All firms with FDI	1963	57.4
	Nayyar (1978)	"	1970	70.0
	Huff (1994, table 11.11)	51 % or more	1975	84.1
		"	1980	84.7
		"	1990	85.8
			1991	91.5
Philippines	ITC (1987)	12.5 % or more	1980	60.8
			1983	57.5
Thailand	Ramstetter (1997)	All firms with FDI	1974	12.0
			1986	15.0
			1988	33.0
Indonesia	Ramstetter (1999)	All firms with FDI	1992	65.0
			1994	71.0

Notes

1 In all cases manufactured exports have been measured using the ISIC-based definition of manufacturing (i.e. ISIC 3) or an approximation of it. Estimates cover direct exports only.

2 Derived from data on exports by foreign invested enterprises given in Naughton (1996), table 3 and value manufactured exports reported in Pomfret (1997), table 2. Estimate for 1996 refers to the first six months.

na Information not available.

There are at least two possible explanations for the observed difference between Taiwan, Korea and Hong Kong, on the one hand, and 'second tier' exporting countries on the other, in terms of the relative share of MNC affiliates in total exports. First, since about the early 1970s, successful exporting firms in the East Asian NIEs have begun to play an important role as direct investors in the labour-intensive export industries of the latecomers (Wells, 1994). Two main factors have contributed to this new development: the erosion of international competitiveness of labour-intensive export products from their home countries as a result of wage increases, and the imposition and gradual tightening of quantitative import restrictions (QRs) by OECD economies on certain labour-intensive exports (mostly textile, garments and footwear). There are indications that, in line with rapid structural transformations taking place in the NIEs, the intermediary role of these 'new' investors in linking late comers to world markets may become increasingly important in years to come. Unlike MNCs from developed countries, these new investors from the NIEs are able to adapt to the more difficult business environment (e.g. poor infrastructure, bureaucratic red tape) in the latecomers.

The second possible explanation is that, as already noted, from about the mid-1980s, assembly activities in global industries have become the most dynamic area for developing countries to participate in international production. This development, which largely post-dates the labour-intensive growth phase of Korea and Taiwan, is part of an adjustment process whereby firms in industrialised countries adapt to the increasing pressures of rising real wages at home and increased import competition from low cost sources. The transfer abroad of component assembly occurs in many industries where the technology of production permits the separation of labour-intensive components from other steps in the production process. Assembly operations related to high-tech electronic industries, semi-conductors in particular, are by far the most important. The other industries with significant assembly operations located in developing countries are electrical appliances, automobile parts, electrical machinery and optical products. Assembly exports from developing countries have grown much faster than total manufactured exports from these countries (Krugman, 1995).

It can be reasonably expected that these overseas production arrangements will continue to remain a dynamic growth area in the foreseeable future. For developed-country MNCs in product areas such as electronics, electrical goods and automobile, whose home operations are severely affected by import competition from low-cost sources, offshore assembly is crucial for their survival. Governments in these countries are also actively encouraging such operations through value-added tariff provisions and other measures, with a view to cushioning domestic economies against disruptions resulting from rapid import penetration. For instance, the US government has created a special tariff structure, which allows goods exported from the US for further processing to be re-imported subject to *ad valorem* tariffs which are levied only on the value added abroad. (While there have been attempts towards assembly automation in developed countries, there is no indication yet of a trend away from offshore production.) In many high-tech industries – notably in electronics – rapid innovation and continuous technical change, which bring about a constant cycle of change and obsolescence, are formidable constraints to rapid automation.

Table 11.5 sheds lights on the export orientation of US multinationals (majority-owned affiliates) in East Asia in a global context. It is clearly evident that the operations of US MNCs in East Asia is much more export oriented than elsewhere in the world, both among developed and developing countries. Within East Asia, affiliates in Singapore and Malaysia stand out for their high export orientation, with exports accounting for 80 per cent or more of total sales. Affiliates in China are the least export oriented, but their export–sale ratio has begun to increase sharply in recent years. The relative importance of domestic sales in total turnover of affiliates in the four NIEs (Taiwan, Korea, Singapore and Hong Kong) has increased over time, reflecting perhaps expanding domestic market opportunities as these countries rapidly catch up with the consumption patterns of mature

Table 11.5 Export–sales ratio and home-country export shares of MOFAs of US multinationals, 1982–93

	1982–83	*1985–87*	*1988–90*	*1991–93*
Export–sales ratio				
All countries	35.8	38.3	38.5	40.8
Developed countries	37.0	38.4	38.3	41.5
Developing countries	29.5	37.6	40.0	37.8
East Asia	62.7	70.3	63.5	62.6
China	0.0	0.0	10.1	27.2
Hong Kong	74.5	70.0	65.5	61.7
Indonesia	14.3	10.3	5.5	10.4
Korea Rep.	58.0	55.5	39.3	28.1
Malaysia	77.7	83.5	75.8	82.2
Philippines	30.3	39.9	35.0	33.9
Singapore	92.1	89.7	85.6	83.5
Taiwan	60.3	59.8	45.4	36.6
Thailand	77.6	66.7	67.1	66.2
Export to USA as a share of total exports				
All countries	34.4	34.9	33.5	29.8
Developed countries	30.1	29.6	27.0	24.5
Developing countries	63.8	67.9	70.0	60.6
East Asia	70.6	68.8	61.1	56.4
China			3.2	1.7
Hong Kong	69.5	55.2	56.0	36.9
Indonesia	9.5	11.8	32.3	75.9
Korea Rep.	81.9	81.5	83.2	78.5
Malaysia	74.9	73.9	55.5	66.5
Philippines	65.1	59.1	52.4	40.2
Singapore	78.4	69.3	64.7	62.4
Taiwan	82.9	73.4	65.2	52.8
Thailand	59.7	50.6	45.6	43.7

Sources: Compiled from US Bureau of Economic Analysis, *US Direct Investment Abroad: Operations of US Parent Companies and Their Foreign Affiliates*, US Department of Commerce (annual).

western economies. As regards the distribution of total sales between the home country (US) and third country destinations, affiliates in East Asia, as well as those in other developing countries, export a larger share to the home country than their counterparts in developed countries. This is understandable because international production in developing countries is fundamentally determined by comparative advantage considerations, whereas scale economies and other market-related factor play a relatively more important role in determining the relocation of production in developed countries. A final observation is that home-country export shares of Malaysia and Singapore have begun to decline in recent years, reflecting the gradual integration of assembly activities located in these two countries into the expanding global production networks of US MNCs.

A widely debated aspect of the trade-FDI nexus concerns export processing zones (EPZs). The early studies, both those focused on selected aspects of EPZs such as employment creation, linkages to the rest of the economy and net foreign exchange earnings as well as the few available systematic cost–benefit analyses selected EPZs, found their developmental contribution to be at best marginal (Hill, 1990: 35–6). A number of recent studies have however identified them as a useful transitional in the process of integrating the national economy within the world economy (ADB, 1997; Athukorala, 1998: chapter 6; Johansson and Nilsson, 1997; Radelet and Sachs, 1997). According to the 'new view', the early studies, given their narrow focus on direct economic impacts (or national profitability), have ignored important *catalyst* effects of EPZs on potential domestic exporters, operating through exposure to marketing know-how and technology, direct demonstration effects and linking, and bringing international buyers to the country. In many countries EPZs failed to generate these externalities and to provide a conducive setting for an export takeoff, not because of any intrinsic limitation of the zones but because they were used as an appendage to a highly regulated domestic economy. Moreover, the 'footloose industry argument' against EPZs (i.e. that they possessed shallow linkages with the rest of the economy and would quickly migrate in response to rising domestic costs) ignored the inevitable time lags involved in the process of linkage formation with the domestic economy by new entrants to EPZs. There is convincing evidence that EPZ firms tend to increase their local purchases and shift over to more sophisticated production process as their operations in the host country mature, provided the local business environment is conducive to such behaviour (Aoki, 1992; Athukorala and Menon, 1996; Lim and Pang, 1991).

FDI and technology

With the growing appeal of the new growth theories, technology has returned to the centre stage of economic development. Along with human capital, expenditure on R&D is now regarded as one of the key factors driving economic development. As a corollary, therefore, the notion of international R&D 'spillovers' attracts great interest – countries can increase their growth rates not only by investing in R&D, but also through commercial relationships with other countries which possess large R&D stocks (Grossman and Helpman, 1991; Coe and Helpman, 1995). Modeling the international effects of one country's R&D effort on others' growth rates is still rudimentary. Owing to data availability, most of this research has concentrated on trade links as the transmission mechanism, but in practice FDI almost certainly has a larger impact. Incorporating FDI into these models is likely to become a major research endeavour as the data base improves.

The literature on FDI spillovers has proceeded in two main directions, a newer one which is macro, econometric and inferential and traditional one which is more micro, qualitative and firm-based.[5] The two approaches are usually particularly data-intensive, and so rarely, unfortunately, are both employed in the one study. The first of these employs a large secondary data set in which foreign and domestic firms are separately identified. It examines productivity (either total or labour productivity) trends among the two groups and across industries to discern whether the foreign presence affects levels and growth rates among domestic firms. These studies are generally not concerned with the transmission mechanism, nor are they able to estimate the relative importance of FDI among other factors explaining productivity growth in domestic firms. However, they do provide presumptive evidence of causation. The results vary across countries and industries, indicating that such spillovers do not occur automatically. It is hypothesised, and sometimes empirically demonstrated, that spillovers will be positively associated with the level of competition (which pushes firms to adopt improved technology) and negatively associated with the productivity gap between foreign and domestic firms (on the assumption that a very large gap renders absorption by domestic firms more difficult).

Some research has begun to test this approach empirically in developing East Asia. Fan and Warr (2000) examined spillovers, as measured by TFP growth, to state-owned enterprises (SOEs) and those which are collectively-owned (mainly the Town and Village Enterprises, TVEs). Their results are very important, and highlight the importance of the domestic policy and absorptive environment in maximising the gains from FDI. Among the SOEs, negative spillovers were detected. They attribute this to these firms' operating environment, including their soft budget constraint, a deteriorating human capital base and the absence of incentives to improve productivity. By contrast, in the flexible and dynamic TVEs, where appropriate incentives structures are in place, the FDI spillovers were found to be positive. In Sjoholm's study of Indonesian manufacturing, in which labour productivity was the key variable, competitive pressures were found to be highly significant in explaining inter-industry variations. Interestingly, domestic competition (that is, a firm concentration variable) was found to be more significant than foreign competition, as proxied by effective protection. Subsequent research of this genre (e.g. Okamoto and Sjoholm, 2000) found the foreign presence to be significantly and positively associated with inter-industry variations in productivity growth (see also Aswicahyono and Hill (1999) on this issue).

Ideally, one would want to supplement these studies by some more detailed industry-level work, to understand better how and why the spillovers work. One such attempt to probe technology transfer mechanisms is Hou and Gee (1993) on Taiwan. They found labour mobility from foreign to local firms to be a key variable. They also pointed to the differences between medium, large and small firms. Whereas the former generally approached technology transfer through formal mechanisms such as joint ventures (including 'reverse engineering' via FDI abroad) and licensing agreements, the latter relied more heavily on informal channels such as copying and informal business liaisons. The latter strategy is similar to that employed by Bali's small–medium garment exporters, referred to above in Cole's (1998) study.

FDI and technology development continue to attract much attention in Malaysia, a country, which has traditionally adopted an open approach towards FDI, and has received very large inflows into its electronics industry. Some observers regard this as a classic case of enclave, 'shallow' industrialisation, in which too little attention has been paid to education, and to extracting the benefits from the MNC presence (see, e.g. several of the chapters in Jomo, ed. 1993). As real wages began to rise quickly before the crisis, the question being asked was whether this strategy was capable of facilitating industrial upgrading. Although it might be argued that Malaysia had under-invested in education and R&D, the country has apparently been developing quite successfully with FDI. Several detailed case studies (Hobday, 1999; Lai and Narayanan, 1997) have demonstrated that Malaysian industry was shifting quite quickly from low to medium–high technology, both in the core electronics firms and in their clusters of support industries. These firms continue to operate well within the technology frontiers, and as Hobday (1999) observes, the innovation is generally incremental in nature, and not the radical R&D-based advances sometimes portrayed in the literature. There are continuing concerns that: heavy reliance on migrant labour is retarding the inevitable process of structural adjustment; Penang (where much of the MNC electronics activity is located) is perhaps a special case in the Malaysian context; the vocational education system remains poorly developed; and the participation of local firms is inadequate. But the broad picture is nevertheless one of rapid industrialisation, and in this respect pre-crisis Malaysia appeared to be following closely a Singapore-style strategy towards FDI and technology transfer.

The option of Korean and Japan-style technology imports, in which FDI plays a minor role in aggregate, is arguably neither feasible nor desirable in the 1990s (Soesastro, 1998). The imperative of globalisation means that highly restrictive FDI policies will have a general deterrence effect on MNCs, and would jeopardise membership of WTO, APEC, ASEAN and other international and regional initiatives.

Moreover, even in Korea, with its strong human capital and R&D base, it is often forgotten that FDI has played a critical role in technological development. As Kim (Kim, 1997) points out, Korea has already surpassed OECD R&D norms in a number of respects. For example, its R&D expenditure as a percentage of GDP has risen from 0.3 per cent in 1971 to 2.6 per cent in 1994, a figure which exceeds the OECD median. However, in the 1980s FDI was seen as a means of facilitating the technological upgrading process in several key Korean industries, including semi-conductors, pharmaceuticals and retail trade. The latter was effectively open to FDI only in 1995, in the face of domestic opposition. Even during Korea's most restrictive phases of FDI policies, it was always recognised that certain forms of advanced technology could only be acquired through direct equity investments (Kim, 1997; Kim and Wang, 1996). There continues to be a debate about the precise mix of government policy and FDI in this upgrading process. Undoubtedly, government-funded research, both general and industry-specific, contributed. But more controversial is the frequent assertion that targeted closure to FDI, combined with off-the-shelf purchase of technology, government support and vigorous exhortation, was instrumental in quickly pushing firms towards the technology frontier. While the case for government support to overcome market failure is well documented (see e.g. Lall, 1996), it is difficult to believe that drastic measures such as prohibition of FDI are cost-effective. Moreover, in some high-tech industries, such off-the-shelf purchases are simply not possible.

As with FDI policy regimes in general, it is important to emphasise that the role of MNCs in the region's technological development has varied considerably across countries and industries. (The 'diamonds' referred to above show this very clearly.) These differences are illustrated in the better comparative case study analysis, such as Hobday's (1995) study of the electronics industry in the four East Asian NIEs. As he reminds us, virtually all combinations of policy regimes have been evident among these four economies – extensive intervention and large firms in Korea and Singapore, which in turn have been distinguished by closed and open policies towards FDI; and small local firms alongside larger foreign ones in Taiwan and Hong Kong, in the context of partially liberal and *laissez faire* FDI and trade policies. It is important, however, to also emphasise the common elements across the four economies: export orientation, strong investments in human capital, generally sound macroeconomic management and liberal policies towards technology imports, if not across-the-board then at least where it was recognised that the local base was inadequate. As argued above, it is not obvious that deliberately restricting firms' access to technology frontiers is an effective means of spurring technological development. The fact that, in the current crisis, Korea is by the worst affected of the four first generation NIEs suggests that its particular mix of industrial policy and selective credit allocations is a high-risk strategy.

There continues to be a debate about the effectiveness of Japanese technology transfer via FDI (Sato, 1998; Tran, 1993). As noted above, the analysis has matured from the somewhat polarised debate in the 1970s, with the general conclusion being that Japanese firms are no better or worse than MNCs from other countries, especially after account is taken of linguistic differences and the industrial location of FDI. In an interesting study of Japanese FDI in the Indonesian auto industry, Sato (1998) finds substantial transfer of managerial know-how from the Japanese investor to, and beyond, the Indonesian partner, which became deeply familiar with the technology, and adapted it to Indonesian conditions. Such a finding is of considerable significance in view of the widespread 'nationalist' sentiment that Japanese companies, long dominant in the industry, have contributed little to its technological development.

One frustrating feature of international technology flows is that it is still virtually impossible to quantify their overall magnitude, let alone the major constituent elements. The closest approximation is royalty payments, but few non-OECD countries publish such data. It is widely assumed that FDI is the most important component of these international transfers (Soesastro, 1998), but the available secondary data are at best indicative. It is not possible to aggregate the various flows with a technology component (e.g. data on FDI, capital goods imports and human capital flows are non-additive). Moreover, it is possible that some very large FDIs (e.g. mining investments) may be enclave in nature with little spillover, whereas smaller manufacturing and service FDIs in the presence of a strong local absorptive capacity may have a significant technology impact.

One final FDI-technology issue, which is now receiving some attention is the relationship between FDI and the location of R&D activities. As Dunning (1998) notes, the traditional model of FDI, which dominated through to the 1970s, involved firms investing abroad on the basis of a competitive advantage which was generally based around an advanced technological competence. During the 1980s, this close association between R&D capacity and outward investment, while still underpinning much FDI, began to evolve in at least two directions. First, as noted, cash-rich companies from East Asia and elsewhere sought to short-circuit the technology upgrading process by 'reverse engineering' investments abroad in firms with a strong R&D capacity. Second, the location of R&D activities within MNCs also became more international. Traditionally, and with few exceptions, such R&D was heavily located at the MNCs' headquarters, owing to the superior human capital base and economies of scope and scale, to maintain synergies between R&D and production, and to safeguard intellectual property rights. However, as comparative advantage factors push production off-shore, the economics of R&D may lead to some international relocation of research activity.

The issue is how much relocation is occurring. Data relating to R&D activities of majority-owned foreign affiliated of US MNCs – the only country which reports such data – are reported in Table 11.6. The data clearly suggest that the East Asian host countries (and of course other developing countries) are yet to benefit from such international reallocation of R&D activity. The internationalisation of R&D activities has been confined mainly to developed countries, as would be expected given the concentration of R&D activities there (Soesastro, 1998). Affiliates located in developing countries accounted on average for a mere 4.6 per cent of the total global R&D expenditures of US MNCs. The percentage accounted for by affiliates in East Asia was 1.5 per cent. Among the East Asian countries, Singapore accounted for the largest share (0.7 per cent) followed by Taiwan (0.3 per cent). The R&D–sales ratios for East Asia and all developing countries were both about 0.4 per cent, compared to 1.5 per cent for developed countries. The estimates for Singapore reported in this table clearly run counter to the general perception in that country (e.g. see Low, 1998) that a significant

Table 11.6 R&D expenditure of MOFAs of US multinationals, 1989–93

	Geographic distribution of R&D expenditure (per cent)	*R&D–sales ratio*
World (excluding USA)	100.00	1.34
Developed countries	95.38	1.50
Developing countries	4.62	0.41
Other Asia and Pacific	1.58	0.39
East Asia	1.54	0.39
China	0.01	0.47
Hong Kong	0.09	0.17
Indonesia	0.04	0.70
Korea Rep.	0.08	0.33
Malaysia	0.09	0.20
Philippines	0.09	0.33
Singapore	0.67	0.61
Taiwan	0.33	0.66
Thailand	0.04	0.13

Sources: Compiled from US Bureau of Economic Analysis, *US Direct Investment Abroad: Operations of US Parent Companies and Their Foreign Affiliates*, US Department of Commerce (annual).

share of R&D expenditure is in the private sector is likely to be mainly MNC activity.

The issue of host-country absorptive capacity draws attention more generally to the importance of the local environment in maximising the benefits of introduced technology. To be effective, the local environment requires a strong human resource base and an internationally integrated economy. The strong R&D efforts of the former Soviet Union and pre-reform India, for example, were dissipated by inward-looking commercial trade policies, whereas small and nimble East Asian economies such as Hong Kong, Singapore and Taiwan, with limited R&D expenditures, have been able to effectively access international R&D capacities.[6] By contrast, one of the criticisms of Indonesia's ambitious high-tech manufacturing investments is that they have aimed for technology self-sufficiency rather than an internationally integrated R&D capacity.

Conclusions

A number of key points deserve emphasis by way of concluding this survey of FDI and East Asian economic development.

- First, there is the apparently inexorable trend towards greater economic integration, both within the region and with the global economy. Rising FDI flows – both absolute values and relative to the size of the host economy – are but one of many manifestations of this phenomenon. This process is almost certainly irreversible. Unless, that is, rising host-country nationalism again becomes a potent force in the wake of increased foreign ownership shares occasioned by post-crisis 'FDI fire sales'.

- Second, all East Asian economies have to varying degrees become more open to FDI, both in the sense of explicit policy liberalisations, and as revealed in actual inflows over time. The special case of China is of course noteworthy since, notwithstanding recent declines, it has emerged as the by far the largest recipient of FDI in the developing world.
- Related to these trends is the fact that, by historical standards, East Asian developing countries are emerging as sources of FDI at relatively low levels of per capita income. As barriers to international commerce continue to fall, this trend is likely to persist, and China in particular can be expected to become a major FDI player.
- Fourth, the production chain is becoming ever more disaggregated across international boundaries, driven by technological development, falling transport costs, and fierce international cost pressures. This trend, which is almost certain to intensify, is most pronounced in the electronics industry and certain service activities.
- Far-reaching implications follow from such an observation, including our fifth key summary point: as international boundaries become more porous, an increasing premium is likely to attach to knowledge of international markets (buying channels, latest production technologies, consumer preferences and the regulatory regime in host countries). This will further strengthen the bargaining power and competitive advantages of firms with such globalised knowledge – or at least access to it – and in particular MNCs. One consequence of this trend is that it will be increasingly difficult for countries to achieve rapid, outward-looking economic development via a policy regime which actively discourages foreign ownership in many sectors. Thus the so-called 'Japanese/Korean' model, of restricted MNC access except for technology and export-intensive activities, is unlikely to be replicated.
- Sixth, the behaviour of the various components of international capital flows has been strikingly different during the recent economic crisis. In particular, short-term flows – portfolio investment and short-maturity loans – fell spectacularly, while FDI held up or even increased in most countries. This is a complex issue, from which strong normative conclusions should be drawn with caution. But the episode has emphasised one key attribute of FDI, namely its much lower volatility as compared with the short-term flows.
- Finally, the interactions between FDI, technology flows and the host-country policy regime have been emphasised. Here the key issue is the link between an open FDI regime, combined with measures to enhance domestic absorptive capacity – principally the human capital base of the host country. One ingredient without the other is unlikely to provide a sustained capacity for technological upgrading.

Notes

* Some of the issues we canvas here were discussed in an earlier paper by the authors (Hill and Athukorala, 1998). This version, written two years on, is now able to offer a more definitive assessment of the impact of the crisis on FDI flows and patterns.

1 For a useful summary, see, for example, Low *et al.*, 1993.

2 In descending order, these were China, Singapore, Malaysia, Thailand, Indonesia and Hong Kong. (Two of these obviously cannot be regarded as 'developing'.) The only countries from outside East Asia to make the list were Mexico and Argentina, ranked fourth and fifth, respectively (see Dunning, 1998: 50).

3 His significant works have recently appeared in an edited collection (see Kojima, 1996).

4 Huff's caution is particularly relevant for the analysis of revealed comparative advantage and the factor content of trade flows based on published trade statistics. For instance, calculations based on SITC-based trade data can 'reveal' a high degree of measured RCA in capital-intensive export production for a country like Malaysia simply because assembly activities are treated as part of the standard category of electronics exports. In reality, what is in aggregate a highly sophisticated capital intensive product line in a high-income economy is generally a very labour-intensive activity in low and middle-income economies, relative to industry averages, and *particularly in electronics.*

5 A widely cited reference in this field is Blomstrom (1989), whose initial work focused on Mexico. See also Blomstrom and Kokko (1998).

6 As a corollary, including international transfers as part of a country's technology base leads to a redefinition of national technology effort, which includes not only the domestic R&D effort but also the imputed equivalent of international transfers. The OECD (1997) has attempted to estimate some of the magnitudes involved, and has found that internationally acquired R&D may be at least as large as that which is domestically generated. In developing countries with a small domestic R&D base and large inflows, the former is probably much more significant. As these international flows data improve, it would be interesting to compute some 'total R&D' figures for developing East Asian economies.

References

Aoki, T. (1992), 'Japanese FDI and the Forming of Networks in the Asia-Pacific Region: Experience in Malaysia and its Implications', in S. Tokunaga (ed.), *Japan's Foreign Investment and Asian Economic Interdependence*, Tokyo: Tokyo University Press, 73–110.

Asian Development Bank (1997), *Emerging Asia: Changes and Challenges*, Manila.

Aswicahyono, H. and H. Hill (1999), '"Perspiration" v/s "Inspiration" in Asian Manufacturing: Indonesia Before the Crisis', *Working Papers in Trade and Development* No. 99/2, Division of Economics, Research School of Pacific and Asian Studies, Australian National University.

Athukorala, P. (1998), *Trade Policy Issues in Asian Development*, London: Routledge.

Athukorala, P. (2000), 'Capital Account Regimes, Crisis and Recovery in Malaysia', *Asian Development Review* 18(1): 17–48.

Athukorala, P. and J. Menon (1997), 'AFTA and the Investment-Trade Nexus in ASEAN', *World Economy*, 20(2), 159–79.

Athukorala, P. and J. Menon (1996), 'Foreign Direct Investment and Industrialisation in Malaysia: Exports, Employment and Spillovers', *Asian Economic Journal*, 10(1), 29–44.

Athukorala, P. and P. G. Warr (1999), 'Vulnerability to a Currency Crisis: Lessons from the Asian Experience', *Working Papers in Trade and Development* No. 99/6, Division of Economics, Research School of Pacific and Asian Studies, Australian National University.

Biggs, Tyler, S. and Brian D. Levy (1991), 'Strategic Interventions and the Political Economy of Industrial Policy in Developing Countries', in D. H. Perkins and M. Roemer (eds), *Reforming Economic Systems in Developing Countries*, Cambridge, Mass.: Harvard Institute for International Development.

Blomstrom, M. (1989), *Foreign Direct Investment Spillovers: A Study of Technology Transfer to Mexico*, London: Routledge.

Blomstrom, M. and A. Kokko (1998), 'Multinational Corporations and Spillover', *Journal of Economic Surveys*, 12(3), 247–77.

Caves, R. E. (1996), *Multinational Enterprise and Economic Analysis*, 2nd edn (1st edn 1982), Cambridge: Cambridge University Press.

Chia S. Y. (1985), 'The Role of Foreign Trade and Investment in the Development of Singapore', in W. Galenson (ed.), *Foreign Trade and Investment: Economic Development in the Newly Industrializing Asian Countries*, Madison, Wis: University of Wisconsin Press, 259–97.

Coe, D. T. and E. Helpman (1995), 'International R&D Spillovers', *European Economic Review*, 39, 859–87.

Cole, W. (1998), 'Bali's Garment Export Industry', in Hill and Thee (eds), 255–78.

Dobson, W. (1997), 'East Asian Integration: Synergies Between Firm Strategies and Government Policies', in Dobson and Chia (eds), 3–27, *Multinationals and East Asian Integration*, Singapore: Institute of Southeast Asian Studies.

Dobson, W. (1997), 'Crossing Borders: Multinationals in East Asia', in Dobson and Chia (eds), 223–48, *Multinationals and East Asian Integration*, Singapore: Institute of Southeast Asian Studies.

Dobson, W. and Chia S. Y. (1997), *Multinationals and East Asian Integration*, Singapore: Institute of Southeast Asian Studies.

Dunning, J. H. (1998), 'Globalization and the New Geography of Foreign Direct Investment', *Oxford Development Studies*, 26(1), 47–70.

Fan, X and P. Warr (2000), 'Foreign Investment, Spillover Effects and the Technology Gap: Evidence from China', *Working Papers in Trade and Development* No. 00/06, Division of Economics, Research School of Pacific and Asian Studies, Australian National University.

Fry, M. J. (1993), *Foreign Direct Investment in Southeast Asia: Differential Impacts*, Singapore: Institute of Southeast Asian Studies.

Grossman, G. and E. Helpman (1991), *Innovation and Growth in the Global Economy*, Cambridge, MA: MIT Press.

Hatch, W. and K. Yamamura (1996), *Asia in Japan's Embrace: Building a Regional Production Alliance*, Cambridge: Cambridge University Press.

Helleiner, G. K. (1988), 'Direct Foreign Investment and Manufacturing for Export in Developing Countries: A Review of the Issues', in S. Dell (ed.), *Policies for Development*, London: Macmillan, 123–53.

Hill, H. (1990), 'Foreign Investment and East Asian Economic Development', *Asian-Pacific Economic Literature*, 4(2), 21–58.

Hill, H. and Athukorala, P. (1998), 'Foreign Investment in East Asia: A Survey', *Asian-Pacific Economic Literature*, 12(2), 23–58.

Hill, H. and Thee K. W. (eds) (1998), *Indonesia's Technological Challenge*, Singapore: Institute of Southeast Asian Studies.

Hobday, M. (1995), *Innovation in East Asia: The Challenge to Japan*, Cheltenham: Edward Elgar.

Hobday, M. (1999), 'Understanding Innovation in Electronics in Malaysia', in K. S. Jomo, G. Felker and R. Rasiah (eds), *Industrial Technology Development in Malaysia: Industry and Firm Studies*, London: Routledge.

Hou, C.-M. and S. Gee (1993), 'National Systems Supporting Technical Advance in Industry: The Case of Taiwan', in R. R. Nelson (ed.), *National Innovation Systems: A Comparative Analysis*, New York: Oxford University Press.

Huff, W. G. (1994), *The Economic Growth of Singapore: Trade and Development in the Twentieth Century*, Cambridge: Cambridge University Press.

Hughes, H. (1993), 'An External View', in Low *et al.* (eds), 1–25.

IMF (International Monetary Fund) (2000), *World Economic Outlook*, April, Washington, DC: International Monetary Fund.

ITC (International Trade Centre) (1987), *Analysis of Trading Channels for the Foreign Trade of the Philippines*, Geneva: ITC.

Johansson, H. and L. Nilsson (1997), 'Export Processing Zones as Catalysts', *World Development*, 25(12), 2115–28.

Jomo, K. S. (ed.) (1993), *Industrialising Malaysia: Policy, Performance, Prospects*, London: Routledge.

Kapellas, J. D. and Liu, H. F. (1990), 'The Growth of ROC Trade and Investment in Southeast Asia', *Journal of Southeast Asian Business*, 6(4), 87–102.

Kim, J.-D. and Y. Wang (1996), 'Towards Liberalization of International Direct Investment in Korea: Retrospects and Prospects', *KIEP Working Paper* 96-02, Korea Institute for International Economic Policy, Seoul.

Kim, L. (1997), *Imitation to Innovation: The Dynamics of Korea's Technological Learning*, Boston: Harvard Business School Press.

Kojima, K. (1996), *Trade, Investment and Pacific Economic Integration: Selected Essays of Kiyoshi Kojima*, Tokyo: Bushindo.

Koo, B. Y. (1985), 'The Role of Direct Foreign Investment in Korea's Recent Economic Growth', in W. Galenson (ed.), *Foreign Trade and Investment: Economic Development in the Newly Industrializing Asian Countries*, Madison, Wis: University of Wisconsin Press.

Krugman, P. (1995), 'Growing World Trade: Causes and Consequences', *Brooking Papers on Economic Activity*, 25th Anniversary Issue: 327–77.

Krugman, P. R. (1997), 'Fire-sale FDI', http:/web.mit.edu/krugman/www/.

Lall, S. (1996), *Learning from the Asian Tigers*, London: Macmillan.

Lai, Y. W. and S. Narayanan (1997), 'The Quest for Technological Competence via MNCs: A Malaysian Case Study', *Asian Economic Journal*, 11(4), 407–22.

Lee, C. H. (1994), 'Korea's Direct Foreign Investment in Southeast Asia', *ASEAN Economic Bulletin*, 10(3), 288–96.

Lim, L. and Pang E. F. (1991), *Foreign Investment and Industrialisation in Malaysia, Singapore, Taiwan and Thailand*, Paris: OECD.

Lin, A.-L. (1996), 'Trade Effects of Foreign direct Investment: Evidence for Taiwan with Four ASEAN Countries', *Weltwirtschaftliches Archiv*, 132(4), 737–47.

Low, L. (1998), 'Science, Technology and the State in Singapore: An Overview, Evaluation and Comparison', *Journal of the Asia Pacific Economy*, 3(2), 183–206.

Low, L., E. D. Ramstetter and H. W. -C. Yeung (1996), 'Accounting for Outward Direct Investment from Hong Kong and Singapore: Who Controls What?', *NBER Working Paper 5858*, Cambridge MA: NBER.

Low, L. *et al.* (eds) (1993), *Challenges and Response: Thirty Years of the Economic Development Board*, Singapore: Times Academic Press.

Mackie, J. A. C. (1992), 'Overseas Chinese Entrepreneurship', *Asian-Pacific Economic Literature*, 6(1), 41–64.

Mead, J. (1951), *The Theory of International Economic Policy, Volume 1: The Balance of Payments*, London: Oxford University Press, chapter XXII.

Nayyar, D. (1978), 'Transnational Corporations and Manufactured Exports from Poor Countries', *Economic Journal*, 88, 59–84.

Naughton, B. (1996), China's Emergence and Prospects as a Trading Nation, *Brookings Papers on Economic Activity*, 2, 293–344.

Nguyen Tuan Dung (1996), 'Foreign Direct Investment in Vietnam', S. Leung (ed.), *Vietnam Assessment: Creating a Sound Investment Climate*, Singapore: Institute of Southeast Asian Studies.

OECD (1997), *Technology and Industrial Performance*, Paris: OECD.

Okamoto, Y. and S. Sjoholm (2000), 'FDI and the Dynamics of Productivity: Microeconomic Evidence', *APEC Discussion Paper Series*, No. 34, Graduate School of International Development, Nagoya University, Nagoya.

Petri, P. A. (1992), 'Platforms in the Pacific: The Trade Effects of Direct Investment in Thailand', *Journal of Asian Economics*, 3(2), 173–96.

Petri, P. A. (1993), 'The East Asian Trading Block: An Analytical History', in J. A. Frankel and M. Kahler (eds), *Regionalism and Rivalry: Japan and the United State in Southeast Asia*, Chicago, IL: University of Chicago Press.

Pomfret, R. (1997), 'Growth and Transition: Why Has China's Performance been So Different', *Journal of Comparative Economics*, 25(4), 422–40.

Radelet, S. and J. Sachs (1997), 'Asia's Reemergence', *Foreign Affairs*, 76(9), 44–59.

Ramstetter, E. D. (1993), 'Prospects for Foreign Firms in Developing Economies in the Asian and Pacific Region', *Asian Development Review*, 11(1), 151–85.

Ramstetter, E. D. (1997), 'Thailand: International Trade, Multinational Firms and Regional Integration', in Dobson and Chia (eds), *Multinational and East Asian Integration*, Singapore: Institute of Southeast Asian Studies.

Ramstetter, E. D. (1999a), 'Comparison of Foreign Multinationals and Local Firms in Asian Manufacturing Over Time', *Asian Economic Journal*, 13(2), 163–204.

Ramstetter, E. D. (1999b), 'Trade Propensities and Foreign Ownership Shares in Indonesian Manufacturing', *Bulletin of Indonesian Economic Studies*, 35(2), 43–66.

Riedel, J. (1991), 'Intra-Asian Trade and Foreign Direct Investment', *Asian Development Review*, 9(1), 111–46.

Riedel, J. (1997), 'Capital Market Integration in Developing Asia', *World Economy*, 20(1), 1–19.

Sato, Y. (1988), 'The Transfer of Japanese Management Technology to Indonesia', in Hill and Thee (eds), *Indonesia's Technological Challenge*, Singapore: Institute of Southeast Asian Studies.

Soesastro, H. (1998), 'Emerging Patterns of Technology Flows in the Asia-Pacific Region: The Relevance to Indonesia', in Hill and Thee (eds), *Indonesia's Technological Challenge*, Singapore: Institute of Southeast Asian Studies.

Tran V. T. (ed.) (1993), *Japanese Management Style and Technology Transfer in Thailand*, Research Report No. 3, Tokyo: Japan Center for Economic Research.

UNCTAD (annual), *World Investment Report*, New York and Geneva: United Nations.

UNCTAD (1998), *The Financial Crisis in Asia and Foreign Direct Investment*, Geneva: United Nations.

UNTCMD (United Nations Transnational Corporation and Management Division) (1982), *World Investment Report 1992: Transnational Corporations as Engines of Growth*, Geneva: United Nations.

Wells, L. T. (1994), 'Mobile Exporters: New Foreign Investors in East Asia', in K. A. Foot (ed.), 173–91, *Foreign Direct Investment*, Chicago: University of Chicago Press.

World Bank (1997), *Private Capital Flows to Developing Countries: The Road to Financial Integration*, New York: Oxford University Press.

World Bank (1999), *Global Development Finance*, Washington, DC: World Bank.

12 IPRs and FDI

Keith E. Maskus

Introduction

The global system of intellectual property rights (IPRs) is changing profoundly. Many developing countries have undertaken significant strengthening of their IPRs regimes. Several regional trading arrangements now address questions of regulatory convergence, particularly in IPRs. Most significant is the introduction of the agreement on trade-related IPRs, or TRIPs, within the World Trade Organization (WTO). Under TRIPs, WTO members must adopt and enforce strong and non-discriminatory minimum standards of protection for intellectual property. Many developed countries are extending strong protection to controversial areas, including biotechnology and electronic databases.

The movement toward much stronger global IPRs is consistent with processes of economic globalization, or the successively closer integration of national and regional markets through the reduction of barriers to trade, investment, and technology flows. In this world, knowledge creation and its adaptation to product designs and production techniques are increasingly essential for competitiveness and growth. This situation takes on political importance because the international mobility of capital and technology have risen markedly relative to that of most types of labor. In turn, globalization pays its largest rewards to creative and skilled workers and places its largest pressures on lower-skilled workers.

Markets are becoming more integrated through changes in both natural forces and government policies. The former group consists of falling transport costs, improving global communications, and massively increasing computing power. The latter group includes trade liberalization, deregulation of investment and licensing restrictions, provision of establishment rights in services, privatization of state-owned enterprises, adoption of freely traded currencies, and tax reform. The central feature of policy making in many emerging economies in the 1990s has been a sharp movement toward improving market access, through both unilateral policy reform and adherence to regional and multilateral trade agreements.

The channels through which globalization affects economies include trade, portfolio investment and foreign direct investment (FDI), and product and technology licensing. FDI is particularly important because it is both a source of capital and a provider of knowledge about production techniques.

The direct impact of globalization is stronger arbitrage of international prices of goods and tradable services and greater access by consumers and firms in each liberalizing country to new and more varied products and technologies on international markets. In turn, such economies experience increases in competition, reductions in domestic market power of formerly concentrated industrial concerns, re-allocations of economic resources into areas of comparative advantage, falling production costs in sectors with increasing returns to scale, and contraction or elimination of uncompetitive firms. Over the long term, competitive pressures encourage adoption of advanced technologies and development of high-quality, differentiated products for both domestic production and export. The stronger markets encouraged by liberalization could lead to a permanently higher growth rate.

There is considerable evidence to support this optimistic view of globalization. However, there are potential costs; greater competition changes demands for labor in each country, with unskilled workers bearing the brunt of competitive pressures. Also of concern are potential abuses of market power to the extent that larger international firms are placed into a position of market dominance by virtue of their marketing advantages or technological superiority.

This brief review suggests that developing countries have rising interests in attracting FDI and technology. However, policies to promote such activities must be accompanied by programs to build local skills and ensure that the benefits of competition emerge. IPRs are an important element in a broader policy package that governments in developing economies could pursue with a view toward promoting dynamic competition in which local firms participate significantly. This broad "cocktail" of policies would include promoting political stability, encouraging flexible labor markets and building labor skills, continuing to liberalize markets, and developing forward-looking regulatory regimes in services, investment, intellectual property, and competition policy.

It is beyond the scope of this chapter to consider each of these issues and their complex interrelationships. Instead I consider the issue of how IPRs influence FDI and technology inflows, which is the subject of the section on econometric evidence on IPRs and FDI. I then overview, in the following section, the available economic evidence about IPRs as a determinant of FDI. In the next section I discuss the potential benefits and costs of incoming FDI and technology transfer, emphasizing information spillovers and diffusion. Throughout, the impact of IPRs is considered. I also present the broad outlines of a pro-competitive strategy for attracting investment and technology. Inevitably, such strategies vary across countries by level of economic development and technological capability, but there are important common denominators. In a final section I discuss outstanding research issues and provide concluding remarks.

Investment and IPRs

The means by which IPRs influence FDI are complex and subtle. Furthermore, strong IPRs alone are not sufficient incentives for firms to invest in a country.

If they were, recent FDI flows to developing economies would have gone mainly to sub-Saharan Africa and Eastern Europe. In contrast, China, Brazil, and other high-growth, large-market developing economies with weak protection would not have attracted nearly as much FDI. And as noted above, IPRs are an important component of the regulatory system, including taxes, investment regulations, production incentives, trade policies, and competition rules. Thus, from a policy perspective, it is the existence of a pro-competitive business environment that matters overall for FDI.

Nonetheless, it is useful first to discuss how the strength of IPRs could affect FDI decisions. Ultimately, what matters to the firm is the likelihood that an investment will raise its expected profits. While there are numerous factors that influence profitability, the issue regarding IPRs is the extent to which the regime affects the firm's perception that it will be able to earn a higher return on its protected knowledge-based assets (KBAs) through FDI, relative to other means of earning such returns.

This complex subject allows few clear conclusions. A firm with a KBA has numerous options in servicing a particular foreign market. It could export the goods through standard channels. It could produce locally within the firm through FDI, thereby directly controlling the production process. It could license or franchise its asset to an unrelated firm and allow local production in return for royalties and fees. Finally, it could enter into a joint venture involving some common production or technology-sharing agreement. These decisions are jointly determined and more than one mode of supply could emerge.

Trade is likely to be the primary channel where transport costs and tariffs are low in relation to FDI and licensing costs. The relationship between export volume and the strength of local IPRs has been analysed by Maskus and Penubarti (1995). Strong IPRs in all forms – patents, trademarks, copyrights, and trade secrets – provide protection for exporting firms against local imitation, thereby increasing the market size facing exporters and inducing them to expand sales. This "market-expansion effect" is likely to be important in countries with large markets and established technical capabilities for imitating products and technologies. However, IPRs permit such firms additional market power, although concerns about the competitive implications of this "monopoly effect" are often exaggerated (Maskus and Eby-Konan, 1994). It is more likely to prevail in countries with small markets and limited imitative abilities. Empirical evidence shows that, other things equal, countries with stronger IPRs do attract more imports, though the effect varies across industries (Maskus and Penubarti, 1995). Stronger trademarks seem particularly significant in increasing imports of clothing and other consumer goods because the low costs of knocking off such products under weak trademarks limits interest of foreign firms in offering them for export. In effect, stronger trademarks reduce exporting costs because a firm is less compelled to discipline local imitators through lower prices. This phenomenon holds also in pharmaceuticals, though they are more likely to be produced under local license than imported. Export volumes in goods that are difficult to imitate, such as certain kinds of machinery, or are less dependent on trademarks, such as basic metal manufactures, are less sensitive to IPRs. These results have been refined by Smith (1998), who reached similar conclusions.

FDI is likely to displace exports where there are high trade and transport costs,[1] low fixed costs of erecting plants, high productivity relative to labor costs, large host market size, and substantial R&D and marketing intensities of the products in question. The last factor, reflecting the intellectual component of the firm's advantage, is an important determinant of horizontal FDI in differentiated goods and advanced technologies.

According to this analysis, IPRs should have variable degrees of importance in different sectors in terms of encouraging FDI. Investment in lower-technology goods and services, such as textiles and apparel, electronic assembly, distribution, and hotels, depends far less on the strength of IPRs than on input costs and market opportunities. Firms investing in a product or technology that is costly to imitate may also place little emphasis on local IPRs in location decisions, though falling imitation costs in many sectors raise the importance of IPRs. Firms with easily copyable products and technologies, such as pharmaceuticals, chemicals, food additives, and software, are more concerned with the ability of the local IPRs system to deter imitation. Firms considering where to invest in a local R&D facility would pay particular attention to protection for patents and trade secrets.

The evidence reported in Mansfield (1994) is consistent with these observations. In a survey of 100 major US firms representing six industries, intellectual-property executives were asked their opinions of the importance of IPRs in their FDI and licensing decisions and their assessments of the adequacy of IPRs in sixteen countries. Table 12.1 shows the survey responses regarding type of investment facility. There is little concern in any industry about IPRs protecting the operation of sales and distribution outlets. In the chemical industry, which includes pharmaceuticals, 46 per cent of firms are concerned about protection for basic production and assembly facilities, 71 per cent for components manufacture, 87 per cent for complete products manufacture, and 100 per cent for R&D facilities. This tendency to

Table 12.1 Percentage of firms claiming that the strength or weakness of IPRs has a strong effect on whether direct investments will be made, by type of facility, 1991

Sector	*Sales and distribution*	*Basic production and assembly*	*Components manufacture*	*Complete products manufacture*	*R&D facilities*	*Average*
Chemicals	19	46	71	87	100	65
Transport equipment	17	17	33	33	80	36
Electrical equipment	15	40	57	74	80	53
Food products	29	29	25	43	60	37
Metals	20	40	50	50	80	48
Machinery	23	23	50	65	77	48
Average	20	32	48	59	80	48

Source: Mansfield (1994).

be more concerned with IPRs, the higher the stage of production, holds in all sectors. Overall, chemicals firms are most influenced in their investment decisions, while in all sectors strong concerns exist about local IPRs in locating R&D operations. In a related analysis, Mansfield (1995) shows that these conclusions hold also for Japanese and German MNCs.

Table 12.2 presents further results for selected countries with weak IPRs. India elicits the greatest concern about IPRs, with 80 per cent of the chemical firms surveyed indicating that they would not engage in joint ventures or transfer new technologies to subsidiaries or unrelated firms due to weak protection. There is little difference between joint ventures and subsidiaries in this regard. Both activities

Table 12.2 Percentage of firms claiming that intellectual property protection is too weak to permit types of investment, 1991

Country	*Chemicals*	*Transport equipment*	*Electrical equipment*	*Food products*	*Metals*	*Machinery*	*Average*
Panel A: Joint ventures with local partners							
Argentina	40	0	29	12	0	27	18
Brazil	47	40	31	12	0	65	32
India	80	40	39	38	20	48	44
Indonesia	50	40	29	25	0	25	28
Mexico	47	20	30	25	0	17	22
Korea	33	20	21	12	25	26	23
Thailand	43	80	32	12	0	20	31
Average[a]	49	34	30	19	6	33	
Panel B: Transfer of newest or most effective technology to wholly owned subsidiaries							
Argentina	44	20	21	12	0	14	18
Brazil	50	40	24	12	0	39	28
India	81	40	38	38	20	41	43
Indonesia	40	20	31	25	0	23	23
Mexico	31	20	21	25	0	22	20
Korea	31	20	28	12	40	22	26
Thailand	60	80	31	12	0	18	20
Average[a]	48	34	28	19	9	26	
Panel C: Licensing of newest or most effective technology to unrelated firms							
Argentina	62	0	26	12	0	29	22
Brazil	69	40	29	25	0	73	39
India	81	40	38	38	20	50	44
Indonesia	73	20	33	25	0	37	31
Mexico	56	20	28	25	0	36	28
Korea	38	20	34	12	40	29	29
Thailand	73	80	36	12	0	25	38
Average[a]	65	31	32	21	9	40	

Source: Mansfield (1994).

Note

a Average over the seven countries listed.

evidently afford chemical firms with similar levels of security about their technologies (though there is more concern about joint ventures in Mexico and Indonesia). However, across all countries licensing to unrelated firms is seen as riskier than joint ventures. This situation seems also to characterize machinery. In the other sectors, however, there is little difference in the willingness to transfer technology through various modes according to weakness in IPRs.

Thus, licensing is perceived to be insecure relative to investment in the high-technology sectors in countries with weak IPRs. This fact illustrates a subtle aspect of intellectual property protection. Firms prefer FDI to licensing when they have a complex technology and highly differentiated products and when there are high costs of transferring technology through licensing (Teece, 1986; Davidson and McFetridge, 1984; 1985; Horstmann and Markusen, 1987). In these situations it is efficient to internalize the costs of technology transfer through FDI in a majority-owned subsidiary. As IPRs improve, licensing costs should fall because it becomes easier to discipline licensees against revelation or appropriation of proprietary technology and against misuse of a trademark. Thus, for a given level of complexity of innovations, we would expect to see licensing supplant FDI as IPRs are strengthened.

A summary of the predictions about IPRs, FDI, and technology transfer is in order. First, investment and technology transfer are relatively insensitive to IPRs in industries with standardized, labor-intensive technologies amd products. Second, FDI representing complex but easily copied technologies is likely to increase as IPRs are strengthened because such rights enhance the value of KBAs, allowing efficient exploitation through internal organization structures. Third, to the degree that stronger IPRs reduce licensing costs, FDI could be displaced by licensing. Finally, whatever the channel, the quality of technologies transferred rises with the strength of IPRs.

An implication of this logic is that rapidly growing developing countries should develop a natural interest in improving their IPRs regime over time as they move up the "technology ladder" to an ability to absorb and even develop more sophisticated innovations. This is perhaps the strongest argument to make in favor of adopting stronger protection in nations such as Korea, Brazil, and Malaysia. In the early stages of their industrial growth, such countries have an interest in being able to imitate imported technologies. As they develop, however, they become increasingly willing to tighten IPRs, both in order to attract the most modern technologies and to encourage local innovation. This prediction is consistent with the international pattern of patent protection (Maskus and Penubarti, 1995).

Nevertheless, the implications of stronger IPRs for technology transfer are ambiguous in principle. Technological information is diffused across firms or countries through several channels. Regarding patents, on the one hand they facilitate information transfer (if not the spread of know-how) by revealing the details of inventions in published applications. This information then may be used by rival firms to develop follow-on products that do not violate the patent scope. As more countries award and enforce patents, there should be additional global innovation and patenting, with a positive impact on follower innovation. On the other hand, patents could reduce technology diffusion by permitting restrictive licensing arrangements for critical technologies. This has long been the view of patents in many developing nations.

Recent theoretical analyses of the effects of patents on technology diffusion in growth models contain mixed messages. In some models, technology is transferred through imitation by firms in technology importers. When the international IPRs system adopts stronger minimum standards, imitation becomes harder as foreign patents are enforced. The rate of imitation declines, which ultimately reduces the global rate of innovation as well because as innovative firms expect slower loss of their technological advantages they earn higher profits per innovation, reducing the need to engage in R&D (Helpman, 1993; Glass and Saggi, 1995).

This result is sensitive to model assumptions. Indeed, Lai (1998) finds that product innovation and technology diffusion are expanded under stronger property rights if technology is transferred through FDI rather than imitation. This finding points up the advantages for developing economies of liberalising restrictions against inward FDI as they strengthen their IPRs. Yang and Maskus (2001) demonstrate that because IPRs reduce contracting costs (associated with information asymmetries), licensing activity and innovation could expand with stronger protection. Vishwasrao (1994) shows in that, while the mode of technology transfer is affected by IPRs protection, with internalization through FDI the preferred solution in countries with weak patents, the quality of technologies transferred rises with stronger IPRs. Taylor (1994) also shows that technology transfer expands with stronger patents when there is competition between a foreign innovator and a domestic innovator. A failure to provide patents removes the incentive for the foreign firm to license its best-practice technologies. Rockett (1990) finds that in cases where local imitation focuses on licensed technology, foreign licensors make available lower-quality technologies. This reduces the licensee's incentive to imitate, limiting both the quality and extent of knowledge transfer.

Studies of international patenting behavior (Eaton and Kortum, 1996) indicate that the value of patent rights varies across countries and technology fields, but is typically significant in important developing countries, suggesting that stronger patents would encourage further R&D, patent applications, and patent working. There are considerable spillovers of technological knowledge through patenting and trade in patented products. Indeed, Eaton and Kortum (1996) claim that OECD countries have derived substantial productivity growth from importing knowledge through patent applications, with US applications serving as the driving force.

The transfer of technology through trade in technical inputs (machinery, chemicals, software, producer services, and so on) is also important. Evidence suggests that such trade accounts for significant productivity gains across borders and is part of the technology convergence among developed economies (Coe and Helpman, 1995). This suggests that emerging economies have a joint interest in trade liberalization and linking their IPRs systems with those of the developed countries. Resulting productivity gains could outweigh costs associated with market power.

A final comment about the emerging system of global IPRs is in order. To the degree that different levels of IPRs across countries are a locational determinant of FDI and technology transfer, the trend toward harmonization of IPRs could offset such advantages. Thus, it would make more attractive those countries that strengthen their IPRs but would reduce the relative attractiveness of countries already providing strong IPRs. This harmonization of global minimum standards presents great opportunities for firms that develop technologies and products because they will no longer have to pay as much attention to localized protection and enforcement problems. Rather, they can focus their R&D programs on those areas with the highest global payoffs. Ultimately, however, it means that IPRs no longer will play much role in determining locational choice.

The discussion so far has presented a narrow interpretation of how IPRs interact with incentives for FDI and technology transfer. However, it could be that effective IPRs play a larger role in signaling to potential investors that a particular country recognizes the rights of foreign firms to make strategic business decisions without government interference (Sherwood, 1990). In this view, trade liberalization is insufficient to provide assurances that an economy is becoming more open to international commerce. Market access could remain blocked by inefficient investment regulations, limited rights of establishment, controls on credit, production, and marketing, arbitrary taxes, licensing restrictions, and weak IPRs. The need to attain market access through rationalization of these internal barriers is now at the top of the international trade-policy agenda (Hoekman, 1997). Some observers also consider IPRs to convey a commitment to move from opaque to transparent legal systems and from corruption to professionalism in public management.

As IPRs take on increasing importance to MNCs, the adoption of stronger regimes has become a primary signal that governments are moving toward a more business friendly environment. The objective is to attract more FDI through this signal, whatever the incentives that may be generated in various industries by stronger IPRs. There is little evidence to date suggesting that FDI is responsive to this signal, but belief in its importance is growing in developing economies. This phenomenon explains why many poor countries have strengthened their IPRs laws and enforcement despite serious questions about the wisdom of doing so. They fear being left behind in the global competition for capital and technology.

Econometric evidence on IPRs and FDI

It is apparent that IPRs could play an important role in FDI decisions. However, they have rarely been incorporated into empirical work on the determinants of investment, largely because of the inherent difficulty of measuring IPRs and their impacts. However, a few economists have recently examined the strength of IPRs in different countries as a potential determinant of FDI.

Three early studies (Ferrantino, 1993; Mansfield, 1993; Maskus and Eby-Konan, 1994) found no relationship between crude measures of intellectual property protection and international FDI by US MNCs. However, their models were limited in specification and plagued by poor measurement, and their results should be discounted.

Two recent studies are worth discussing. Lee and Mansfield (1996) surveyed American MNCs to develop an index of perceived weakness of IPRs in destination countries. They regressed the volume of US direct investment in various countries over the period 1990–92 on this index, along with measures of market size, the past investment stock, the degree of industrialization, a measure of openness, and a dummy variable for Mexico. In their work, weakness of IPRs was found to have a significant negative impact on the location of American FDI. Further, among MNCs in the chemical industry the percentage of FDI devoted to final production or R&D facilities was negatively and significantly associated with weakness of protection. The weakness of IPRs had less impact on the decisions of firms with minority ownership of local affiliates because such firms would be unlikely to transfer their most advanced technologies in any case. Thus, it appears that both the quantity and technological sophistication of FDI are reduced in countries with limited IPRs.

Maskus (1998) argued that analysts must recognize the joint decisions made by MNCs. Firms may choose to export, increase sales from foreign operations, raise investment, or transfer technology directly in response to stronger patent rights. He estimated a set of simultaneous equations to measure these joint

Table 12.3 Elasticities of modes of supply with respect to domestic characteristics and policies

Variable	*Asset stock*	*Affiliate sales*	*Intrafirm exports to Aff.*	*Patent apps.*
Real GDP	0.25	0.30	0.13	0.19
Tariff level	−0.02	−0.00[a]	−0.01	−0.01
Affiliate R&D	0.27	0.29	0.15	0.07
Distance	−0.25	−0.02	−0.03	0.02
Incentives	0.97	0.24	0.13	0.17
Disincentives	−0.25	−0.02	0.02	−0.01
Patent strength in developing countries	0.45	0.05	−0.02	0.69

Source: Adapted from Maskus (1998).

Note

a Coefficient is not significantly different from zero. Asset stock is total assets of foreign non-bank affiliates of US parents in $ millions; Affiliate sales is total sales of foreign affiliates in $ millions; Intrafirm exports to affiliate is US exports shipped to affiliates in $ millions; Patent applications is number filed in the host country; Real GDP in the host country is in $ billions; Tariff level is tariff revenues divided by total imports; Affiliate R&D is expenditure on R&D by foreign affiliates in $ millions; Distance is kilometers of capital city from Washington, DC; Incentives is the number of affiliates that received tax concessions in the host country divided by the number that received tax concessions in all the sample countries; Disincentives is number of affiliates required to employ a minimum amount of local personnel divided by the number of affiliates that are so constrained in all the sample countries; Patent strength is an endogeneity-corrected index of patent laws and enforcement.

impacts, controlling for market size, tariff protection, the level of local R&D by affiliates, distance from the United States, and investment incentives and disincentives provided by local authorities. This was done for a panel of 46 destination countries over the period 1989–92. The index of patent strength was the same as that in Maskus and Penubarti (1995).

Table 12.3 lists his preferred specifications, with coefficients transformed into elasticities. From these results it seems that FDI, as measured by the asset stock, reacts positively to patent strength in developing countries. The data suggest that a one-percent increase in the degree of patent protection would expand the stock of US investment in that country by 0.45 per cent, other things equal. This elasticity is significantly positive and is second in magnitude only to the impact of incentives. While these results need to be subjected to robustness tests, they suggest that FDI is sensitive to IPRs.

Policies to attract beneficial FDI and technology transfer

This analysis points out that, in theory, investment and technology transfer do not necessarily expand with stronger IPRs, but there is emerging evidence in favor of that view. It is increasingly assumed around the globe that FDI and licensing are beneficial for the recipient country. As discussed in this section, there is a strong presumption in this direction but it is not a necessary outcome in all situations. Rather, it is important that such flows result in stronger competition on local markets, which tends to promote long-run gains. After a brief review of the potential benefits and costs of these activities, I discuss components of a broad policy framework for raising the likelihood that stronger IPRs contribute to greater dynamic competition.

Benefits and costs of inward FDI and licensing

Although their impacts differ across countries, FDI and licensing bear great promise for improving efficiency and expanding growth in developing countries, particularly those that are scarce in capital, are far from the efficient production frontier, and have limited managerial and entrepreneurial talents. These flows provide access to the technological and managerial assets of foreign MNCs, which provide both a direct spur to productivity and significant spillover benefits. These benefits from diffusion obtain through several mechanisms, including the movement of trained labor among firms, the laying out of patents, product innovation through the legitimate "inventing around" of patents and copyrights, and the adoption of newer and more efficient specialized inputs, such as software, that reduce production costs. Further, competition with subsidiaries of efficient international enterprises can stimulate local entrepreneurship and innovation. There may also be beneficial demonstration effects for local firms.

Thus, exposure to competition-enhancing FDI and licensing should improve the knowledge base of the economy and move it toward the globally efficient production frontier. There is clear evidence that developing countries suffer from lagging labor productivity and managerial efficiency, related in part to a failure to adopt newest technologies (Trefler, 1995; Baumol *et al.*, 1992). Recent experiences in numerous developing economies indicate that liberalization of trade policies and investment regimes can have significantly positive growth impacts in the medium term, even if there is some initial economic adjustment period. Further, a major source of relatively rapid economic growth and industrial restructuring in East Asia in recent decades has been access to foreign technologies through both licensing and FDI in addition to importation of advanced machinery and other technical inputs (World Bank, 1993). Additional benefits include access to a wider variety of specialized products, inputs, and technologies, a deeper and better-trained skilled labor pool, and rising real wages.

These beneficial impacts of inward FDI and technology transfer do not come without costs. If there are not important linkages to other economic sectors, FDI may operate in enclaves and have few spillovers into technologies adopted and wages earned by local firms and workers.[2] This limited diffusion could be insufficient to compensate the economy for the profits taken out by the MNC. That is, because profit repatriation and license fees are the payments emerging countries make for incoming capital, technology, and advanced producer services, the terms of this exchange could be unfavorable in a social sense, if not in a private sense. This situation is exacerbated to the degree that MNCs engage in abusive practices of their protected market positions in exploiting stronger IPRs. Such abuses could emerge in setting restrictive licensing conditions, requiring technology grant-backs, engaging in tied sales, tying up technology fields through cross-licensing agreements, establishing vertical controls through distribution outlets that prevent product competition, price discrimination, and predation against local firms. Thus, countries could find certain sectors of their economies coming under increasing control of MNCs through exploitation of their specific advantages, including brand names, patented technology, marketing skills, and economies of scale.

While these costs are possible, there is little evidence that they are systematic problems in many countries. Fundamentally, they stem from an economy's failure to build a policy system that promotes the maximum gains from FDI. For instance, enclave production emerges when the subsidiary is encouraged to produce only for export rather than to compete locally. Firms that are provided access to local and regional markets are more likely to erect complementary business systems, involving production, distribution, and services, that compete widely in the economy and generate spillover benefits. Abusive practices are possible only to the extent that monopoly positions are protected and not disciplined. Many countries have not yet developed appropriate competition rules to deal with these issues.

IPRs

Seen properly, IPRs do not necessarily generate monopoly market positions that result in high prices, limited access, and exclusive use of technologies. They are more similar to standard property rights, in that they define the conditions within which a right owner competes with rivals (UNCTAD, 1996). Except in particular sectors, cases are infrequent in which a patent holder or copyright owner becomes a strong monopolist. There are still competing products and technologies, including new ones that do not infringe the property right. In this context, much depends on the scope of the product and process claims protected and on the technical characteristics of the invention. For example, narrow patent claims are relatively easy to invent around in generating follow-on innovation.

Thus, IPRs encourage dynamic competition, even if they sometimes diminish static competition among existing products. Advocates of strong IPRs maintain that they create competition with long-run consumer benefits. For example, survey evidence indicates that patent disclosure requirements are significant mechanisms for diffusing technical information to competitors within a short period (Mansfield, 1985). The information may then be used to develop a new product or process that competes with the original. This incremental nature of innovation is a key fact in most technical progress and generally builds dynamic competition rather than investing impenetrable market power. Thus, IPRs can raise imitation costs but likely do not significantly slow down competing product introduction. Moreover, patents and trademarks provide greater certainty to firms, lower the costs of transferring technology, and facilitate monitoring of licensee operations. Additional licensing could then result in greater adaptive innovation in user firms.

In this view, stronger IPRs in developing economies promise long-term benefits as they attract FDI and licensing and encourage follow-on innovation and technology spillovers. This outcome is only likely to emerge if the implementation of stronger IPRs is accompanied by complementary policies that promote dynamic competition.

Broader policy approaches

Freer market access, together with sensible competition rules and related regulatory systems, promise to promote the greatest net benefits from incoming investment. Thus, economies that wish to increase their attractiveness to foreign investors would be advised first to undertake significant market liberalization. While the Uruguay Round committed most countries to cutting trade barriers, further reduction of tariffs and removal of NTBs on a credible schedule would provide an important signal to foreign investors. Regional trade integration, particularly with developed economies that could be the source of additional FDI, could assist in this process. However, such agreements also bear potential for trade and investment diversion and should be considered carefully in each instance.

Developing countries should also establish and encourage rights of establishment in services, in light of the complementary nature of FDI in production and services with trade. Removal or rationalization of investment regulations, such as equity restrictions, content requirements, and limitations on profit repatriation, would expand incentives to invest. It is likely that such regulations generate net welfare losses for the countries imposing them. Finally, privatization of state-owned enterprises could attract further capital as it raises domestic competition.

It is important for emerging economies to pursue sound and stable macroeconomic policies. Development of modern and efficient infrastructure could be instrumental in promoting agglomeration gains that attract cumulatively higher amounts of both domestic and foreign investment. There is also evidence that FDI flows are sensitive to international variations in taxes and incentives (Grubert and Mutti, 1991). While this provides some argument for fiscal advantages, such as tax holidays and accelerated depreciation allowances, it clearly suggests the gains from establishing relatively low tax rates and uniform tax treatment of all investors without discrimination. Certainty and stability in taxes are more effective in promoting investment than are discriminatory and arbitrary policies, while uniform tax schedules can generate considerable efficiencies in resource usage.

A critical component of any program to attract high-quality FDI and technology transfer is the development of a strong indigenous technological capacity. This calls for public and private investments in education and training and the removal of impediments to the acquisition of human capital. It also points toward the development of national innovation systems that promote dynamic competition (UNCTAD, 1996). Such programs include support for basic research capabilities, removal of disincentives for applied R&D and its commercialization, establishment of incentive structures to help stimulate local innovation, and access to scientific and technical information that exists within the global information infrastructure.

Finally, IPRs are important in technology development programs. In implementing stronger IPRs, emerging economies need to find an appropriate balance between needs for technology acquisition, market access, and information diffusion. Most nations will wish to adopt a set of IPRs that do not significantly disadvantage follow-on inventors and creators, allowing sensible fair-use exemptions, issuing compensated compulsory licenses under tightly defined conditions, and carefully defining the scope of protection. Furthermore, it will be important to implement effective competition rules to ensure that IPRs systems are pro-competitive. Each of these policy initiatives requires the development of considerable administrative and judicial expertise. For example, countries may wish to monitor the terms of key technology licensing agreements or to intervene in contracts for the development of indigenous public resources.

Issues for research

This chapter has reviewed theory and evidence on how IPRs may influence decisions on FDI and technology transfers. The message is that, while there are indications that strengthening IPRs can be an effective incentive for inward FDI, it is only a component of a broader set of factors. Policy makers should recognize the complementarities among IPRs, market liberalization and deregulation, technology development policies, and competition regimes. These are complex issues, leading to complicated tradeoffs for market participants. Governments may wish to devote considerable attention and analysis to devising means for assuring their countries will achieve net gains from stronger IPRs and additional IPRs and licensing over time.

In this context, considerable scope remains for research into the linkages between IPRs and FDI. The empirical evidence to date suffers from three primary problems. First, data on international FDI flows remain scarce. Beyond the United States, few countries publish more than minimal information on inward and outward investment and the operations of MNCs in terms of employment, sales, and intra-firm trade. In the intellectual property area, the need is acute for sectoral breakdowns of investment in as many nations as possible, both as source and host countries. Second, measurement problems are endemic in this area. It is difficult to capture the economic incentives afforded by a system of laws, regulations, and enforcement, such as IPRs, in a meaningful international index. Unlike taxes and tariffs, which establish measurable price wedges that may be removed in assessing their economic impacts, IPRs form part of the business framework and may have variable impacts in different situations. For example, it would be useful for analytical purposes to understand the "tariff-equivalent" price effects of strengthening IPRs, but these would depend on local market structure and collateral regulation. Thus, economists could devote more effort to characterising the competitive impacts of IPRs in different situations, with a view to understanding the resulting incentives for FDI.

A third problem is that econometric model specification to date has been inadequate to delve deeply into the relationships among FDI and IPRs. Virtually all studies of the international economic flows induced by international variations in IPRs have been static in nature, ignoring the inherently dynamic impacts on innovation, diffusion, and FDI. This points again to the need for more extensive data (across countries and sectors and over time) on investment. Moreover, as discussed earlier, econometric models need to account more carefully for the multiple and simultaneous channels through which international firms operate, including investment, trade, licensing, and registering for patents, and trademarks. Each of these flows depends on each other and on the evolving structure of IPRs, in ways that economic theory is only now beginning to explore. Thus, considerably more econometric work at the international level is needed to be confident about such impacts. In doing so, however, economists will encounter further data problems, such as scarcity of information about licensing contracts.

Finally, it bears repeating for research purposes that IPRs do not operate in isolation, but rather interact with market structures, competition rules, and deregulation of trade and investment to determine the effective strength of those rights and the resulting incentives for FDI. A substantial, but nevertheless rewarding, research agenda arises for comparative analytical and econometric studies of these linkages across countries.

Notes

1 This is a relative comparison. It is not that raising trade barriers would attract FDI, but rather that high tariffs in relation to fixed costs are associated with FDI.
2 For example, Aitken *et al.* (1996) provide evidence that US multinationals operating in Mexico and Venezuela pay significantly higher wages than average to their own employees but these wage impacts have not spread to other parts of the economy.

References

Aitken, Brian, Ann Harrison, and Robert E. Lipsey (1996), "Wages and Foreign Ownership: A Comparative Study of Mexico, Venezuela, and the United States," *Journal of International Economics*, 40: 345–72.

Baumol, William J., Sue Anne Batey Blackman, and Edward N. Wolff (1992), *Productivity and American Leadership: The Long View*, Cambridge: MIT Press.

Coe, David and Elhanan Helpman (1995), "International R&D Spillovers," *European Economic Review*, 39: 859–87.

Davidson, William H. and Donald G. McFetridge (1984), "International Technology Transactions and the Theory of the Firm," *Journal of Industrial Economics*, 32: 253–64.

—— (1985), "Key Characteristics in the Choice of International Technology Transfer Mode," *Journal of International Business Studies*, Summer, 5–21.

Eaton, Jonathan and Samuel J. Kortum (1996), "Trade in Ideas: Patenting and Productivity in the OECD," *Journal of International Economics*, 40: 251–78.

Ferrantino, Michael J. (1993), "The Effect of Intellectual Property Rights on International Trade and Investment," *Weltwirtschaftliches Archiv*, 129: 300–31.

Glass, Amy and Kamal Saggi (1995), "Intellectual Property Rights, Foreign Direct Investment, and Innovation," Ohio State University, manuscript.

Grubert, Harry and John Mutti (1991), "Taxes, Tariffs, and Transfer Pricing in Multinational Corporate Decision Making," *Review of Economics and Statistics*, 71: 285–94.

Helpman, Elhanan (1993), "Innovation, Imitation, and Intellectual Property Rights," *Econometrica*, 61: 1247–80.

Hoekman, Bernard (1997), "Focal Points and Multilateral Negotiations on the Contestability of Markets," in K. E. Maskus, P. Hooper, E. E. Leamer, and J. D. Richardson (eds), *Quiet Pioneering: Robert M. Stern and His International Economic Legacy*, Ann Arbor: University of Michigan Press.

Horstmann, Ignatius and James R. Markusen (1987), "Licensing Versus Direct Investment: A Model of Internalization by the Multinational Enterprise," *Canadian Journal of Economics*, 20: 464–81.

Lai, Edwin L. C. (1998), "International Intellectual Property Rights Protection and the Rate of Product Innovation," *Journal of Development Economics*, 55: 115–30.

Lee, Jeong-Yeon and Mansfield, Edwin (1996), "Intellectual Property Protection and U.S. Foreign Direct Investment," *Review of Economics and Statistics*, 78: 181–6.

Mansfield, Edwin (1985), "How Rapidly Does Industrial Technology Leak Out?" *Journal of Industrial Economics*, 34: 217–23.

—— (1993), "Unauthorized Use of Intellectual Property: Effects on Investment, Technology Transfer, and Innovation," in M. B. Wallerstein, M. E. Mogee, and R. A. Schoen (eds), *Global Dimensions of Intellectual Property Rights in Science and Technology*, Washington, DC: National Academy Press.

—— (1994), *Intellectual Property Protection, Foreign Direct Investment, and Technology Transfer*, International Finance Corporation, Discussion Paper 19.

—— (1995), *Intellectual Property Protection, Direct Investment and Technology Transfer: Germany, Japan, and the United States*, International Finance Corporation, Discussion Paper 27.

Maskus, Keith E. (1998), "The International Regulation of Intellectual Property," *Weltwirtschaftliches Archiv*, 123: 196–208.

Maskus, Keith E. and Denise Eby-Konan (1994), "Trade-Related Intellectual Property Rights: Issues and Exploratory Results," in Alan V. Deardorff and Robert M. Stern (eds), *Analytical and Negotiating Issues in the Global Trading System*, Ann Arbor: University of Michigan Press.

Maskus, Keith E. and Mohan Penubarti (1995), "How Trade-Related are Intellectual Property Rights?" *Journal of International Economics*, 39: 227–48.

Rockett, Katharine (1990), "The Quality of Licensed Technology," *International Journal of Industrial Economics*, 8: 559–74.

Sherwood, Robert M. (1990), *Intellectual Property and Economic Development*, Boulder, CO: Westview Press.

Smith, Pamela J. (1998), "Are Weak Patent Rights a Barrier to U.S. Exports?" *Journal of International Economics*, 48: 151–77.

Taylor, M. Scott (1994), "Trips, Trade, and Growth," *International Economic Review*, 35: 361–81.

Teece, David J. (1986), *The Multinational Corporation and the Resource Cost of International Technology Transfer*, Cambridge: Ballinger.

Trefler, Daniel (1995), "The Case of the Missing Trade and Other Mysteries," *American Economic Review*, 85: 1029–46.

United Nations Conference on Trade and Development (1996), *The TRIPS Agreement and Developing Countries*, Geneva and New York: United Nations.

Vishwasrao, Sharmila (1994), "Intellectual Property Rights and the Mode of Technology Transfer," *Journal of Development Economics*, 44: 381–402.

World Bank (1993), *The East Asian Miracle: Economic Growth and Public Policy*, Oxford: Oxford University Press.

Yang, Guifang and Keith E. Maskus (2001), "Intellectual Property Rights, Licensing, and Innovation, in an Endogenous Product Cycle Model," *Journal of International Economics*, 53: 169–87.

13 FDI and the environment

The link between FDI and the environment[1]

Bijit Bora

The rapid growth of private foreign direct investment (FDI) has raised the interest in the link between it and environmental protection. In particular, there is the strong concern that these increased flows will accelerate the deterioration of the earth's environment.[2] At the same time, FDI has been shown to affect economic growth positively, which offers new opportunities to reduce its environmental impact, by changing consumption patterns and allowing the use of more advanced environmental technologies.

This link, however, has not been static. More importantly, rapid changes in the global economy in the past fifteen years such as technological innovation and trade and investment liberalisation have changed the environment within which transnational corporations (MNC) and government operate. There are four major changes in the analysis and understanding of these issues.

First, the relationship between the environment and development has evolved.[3] The environment used to be considered a necessary expense for economic growth.[4] Today, however, with economic development defined to be a broadening of choice, protecting the environment is a major objective of developing countries. It is now commonly accepted that both can, and should, be achieved simultaneously.[5] This approach is being adopted by many actors, including MNC and has resulted in them becoming actively involved in environmental issues.[6]

Second, the accepted definition of 'environmental damage' is now wider. Traditionally, environmental damage was associated with process issues such as the degradation of air, land and water caused by chemical or pulp and paper mills, or with the excessive extraction of renewable and non-renewable resources. Today, there is a belief that protecting the environment requires the whole range of production processes and products to be environmentally friendly. Hence, manufacturing firms are now concerned with their product's 'environmental footprint'. This means embracing environment issues at the design stage so that a product allows a greater use of recycled material, uses production processes that minimise environmental damage and methods of disposal that involve limited contamination.

Third, consumers are now more environmentally conscious and concerned about these impacts in their purchasing decisions. This has created both a market for 'green' products and created another avenue by which firms can be pressured to respond to environmental concerns (Schmidheiny *et al.*, 1997). For example, companies selling household products have found that their environmental footprint is largest outside their direct activities, and lies in the raw materials they use and in the disposal of their products. Hence, in response, they are careful to identify the environmental damage caused by activities related to their company's core activities. For example, the famous dolphin label on cans of tuna reflects the fact that the harvesting of the tuna was done without harming dolphin stocks.

Fourth, many firms are finding that environmental reduction and competitiveness are not mutually exclusive. It is possible to be eco-efficient: that is to reduce both environmental impact and costs simultaneously. For example, since 1975 3M has reduced by 1.4 billion pounds its releases to the environment and saved over $750 million (Schmidheiny *et al.*, 1997). Similarly, since 1992 SC Johnson has reduced its waste output by 420 million pounds and reduced costs by $125 million.[7]

Despite these four changes that define the new context, it is important to note that the fundamental tension between the profit motive of private firms and the public interest in protecting the environment has not completely vanished.[8] They are positive changes, but on their own are not sufficient to ensure an equitable intergenerational access to the world's resources. Market failures continue to persist in the use of the environment due to a number of factors such as: the inability to properly define property rights, bargaining costs between relevant parties, or valuation of the environmental damage (UNCTAD, 1992; World Bank, 1992).

Although recently, the regulatory framework for environmental issues has improved for a number of countries, protecting the environment nevertheless remains a challenging task. Policy decisions are often made in response to immediate employment and output objectives. The pressures of delivering high economic growth rates and securing FDI, especially in environmentally vulnerable developing countries, may tempt them to accept environmentally risky activities. This problem is particularly acute in developing countries who have many concerns related to their ability to protect their environment. They generally lack the resources[9] and technical expertise needed to design and implement appropriate environmental legislation to combine growth with protecting the environment. Once enacted, environmental legislation has to be implemented; developing countries face problems of inspection, monitoring, enforcement and prosecution. This chapter analyses the role played by FDI and in particular the operations of MNCs that affect the environment.

The environmental strategies of MNCs

The environment is an input into the production process whose importance to MNCs ranges from critical for mining and other natural resource industries, to less important for industries such as financial services where there is a lower potential for environmental damage. As with other inputs, especially human resources MNCs have had to reconsider their approach. In the new context, defined by the above changes, the MNCs approach to handling environmental issues has come under increasing pressure for changes. This pressure has emerged from a cross-section of the community and is a direct result of the visibility of MNCs and their potential to both harm and protect the environment. Members of civil society such as NGOs and consumer groups have been quite vocal, but there are also pressures from both shareholders of companies and financial institutions that lend credit to many MNCs. In the old context, shareholder value was usually represented as a return on equity (UNCTAD, 1998); today, shareholders are increasingly asking firms for a more responsible attitude to the environment and other social issues. Social concerns are often reinforced by sound business considerations. Investors always seek to reduce their credit risk, and they are now concerned about the corporate ability to manage environmental risk. This demand for change from MNCs with regards to their role in the environment is not without reason. For example, Agenda 21, the call for action from the 1992 United Nations Conference on Environment and Development, contains 52 provisions across five chapters directly relating to MNCs.

The MNCs' response to environment issues differs in one important respect from that of uninational firms. In addition to managing the environment through pollution abatement practices, environmental management systems, education and training, MNCs must also manage their affiliates across international borders. Hence, an added dimension for them is cross-border environmental management, which is a key issue in assessing their impact on the environment in host developing countries.[10]

In terms of managing the environment, MNCs have at their disposal the same type of strategies available to other firms. They can be either end-of-pipe, where the focus is on disposal and clean-up, process-oriented where environmental damage through process is addressed, or product-oriented where both product and process issues are addressed. While not necessarily a continuum these approaches do reflect business perceptions of environmental issues. On one end the notion that environmental issues is a burden will result in end-of-pipe activities. Whereas, if the perception of environmental protection and business profitability is perceived to be a challenge, firms will have product-oriented environmental management strategies.

The way in which these ranges of environmental management approaches are handled within an MNC system has implications for host developing countries. Again, there is a range of options. At one extreme is the complete decentralisation of environmental issues between the parent and the affiliate. The affiliate here has a minimal commitment to the environment. If the host country does not have strict environmental legislation in place, the affiliate chooses the least cost strategy; where the legislation is more stringent, it complies accordingly. The affiliate is aware that it has a legal responsibility for environmental care, but considers environmental protection a net cost and a burden. This is essentially a satisfying approach to comply passively with existing regulations. While such a minimalist strategy does little to assist developing countries with pollution intensive industries it can still be sufficient for industries with low environmental damage.

A second strategy is to centralise all environmental decisions for the MNC system. This would ensure that the environmental activities of an affiliate in one host country do not have an adverse impact on other affiliates or the parent. Within this centralisation strategy, however, there could be different approaches.

- The parent could pursue minimum standards, with a regulatory floor for all affiliates. Affiliates would be free to deviate from this floor, but only upwards, towards better environmental practice.
- The parent could establish uniform standards across the entire MNC system, compatible both with each host country as well as the home country. Thus, the highest national levels of all the countries in which the MNC operates sets the standard.
- The parent could establish uniform standards across not only the entire MNC system, but also across to input suppliers, regardless of ownership. This would ensure all environmental risks and liabilities are internalised. For example, Hewlett-Packard has in place a product stewardship program, which embraces the design, manufacture, distribution, use, take-back, disassembly, reuse, recycling and ultimate disposal of constituent parts and materials (von Moltke *et al.*, 1998).

The choice of strategy depends on a complex mix of considerations. One significant factor is the implications for the competitiveness of the affiliate and the MNC as a whole. This goes beyond the direct cost of environment technologies. These costs need not deter the adoption of a comprehensive environmental strategy: there may exist other incentives for firms, national or transnational, to adopt environment protection technologies. The threat of liability, for instance, is a major consideration for MNCs in implementing environmental protection. The potential liability of environmental litigation can be more important to firms than the cost of implementation (UNCTAD, 1996a). In addition to the public embarrassment of being caught deploying poor environmental technology and the threat of consumer boycotts, there is even a possibility that company executives could be extradited to face trial in the host country.[11]

Another important factor is uncertainty with respect to host government policy. While a decision to implement poor quality technology in an affiliate may seem appropriate where it meets existing host country legislation, this could be short sighted. A host country government could later move its regulations to those of more advanced countries, requiring the affiliate to upgrade its technology and incur the costs of complying with the new regulation (Hansen, 1998; Adams, 1997). It may be cheaper to anticipate the upgrading of environmental legislation by installing the latest technology.

A third factor is the role of customer markets. In some cases, the shift towards a comprehensive centralised strategy is due to the perception that there are competitive advantages in being green. For example, the following products are now being advertised as being environment friendly;

- household products such as soaps and cleaners that are phosphate free;
- packaging of consumer products that require less landfill; and

- consumer electronic equipment such as computers that are energy efficient, use more recycled material for input, and create less waste when being disposed.

Fourth, abatement costs tend to be a small percentage of total costs.[12]

The nature of costs also matter especially in the application of environmentally sound technologies and environmental management systems; in particular, it is important to distinguish between the size and type of costs (Adams, 1997). Fixed costs such as the installation of equipment to reduce emissions have a different effect on the choice of strategy from variable costs such as compliance checks or the use of more costly inputs. The existence of fixed costs means that there are scale economies in implementing clean technologies. Thus, it may be cheaper for an MNC to implement the same high-level environmental technology across its entire system than to tailor the technology to each affiliate (Hansen, 1998).

In summary, an MNC can pursue a wide range of environmental strategies, from comprehensive to ensure that its 'environmental footprint' is fully internalised to minimalist that only ensures compliance with existing regulations. The implications for a host country government depends on the type of strategy pursued by an MNC and the environmental damage associated with the production and consumption of their product. The worst case scenario is a decentralised minimalist approach for affiliates operating in environmentally sensitive industries. In the next section, the impact that MNCs can have on the environment is examined.

Pollution intensity of FDI

Environmental degradation in host developing countries is a consequence of both production and consumption patterns within countries and also increasingly of the consumption patterns of export markets. The effect that production processes can have on the environment depends considerably on the industry involved. Some industries are highly pollutive in the sense that they can have large negative effects on the air, water and land, while others have minimal effects. Studies to identify these industries use different criteria, but still arrive at similar conclusions:[13] the highly pollutive industries include chemicals and allied products, mining for minerals and metals, fabricated and non-fabricated metals, cement, glass and ceramics.

The share of these industries in the total industrial activity of a country depends on many national characteristics such as the level of development and the factor endowment profile. Different countries would then be expected to have different propensities to attract both foreign and direct investment in pollution intensive industries.[14] Therefore, if these general national characteristics are important for determining location, then by definition there should be some differences between the structure of domestic production in pollution intensive industries and the structure of foreign production by domestic firms in those same industries.

Poor quality FDI data has made it difficult for researchers to provide an adequate answer to question. However, to provide some insight into some general trends that may assist in finding a response, data from the United States is used.

These data differ from the conventional approach of using FDI data. It is production data of affiliates of US companies. This allows for a closer correlation between production structures than finance data collected on an aggregate basis.

The data shows that the share of value-added of majority-owned-foreign affiliates (MOFAs) of United States MNCs engaged in pollution intensive industries[15] in the total value-added of these affiliates has risen slightly over time (Figure 13.1). However, this picture differs considerably across regions: the share of pollution intensive production in total affiliate production is the highest in developed countries and has been so far in the past decade and a half (Figure 13.2). The Western Hemisphere has a comparatively high share, while all other regions have very low shares, with the Middle East the lowest. Nevertheless, when this overall trend is compared with the same figures for production in the United States itself, the pollution intensity of these foreign affiliates has remained slightly higher during the past fifteen years. Conclusions about the environmental friendliness of United States international production are difficult to make from this chart since it does not give any information on the environmental impact or production. This would vary depending on the availability of technology and the regulatory environment.[16]

Another way to examine the environmental profile of FDI is to compare foreign affiliate production with total host country production (Figure 13.3). Again, this can only be accomplished with data for the operations of affiliates of United States parent companies. Countries where a higher proportion of their manufacturing GDP is accounted for by affiliates from the United States, such as Australia and Canada, reflect their comparative advantages in pollution intensive industries. The ratios for developing country industries are very low with no clear

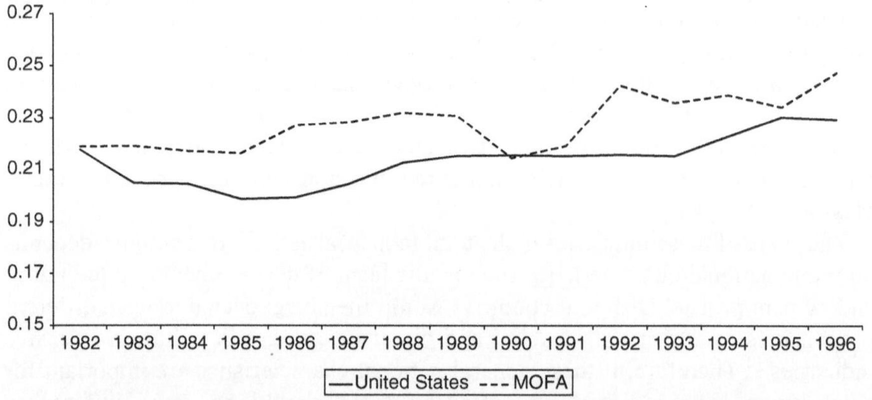

Figure 13.1 Share of pollution intensive manufacturing production in total manufacturing production: United States and for United States MOFAs (per cent).

Source: Based on United States Department of Commerce data.

a Pollution intensive industries are the sum of the chemicals and allied products and primary and fabricated metals.

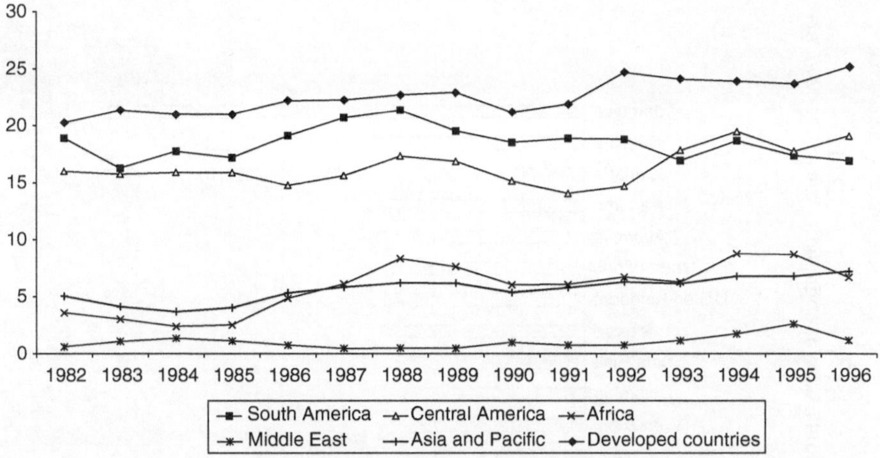

Figure 13.2 Share of United States MOFA GDP in manufacturing pollution intensive industries in total United States manufacturing GDP, by region, 1982–96.

Source: Based on United States Department of Commerce data.

a Pollution intensive industries are the sum of chemicals and allied and primary and fabricated metals.

upward trend. This is an important point since, in the new context, many of these pollution-intensive industries have incorporated aspects of centralised comprehensive environmental strategies, including adoption of industry wide codes (UNCTAD, 1996b). The shares of output in these industries are low, implying that their environmental impact will be largely determined by regulatory stringency.

Caution needs to be exercised in interpreting these data. That there is FDI in pollution-intensive industries at all means that environmental stress is increased. But changing shares in and by themselves say little about the environmental impact of FDI. Changes in the volume of FDI can be attributed to a number of factors, including structural change through economic growth. Thus, host countries may be setting up pollution-intensive industries in their drive to develop heavy industry, regardless of the role played by MNCs (Mani and Wheeler, 1999). Furthermore, as mentioned above there is a negative relationship between economic growth and some pollutants over a range of per capita incomes. The data also do not capture the possibility that there are varying *degrees* of environmental damage. Substantive environmental problems can arise in many industries that are not heavy polluting overall, for instance, textiles and clothing, semiconductors or primary product exports such as fresh fruit and flowers, all activities in which foreign affiliates are quite active in the developing world. The total impact on the environment depends on the scale of activity, their pollution content and

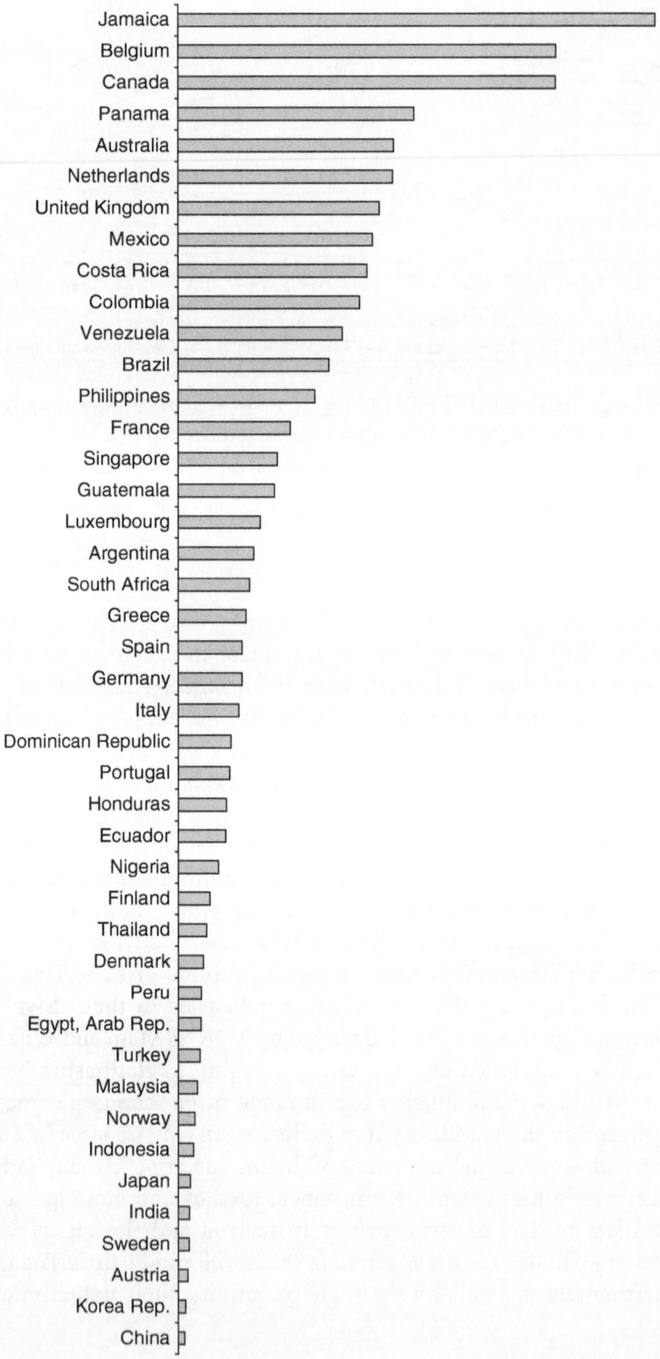

Figure 13.3 Share of pollution intensive production by affiliates of United States parent companies in host country production: selected countries, 1995.

Source: Author's calculations.

the control measures used. Low pollution content activities with large outputs and poor environmental control can do significant environmental damage.

The environmental vulnerability of countries varies too. Many developing countries are environmentally vulnerable beyond industrial pollution. Small island host countries, for example, depend heavily on tourism and a narrow range of primary products such as fisheries (ADB, 1992). MNCs affect the environment in many of these activities, if not directly then through their sourcing of intermediate inputs – they can leave a large 'environmental footprint' on the resources of these countries.[17] Similar concerns exist as regards forestry management. Almost 90 per cent of logging operations in Gabon and Cameroon are foreign owned (French, 1998). Growing demand for forest products has also drawn foreign firms (some from developing East Asia) to Brazil, Cambodia, Congo, Guyana, Nicaragua, Papua New Guinea, the Solomon Islands and Suriname (French, 1998). Labour-intensive manufacturing, too, can raise environmental concerns. For example, textile manufacturers use numerous chemical liquid effluents for washing, dyeing and bleaching in the finishing stage. These effluents can lower oxygen levels in the water and threaten aquatic life (van Moltke *et al.*, 1998). Semiconductor products, critical to the exports from East Asian developing countries, contain hazardous materials such as lead, use toxic chemicals in assembly and cleaning, and produce harmful waste and emissions. As MNCs disperse their production and sourcing geographically, developing countries need to watch the associated environmental effects.

The question of whether MNCs shift the location of their production in response to lax environmental standards has created a lively debate.[18] While there are cases in which firms appear to have shifted this production activities to take advantage of lower environmental standards elsewhere, it is difficult to establish conclusively whether MNCs *in general* exploit environmental laxity (Zarsky, 1999).[19]

There have been two approaches to testing the general 'pollution haven' hypothesis (Adams, 1997). The first has been to correlate outward FDI with environmental standards. The results have found no support for the 'pollution haven' hypothesis, that is, that MNCs direct their investment to countries with lax standards (Leonard, 1988; Repetto, 1995; Eskeland and Harrison, 1997). One study (Xing and Kolstad, 1997) does find the predicted effect, but its robustness has been questioned because of the use of sulfur dioxide emissions as a proxy for environmental stringency (Adams, 1997; Zarsky, 1999). The second approach has been to embed environmental regulation in a larger model of locational choice. Again, the studies find that the environmental variable is rarely significant. The most important variables remain the traditional ones of locational choice: factor endowments, infrastructure quality, distance and market size (Eskeland and Harrison, 1997).

There is also a third approach – to use case studies. This approach, which examines specific company decisions has proven to be more successful in finding cases that support the notion that environmental standards are a factor in MNC location decisions (WWF, 1998). Examples of both governments failing to enforce environmental legislation and firms acknowledging that lower environmental standards were a factor were found in: Costa Rica, Mexico, India, Indonesia, Papua New Guinea and the Philippines (WWF, 1998; 1999).

All three approaches have inherent difficulties. The first two suffer from precise measurement of the variables, such as environmental stringency and the difficulties plaguing FDI data and affiliate production data in general. The third from selection bias – only firms that have actually shifted are documented.

In general, however, the existing research has found little evidence to support the 'pollution haven' hypothesis. Possible explanations for the lack of a correlation between environmental standards and the location decisions by MNCs include the following:

- Other locational variables are more significant in making the choice.
- The costs of compliance with environmental regulations in both home and host countries are a small share of total costs, and so do not affect the final decision.
- The cost of applying common standards across an MNC system may be lower than the cost of differentiating standards by country.
- The measures used in the analyses of environmental stringency and its impact may be deficient and need improvement.
- MNCs are now more visible, and environmental issues more closely monitored; thus, the risks associated with environmental negligence are too high for firms to bear.

More generally, it is difficult to isolate the environmental profile of FDI and international production from normal industrial restructuring. In the new context, MNCs that are active in pollution intensive industries will seek to take advantage of new opportunities to locate production in developing countries, as would any other firm seeking to improve its competitiveness. What is important in the context of assisting developing countries to protect their environment is not the fact that MNCs are present, but how environmentally responsible they are. This question is taken up in the next section.

Transfer of environmentally sound technology

MNCs possess a number of advantages and disadvantages for host developing countries attempting to achieve their sustainable development objectives. This section examines whether or not ownership matters for sustainable development under key headings. It is important to note at the outset that a direct comparison of affiliates and local counterparts may not provide an accurate picture of the impact of MNCs on the environment more broadly. There may be substantial foreign control in some activities without direct foreign equity participation, for instance by subcontracting or licensing relations. It is then difficult to distinguish the real environmental impact of MNCs: the affiliate may have high environmental standards while suppliers or licensors do not. The substantive issue is MNCs' 'environmental footprint' regardless of whether or not they actually own the activities.

Environmental management

While combining, firm competitiveness and environmental protection is now possible in the new context, it is still not automatic for all industries and all firms. Implementing advanced environmental management systems comes with costs and this could imply a loss of competitiveness. One advantage of MNCs is their trend towards enhanced environmental management practices, especially among those in highly pollution intensive industries such as chemicals. For example, the industry guidelines for the International Councils on Metals and the Environment and the Canadian Chemical Producer's Association have been assessed positively against the Agenda 21 provisions (UNCTAD, 1996b). Some cases does require the application of standards above those required in the host country (UNCTAD, 1996b).

There is evidence to suggest that foreign affiliates have higher environmental standards than domestic counterparts.[20] However, foreign ownership is not a significant factor in the adoption rate of ISO14000 environmental management standards in Mexico (Dasgupta *et al.*, 1998). Nor are other overseas links through trade, management training or management experience. The most important factors are the skill level of plant managers and staff awareness of environmental issues. Foreign ownership is also insignificant in plant-level abatement practices in South and Southeast Asia (Hettige *et al.*, 1996). Again, the key factors are scale, productive efficiency and the use of new process technology.[21] In general, the results of analysis comparing the relative environmental practices of local and foreign firms, points to factors other than ownership, such as the size and age of the plant, skill levels as being important. These findings would suggest that an MNC advantage in this area exists, but is not widespread.

A disadvantage of MNCs in this area is that the adaptation of environmental management practices to a host country environment is not always easy. This requires an acknowledgement and understanding of differences in laws, customs, culture and practices. Efforts of MNCs to surmount these difficulties may not always result in the most efficient practice.[22] The end result could be the use of management practices that are below the potential of MNCs to protect the environment. A domestic firm with similar resources and capabilities maybe better situated to implement more efficient practices.

A related issue, which is a core part of the new context is the environmental management responsibilities of MNCs and their customer and supplier relationships. MNCs have a clear advantage in assisting their suppliers to upgrade their environmental management practices and consumers to change their consumption habits. Most of the developments in this area relate to the consumer demand in developed countries (van Moltke *et al.*, 1998). Their increased demand for environmentally friendly products is a challenging task, but contracted suppliers to MNCs must also be able to meet these demands. MNCs have the advantage of being able to communicate the changing consumption patterns as they relate to process to developing host country firms. They also have the advantage of being able to train input suppliers in changing their production processes to exploit these market opportunities. Notable examples here are the activities of MNCs in the area of eco-labelling. If developed country customers place a premium on eco-labelling suppliers, regardless of ownership suppliers need to meet the certification requirements.

An obvious disadvantage of MNCs, however, is that their suppliers will have to invest resources to meet the higher system wide requirements. In some instances there are MNCs actively assisting their suppliers in the form of technical workshops, training courses, and ISO14,000 certification. Intel insists that their suppliers conform to their rigorous in-house environmental standards (van Moltke *et al.*, 1998).

Spillover effects

The actual pollution abatement technology employed within a plant depends on a complex mix of regulatory, market and non-market forces. An advantage held by MNCs in this area is they respond to their home country standards (UNCTAD, 1993).[23] This is important as a general issue in that developed countries also have the most significant environmental impact from their production and consumption (WRI, 1998). Hence, affiliates of foreign firms can act as conduits to transmit efforts to reduce similar impacts in developing countries.

The question of whether or not affiliates use the most efficient environment technology cannot be answered in a straightforward manner. Much depends on the type of technology and the nature of the installation costs. For heavy polluting industries implementation of a more environment friendly process and product technology can be quite expensive. Hence, there is an incentive when planning a new production facility to forecast regulatory stringency in the future. In this case, the vintage of the facility becomes a critical factor in the application of the best available technology. Strong evidence from the Chilean pulp and paper industry supports this fact (Herbert-Copley, 1998). A similar response has also been found in the mining industry, which is also characterised by very high fixed costs. In this case companies were found to implement the latest technology, as opposed to 'dumping' old technology.

These results to some extent have been generalised by using the consumption of energy and environmentally 'dirty fuels' as a proxy for pollution intensity. After controlling for other factors, foreign manufacturing plants in Mexico, Venezuela, Morocco and Côte d'Ivoire were significantly more energy efficient than their domestic counterparts (Eskeland and Harrison, 1997).

All these studies should be interpreted with caution. They are point-in-time estimates, and do not identify when environmentally sound technologies or practices were implemented. This may overstate the positive environmental impact or practices of affiliates. In many cases, the move from decentralised to centralised environmental strategies is very recent. A disadvantage of MNCs in this area is that there is evidence that they adopt environmentally sound practices only *ex post*, in response to community pressure on their parents; they could have improved earlier but did not (Hettige *et al.*, 1996).

Sustainable consumption patterns

MNCs based in developed home country markets, or those that serve these markets have an advantage over uninational firms when it comes to affecting consumption patterns. Since the income elasticity of demand for environmentally friendly products is high, consumers in developed countries are demanding these products. While servicing these markets MNCs can affect the consumption patterns of developing host countries, as well as production processes.

At the same time MNCs could be a disadvantage in this area. MNC in the pursuit of competitiveness would attempt to exploit any advantage including cultural and locationally specific consumption characteristics. Imposing the consumption preferences of a developed country on a developing country maybe difficult. For example, switching to environmentally friendly products could result in an increase in price. Given the low level of incomes in developing countries, many consumers could simply not be able to afford these products, despite the premium may place on environmentally sustainable consumption.

Market structure of the polluting industry

A key feature of the economics of sustainable development is the market structure of the industry. In cases where the switch to environmentally sound technology raises costs, both foreign and domestic firms, will attempt to pass this increase through to consumers in the form of higher prices. Furthermore, when firms, are able to be eco-efficient, the cost savings may not necessarily be transferred to consumers. The extent of this pass through depends on the market structure of the industry and also on the application of competition policy.

If there are commercial benefits to being environmentally friendly, the use by affiliates of new environment technologies may spur domestic competitors to acquire clean technologies (Wheeler and Martin, 1992). Moreover, to preserve the 'image' of an industry as a whole, MNCs may have an incentive to ensure that all firms in the industry follow good environmental practice.

Scale of foreign investment

While larger production operations bring with it benefits to host countries such as scale economies, increasing in employment, increasing export opportunities, there is a disadvantage when it comes to the environment. Many developing economies, especially some of the most environmentally vulnerable, receive FDI in industries that can do significant and irreversible environmental damage. Some developing countries are often quite proud of their achievements in attracting these large-scale FDI projects in a competitive environment. The environmental impact of these efforts, are sometimes not considered in the drive to be competitive. FDI can have a 'herding' effect on foreign investors, often creating specific industrial areas through backward and forward linkages. As these areas grow and attract further FDI, there is potential for the environmental effects to escalate.

For many developing countries it is difficult to balance the positive economic benefits from the FDI with the negative environmental effects. This problem is further exacerbated in industries where domestic firms can rarely achieve the minimum scale required, such as in mining projects in Papua New Guinea. Or, large-scale tourism resorts in island economies. In these cases, with no direct domestic counterpart, the environmental damage is not only large scale, but also due specifically to the foreign investor. Another example is the banana cultivation industry in Costa Rica. Despite evidence that the environmental management practices of the industry, with the help of foreign firms is sound (Gentry, 1998), bananas are a mono-crop. This means that in order to achieve the required scale there is a heavy use of pesticides, which is not sustainable (Zarsky, 1999).

A further disadvantage of MNCs is that if there is an imbalance between the scale of the operation and the size of the country, the MNC holds the bargaining advantage in negotiations concerning regulatory frameworks. Host developing country governments out of fear of losing the positive economic benefits associated with the FDI would be willing to concede environmental laws (WWF, 1998). This has been prevalent in some free-trade zones and in some mining projects in the Asia Pacific (WWF, 1999).

In summary, FDI can have a direct impact on the environment by affecting the production of specific pollution intensive industries and indirectly on the environmental effects that accompany economic growth. The evidence on the impact of FDI on the ability of host countries to protect their environment is mixed and it is not clear that in general ownership matters. Some MNCs are clearly international leaders in mitigating the environmental impact of their entire range of activities. Others fail to utilise their full potential for environmental protection by using a decentralised strategy. The evidence shows that a large number of factors in addition to foreign ownership will affect the environmental performance and management strategies of affiliates and domestic firms in developing countries.

There are instances where ownership does matter, such as cases where there are only a few firms operating and the scale of the industry is quite large. In these instances, there is a role for government policy to target specifically these industries and firms to minimise their environmental damage.

It is also important to note, that despite the existence of specific evidence allowing for a general conclusion about the importance of ownership, an advantage held by foreign firms is their basic ability to respond and adapt to changes. In the changing regulatory framework for environment issues in both home and host countries this could be the greatest impact of foreign firms.

Implications for research

As the absolute volume of FDI and the general public's sensitivities to environmental issues increase, the debate on whether or FDI and environmental protection are mutually exclusive will become more intense. This chapter has shown that the empirical evidence to support an informed debate on this link is less than conclusive. In this last section approaches to a research agenda are identified, with a specific focus on difficulties for researchers.

One of the defining features of this area is its appeal to a broad range of researchers. The literature reviewed in this chapter was sourced from management researchers with a case study approach to research questions to other researchers that rely on cross-section and time-series data. In same cases, such as in the pollution haven question, or transfer of environmentally sound technology, their conclusions are often in direct contrast to each other. These two approaches need to be made more complementary, but this is difficult due to the inherent different approaches.

One way to proceed would be to deal with the aggregate issue of FDI data, but that is difficult. It is almost impossible to develop indicators of the pollution intensity of FDI. Only a handful of countries, led by the United States, collect FDI data at the three digit level, which would allow an adequate identification of pollution intensive industries. This problem is also compounded by a lack of disaggregation in the destination countries for FDI. This makes it difficult to isolate the particular national characteristics that may be conducive to hosting higher relative shares of FDI. While incredibly helpful, these data improvements do not adequately address all the issues identified in the chapter. What the data provides is a profile of pollution intensive sectors, whereas, what is important is to find out what firms, both domestic and foreign, are doing to actively minimise their environmental damage. This type of analysis lends itself to case-study approaches that are common in the business management field.

One way to advance the research agenda would be to invest resources into a large-scale cross-country management study. For example, instead of focusing on one particular company's activities in one particular country, what could happen is a number of countries could be studied simultaneously. Such a large-scale project involves considerable time and resources including time spent on developing a common template for analysis. However, what it would do is identify common elements among those firms in areas such as environmental strategy, including environmental accounting, transfer of environmental sound technology and product design strategies that reduce the consumption of environmental damaging products.

Notes

1 A substantially revised version of this chapter was published as chapter X in UNCTAD 1999.

2 The achievement of environment objectives has opportunity costs in terms of goods and services (World Bank, 1992).

3 Environmental disasters involving MNCs, such as the Bhopal disaster in India (1984) which killed thousands of people and the oil spill from the Exxon Valdez in Alaska (1989) which destroyed a pristine environment, have contributed to the increased the awareness of environmental issues.

4 The formal title of the report published by The United Nations World Commission on Environment and Development report entitled is *Our Common Future* (informally

known Bruntland Commission's) together with the United Nation's Conference on Environment and Development (1992) have been important in changing perceptions.

5 There are several arguments against a simple tradeoff between growth and environment. Some evidence suggests, for instance, an inverted-U relationship between local air pollution and income per capita (Grossman and Krueger, 1994). Over lower ranges of per capita income, environment quality deteriorates with growth, but after a threshold level it improves. If the components of environmental quality are decomposed into specific categories of pollutants, there is no aggregate relationship at all with growth (World Bank, 1992). Thus, the relationship can be very complex, especially if the definition of 'sustainable development' is wider than the traditional one of the depletion of natural resources and waste disposal of manufacturing firms.

6 Representatives from 179 governments attended the official function, while almost 20,000 people attended the non-governmental forum. The event was covered by more than 8,000 media personnel.

7 www.wbcsd.ch/eedata/eecsindx.htm.

8 This is commonly referred to as an externality: when the consumption or production decisions of an individual, household, firm or government do not reflect the wider costs or benefits to society. If the price of goods, be they consumption or intermediate goods are not priced to reflect their value to society their production and consumption could result in harm to the environment.

9 This issue reflects the income elasticity of demand for environmental protection, which is estimated to be quite high (Mani and Wheeler, 1999). Developed countries are able to demand and obtain better environmental protection than do developing countries. One reason for this is the relationship between per capita income and environmental damage as discussed in Note 4.

10 This is not to say that uninational firms are single-plant firms.Uninational firms could not only have multiple-plants, but could also have them in different states or provinces. To the extent that environmental regulation varies across subnational states, uninational firms also face the dual problem of managing environmental concerns and managing their affiliates.

11 Another related issue is whether or not in cases of environmental negligence a case against an affiliate can be tried in the home country.

12 Pollution abatement capital expenditures are less than 5 per cent of total investment costs for most industries, though for heavy polluting industries such as petroleum and coal the figure is much higher. Even then, the share of these expenditures in total revenue is very low (Wheeler and Martin, 1992; Low and Yeats, 1992).

13 Most of these studies use data from the United States Toxic Release Inventory (TRI). This inventory contains over 200 substances of varying toxicity that can be discharged into the environment. With these data, the emissions intensity of a discharge or transfer can be measured in volume terms. It is important to note that emission intensity is not the same as toxic intensity (Olewiler and Dawson, 1998). The latter measure includes the toxicity of each discharge.

14 Recent work by Olweiler (1999) in developing an index to capture these characteristics shows such a profile. These include population density, energy consumption (GDP per kilogram oil equivalent), sanitation and clean water (per cent of population covered), water pollution (kilograms per day per unit GDP), and land area (thousands of square kilometres). The values for each category are ranked from 1 (low ECA) to 10 (high ECA), where low means that a country is least likely to become a pollution haven because it has the lowest value of all forty countries of the variable in question. Calculating the average of the ranking for each characteristic then creates an index.

15 Defined as the sum of fabricated metals and allied chemicals.

16 In contrast to Figure 13.1, there is evidence to suggest that the downward trend in the production share of some pollution-intensive industries has been declining in some developed countries (Mani and Wheeler, 1999).

17 For example, Unilever sources fish and fish products through contractual arrangements. In order to lessen its 'environmental footprint' it has combined with the World Wildlife Fund to support the Marine Stewardship Council. That Council has a voluntary certification programme for sustainable fishing (www.msc.org).

18 There is a parallel in the debate on this issue with the debate on the effectiveness of fiscal incentives to affect location decisions. The extensive literature on that issue has shown that incentives are not a significant determinant of location (UNCTAD, 1996c; Pirnia, 1998). A similar result can be found in the now extensive literature on the existence of 'pollution havens' (Adams, 1997; Zarsky, 1999; Hansen, 1998).

19 These are cited in a review of the pollution haven hypothesis done by the World Wildlife Federation, 1998. Most of the cases have to do with developing host countries exempting MNCs from local environmental laws and the relevant MNC being denied permission to operate in their home country. Another area where the pollution haven hypothesis is likely to be confirmed is in free trade zones (Sierra Club, 1993).

20 See Leonard (1988) on US MNCs in Ireland, Spain, Romania and Mexico, and Pearson (1987) on Indonesia, Brazil, Korea, Turkey, Mexico, Malaysia and the Philippines. Gentry (1998) reviews five case studies in Brazil, Costa Rica and Mexico, and concludes that MNC affiliates made improvements in their environmental standards and performance.

21 There are other studies showing that affiliates employ lower environmental standards than at home (ESCAP, 1988): some MNCs use environmental 'double standards', or have decentralised managerial systems that allow affiliates to suit their systems to local regulations.

22 For example, Union Carbide's Bhopal plant, which had been cleared by the state pollution board. However, its safety systems were apparently inferior to those of an identical plant in the USA, it lacked computerised logging systems and its management training was deficient (Gladwin, 1987).

23 Although it should be pointed out that when home and host countries are developing countries, there could be a situation where the environmental standards are low in both countries.

References

Adams, Jan (1997) 'Environmental policy and competitiveness in a globalised economy: conceptual issues and a review of the empirical evidence', in *Globalisation and Environment, Preliminary Perspectives*, Paris: OECD.

——(1999) 'Foreign direct investment and the environment: the role of voluntary corporate management', Paris: OECD.

Asia Development Bank (1992) *Environment and Development: A Pacific Island Perspective*, Manila: Asia Development Bank.

Dasgupita, A., H. Heltige and D. Wheeler (1998) 'What improves environmental performance? Evidence from Mexican industry', Washinton, DC: The World Bank, mimeo.

Eriksen, L. and Michael Hansen (1999) 'Environmental aspects of Danish direct investment: managing the environment in an open economy', Copenhagen: Copenhagen Business School, mimeo.

Eskeland, Gunner and Ann Harrison (1997) 'Moving to greener pastures? Multinationals and the pollution haven hypothesis', Washington, DC: The World Bank, mimeo.

French, Hilary (1998) *Investing in the Future: Harnessing Private Capital Flows for Environmentally Sustainable Development*, World Watch Paper 139, Washington, DC: World Watch Institute, mimeo.

Gentry, B. (ed.) (1998) *Private Capital Flows and the Environment, Lessons from Latin America*, Cheltenham: Edward Elgar Publishing.

Gladwin, T. (1987) 'A case study of the Bhopal tragedy', in C. Pearson (ed.), *Multinational Corporations, the Environment and the Third World*, North Carolina: Duke University Press.

Grossman, G. and A. Krueger (1994) 'Economic growth and the environment', NBER Working Paper No. 4634, Cambridge: NBER, mimeo.

Hansen, Michael (1998) *Transnational Corporations and Sustainable Development: An Appraisal of the Environmental Implications of Foreign Direct Investment in Less Developed Countires*, Copenhagen: Copenhagen Business School, PhD Thesis.

Herbert-Copley, B. (1998) *Innovation, Regulation and Environmental Management in the Chilean and Canadian Pulp and Paper Industries*, Ottawa: Carleton University, PhD Thesis.

Hettige, M., M. Huq, S. Pargal and David Wheeler (1996) 'Determinants of pollution Abatement in developing countries: evidence from south and southeast Asia', *World Development*, 24(12): 1891–904.

Jaffe, A.B., S.R. Peterson and P.R. Portney (1995) 'Environmental regulation and the competitiveness of United States manufacturing: what does the evidence tell us?' *Journal of Economic Literature*, 33: 132–63.

Leonard, D. (1988) *Pollution and the Struggle for the World Product*, Cambridge: Cambridge University Press.

Low, P. (1992) *International Trade and the Environment*, Washington, DC: The World Bank.

Low, P. and S. Yeats (1992) 'Do dirty industries migrate?', in P. Low (ed.), *International Trade and the Environment*, Washington, DC: The World Bank.

Mani, M. and D. Wheeler (1999) 'In search of pollution havens: dirty industry in the world economy, 1960–1995,' Washington, DC: The World Bank, mimeo.

Olewiler, N. and K. Dawson (1998) 'Analysis of national pollutant release inventory data on toxic emissions by industry', Working Paper 97–16, Ottawa: Department of Finance.

Pearson, C. (ed.) (1987) *Multinational Corporations, the Environment and the Third World*. North Carolina: Duke University Press.

Pirnia, N. (1998) 'The relative impact of investment incentives on FDI: a literature review', in D.J. Encarnation and B. Velic (eds), *Competing for FDI: Government Policy and Corporate Strategy in Asia*, New York: Oxford University Press.

Repetto, R. (1995) *Jobs, Competitiveness and Environmental Regulations: What are the Real Issues?* Washington, DC: World Resources Institute.

Sierra Club (1993) *Analysis of the North American Free Trade Agreement and the North American Agreement on Environmental Cooperation*, Washington, DC: Sierra Club, mimeo.

Schmidheiny, S., R. Chase and L. De Simone (1997) *Signals of Change: Business Progress Towards Sustainable Development*, Geneva: World Business Council for Sustainable Development.

United Nations Commission on Environment and Development (1987) *Our Common Future*, Oxford: Oxford University Press.

United Nations Conference on Trade and Development (1992) *World Investment Report 1992: Transnational Corporations as Engines of Growth*, New York: United Nations.

United Nations Conference on Trade and Development (1993) *Environmental Management in Transnational Corporations: Report on the Benchmark Corporate Environmental Survey*, New York and Geneva: United Nations.

United Nations Conference on Trade and Development (1995) *Transnational Corporations and Competitiveness*, New York and Geneva: United Nations.

United Nations Conference on Trade and Development (1996) *Incentives and Foreign Direct Investment*, New York and Geneva: United Nations.

United Nations Conference on Trade and Development (1996a) *International Accounting and Reporting Issues, 1995 Review: Environmental Accounting*, New York and Geneva: United Nations.

United Nations Conference on Trade and Development (1996b) *Self-Regulation of Environmental Management: Analysis of Guidelines set by World Industry Associations for New Member Firms*, New York and Geneva: United Nations.

United Nations Conference on Trade and Development (1998) *Linking Environmental and Financial Performance: A Survey of Best Practice Techniques*, Geneva: United Nations, DITE/EDS/Misc 9.

United Nations Economic and Social Commission for Asia and the Pacific (1988) *Transational Corporations and Environmental Management in Selected Asian and Pacific Developing Countries*, New York and Bangkok: United Nations.

Von Moltke, K. and O. Kuik, N. van der Grijp, C. Salazar, T. Banuri, C. Mupimila, C. Inman, N. Mesa, R. Oleas and J. Jose de los Santos (1998) *Global Product Chains: Northern Consumers, Southern Producers, and Sustainability*, Geneva: United Nations Environment Program.

Wheeler, D. and P. Martin (1992) 'Prices, policies and the international diffusion of clean technology: the case of wood pulp production', in P. Low (ed.), *International Trade and the Environment*, Washington, DC: The World Bank.

World Bank (1992) *World Development Report: The Environment and Development*, Oxford: Oxford University Press.

World Resources Institute (1998) *World Resources 1998–1999: Environmental Change and Human Health*, Oxford: Oxford University Press.

Worldwide Fund for Nature (1998) 'Pollution havens: examining the evidence and redefining the problem', Surrey: Worldwide Fund for Nature.

Worldwide Fund for Nature (1999) 'Foreign investment in the Asia Pacific mining sector: national policies, economic liberalisation and environmental and social effects', Gland: Worldwide Fund for Nature.

Xing, Y. and Kolstad, C. (1997) 'Do Lax environmental regulations attract foreign investment?', Working Paper in Economics #6–95R, Santa Barbara: University of California, mimeo.

Zarsky, Lyuba (1997) 'Stuck in the Mud? Nation-States, Globalisation and Environment', in *Globalisation and the Environment, Preliminary Perspectives*, Paris: OECD, pp. 27–52.

Zarsky, Lyuba (1999) 'Havens, Halos and Spaghetti: Untangling the Evidence about Foreign Direct Investment and the Environment', Paris: OECD, mimeo.

Part III

Analytical and policy issues

14 Modelling FDI in a computable general equilibrium framework

Susan F. Stone and Patrick A. Jomini

This chapter discusses the insights gained from, and the issues involved in, incorporating the activities of multinational corporations (MNCs) into a single country, regional or world economic model, through foreign direct investment (FDI). Specifically, we will deal with general equilibrium (GE) models, but many of these issues arise irrespective of modelling technique. The chapter will proceed as follows: the first section will discuss the insights to be gained by including FDI in a GE model. The second section discusses some of the issues involved in modelling FDI in a GE framework. The third section outlines data problems and constraints. In the fourth section we examine some applications in a GE framework and the fifth section summarises and makes suggestions on potential future work.

Insights gained from including MNCs in GE models

In the past twenty years international capital flows have grown at a faster rate than both global output and trade. Generally, international capital flows are broken into two distinct categories: portfolio and direct. While there have been GE models which incorporate international capital mobility (e.g. Brown *et al.* 1996, McKibbin and Wilcoxen 1996, Bora and Guisinger 1997, Hanslow *et al.* 1999) they do not explicitly consider MNC activity or their microeconomic impacts on an economy. Neither do they distinguish between the effects of portfolio and direct investment. Some more recent attempts to differentiate foreign and domestic firms within a GE framework are discussed later in this chapter.

The growth in the role of MNCs in the world economy underlines the need for a better understanding of how MNCs operate, including their effect on the economies in which they operate. Multilateral trade negotiations are tackling increasingly intricate themes, such as liberalising trade in services (GATS) and concerns over intellectual property rights (TRIPs). These issues give rise to significant conceptual and measurement difficulties that directly affect negotiations. Multilateral agreements are also moving beyond barriers to the free movement of goods and services to include international trade in factors of production. MNCs are intimately involved in all these developments.

The implications for MNC activity in a multi, as well as single, country framework go beyond trade analysis. FDI can change a country's comparative advantage and resource allocation and thus require changes in existing domestic, as well as multinational, policies. These policies may address three types of barriers to international capital flows. First are direct barriers that are due to differing legal standards between foreign and domestic firms. Examples would be ownership restrictions and differential tax treatment. Second are indirect barriers, including differences in accounting standards and information access. Finally, there are market specific barriers stemming from issues such as degree of liquidity of the investment, economic policy and political risk. While there are arguments that such risks are captured in prices or diversification, surveys of institutional investors in developed markets found liquidity problems to be a major impediment to international investment flows.[1] A GE framework incorporating MNC activity allows an analysis of these issues to account for a number of interaction and feedback effects.

An early extension of trade liberalisation analysis incorporating MNC activity was Markusen *et al.* (1995). They developed a GE model which included trans-border pricing and output decisions by MNCs. Firms maximise profits across multiple plant locations, thus a firm's market share now includes imports from its overseas branches. Their findings suggest that a strictly national enterprise model may overestimate welfare gains from trade liberalisation.

A more recent example of work incorporating MNC activity is that on the liberalisation of trade in the service sector. In order to capture more fully the policy implications for liberalising trade in services, it is important to consider method of delivery. Services are often delivered through commercial presence, that is, FDI. Barriers to commercial presence are distinct from those affecting other modes of service delivery – cross border supply, consumption abroad, and the movement of persons. Service delivery via commercial presence is modelled as a movement of capital across international borders, while delivery via the other modes of supply can be modelled as trade in industry output. Barriers affecting foreign suppliers should be distinguished from those that affect foreign and domestic supply equally. Thus, the operations of these sources of supply must be separated in any modelling exercise (See Dee and Hanslow 2000).

Key questions concerning MNCs involve how their activity affects the host and home economy and the relevant trade-offs.[2] MNCs are often accused of precipitating a 'race to the bottom'; that is, a race to the country employing the lowest labour and/or environmental standards, as well as government tax rates and services. This race, it is sometimes argued, will lower standards the world over and cause a 'beggar-thy-neighbour' approach to world economic growth. On the other hand, MNCs are also seen as the driving force in increasing technological innovation, and the dissemination of this technology worldwide.[3] In order for economists to have anything of substance to say on these issues, they need to be explicitly considered in models of economic behaviour.

Four areas of interest

Major issues surrounding MNC activity include labour market standards, taxes and tariffs, the environment and technology transfers. We will briefly consider each of these in turn.

Labour markets

MNCs have often been accused of 'exploiting' labour in developing countries and 'exporting jobs' in the developed world. However, it is generally accepted that foreign investment does not permanently change the level of unemployment, but it can have short-run effects on unemployment and result in permanent changes in real wages (Caves 1996).

It is not always clear to what extent labour costs play a role in the location decision of MNCs. While some studies show wages paid by MNCs are about the same as those of comparable local firms, this appears to hold true more so for developed countries. Research by Harrison (1994) on wage-setting by MNCs in the United States, Mexico and Venezuela suggests that MNCs generally pay higher wages than domestic firms, leading to increases in overall wages in the host country.

Beyond the effects on overall wages and income distribution, MNCs may change the welfare of workers through employment polices and their stance on collective bargaining. MNC access to alternative overseas production sites (and labour markets) may make their demand for labour more elastic and thus more resistant to unions' wage demands at home (Caves 1996). Two studies by Hatzuis (1997a,b) show that British, German and Swedish domestic economies all experienced rising labour demand elasticity as a result of increased FDI. These findings have implications for workers' bargaining power and employment levels in both home and host markets. A GE model would provide a framework to understand and measure the trade-offs and interactions of home and host wages and employment levels.

Taxes and tariffs

In addition to the relative impact on wages and employment, there are insights to be gained in modelling MNCs' effects in the area of taxation. Many domestic governments are concerned about what they see as tax avoidance measures employed by MNCs. These measures are usually analysed under the topic of transfer pricing, but can go beyond that in to such areas as tax havens and e-commerce. MNCs can manipulate the prices attached to intra-corporate transactions (e.g. royalty payments) by moving taxable profits into jurisdictions where they pay a lower tax (Caves 1996).

Modelling MNC activity would allow for explicit consideration of transfer pricing and its impact on where, and how much, taxes and tariffs are paid. In a multicountry GE model, bilateral or multilateral trade-offs of different tax regimes could be analysed. Tax havens and harmful preferential tax regimes, affect the location of financial and other service activities, erode the tax bases of other countries, distort trade and investment patterns and undermine the fairness, neutrality and broad social acceptance of tax systems generally (OECD 1998).

Tariffs have also been used to encourage local production. Foreign exporters have historically found it more profitable to establish production facilities within the tariff wall (jump the tariff) than to service the market from an overseas location

(Caves 1996, Wong 1995, for examples). While this has been a more traditional area of GE modelling, adding MNC activity may affect the estimated welfare gains and losses (Markusen *et al.* 1995).

Environment

Of increasing concern to the world economy is the emission of harmful pollutants often associated with manufacturing activity. During the negotiations for the North American Free Trade Area, environmental and labour standards were two key areas of debate. Indeed, separate clauses on these issues were ultimately attached to the final treaty.[4]

MNCs have been criticised for:

- promoting international trade in hazardous wastes (Scherr 1987, Strohm 1992);
- avoiding environmental regulations in 'pollution havens' (Pearson and Pryor 1978, Pearson 1985, Low and Safadi 1992, Daly 1993, Charnovitz 1993); and
- impeding international environmental agreements through their influence on host country governments (Prakash *et al.* 1996).

Differences in environmental standards between countries may influence MNCs to invest in 'dirty' industries in countries with low environmental standards exacerbating environmental degradation that may already be occurring (Low and Yeats 1992). This follows the 'pollution haven' hypothesis which assumes that the differences in abatement costs between countries are such that they affect the location and level of FDI (i.e. low environmental standards act as an incentive for FDI in 'dirty' industries).[5]

Low and Yeats present comparative evidence that shows that 'dirty' or polluting industries accounted for an increasing share of exports of some developing countries between 1966–68 and 1986–88. This suggests that environmental policies among different countries are a cost factor that can influence the location of investment in 'dirty' industries by MNCs.

By explicitly modelling the operations of MNCs production technology, one could gauge their responses to changes in markets, and the environmental impacts of such responses.

Technology transfer

Finally, technology transfer can be an important source of growth for many economies. Generally speaking, in the technology life cycle model, advances are made in industrialised economies and provided to lesser developed economies through the export of products. In the case of service, it is often delivered through FDI so that MNCs can maintain control over the new technology. Once the technology has become more standardised, joint ventures or licensing agreements are established as the company owning the technology attempts to recoup more of its development costs. In this process, local firms learn and adopt the technology.

Soon, it spreads to other host economy firms and becomes, more or less, 'standard practice'. Thus, a local firm may improve its productivity by copying technology used by MNC affiliates operating in the local market (Blomström and Kokko 1996, p. 3).

This process allows the developing world to gain access to technology that it would, with its given resource constraints, have been unable to develop on its own. The theory of contagion implies that FDI may be a very effective vehicle for transferring and diffusing technology due to the potential contacts and networks that MNCs establish in a host country (Wong 1995). This is often seen as one of the main benefits to host economies of allowing MNC activity.

MNCs may also facilitate the transfer and diffusion of technology by signalling to local firms that certain products exist, that there is a market for them and how to produce them – the so called 'demonstration effect' (Wong 1995). The entry of MNCs may lead to technology spillovers through competition in that MNCs may force local firms to search for and implement more efficient technologies (Blomström and Kokko 1996).

MNCs may need to undertake research and development (R&D) to adapt parent company technologies for products to suit the local market. This R&D may be extremely valuable to local firms because it makes the technology more readily adaptable to local conditions (Wong 1995). Technology transfer also refers to techniques for inventory and quality control that standardise and improve distribution channels (Blomström and Kokko 1996).

Incorporating MNC technology into a GE framework allows the modeller scope to capture some of the spillover effects of this activity. Estimating outcomes from liberalisation in trade and investment regimes will then more accurately reflect this welfare enhancing process.

Issues in incorporating MNC activity

The framework for most GE models starts with a country or region's input–output table. Figure 14.1 illustrates such a basic table. The left-hand side represents a region's input structure. A modeller must determine the functional relationship between intermediate inputs and primary factors that produce each industry's output. These relationships include degree of substitution and source of input, that is, domestic versus imports. The output is then spread across the various sources of final demand.

On the input side, issues surrounding incorporating MNCs into a GE model include determining the cost structure of MNCs as distinct from the cost structure of domestic firms in the industry. The underlying premise is that MNC cost structures differ from their domestic counterparts (see Mahajan *et al.* 1996). Even in cases where firms invest to take advantage of relative input cost savings, it is reasonable to expect that MNCs employ a different technology than domestic firms. MNCs locating in a new economy encounter many operational constraints not faced by local firms. These include the need to overcome a lack of knowledge of the local market and a possible domestic resistance to 'foreign' firms. MNCs

		Intermediate inputs					Final demand					Total sales
C		1	2	3	…	*n*	C	I	G	X	M	
O	1											
M	2											
M	…											
	n											
		Value-added										
Labour												
Capital												
Tax												
		Industry output										

Figure 14.1 Input–output table structure.

must have some comparative advantage to make such a move profitable. In many cases, this will be a type of monopoly power in a production process or brand name, and may be reflected in the different cost structures. Estimates of intermediate inputs, labour and capital usage all need to be determined. Researchers need to account for differing ownership structures available across industries, and the effect this has on such issues as the repatriation of profits.

The cost structure of an MNC in a host economy will be informed by the motivation behind the investment. A company has several choices as to how it delivers its good or service to the local market. It can export, set up an affiliate to deliver its product to the local market or set up some sort of joint venture or licensing agreement with a local company. The 'eclectic theory' (Dunning 1977) summarises the motivation behind FDI over some other form of entry, including export. The three factors involved in this theory, *internalisation, location* and *ownership*, are outlined in Table 14.1. *Internalisation* refers to the need to keep certain operational aspects of the company's business in-house. This leads to the need for a company to have a physical presence at the site of consumption. This could stem from a desire to secure supply (such as Japanese extracting companies operating through wholly owned subsidiaries) or service quality. *Location* is associated with resource or some other market advantage in the host economy. Ensuring access to markets in the face of high tariffs or low relative cost labour would fall into this category. Finally, *ownership* refers to product or process differentiation that gives an MNC a market advantage over its rivals. This can manifest itself in terms of patents or specific methods of production. By locating operations in the host economy, the firm maintains control over the process or product. These characteristics are manifested in so-called 'high tech' companies, or companies with high profile brand names. The motivation for FDI will help inform modellers as to the degree, or type, of cost structure differentiation appropriate.

Table 14.1 Motivations of FDI and consequent modelling considerations

FDI motives type	*Example*	*Assumptions*
Internalisation – usually associated with vertical integration in an attempt to reduce transaction costs and/or increase control	• Resource supplies or reputation ('quality') • Mining – secure supply • Services – ensure quality	• May import technology; tendency to export • May import technology; tendency to import • No *a priori* assumptions as to rate of return
Location – associated with resource advantage or market advantage	• Low cost labour; access to market • Tariff jumping • Low cost unskilled labour • Low cost skilled labour	• Tendency to local usage; against exports • Local cost structure; tendency to export • Home country cost structure; tendency to export • No *a priori* assumption of higher rates of return
Ownership – associated with some company specific factors	• Technology, trademarks, management skills, etc • 'High tech' • Brand names	• Tendency to imported cost structure • *A priori* assumption of higher rates of return

Another issue when comparing the cost structures of domestic and foreign firms deals with the degree of specialisation adopted by the MNC. In a general equilibrium framework, industry costs are often the average of several different processes (e.g. communication may include telecommunication and post offices). Foreign activity may be concentrated in a very small part of the industry (e.g. telecommunications).

Once the cost structure of an MNC has been determined, distinct from its domestic counterpart, model parameters must also be examined. Given MNCs' access to global resources, factor substitution elasticities will most likely differ. As alluded to earlier, transfer pricing may also affect relative prices of intermediate inputs. A researcher must determine the entire functional relationship for each industry in which MNCs operate in the host economy.

Input demands and cost structures

Expanding a standard input–output structure to account for MNC activity requires determining the size of the foreign contribution to each sector as well as the structure of the expanded inter-industry table.

Determining the share of industry activity accounted for by MNCs

The first issue with which a modeller must deal is to determine for each sector in the input–output table, how much activity within that sector is accounted for by

MNCs. The value of industry output associated with FDI might conceptually be obtained in a number of different ways. Two approaches may be a 'top down' and a 'bottom up'. In principle, the major difference between the two is how a modeller determines the scale of operation and the reliance on potentially incompatible data sources.

A top down approach might use ratios of foreign affiliate output to the host economy's total output in each sector. Intermediate, capital and labour inputs would then be determined through appropriate ratios (such as capital–output ratios). Most often these ratios would be based on the host technology. While this method makes blanket assumptions about input–output relationships and implies similar cost structures for MNCs and domestic firms, it has the benefit of relying on relatively little new data and being more general in its implementation.

The bottom up method requires more information, but also allows the researcher more leeway in its application. With this approach individual input determinations are made regarding the MNCs cost structure. It most often relies on capital as its starting point. Each sector would apply a combination of factors driven by its source of capital, that is, foreign or domestic. This unique combination of inputs would be summed to determine total output. This approach has the appeal of allowing each MNC in the sector to adopt a unique production process, including import scheme and captures the elements of both the internalisation and ownership motivations for FDI. However, its most promising feature is also its most detrimental: it is more detailed and thus the more data-intensive method.

A possible method for incorporating FDI into a general equilibrium model is illustrated in Figure 14.2. Following the bottom up method, it begins by obtaining

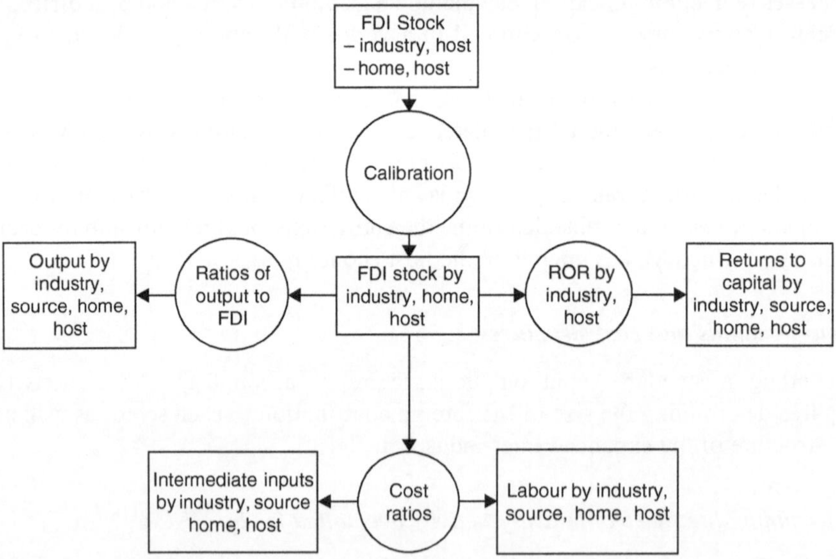

Figure 14.2 Adding FDI into a GE framework.

FDI stock data for each sector, by home and host economy.[6] The sources of FDI stock data and its applicability in a GE framework will be discussed in more detail in the next section. For now, assume we have FDI stock information that accurately reflects the financial position of the home country in the host country. Information on the amount of FDI in each sector by home and host economy is not readily available. Thus, some calibration method (such as RASing) must be applied to obtain FDI stocks by industry, home and host.

When using total capital stock for each sector of the host economy, two things must be kept in mind. First, we are deriving the number in order to obtain foreign stock values to produce an estimate of returns to foreign investors. We then subtract the foreign returns from the total returns reported in the input–output table to obtain returns to domestic investors. Therefore, we must make sure the FDI stocks and the total capital stocks derived from the original national accounts are consistent. Second, the returns to capital by sector in an input–output table are defined as gross operating surplus (GOS). GOS is the excess of gross output over the costs incurred in producing that output before allowing for the consumption of fixed capital. Put another way,

$$\text{GOS} = \text{taxable income} + \text{net interest paid} + \text{depreciation}\,.$$

This means that the rates of return that are applied to the capital stock numbers need to be calculated on an EBITD (earnings before interest, taxes and depreciation) or gross value. Foreign returns to capital are calculated by applying the rates of return to the foreign capital stocks and thus allowing the split of foreign and domestic returns. Applying a capital–output ratio,[7] one can obtain output associated with each source of capital.

FDI stocks

The FDI stocks reported by most sources include equity investments of more than 10 per cent. However, not all values of FDI stock reported include debt. Some include only debt between parent and subsidiary. While when dealing with purely domestic firms, in so far as a parent and subsidiary operate in the same sector, the fact that there exist inter-company loans and equity swaps does not affect the national accounts. Also, for the most part, debt obtained from third party sources is not included in FDI stock numbers. Returns derived from FDI stocks may seriously understate the true capital position of the MNC operating in the host economy.

Rates of return

There are many issues surrounding the topic of rates of return. It is not immediately clear what rate of return should be applied to foreign stocks. Is it the rate prevailing in an industry in the host economy, or is the rate of return determined in the home economy, the original source of capital? If firms are maximising rates of return in order to attract investors, they must know where their potential investors originate and what their opportunity cost is. There is evidence of a home country bias when investors calculate opportunity costs, thus lending support for using home-based rates of return (Gokkent 1999). Yet, foreign firms are competing with domestic firms in the host region. If they are attracted to that market due to the ability to earn 'superior' returns, then the basis of comparison is the host economy. It is also possible that the unique combination of resources available to the MNC by operating in the host economy allow it to earn returns superior to both those prevailing in the host or home economies.

If the MNCs' required rate of return is based on a home country's returns, then MNCs and domestic firms have the potential to earn different returns, even within the same sector and region. In such a case, the same rate of return should not be applied to both foreign and domestic sources of capital. There is no guarantee MNCs should, *a priori*, have superior rates of return to their domestic counterparts. An example might be resource-seeking FDI. An MNC, driven by securing means of supply, is motivated to reduce the risk of disruption and not, necessarily, driven by divergent rates of return between home and host economies. Indeed, empirical evidence has shown that foreign affiliates often earn inferior returns to those of their domestic counterparts (see, for example, Landefeld *et al.* 1992). When determining what return to apply, modellers must consider that the observable rate of return in the domestic market may not be the appropriate benchmark. Rather the firm seeks some unobservable internal rate of return.

The potential for disparity between foreign returns, joint venture returns, and strictly domestic capital returns, can arise due to firm specific issues as well as the environment in which they operate. In the extreme, if the risk adjusted foreign rate of return is greater than the domestic rate of return, all domestic capital will flow to the foreign investment. Since we do not observe this phenomenon, barriers must be in place which are preventing this from occurring. If we assume that impediments are imposed to capture superior 'technology' of MNCs, then the pre-impediment rates of return may not diverge but post returns will. The relative rate of return will affect the rate at which foreign and domestic capital mix. It will determine how that mix changes in response to changes in returns as well as the barriers affecting the returns. Possible wedges in rates of return imposed by direct impediments are outlined in Table 14.2.

Cost structure

Even if one were able to obtain returns to capital completely representing the return to all foreign capital in the host economy, one would still need to deal with the issue of the appropriate cost structure.

Many of the interesting questions researchers have about MNCs arise from the fact that they are presumed to have a different cost structure than domestic firms. That is, they often employ a different technology than that of the domestic production process. MNCs import their intermediates in a different proportion than host economy firms and often pay a different price for those intermediates. They

Table 14.2 Direct barriers

Impediment type	*Issues*	*Implications*
Regulation	• Increases cost of operations in host • Impediment implemented in host/source	• Possible disparity between joint venture and domestic-only returns • Rents accrue to host economy
Quotas/Restrictions	• Limits supply of capital • Raises the cost of capital	• Possible disparity between joint venture and domestic-only ventures • Rents can accrue to host or source economy
Taxes	• Raises the cost of capital	• Possible disparity between joint venture and domestic-only returns • Rents accrue to host economy

employ a different proportion of labour, and often import more skilled labour. Their capital requirements and returns, as discussed above, differ as well. All of these combined is what makes explicitly modelling MNCs so interesting and so difficult.

When breaking up intermediate and labour inputs into those used by foreign and domestic sources, one must consider the underlying assumptions involved if using pro-rata shares based on capital–output ratios. The researcher could argue, on the grounds of localisation, that the MNC would adopt the host economy's technology. If the MNC were operating in that host economy to take advantage of a cheap resource, this assumption might apply. But this may not be the case if the investment was to deliver a service, or secure a source of supply. Much would depend upon the MNC, the type of service and the operations of the MNC itself. For example, Japanese firms have a reputation for applying the parent company's methodology no matter where they operate, while firms from the US have been shown to vary their technology in response to local conditions.

In Table 14.3 some of the issues surrounding the implementation of MNC activity into the input side of the input/output table are summarised. Along the top, we assume there are three types of firm, domestic (Australian), and two MNCs, one Japanese owned, the other American owned. The first columns lists the input items. The centre lists three possible strategies for differentiating inputs between foreign and domestic firms. The first would assume that the host economy (in this case Australia) determines the technology, or input mix, for all firms which operate in that economy. This would then entail a simple share weighting of the input table between the various firms. The second option is to model a production technology based on Japanese and/or American foreign affiliate data. The third is to use some third party (such as OECD or UN) data. Some of the considerations discussed above are listed in the third column.

Table 14.3 Sample input structure for an industry with FDI located in Australia

	Australia owned	*Japan owned*	*USA owned*	*Considerations*
Domestic				
Commodity inputs	Possible setups: 1 assume destination cost structure for foreign affiliates and local industries (only differentiation is in level of foreign ownership) 2 Input new cost structure using foreign affiliate data 3 Input new cost structure using third-party data			Tendency of foreign affiliates to substitute for imported variety
Imported				
Commodity inputs				Tendency of foreign affiliates to import from home country
				Tendency to be the same across firms
Services				Tendency of foreign affiliates to use highly skilled labour
Skilled labour				
Unskilled labour				Cost-driven FDI
Local capital returns				Form of FDI, Host policy
Foreign capital returns				Form of FDI
Total Capital returns				Policy
(Shadow)Tax on foreign capital and domestic				Policy
Total costs	Ratio of output to FDI			Level of FDI

Final demand

Aside from the production process, differentiating final demand between foreign and domestic firms is also important. Private and public consumption and investment goods can now be procured from domestic firms, foreign firms or from imports. There is also evidence that MNCs often export more of their output than do host economy firms (APEC 1995). These characteristics of MNC activity must be reflected in the database and model theory when incorporating MNCs in a GE framework.

MNC activity enhances the variety of output available to the host economy. Therefore, when structuring a final demand sector including MNC activity, researchers should consider theories explaining product differentiation. There is an extensive literature on exploring properties of firm level product differentiation, including models building on the theoretical work of Ethier (1986) and Krugman (1980) include Brown (1994) and Francois *et al.* (1997).

Data problems and constraints

The difficulties and potential pitfalls in modelling FDI become clear as soon as one begins to collect data. When dealing in a single-country environment, data issues are generally less overwhelming. Countries such as the United States, Japan and the Netherlands provide annual, detailed statistics on foreign firms operating within their economies, as well as domestic firms operating overseas. However, in a multicountry framework, matters of consistency between respective countries or regions, and completeness become of much greater concern.

The problem can be broken into two basic components: *what* a country reports and *how* it reports it. *How* a country reports refers to its definition of FDI. This varies across countries. The EU defines direct investment as

> … an incorporated or unincorporated enterprise in which a foreign investor owns 10% or more of the ordinary shares or voting power of an incorporated enterprise or the equivalent of an unincorporated enterprise or has an effective voice in the management of the enterprise.
>
> European Union Direct Investment Yearbook 1997 (p. 355)

This definition has some 'flexibility' across countries to 'fit circumstances.' European Union Direct Investment Yearbook 1997, p. 355). The definition of FDI stock, according to the UNCTAD, is

> … the value of the share of their (FDI enterprise) capital and reserves (including retained profits) attributable to the parent enterprise, plus the net indebtedness of affiliates to the parent enterprise.
>
> World Investment Report 1999 (p. 465)

An 'FDI enterprise' is defined as one whose 'stake permits a lasting interest in the management of that enterprise (an equity stake of 10 per cent for incorporated enterprises or its equivalent for unincorporated).' However, this definition is not always adhered to, and the data depend on the various reporting standards of the respective country. For example, Thailand's statisticians generally define foreign affiliates as firms having at least 25 per cent equity participation and do not include reinvested earnings in their calculations. In Indonesia, FDI flows are defined as the equity contributions of both foreign and domestic enterprises and loan capital. Thus, in Indonesia, all equity shares in joint ventures are included in data on FDI. Japan reports inward FDI stock of firms with equity shares of more than 50 per cent. These inconsistencies between national statistics affect international comparisons that are based on national reports.

There is disagreement on the definition of an 'investment'. Indonesia includes all capital investment (foreign and domestic) in its reported values of FDI stocks and flows. While OECD countries all adhere to the 10 per cent value, they differ in their definition of investment. Some countries include retained earnings, other only include parent-related debt and equity.

On a practical level, conflicting definitions and reporting standards lead to disagreement between reported values of inward versus outward FDI flows and stocks between two countries. A researcher must determine the degree to which the two must be, or can be, reconciled. One way to approach it is to ask which flows are more closely tracked by reporting agencies. Generally, governments are more concerned with what happens within their borders, thus focus on incoming FDI. If that is true, inflows or inward stock would be more accurate. Or one could use the 'OECD rule' and choose the numbers reported by definition – complying OECD countries over all other flows. If that is the case, again, do we rely on inward reported flows or outward? As the example in Box 14.1 illustrates, even when dealing with OECD countries the numbers do not necessarily agree.

The notion of *what* a country reports deals with the broader concept of what constitutes control. FDI is meant to be distinguished from portfolio investment

Box 14.1 Reporting FDI numbers for Australia: which to use?

It is usually assumed that developed countries have higher reporting standards and consistency than developing countries and thus higher quality data. Thus, when in doubt, most researchers will choose the number reported by an OECD country. However, this method is not always foolproof, especially when dealing with FDI. Take Australia for an example. (All numbers reported are in millions.)

The Australian Bureau of Statistics (ABS) reported in their 14 August 1998, Balance of Payments and International Investment Position that in 1993 Australia had a total investment position abroad of A$47,969, while the total foreign investment in Australia stood at A$114,297. This translates (using consistent exchange rates) into US$35,760 and US$85,210, respectively. In 1995 it was A$54,156 and A$123,409 or US$40,373 and US$92,002, respectively. *International Direct Investment Statistics Yearbook* published by the OECD puts Australian inward investment in 1993 (most recent year available) at A$112,244, and its position abroad at A$45,196. UNCTAD's World Investment Report 1998 indicates that Australia's inward FDI stock in 1995 was US$96,811, while outward stock was reported to be US$39,107 (they do not report numbers for 1993). Finally, APEC's FDI and APEC Economic Integration reported in 1992 Australian inward stock valued at US$71,888 and outward stock of US$29,400.

The problem progresses when we move to bilateral relationships. Taking just the OECD publication, Australia reports its investment in the United States in 1993 stood at US$7,840 while the US reports in the same publication, Australia's inward FDI at US$7,278. The United States is reporting to have US$18,437 invested in Australia while Australia is reporting US$23,332.

These discrepancies exist between two countries considered to have consistent and somewhat diligent reporting institutions. The differences are even greater when we move to countries like China and Indonesia.

by indicating some degree of control by the foreign firm, as well as being an indication of a 'lasting interest.' What level of participation does a firm need to reach in order to achieve this standard? Can there be one? In reporting activities of foreign affiliates, the OECD relies on a definition based on an equity investment greater than 50 per cent.[8] Yet it uses the 10 per cent value to determine whether an investment is FDI or not. This implies that on an operational level, an investor must have a stake greater than 50 per cent to be considered an affiliate but over 10 per cent to be 'lasting' or 'influential'. The importance of this distinction depends on the purpose of the modelling exercise.

The question becomes: what constitutes foreign investment and does one apply a 'universal' definition and thus rely on one source, say OECD, for data? This way we only use stocks reported by countries in compliance with that definition. Or does one use the country-specific numbers under the argument that each country has its own definition of control and thus, the level of investment needed to obtain control is regionally dependent.

The best source of cost structure is that reported by foreign affiliates. While the reporting standards are still rather loose, OECD now has an *Activity of Foreign Affiliates in OECD Countries* biennial publication. However, not all countries have chosen to participate. Table 14.4 lists a number of multinational data sources for FDI.

Existing studies

Few studies have attempted to explicitly incorporate FDI in a general equilibrium framework. As outlined above, the reasons stem in large part from the lack of consistent and detailed data. Some attempts to model distinction between foreign and domestic firms are outlined in Table 14.5.

Petri (1997) introduced FDI into his model of trade liberalisation in the APEC region. This model distinguishes foreign and domestic firm operations at a microeconomic level. Production linkages between parent and subsidiary are modelled by identifying inputs specifically sourced from parent. Both country of ownership and place of production differentiate demand. Petri found substantial benefits from trade liberalisation and estimated that 40 per cent of those gains were due to investment liberalisation. This is a result not explicitly captured in earlier models.

Table 14.4 Main sources of data

1	*Foreign Direct Investment*, APEC Economic Integration. APEC 1997
2	*World Investment Report*, United Nations Conference on Trade and Development, annual publication
3	*International Direct Investment Statistics Yearbook*, 1995, 1997, Organisation of Economic Cooperation and Development
4	*Activities of Foreign Affiliates in OECD Countries, 1985–1994*, Organisation of Economic Cooperation and Development
5	Multicountry Input/Output databases such as GTAP
6	*European Union Direct Investment Yearbook*, Eurostat

Table 14.5 Models distinguishing between foreign and domestic firms*

Markusen *et al.* (1995)	Analysis of trade liberalisation in the automobile industry in the NAFTA countries, using a model with multinational firms or national firms responding to changes in their market shares.
Markusen *et al.* (1996)	Conceptual static and dynamic CGE model used to analyse how inward FDI in producer services may complement domestic skilled labour, affect the pattern of trade in goods, and determine the characteristics of the dynamic adjustment path.
Petri (1997)	Based on 6-region, 3-sector CGE model, using 1992 GTAP dataset, with FDI distinguished between activities of domestic and foreign-owned firms. Products differentiated by both country of ownership and place of production. Capital allocation between sectors and between domestic and foreign investments responds to changes in rates of return and to investor preferences. Barriers to FDI modelled as a tax on FDI profits.
Benjamin and Diao (1997)	Based on 10-region, 11-sector CGE model, using data for the early 1990s, with the focus on liberalisation of cross-border trade of other private services in APEC. Service providers in the single services sector are imperfectly competitive and have fixed costs, and are able to price discriminate across countries. Liberalisation is modelled as both reducing fixed costs and removing the market segmentation that permits price discrimination. FDI is not modelled explicitly, but it could be.
Dee and Hanslow (1999)	Based on 19-region, 3-sector, 1995-reference year CGE model, with modifications of Petri's (1997) framework and updating of data on FDI stocks, output, and rates of return. Used averages of services barriers for banking and telecommunications services contained in Kalirajan *et al.* (1999) and Warren (2000).
Brown and Stern (1999)	Based on an 18-country update of the Michigan Model of World Production and Trade with each MNC production location producing a differentiated product. Labour is mobile between sectors but not across borders while capital is internationally mobile.

* Based on Brown and Stern (1999).

Dee and Hanslow (2000) used measures of barriers to services trade in a 19-region 3-sector model of world trade. This was based on an expansion of the GTAP model called FTAP. This model differed from Petri in the preference ordering applied. Petri's treatment assumes that US owned firms are closer substitutes for each other than, for example, Australian firms, irrespective of location. Dee and Hanslow's treatment assumes a US MNC located in Australia is a closer substitute for an Australian owned firm than it is for a US firm located in the United States. They, like Petri, found those economies that had the most highly protected service sectors experienced the largest gains in welfare from the liberalisation of those barriers.

Finally, a study by Brown and Stern (1999) also applied a general equilibrium model with explicit MNC behaviour to evaluate the effects of liberalisation of trade in services. They also found large welfare gains under liberalisation. Further, they point out that capital formation plays a 'far more important and substantive role than consumer distortions' in determining welfare effect.

Conclusions

In summary, incorporating MNC activity in a general equilibrium framework affects the measurement of benefits and changes in trade policy, environmental regulation, factor movements and technology transfers. As shown in the above studies, differentiating between foreign and domestic firms has implications for measuring the benefits of trade liberalisation. As long as MNCs face different operating constraints from domestic firms the impact of any policy change on the host and home economies will best be estimated by modelling MNC activity specifically.

The differing cost and sales structure of MNCs need to be estimated when attempting to incorporate their activity into a model. The motivation and role of technology will determine the effect on the data structure of MNC activity relative to domestic firms. These will impact returns to labour and capital and the use of intermediate inputs. The differing import and export propensities of MNCs may have a large effect on model estimates and resulting sectoral, economy-wide and trade outcomes.

The biggest constraint on modellers is data. None is directly compatible with the input–output structure that underlies a GE model. FDI flows and stocks are not reported on a consistent, detailed basis. Even FDI stocks, which are often considered reliable, differ in characteristics (equity versus debt) and definition (10 per cent versus 50 per cent). What is needed is a consistent (both over time and definition) and detailed effort by international statistical agencies to collect data on FDI. The OECD through its *Affiliate* publications has made a necessary first step. However, beyond affiliate data, organisations such as UNCTAD need to report statistics not only on a bilateral basis (for country or industry) but on a three-dimensional basis, covering flows between home and host by industry.

Incorporating MNC activity into models of international economic activity affects estimates of welfare outcomes from modelled policy changes. The studies cited in this chapter found substantial changes in welfare measurements when MNC activity was included. While data developments lag behind modelling attempts, data collection agencies will hopefully be able to improve the reliability, detail and consistency of data on MNC activity.

Notes

1 See, for example, the World Bank's Development Economic Research Group's investor surveys.

2 We will adopt the usual convention of identifying the 'home' economy as the location of the MNCs headquarters and the 'host' economy as the location in which one of its affiliates operates.

3 The internet has allowed more companies to operate globally than ever before. But this trend has also raised concerns of tax and regulation avoidance.

4 For a GE analysis of the NAFTA agreement, including labour and environmental standards see, for example, Francois and Shiells (1994).

5 Advocates of the harmonisation of environmental standards claim that free trade in the presence of divergent environmental standards provides the nation with the lowest standard with a competitive advantage. As a result, pollution havens will emerge and nations try to undercut the environmental standards of their competitors (Cole 2000).

6 This discussion follows the method applied by the Productivity Commission to expand the Global Trade Analysis Project, or GTAP, model to include FDI. The resulting model is referred to as FTAP. See Hanslow *et al.* (1999) for details.

7 Capital–output ratios can be obtained from the host or MNC data. Using the host economy's input–output table, a modeller can calculate the ratio and apply it to the MNC. One can also use reports on MNC activity supplied by various OECD countries.

8 France and the United States are the exception to this. They report activities of foreign affiliates based on any firm that has a foreign equity investment of greater than 10 per cent.

References

APEC, 1995, *Foreign Direct Investment*, Singapore: APEC Secretariat.

Blomström M and Kokko A, 1996, 'Multinational Corporations and Spillovers', *Journal of Economic Surveys*, 12(3): 247–77.

Bora B and Guisinger S, 1997, *Impact of Investment Liberalisation APEC*, Adelaide: Flinders University.

Brown D, 1994, 'Properties of Applied General Equilibrium Trade Models with Monopolistic Competition and Foreign Direct Investment in Modelling Trade Policy' *in* Francois J and Shiells C (eds), *AGE Models of North American Free Trade*, Cambridge: Cambridge University Press.

Brown D, Deardoff A and Stern R, 1996, 'Modelling Multilateral Trade Liberalisation in Services', *Asia Pacific Economic Review*, 2(1): 21–34.

Brown D and Stern R, 1999, 'Measurement and Modelling of the Economic Effects of Trade and Investment Barriers in Services', presented at the *Coalition of Service Industries World Services Congress*, Atlanta, November 1–3.

Caves R, 1996, *Multinational Enterprise and Economic Analysis (second edition)*, New York: Cambridge University Press.

Charnovitz S, 1993, 'Environmental Harmonisation and Trade Policy' *in* Zaelke, Orbuch and Housman (eds), *Trade and the Environment: Laws, Economics and Ethics*, Washington, DC: Centre for International Environmental Law.

Cole M, 2000, *Trade Liberalisation, Economic Growth and the Environment*, Cheltenham: Edward Elgar Publishing.

Daly H, 1993, 'Problems with Free Trade: Neoclassical and Steady State Perspectives' *in* Zaelke, Orbuch and Housman (eds), *Trade and the Environment: Laws, Economics and Ethics*, Washington, DC: Centre for International Environmental Law.

Dee P and Hanslow K, 2000, *Multilateral Liberalisation of Services Trade*, Productivity Commission Staff Research Paper, Canberra: Productivity Comission.

Dunning J, 1977, 'Trade, Location of Economic Activity and the Multinational Enterprise: A search for an Eclectic Approach', *in* Ohlin, Hesselbar and Wilkman (eds), *The International Allocation of Economic Activity*, London, MacMillan, pp. 395–418.

Ethier WJ, 1986, 'The Multinational Firm', *Quarterly Journal of Economics*, 101: 805–33.

Eurostat, 1998, *European Union Direct Investment Yearbook 1997*, Belgium: European Communities.

Francois J, Roland-Holst D, 1997, 'Scale Economics and Imperfect Competition', *in* Francois J and Reinert K (eds), *Applied Methods for Trade Policy Analysis*, Cambridge: Cambridge University Press, pp 331–63.

Francois J and Shiells C, 1999, *North American Free Trade*, Cambridge: Cambridge University Press.

Francois J and Shiells C, 1994, *Modelling Trade Policy: Applied General Equilibrium Assessments in North American Free Trade*, Cambridge: Cambridge University Press.

Gokkent G, 1999, 'Simultaneous Home Bias and Cross-Holding of Assets under Information Asymmetry,' *Economia Internazionale*, 52(1): 15–44.

Hanslow K, Phamduc T and Verikios G, 1999, 'The Structure of the FTAP Model' Research Momorandum MC-58, Productivity Commission, Canberra, August.

Harrison A, 1994, 'The Role of Multinationals in Economic Development: The Benefits of FDI', *Columbia Journal of World Business*, 29(4): 6–11.

Hatzius J, 1997a, 'Foreign Direct Investment Capital Formation and Labour Costs: Evidence from Britain and Germany', CEP Discussion Paper No 336, London: CEPR.

—— 1997b, 'Domestic Jobs and Foreign Wages: Labour Demand in Swedish Multinationals', CEP Discussion Paper No 332, London.

Krugman P, 1980 'Scale Economies, Product Differentiation and the Pattern of Trade', *American Economic Review*, 70(5): 950–9.

Landefeld S, Lawson A and Weinberg D, 1992, 'Rates of Return on Direct Investment', *Survey of Current Business*, Washington, DC: 79–86.

Low P and Yeats A, 1992, 'Do "Dirty" Industries Migrate?' in Low, P (ed), *International Trade and the Environment*, World Bank Discussion Paper No 159, Washington, DC: World Bank.

Low P and Safadi R, 1992, 'Trade Policy and Pollution', in Low, P (ed), *International Trade and the Environment*, World Bank Discussion Paper No 159, Washington, DC: World Bank.

Mahajan A, Rangan N and Zardkoohi A, 1996, 'Cost Structures in Multinational and Domestics Banking', *Journal of Banking and Finance*, 20: 283–306.

Markusen J, Rutherford T and Hunter L, 1995, 'Trade Liberalisation in a Multinational Dominated Industry,' *Journal of International Economics*, 38: 95–117.

Markusen J, Venables A, Konan D and Zhang K, 1996, 'A Unified Treatment of Horizontal Direct Investment, Vertical Direct Investment, and the Pattern of Trade in Goods and Services', National Bureau of Economic Research Working Paper No 5696, Cambridge, MA: NBER.

McKibbin W and Wilcoxen P, 1996, 'The Role of Services in Modelling the Global Economy', *Asia Pacific Economic Review*, 2: 2–13.

OECD, 1998, *Harmful Tax Competition: An Emerging Global Issue*, Paris: OECD.

Pearson C, 1985, *Down to Business: Multinational Corporations, the Environment, and Development*, Washington, DC: World Reserve Resources.

Pearson C and Pryor A, 1978, *Environment North and South*, New York: John Wiley.

Petri P, 1997, 'Foreign Direct Investment in a Computable General Equilibrium Framework', presented at *Making APEC Work: Economic Challenges and Policy Alternatives*, March 13–14, Tokyo: Keio University.

Prakash A, Krutilla K and Karamanos P, 1996, *Multinational Corporations and International Environmental Policy*, Indiana Centre for Global Business Discussion Paper No 125, Indiana: Indiana University.

Scherr J, 1987 'Hazardous Exports: US and International Policy Development', *in* Pearson C (ed), *Multinational Corporations, Environment and the Third World*, Durham, NC: Duke University Press.

Strohm L, 1992, 'Environmental Politics of the International Waste Trade', *Journal of Environment and Development*, 2(2): 129–53.

United Nations, 1999, *World Investment Report, Foreign Direct Investment and the Challenge of Development*, Geneva and New York: United Nations.

Wong K, 1995, *International Trade in Goods and Factor Mobility*, Cambridge, MA: MIT Press.

15 Measuring and modelling barriers to FDI

Alexis Hardin and Leanne Holmes

Introduction

In recent years many governments have removed or reduced some restrictions on foreign direct investment (FDI), often as part of broader reform agendas, and committed to limit the introduction of further restrictions, in multilateral fora such as the General Agreement on Trade in Services (GATS). However, all APEC, OECD and World Trade Organisation (WTO) member economies continue to place some restrictions on inward FDI.

Policies to control or influence FDI are designed to achieve a range of economic, political and social objectives. For example, restrictions on FDI in key service sectors such as broadcasting, telecommunications or transport may be designed to address national security or national sovereignty concerns. These policies distort the market signals which drive foreign investment, and could potentially have a significant impact on trade in services. For example, restricting foreign investment in certain markets may result in less competition in those markets, higher prices and less diversity and innovation in the goods and services offered. These types of economic costs must be balanced against the perceived benefits of maintaining control over FDI.

The challenge for researchers and policy advisers is to provide information and analysis on the nature and extent of barriers to FDI and the possible gains from removing them. For example, are the barriers relatively high in particular sectors or economies? What are the possible economic impacts of removing restrictions on FDI in, say, the transport and communications industries?

Considerable progress has been made in recent years in the analysis of barriers to goods trade, and to a lesser extent services trade (see Hoekman and Braga 1997, Hufbauer 1996, OECD 1997, Deardorff and Stern 1997). Estimates of the possible gains from trade liberalisation have helped to provide impetus for the reform process. In contrast, there are still major gaps in the information base and tools for analysis of FDI policies.

The aims in this chapter are to examine the issues involved in measuring FDI barriers and modelling their impact, and to suggest options for dealing with some of the problems. The emphasis is on barriers to FDI in the services sector. Services industries tend to be the most heavily restricted in most countries, with even the most open economies maintaining some control over FDI in key service industries such as transport, telecommunications, broadcasting and financial services (Hardin and Holmes 1997). The focus on the services sector is also useful because FDI plays a particularly important role in many service industries, allowing foreigners to supply services which cannot be traded across borders. These economic characteristics of FDI in the services sector raise some challenging issues for modellers.

The information base

The first major hurdle in the analysis of FDI barriers is the lack of information on the restrictions imposed in each economy. Some initiatives in recent years have helped to increase transparency, although the new sources of information still have some shortcomings. For example, FDI policies in APEC member economies are now documented and updated in the *Guide to Investment Regimes of Member Economies* (1998 version now available on the internet) and APEC members' Individual Action Plans (most recently released in November 1997). However, these information sources are self-reported and often incomplete. WTO members' listing of some FDI restrictions in the GATS has also helped to improve transparency. However, the 'positive list' approach, with members only scheduling those restrictions to which they intend to apply the market access and national treatment principles, means that many restrictions, particularly those in sensitive sectors, are not included (see Hardin and Holmes 1997 for a discussion).

A further difficulty with establishing an information base on FDI barriers is that a vast range of measures is applied throughout the world, often on a vague case-by-case nature. For example, UNCTAD has identified a total of fifty-seven different types of FDI restrictions applied throughout the world (UNCTAD 1997). These must be identified, classified and summarised in some way before any analysis can proceed. Using the three part classification system suggested by UNCTAD (1996) – restrictions on market entry, ownership and operations of the foreign firm – Hardin and Holmes (1997, table 4.2) list the major restrictions on inward FDI in service sectors in selected APEC economies.

While the details vary, some common characteristics seem to be:

- application of some form of screening or registration process, involving various degrees of burden for the foreign investor;
- restrictions on the level or share of foreign ownership, particularly in some service sectors, and often in the context of privatisations;
- widespread use of case-by-case judgements, often based on vague national interest criteria;
- widespread use of restrictions on ownership and control (e.g. restrictions on board membership), particularly in sectors such as telecommunications, broadcasting, banking; and
- relatively limited use of performance requirements or input controls in services sectors.

Quantifying barriers to FDI

While the details of FDI restrictions vary widely across economies and sectors, in essence they involve some restriction on the value of foreign investment (say a limit on the share of foreign ownership in a sector or firm), or some measure which makes the foreign investment more costly (say by requiring the investor to go through a screening process, or by restricting the inputs used by the foreign firm).

In principle, the impacts of these restrictions on asset prices or prices for the services in the restricted markets would be useful measures of the extent or size of the FDI barriers. These 'tariff equivalents' could provide a basis for comparing FDI regimes across economies, and would be a useful starting point for modelling the general equilibrium effects of liberalisation.

However, there are a range of practical and conceptual difficulties in estimating tariff equivalents for FDI barriers. The wide variety of forms of restrictions and their often case-by-case nature complicates the task. Even for relatively direct types of restrictions such as limits on the share of foreign ownership the analysis is complicated, with different limits often applying to different firms in a sector, to different types of foreign investors, and to individual and aggregate foreign investment. As is the case for non-tariff barriers to goods trade, alternatives to simple price or cost wedges often have to be used to summarise the extent of FDI restrictions. The difficulties with estimating tariff equivalents, or price wedges, are outlined in the following section and some alternatives are then considered.

Tariff equivalents

Restrictions on foreign ownership are applied in selected sectors by all APEC and WTO member economies. In some cases, no foreign investment is allowed in certain sectors, while in others foreigners may own up to some maximum share of equity in firms within a sector.

These types of restrictions are similar in many ways to quotas on imports of goods. They, therefore, provide a useful starting point for assessing the extent to which the techniques used in assessing goods trade barriers can be applied to calculating tariff equivalent type measures for FDI barriers.

In general, a restriction on the supply of imports (of goods or capital) will lead to some price adjustment to ration the limited supply, and some switching to the next best alternative product or asset – usually a domestically produced good or capital from domestic investors.

Where the FDI is being undertaken to gain access to service markets in a country, the next best alternative may be some other mode of supply, such as delivering financial services via the internet or sending professional staff temporarily to the country to provide services to clients, without the firm investing directly. In some cases, the next best alternative to the supply of services via foreign investment may be supply using domestic resources.

The quantity restriction on imports translates into some increase in prices or rates of return. Assuming the next best alternative is a very close substitute for the restricted product or asset, the wedge that is driven between the restricted and unrestricted prices or returns measures the tariff equivalent of the quota. The size of the wedge depends on the nature of supply and demand in the restricted market. In Box 15.1, this is illustrated for the case of a restriction on the supply of foreign capital, where domestic capital is a perfect substitute for the restricted foreign capital. The restriction results in an increase in the rate of return, a reduction in total capital flows and an increase in the share of domestic capital in the total.

If the next best alternative to services delivered via FDI is services delivered by some other mode, the simple partial equilibrium model in Box 15.1 can be re-interpreted in terms of a services market, rather than a capital market. The demand would be for services, while supply would be via FDI or an alternative mode. The restriction would increase the price of services, and increase the share of the alternative (and more costly) mode of supply in total service supply.

Moving beyond the simple model to a practical tariff equivalent measure can be difficult. For example, what rates of return or service prices should be compared, and can all the differences be attributed to the effects of the investment restriction? It is likely that observed price or rate of return wedges will reflect factors other than just FDI restrictions. For example, differences in rates of return in the telecommunications sector in Australia or New Zealand, where foreign investment is restricted, and the United Kingdom, where it is not restricted, could be due to a range of factors, including different regulatory regimes in telecommunications. Observed differences in rates of return could not be attributed fully to the different foreign investment policies. Removing the FDI barriers may not eliminate the wedge. The wedge may also remain if the domestic and foreign capital are not perfect substitutes, although it would be reduced by removal of the barrier.

The underlying assumptions about perfect substitutability are particularly relevant when applying the simple model to the case of FDI. The above analysis is based on a very simple representation of capital (or services) markets. There is demand for capital (or services) in the domestic market, and this can be met from one of two sources. The two sources are perfect substitutes, so that domestic capital (or services supplied via some mode other than FDI) can meet any demand not satisfied by restricted foreign capital.

However, FDI often involves transfer of firm-specific assets, such as human capital, technology and international reputation. It is these assets which give the international firm an advantage over domestic firms, making FDI profitable despite the additional costs that must be incurred in managing affiliates in different countries.

In the services sector in particular, the FDI may be driven by the desire to establish a commercial presence in a market, where it is the most technically feasible and profitable way to supply a service. Furthermore, service suppliers often compete on non-price terms, with FDI in a range of countries giving them

Box 15.1 The impact of a limit on the share of foreign ownership

To illustrate the effects of a limit on the supply of foreign capital, assume that the demand for capital in the sector is a declining function of the rate of return (see D_1 figure below), and the domestic supply of capital increases with increases in the rate of return. Domestic suppliers of capital to the sector need to be offered higher returns to divert more capital to the sector, to offset any additional risks they may take by reducing their portfolio diversification. Since the domestic economy is small, foreign capital supply is assumed to be perfectly elastic – any amount is available at the world rate of return.

If there were no restrictions on foreign capital, it would meet demand beyond Q_d, up to Q_t. Domestic capital can be supplied at below the world rate of return up to Q_d, but beyond that the foreign capital meets all demand as it is cheaper.

However, now say there is a 25 per cent limit on the share of foreign capital in the market. This effectively places a limit on the amount of foreign capital that can be supplied beyond Q_d. For an increase in foreign capital by 1 unit, 3 additional units of domestic capital must be used. Three quarters of any increase in capital must be met from the domestic market.

The demand curve for domestic capital can therefore be derived (D_2 in the figure below). Domestic demand is three quarters of total demand, at each price. The domestic demand curve has a slope of 4/3 of the total demand curve. The level of domestic capital supply is set where the domestic demand and supply curves intersect (Q_{dr}), and imports then meet the additional demand (up to Q_{tr}).

With the restriction in place, the rate of return increases, less capital is used, but more of it comes from domestic sources. A measure of the size of the investment barrier is the implicit tariff, which is given by the difference between the actual rate of return in the restricted sector (R_r) and the return on the world market (R_w).

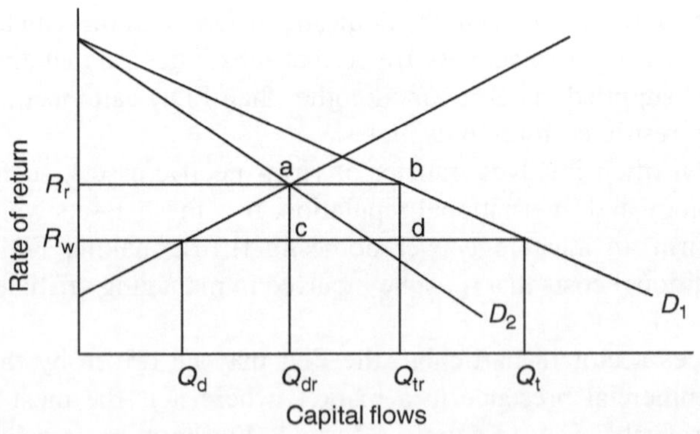

some competitive advantage over purely domestic firms. For example, American Express may be able to differentiate its products and services from others because of the international facilities it offers, and remain competitive even if it does not offer the lowest prices.

Given these economic factors driving FDI, an observed price or rate of return wedge could not necessarily be interpreted as the result of the restriction on foreign capital. It may reflect the less than perfect substitutability between FDI and domestic capital (or FDI and the next best mode of service supply).

The basic concepts illustrated in Box 15.1 are still relevant, as they show that the quantity restriction translates into some equivalent price or rate of return distortion, and the size of the distortion depends on supply and demand in the relevant market. But the difficult parts in assessing FDI barriers are deciding the appropriate market in which to conduct a partial analysis, and deciding how much of any observable price wedge reflects the restriction (as opposed to the less than perfect substitutability), before proceeding to trace the effects through the economy.

The problems in measuring and interpreting price wedges, or tariff equivalents, become even more significant when we move from the simple case of a 25 per cent restriction on the share of foreign capital to more complicated real world regimes. For example, different foreign ownership limits may apply to different firms within a sector – say Telstra and Optus. A restriction on foreign share ownership may also be coupled with other operational or establishment restrictions – say requirements that local labour and other local inputs be used.

In short, while conceptually appealing, tariff equivalents of FDI restrictions are likely to be very difficult to measure and interpret. As is the case in assessments of non-tariff barriers to goods trade, alternatives generally have to be used. Commonly used measures include coverage ratios (the proportion of trade covered by barriers) and frequency ratios (the number of barriers in each sector) (see PECC 1995).

Frequency-based measures

Hoekman (1995) used frequency ratios as a starting point for estimating 'tariff equivalent' measures of the relative degree of restriction of services trade across countries and sectors. The measures were based on information contained in each country's schedule of GATS commitments. Hoekman arbitrarily defined a set of benchmark 'guesstimates' of tariff equivalents for each sector to reflect a country that is highly restricted with respect to market access. A value of 200 per cent was chosen for the most restricted sectors such as postal and telecommunications services, while values between 20 and 50 per cent were assigned to more open sectors such as tourism and education services. Each country and sector was then assigned a value related to that benchmark. For example, the benchmark for postal services was set at 200, then if a country had a frequency ratio of 50 per cent for postal services, its tariff equivalent for that sector was 100. For countries which made no commitments for postal services, such as Australia, the frequency ratio was zero and the tariff equivalent for the sector was 200.

Different overall country and sector measures can then be calculated, with the values depending on the weights chosen for different sectors and countries. While these 'tariff equivalents' provide some indication of the relative degree of restriction of services trade across sectors and countries, their usefulness as a basis for policy development, country comparisons and modelling of the economic effects of FDI barriers is limited, for several reasons.

First, interpreting 'no commitment' in a GATS schedule as meaning that restrictions exist may lead to misleading or biased results. There are many cases where a country does not have restrictions, but has not made commitments for the sector in the GATS. For example, Singapore does not apply restrictions in civil aviation (APEC 1998). However, it does not schedule the sub-sector in the GATS, and is therefore recorded as applying restrictions (with a tariff equivalent of 200) in Hoekman's estimates. Some countries may not schedule some sectors or make commitments simply because they do not have the relevant sectors or activities in their economies. For example, space transport services are scheduled only by three countries. Other services such as maritime transport and inland waterway transport are simply not relevant for some countries, and therefore no commitments are made. (Australia does not schedule space transport or inland waterway transport.) Furthermore, developing countries make, on average, far fewer commitments than higher income countries, in part reflecting their relatively undeveloped services sectors. In short, a higher score may not necessarily reflect a less open or liberal policy regime.

Second, all types of restrictions listed in the country schedules are given equal weight in the index. For example, a country that lists a market access restriction in the form of a 49 per cent limit on foreign ownership gets the same score as a country that lists a screening process. No account is taken of the likely differences in economic impact of different types of restrictions. Hoekman does distinguish between measures which are scheduled as unbound, and those which are unscheduled, with the former assigned a score of 0.5 in the index and the latter 1. The implicit assumption is that more substantial restrictions are in the unscheduled sectors. However, as noted above, this may not be reasonable.

Third, the 'tariff equivalents' are simply benchmarks. For example, the 200 per cent for postal services does not mean that prices or returns in the sector are 200 per cent higher than they would be in the absence of restrictions. The restrictions on postal services are simply twice as widespread or frequent as they are in a sector where the tariff equivalent is 100.

Fourth, the tariff equivalents only include market access restrictions, not national treatment. They, therefore, provide an incomplete indication of the extent of restrictions.

Finally, these GATS-based tariff equivalents combine measures which restrict all modes of service delivery, not only commercial presence and FDI. It is, however, important to distinguish between barriers to FDI and barriers to the other modes of supply, as they are likely to operate through different channels and will need to be modelled in different ways. For example, a particular FDI restriction may be best treated as a tax on foreign investor profits, whereas restrictions on cross-border services trade may be better treated as a wedge between domestic and foreign service prices. Further, the links between cross-border trade restrictions and FDI restrictions cannot be analysed if the two types are lumped together. It is also important to distinguish between FDI and other restrictions for the purposes of policy development. FDI may raise national sovereignty concerns and may, therefore, need to be addressed separately from cross-border trade.

Hoekman's estimates have already been used in several studies of trade and investment liberalisation (e.g. Petri 1997, Brown *et al.* 1995, 1996, Dee *et al.* 1996). In each case, the authors note the limitations of the tariff or tax equivalent measures used. For example, Petri (1997) models FDI barriers as a tax on foreign profits. He uses Hoekman's tariff equivalents for the service sector but notes that these estimates need to be treated with caution (in the primary and manufacturing sectors he assumes barriers to FDI are half as high as tariff equivalents on goods). If indices could be derived which better reflect the size or economic significance of FDI barriers, relative to an unrestricted benchmark, they could potentially provide the basis for calculation of tax rates on profits for foreign capital in various sectors. These tax rates, or tariff equivalents, could then be substituted into a Petri style framework.

An index of the degree of restrictiveness of FDI regimes

Alternative indices of the degree of restrictiveness of FDI have been developed by Hardin and Holmes (1997). They are basically extensions of the simple frequency index, addressing several of the shortcomings of Hoekman's approach. For example, instead of being based on the information contained in the positive GATS schedules, and the assumption that unscheduled sectors are restricted, they are based on information on actual restrictions (drawn largely from the APEC Individual Action Plans and the APEC *Guide to Investment Regimes of Member Economies*). Information on the types of barriers and their likely relative economic impacts is incorporated, so that the measures provide a more useful basis for modelling the effects of FDI liberalisation. Furthermore, FDI impediments are identified separately from restrictions on other modes of service delivery, and restrictions on all aspects of FDI, not only market access, are incorporated.

The indices of the relative degree of restriction (by economy or sector) can be translated into some tariff equivalent or tax equivalent. Here, a completely open FDI regime is assigned an index value of zero, and the corresponding tax rate could be zero, while at the other extreme a complete ban on FDI is assigned an index value of 1, and the corresponding tax rate could be 100 per cent.

There are a range of issues to address in devising sensible and useful indices. These include:

- which impediments to include as separate components of the index;
- the weights to assign to each type of barrier (e.g. what should the relative weights be for a screening process involving some vague national interest

assessment and a restriction on the ownership or operations of a foreign company?); and

- the weights to assign when aggregating across sectors or countries.

Barriers to include in the index

The components of the index capture the major types of barriers or impediments, as discussed earlier: restrictions on entry and establishment; restrictions on control and management; and restrictions on operations. These broad categories can be further disaggregated, to take account of the relative restrictiveness of different barriers. Restrictions on entry and establishment are broken into limits on foreign ownership and requirements for screening and notification. Limits on foreign ownership are further to be divided into cases where no foreign ownership is allowed, those where it is allowed up to some maximum, say 49 per cent, and finally those cases where investment in an existing firm is limited, but the same limits do not apply to greenfield investment.

Screening and approval is divided further into: simple requirements that the investor notify the relevant authority and register the investment; approval unless judged contrary to the national interest; and approval only if the investor can demonstrate that the investment will result in a net economic benefit for the country.

There is also substantial variation in the nature and extent of restrictions in the other two broad categories: management and control; and inputs and operations. Separate components of the index could be used to capture these. For example, in terms of ownership and control, a limit on the number of foreign board members may be less onerous than a requirement that the government appoint one board member or that it have the right to veto management decisions. However, making these types of distinctions requires detailed information on FDI regimes in each country and requires a substantial degree of judgement, which complicates the task.

Aggregating across different types of impediments

In assigning weights to different types of barriers, the aim is to ensure that the indices make economic sense. The weights are set to reflect the relative economic costs of different types of restrictions. For example, a restriction on board membership is likely to be less important in terms of distorting investment patterns and levels than a ban on foreign ownership, and the index does not assign equal weights to these types of measures. Similarly, the index should not have the property that more types of restrictions necessarily result in a higher index value. A single restriction in the form of a complete ban on foreign ownership could involve a higher economic cost than a package of several less onerous restrictions, such as screening requirements and limits on board membership. Fewer restrictions are not necessarily better, and the index reflects this. The suggested set of weights is presented in Table 15.1.

Table 15.1 Components of an index of FDI restrictions

Type of restriction	*Weight*
Foreign equity limits on all firms	
No foreign equity permitted	1
Less than 50 per cent foreign equity permitted	0.5
More than 50 per cent and less than 100 per cent foreign equity permitted	0.25
Foreign equity limits on existing firms, none on greenfield	
No foreign equity permitted	0.5
Less than 50 per cent foreign equity permitted	0.25
More than 50 per cent and less than 100 per cent foreign equity permitted	0.125
Screening and approval	
Investor required to demonstrate net economic benefits	0.1
Approval unless contrary to national interest	0.075
Notification (pre or post)	0.05
Control and management restrictions	
All firms	0.2
Existing firms, none for greenfield	0.1
Input and operational restrictions	
All firms	0.2
Existing firms, none for greenfield	0.1

A maximum score of 1 is assigned when there is a complete ban on foreign ownership. A score of 1 is also possible when there is a partial ban on foreign ownership as well as stringent approval, management and operational restrictions. In contrast, a country which applied no restrictions would score zero, while one that used only a simple notification process would score 0.05.

The suggested weights are of course arbitrary, and may not be particularly relevant to some cases. For example, to deal with situations where foreign ownership limits apply to investment in existing firms but not new ones (or to one existing firm but not another, as with Telstra and Optus), the foreign equity weight is halved (Table 15.2). The suggested weights also imply that a limit on foreign ownership could be more restrictive than other impediments, such as input and operational restrictions (0.2) in the form of a local content requirement. In practice, the input restriction may be more distortionary than the equity limit, particularly if the foreign equity limit is not binding. But equally, the local content requirement may not be particularly onerous in some situations. Further, local content and other trade related investment measures tend not to be applied widely in services sectors.

While there may be some inconsistencies in the results obtained using the suggested categories and weights, they provide a simple and transparent starting point, and a useful alternative to measures which treat all types of barriers equally. The sensitivity of the results to the weights chosen is examined in Hardin and Holmes (1997, appendix A).

Table 15.2 FDI restrictiveness indices, selected APEC economies and GATS sectors and sub-sectors

	Australia	*Canada*	*China*	*Hong Kong*	*Indonesia*	*Japan*	*Korea*	*Malaysia*	*Mexico*	*New*	*Papua New Zealand*	*Philippines Guinea*	*Singapore*	*Thailand*	*United States*
Business	0.183	0.225	0.360	0.015	0.560	0.062	0.565	0.316	0.289	0.086	0.300	0.479	0.261	0.775	0.005
Communications	0.443	0.514	0.819	0.350	0.644	0.350	0.685	0.416	0.739	0.434	0.475	0.758	0.518	0.838	0.345
Postal	1.000	1.000	1.000	1.000	1.000	1.000	1.000	1.000	1.000	1.000	1.000	1.000	1.000	1.000	1.000
Courier	0.175	0.200	0.275	0.000	0.525	0.050	0.550	0.075	0.775	0.075	0.300	0.475	0.250	0.775	0.000
Tele-communications	0.300	0.325	1.000	0.200	0.525	0.100	0.550	0.375	0.705	0.425	0.300	0.975	0.571	0.804	0.200
Audio visual	0.295	0.530	1.000	0.200	0.525	0.250	0.640	0.215	0.475	0.235	0.300	0.580	0.250	0.775	0.180
Construction	0.175	0.200	0.400	0.000	0.525	0.050	0.750	0.775	0.450	0.075	0.300	0.475	0.250	0.775	0.000
Distribution	0.175	0.200	0.275	0.050	0.525	0.050	0.625	0.075	0.325	0.075	0.300	0.475	0.250	0.775	0.000
Education	0.175	0.200	0.525	0.000	0.525	0.200	0.550	0.075	0.450	0.075	0.300	0.475	0.250	0.775	0.000
Environmental	0.175	0.200	0.275	0.000	0.525	0.117	0.700	0.075	0.075	0.075	0.300	0.475	0.250	0.775	0.000
Financial	0.450	0.375	0.450	0.233	0.550	0.358	0.875	0.608	0.554	0.200	0.300	0.954	0.378	0.875	0.200
Insurance	0.275	0.425	0.475	0.400	0.575	0.450	0.838	0.600	0.575	0.125	0.300	0.975	0.250	0.775	0.000
Banking	0.625	0.325	0.425	0.067	0.525	0.267	0.913	0.617	0.533	0.275	0.300	0.933	0.506	0.975	0.400
Health	0.175	0.200	0.275	0.000	0.525	0.050	0.550	0.317	0.408	0.075	0.300	0.475	0.250	0.775	0.000
Tourism	0.175	0.200	0.283	0.000	0.525	0.050	0.617	0.542	0.275	0.075	0.300	0.808	0.317	0.775	0.000
Recreational	0.175	0.200	0.275	0.000	0.525	0.050	0.550	0.175	0.075	0.075	0.300	0.475	0.250	0.775	0.000
Transport	0.204	0.235	0.455	0.093	0.525	0.114	0.573	0.122	0.283	0.131	0.300	0.975	0.250	0.780	0.025

Aggregating across sectors and economies

The initial index numbers are calculated for individual GATS sub-sectors in individual economies. To get an overall FDI restrictiveness index for a country, sector scores would need to be added, and in doing this the relative importance of sectors must be taken into account. The most obvious way to aggregate would be to weight each sector according to its share in the total value of service sector output in the country. In practice this is difficult, as disaggregated services output data are not always available. An extension would be to assign higher weights to sectors which supply intermediate inputs (such as transport), to reflect the relatively high economic cost associated with distorting intermediate input markets.[1]

When aggregating across economies, to get an indication of the relative degree of restrictiveness in selected sectors, the most obvious way to weight would be according to the contribution of the economy to the value of world services output (or the value for the relevant group of economies, such as the OECD or APEC). This may also be constrained by data availability.

However, often the aggregation issue will not arise, because sub-sector measures for each economy will be more useful than aggregated sector or economy measures.

Results for selected APEC economies

Using the weights for different types of barriers shown in Table 15.2, FDI restrictiveness indices have been calculated for fifteen APEC economies and eleven of the twelve GATS sectors ('other services' are not included). The sectoral results are simple rather than weighted averages of the results for the GATS sub-sectors. The index values are summarised in Figure 15.1.

Across the sectors, the indices indicate that communications and financial services tend to be subject to the most stringent FDI controls. Scores are particularly high for the communications sector because many economies impose ownership limits in both telecommunications and broadcasting and also have their postal services closed to foreign entry. The least restricted sectors include business, distribution, environmental and recreational services.

Across the economies examined, Korea, Indonesia, Thailand, China and the Philippines score relatively high, reflecting the foreign ownership bans applied in several sectors, along with restrictions on the management and operation of foreign firms. The United States and Hong Kong tend to have the lowest index values. For Australia, the index value is 0.175 for many sectors, reflecting horizontal restrictions.[2] This index value comprises 0.075 for the approval process (with approval unless the project is contrary to the national interest) plus 0.1 for the management and control restriction that at least two board members of a public company must be Australian. Australia's highest scores are for the communications and financial services sectors.

Figure 15.1 shows index values for communications services (postal, courier, telecommunications and audio visual services) in selected APEC economies.

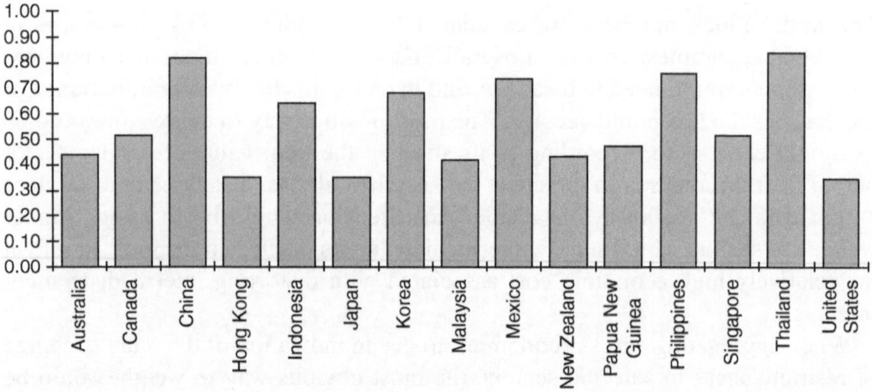

Figure 15.1 FDI restrictiveness indices for communications services in selected APEC economies.

According to these indices, Thailand has the most restricted communications sector followed by China, the Philippines and Mexico. These countries tend to have highly restrictive horizontal commitments which result in a high score for all sectors, plus specific restrictions on communications. For example, Thailand imposes foreign equity restrictions, management restrictions and approval requirements at the horizontal level, giving a minimum score of 0.775 for all sectors. In addition, postal services are completely closed and there are operational restrictions on two telecommunications sub-sectors, which increase Thailand's score for the communications sector as a whole to 0.838. The United States has the least restricted communications sector, followed by Hong Kong and Japan. Australia scores 0.443 for communications services, reflecting limitations on the foreign ownership of Telstra, a closed postal sector and foreign ownership and control restrictions on television broadcasting.[3]

The results for the GATS communications sector highlight a number of problems with the indices of restrictiveness for FDI. First, calculating the index for the whole communications sector as a simple average of the sub-sector scores means that restrictions (or lack of them) in important sub-sectors, such as telecommunications, are given insufficient weight. Instead, the index for the sector as a whole is unduly affected by the often relatively tight restrictions in the much smaller postal sub-sector. For example, the telecommunications sector in Hong Kong has a restrictiveness index of 0.2, but because FDI in postal services is prohibited and sector scores are derived as the simple average of sub-sector scores, the restrictiveness index for Hong Kong's communications sector as a whole is 0.35.

Thus, in some cases it may be more useful to examine sub-sector scores, rather than the broad GATS sector scores (some sub-sector scores are also provided in Table 15.2). Figure 15.2 shows FDI restrictiveness indices for the telecommunications sub-sector, which reveal greater variation than those for the total

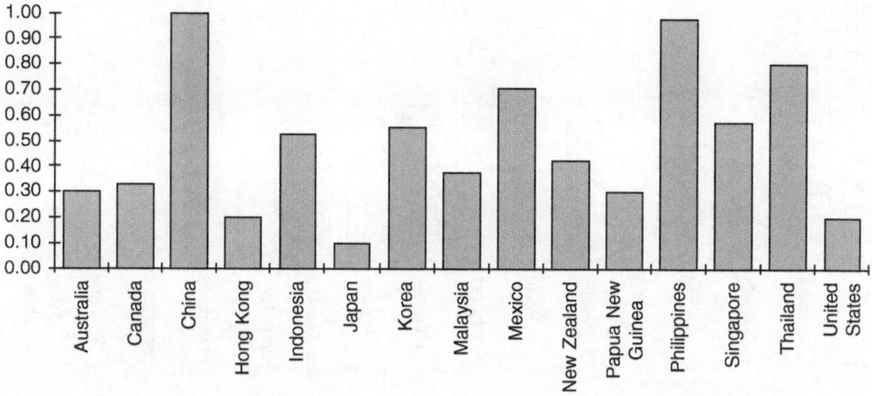

Figure 15.2 FDI restrictiveness indices for telecommunications services in selected APEC economies.

communications sector. The index for Singapore is relatively high, reflecting Singapore Telecom's monopoly rights on the provision of wire-based local and international telecommunications services until 2000. Japan's index for telecommunications is low because the index for its highly restricted voice telephony market is offset by its unrestricted value-added and non-voice telecommunications markets.

Second, countries which do not schedule a sector in the GATS and do not supply information in the APEC Investment Guide or Individual Action Plans are assumed to have no restrictions on that sector. This is the case for the telecommunications sector in Malaysia and Papua New Guinea (for which only limited information is available), resulting in implausibly low index values.

Third, to restrict the value of the index between zero and one, multiple restrictions of the same type are counted only once. This may lead to an underestimate of FDI restrictiveness for economies which apply many restrictions of the same type, compared with economies which may impose fewer restrictions of different types. For example, Mexico and New Zealand receive the same score for operational restrictions applying to the motion picture projections sub-sector, but Mexico imposes four different operational restrictions on motion picture projections while New Zealand applies only one operational restriction. Also, the severity of restrictions is assumed to be the same, yet in practice there may be considerable variation across economies. For example, in the above case, one of Mexico's restrictions requires that 30 per cent of screen time must be devoted to Mexican films, while the New Zealand requirement is less restrictive, with 6 per cent of the New Zealand Broadcasting Commission budget to be allocated to Maori programming.

Finally, the values of the indices are dependent on the weights that are assumed to apply to different restrictions. The sensitivity of the restrictiveness indices to

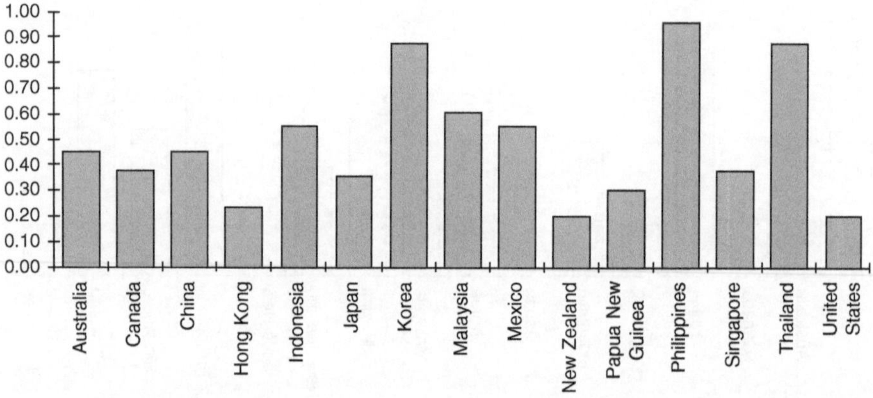

Figure 15.3 FDI restrictiveness indices for financial services in selected APEC economies.

variations in the weights is examined in Hardin and Holmes (1997, appendix A). Index values for the financial services sector are presented in Figure 15.3. According to these indices, the Philippines, Korea and Thailand have by far the most restricted financial service sectors. The Philippines scores 0.954, reflecting horizontal restrictions (worth 0.475) plus foreign equity restrictions for insurance, banking and other financial services. New Zealand, the United States and Hong Kong have the least restrictive financial sectors according to the indices, all imposing operational and/or management and control restrictions on some financial services. Australia scores 0.450 for financial services, reflecting limitations on foreign ownership of the four major banks (large-scale transfer of ownership to foreigners is considered contrary to the national interest (Costello 1997)), and some operational restrictions. China's index for financial services is relatively low, even though many restrictions are imposed on its insurance and banking sectors. This is because China applies many restrictions of the same type, imposing five operational restrictions on FDI in its banking sector and seven operational restrictions on FDI in insurance and related services. In each case, only one operational restriction is counted in the index.

In contrast to communications and financial services, the indices for business services indicate that foreign investment in this sector tends to be relatively unrestricted. The United States, Hong Kong, Japan and New Zealand score very low index values for business services, reflecting few FDI restrictions in this sector (Table 15.2). Countries with high index values for business services (Thailand, Korea, Indonesia and the Philippines) tend to have a high score for their horizontal commitments, with few or no additional restrictions on business services specifically. Australia scores an index of 0.183 for business services, only marginally above the horizontal score (0.175), the difference reflecting management and control restrictions on law and accounting services.

As noted above, the indices are based on information contained in the GATS schedules, the APEC Individual Action Plans (November 1997) and the APEC *Guide to Investment Regimes of Member Economies* (APEC 1998). In recent months, some Asian economies have announced plans for major economic reform packages, as a condition for securing financial support from the International Monetary Fund (IMF). Some elements of these reform packages will have implications for restrictions on FDI and will need to be incorporated in the indices as they are introduced (see Hardin and Holmes 1997).

Modelling the gains from removal of FDI barriers

Once some estimates of the size of FDI barriers are available, the next step is to use these to model the impacts of further liberalisation. Few attempts have been made to model the impacts of investment liberalisation in a general equilibrium framework. Some studies have modelled barriers to services trade generally and have, therefore, implicitly included barriers to FDI, as it is one mode of service supply (e.g. Brown *et al.* 1996, Dee *et al.* 1996). However, they have not taken account of the particular characteristics of FDI as a mode of service supply, and have not separated FDI barriers from barriers on the other modes of service supply which have quite different policy implications. Other studies have explicitly modelled financial market liberalisation, treating all forms of foreign investment as a flow of financial capital, with barriers to capital flows represented as limitations on capital mobility and violations of interest parity conditions (e.g. McKibbon 1997, Donovan and Mai 1997). They have, therefore, been relevant to portfolio investment, but have not taken account of some of the economic factors driving FDI and its role in services trade.

To be policy relevant, the modelling framework should reflect the theoretical and empirical evidence on the role of FDI and the economic factors driving it. For example, FDI often involves firms investing to take advantage of some specific assets, such as particular expertise, that the parent may have. It is, therefore, important to model the links between the parent and the foreign affiliate. Further, the foreign firm may be able to distinguish the services it supplies from those of domestic firms, say due to its international reputation, and it is, therefore, important to distinguish between output from the foreign affiliate and domestic firms.

In addition to the modelling framework, the other key requirements for modelling the economy-wide effects of FDI barriers are measures of the size of the barriers and data on FDI and services trade. While some progress has been made recently, the availability of each of these continues to constrain progress in modelling FDI barriers.

A modelling framework

The general equilibrium modelling framework developed by Petri (1997) captures some of the features of FDI identified in the theoretical literature which are important when examining the impacts of liberalisation. Petri's framework recognises that foreign-owned firms benefit from their parents' assets by modelling them as distinct from domestic-owned firms, both in terms of demand and production characteristics. Petri also allows foreign affiliates to be linked to parents through intermediate input flows. Petri's model distinguishes between varieties produced by the foreign affiliate and those produced by domestic firms of the host economy or by subsidiaries of other parents.

Reducing FDI barriers in Petri's model is equivalent to reducing taxes on the profits earned by foreign affiliates. As profits increase, foreign affiliates can offer lower prices to domestic consumers. Increased profits also attract FDI flows to the liberalising economy, which increases competition and the demand for inputs from both the host and home economies.

All of these links should be incorporated when modelling the impacts for Australia of FDI liberalisation in the services sector. The inclusion of trans-border price and output coordination by multinationals identified by Markusen *et al.* (1995) also needs to be considered. The relevance of multinational coordination will depend on the sector and countries being analysed. It may be more likely to occur in the North American auto market (which Markusen *et al.* modelled) than for other types of FDI, such as that in service industries.

Petri notes a further interaction that is identified in the theory but not incorporated into his FDI model. That is the interaction between foreign affiliates and their host economy through various dynamic relationships, including externalities associated with scale or technological spillovers. Theoretical literature suggests that these could be important implications of FDI (see Blomström and Kokko 1997). Also, Petri's model specification does not capture the benefits for consumers of increased product variety which is likely to be an important outcome of FDI liberalisation.

Developing a global modelling framework similar to Petri's is a large task. An alternative, smaller task may be to apply Petri's framework to a model of the Australian economy. This would allow the impact of FDI liberalisation in Australia to be examined without requiring information for other individual regions. The microeconomic distinctions between domestic and foreign firms made by Petri would still have to be incorporated, although only for the Australian economy. A major drawback of this approach is the limitations a single country model places on the liberalisation scenarios that can be examined. Using a model of the Australian economy means that only unilateral FDI liberalisation scenarios can be considered. While these scenarios will provide a starting point for examining FDI liberalisation, useful policy results will require modelling multilateral FDI liberalisation in the context of the GATS and other investment agreements.

A second alternative is to build on Petri's multiregional model of FDI. This would allow a range of FDI scenarios to be examined including unilateral liberalisation. A separate region for Australia would need to be identified and a disaggregated service sector would be beneficial. The method outlined in this chapter for quantifying investment barriers could also be used.

Quantifying investment barriers

Measures of FDI barriers are vital for sensible modelling of FDI liberalisation. Several studies have used Hoekman's tariff equivalent estimates when modelling services trade liberalisation (e.g. Brown *et al.* 1995, 1996, Dee *et al.* 1996). These studies have modelled services trade generally, rather than that associated explicitly with FDI. As discussed above, the Hoekman tariff equivalents used in these studies are based on a number of arbitrary assumptions and include not only barriers to FDI but also barriers to services traded cross-border.

The method outlined in the previous sections of this chapter, essentially an extension of Hoekman's frequency-based measures, addresses several of the shortcomings of Hoekman's approach and allows barriers to FDI to be identified separately from other barriers to services trade. The indices can be used as a basis for estimating tariff equivalents for each of the services industries identified within the model, to allow a full examination of the impacts of services sector FDI liberalisation to be undertaken.

As an input into general equilibrium modelling, the indices could be applied in a variety of ways. Following Petri's (1997) approach, the indices could be translated into a tax on the returns to foreign investment (FDI profits). An index value of 1.00, which reflects either a total prohibition on FDI or a highly restricted sector, could be translated into a tax rate of, say, 100 per cent. An FDI regime involving only screening with approval unless the investment is contrary to the national interest would translate into a tax rate of 7.5 per cent. This could be thought of as the cost impost associated with going through the approval process. If the indices are applied as a tax on FDI profits, the allocation of the tax revenue needs to be considered. It may be distributed to the government or to domestic producers, or may simply be retained by foreign service providers. Alternatively, the indices could be applied as an increase in a foreign investor's production costs or a fall in their productivity.

Data

Limited FDI and services trade data continue to be major constraints on progress in modelling FDI liberalisation. To model the gains from multilateral liberalisation, data on bilateral investment stocks and flows are required, together with data on the value of services traded via FDI (as opposed to the other modes of supply, cross-border trade and temporary movement of people), and data on the activities of foreign affiliates, so that their inputs and outputs can be distinguished from those of domestically owned firms.

Petri has made some progress in addressing these data constraints by constructing a database showing the role of FDI in six broad regions and three sectors (agriculture, manufacturing and services), drawing on the 1992 GTAP database (Hertel 1997) and detailed survey data for Japan and the United States. However, considerable extensions to this, involving further assumptions and estimates, would be required if the model was to be extended to incorporate Australia separately and to disaggregate the services sector.

If an Australian model was used for unilateral liberalisation simulations, rather than building on Petri's existing global model, the required amount of information on FDI flows, stocks and activities would be reduced substantially. However, a more detailed industry disaggregation than Petri's could be adopted so that the impact of removing FDI barriers from individual service industries could be modelled.

An existing model of the Australian economy could be used as the basis of the Australian FDI model. While the dataset of an existing model would cover the activities of both domestic and foreign firms, it would not distinguish between them. Therefore, the dataset would need to be split into domestic and FDI components using information on the scale and structure of FDI from other sources.

First, the overall output associated with FDI stocks in Australia would need to be estimated. This could be done following Petri's methodology, which involves multiplying total capital stock associated with FDI by rates of return to estimate the capital incomes expected from FDI activities, and then multiplying these by ratios of output to capital income to estimate outputs associated with FDI. Petri calculates rates of return and ratios of output to capital income from GTAP input–output data.

Second, information on the production technology of FDI activities would be required. For this, Petri used estimates from US and Japanese surveys of outward FDI investment and it is likely that these estimates would have to be used in the Australian FDI model. FDI activities are linked to home firms through purchases of intermediate inputs. Ratios of such inputs to FDI output are estimated by sector and region from US and Japanese survey data. These ratios are applied to estimated FDI output to derive trade flows that result from home sourcing. The foreign affiliates' remaining intermediate inputs are allocated to products purchased in the host country's markets (including imported products), with a composition based on that of domestic firms. Value added coefficients of affiliates are also assumed to be the same as those of domestic firms.

Finally, the distribution of FDI sales across different markets is used to specify the demand side of the system. Based on survey data, Petri distinguishes between local sales, home market sales and third market sales. In the Australian model, it would only be necessary to distinguish between local and overseas sales. In the absence of information indicating that Australian-based foreign affiliates behave differently from those based in Japan or the United States, Petri's US and Japanese survey data could be used to estimate the shares of FDI output in Australia that are sold locally and abroad.

Additional modelling requirements

It is important to distinguish between barriers to FDI and those affecting other modes of supply, so the impact of liberalising FDI can be isolated from the effects of reducing other trade barriers. However, to examine the interactions and make comparisons between FDI liberalisation and the reduction or removal of barriers on other modes of supply, it will also be necessary to have information on restrictions on other modes of service supply.

The substitution between different modes of service supply also needs to be incorporated when modelling barriers to services trade, and further analysis of this important area is required. For example, some services can be delivered easily by either FDI or cross-border trade. Reducing or removing barriers to FDI may result in more of these services being delivered by FDI and less being delivered cross-border. For other services which are not easily traded by an alternative mode of supply, liberalising FDI will have little effect on how they are delivered. Rapid technological developments which create new opportunities for delivering services across international borders will complicate the task of specifying the degree of substitutability between modes of service supply.

Notes

1 For Hoekman's (1995) tariff equivalents, weights for the GATS sectors were estimated as the share of the sector's output in the total value of service sector output for an 'average' industrialised country. An interesting feature of the estimates is the relatively low weights for some services which are important intermediate inputs. For example, transport and communications services have lower weights than business services.

2 Horizontal restrictions, as defined in the GATS, are those which apply across all sectors.

3 The index value will not change with approval for the sale of further Telstra shares to foreigners. The score for voice telephone services is currently 0.25, because there is no formal limit on foreign ownership of Optus and foreign ownership of Telstra is limited to one-third of the 35 per cent sold to the public (around 12 per cent of the total). In terms of the index, foreign ownership of Telstra is limited to less than 50 per cent. The index score is 0.25, because the limit only applies to one of the firms in the market (i.e. Telstra, but not Optus). If foreigners are allowed to own one-third of all Telstra shares, that is still less than 50 per cent, so the index score is still 0.25.

References

Asia Pacific Economic Cooperation (APEC) 1998, *Guide to the Investment Regimes of Member Economies*, APEC Committee on Trade and Investment, Singapore: APEC Secretariat.

Blomström, M. and Kokko, A. 1997, 'How foreign investment affects host economies', *Policy Research Working Paper 1745*, Washington, DC: World Bank.

Brown, D., Deardorff, A. and Stern, R. 1996, 'Modelling multilateral trade liberalisation in services', *Asia Pacific Economic Review*, 2(1): 21–34.

Brown, D., Deardorff, A., Fox, A. and Stern, R. 1995, 'Computational analysis of goods and services trade liberalisation in the Uruguay Round', in Martin, W. and Winters, L. A. (eds), *The Uruguay Round and the Developing Economies*, World Bank Discussion Paper 307, Washington, DC: World Bank.

Costello, P. (Federal Treasurer) 1997, Release of the Report of the Financial System Inquiry and Initial Government Response on Mergers Policy, Media Release, 9 April.

Deardorff, A. V. and Stern, R. M. 1997, 'Measurement of non-tariff barriers', *OECD Economics Department Working Paper No. 179*, OECD, Paris.

Dee, P., Geisler, C. and Watts, G. 1996, *The Impact of APEC's Free Trade Commitment*, Staff Information Paper, February, Canberra: Australian Government Publishing Service.

Donovan, D. and Mai, Y. H. 1996, 'APEC trade liberalisation: the impact of increased capital mobility', *Australian Commodities*, 3(4), Canberra: ABARE.

Hardin, A. and Holmes, L. 1997, *Services Trade and Foreign Direct Investment*, Industry Commission Staff Research Paper, Canberra: Australian Government Publishing Service.

Hertel, T. (ed) 1997, *Global Trade Analysis: Modeling and Applications*, Cambridge: Cambridge University Press.

Hoekman, B. 1995, 'Assessing the General Agreement on Trade in Services', in Martin, W. and Winters, L. A. (eds), *The Uruguay Round and the Developing Economies*, World Bank Discussion Paper 307, Washington, DC, pp. 327–364.

Hoekman, B. and Braga, C. 1997, 'Protection and Trade in Services', *Policy Research Working Paper 1747*, Washington, DC: World Bank.

Hufbauer, G. C. 1996, 'Surveying the Costs of Protection: a Partial Equilibrium Approach', in Schott, J. J. (ed.) *The World Trading System – Challenges Ahead*, Washington, DC: Institute for International Economics.

Markusen, J. R., Rutherford, T. F. and Hunter, L. 1995, 'Trade liberalisation in a multinational dominated industry', *Journal of International Economics*, 38(1–2): 95–117.

McKibbon, W. J. 1997, 'Some global consequences of financial market liberalisation in the Asia Pacific region', paper presented at the EMBA conference, *Investment Liberalisation and Financial Reform in the Asia Pacific Region*, 29–31 August, Sydney.

OECD (Organisation for Economic Co-operation and Development) 1997, *Indicators of Tariff and Non-tariff Trade Barriers*, OECD: Paris.

Pacific Economic Cooperation Council (PECC) 1995, *Survey of Impediments to Trade and Investment in the APEC Region*, Singapore: PECC.

Petri, P. A. 1997, 'Foreign direct investment in a computable general equilibrium framework', paper prepared for the conference, *Making APEC Work: Economic Challenges and Policy Alternatives*, 13–14 March, Tokyo: Keio University.

United Nations Conference on Trade and Development (UNCTAD) 1996, *World Investment Report 1996: Investment, Trade and International Policy Arrangements*, New York and Geneva: United Nations.

16 The impact of tax policy and incentives on FDI

Jacques Morisset and Nedia Pirnia[1]

Introduction

In a world where an increasing number of governments compete hard to attract multinational corporations, fiscal incentives have become a global phenomenon. Poor African countries rely on tax holidays and import duty exemptions, while industrial Western European countries allow investment allowances or accelerated depreciation (Table 16.1). This trend seems to have grown considerably since the early 1990s as evidenced by the number of high profile foreign investments, such as Toyota in Northern France or Mercedes-Benz A.G. in the US State of Alabama. These have generated considerable debate about whether governments have offered unreasonably large incentives to entice those firms to invest in their area. Still, this debate about the effectiveness of tax incentives is hardly new and has accumulated a long history.[2]

The objective of the paper is to review the existing literature on tax policy and Foreign Direct Investment (FDI) as well as to explore possibilities for future

Table 16.1 Types of incentives used by region

Region/Major incentives (countries)	*Africa (23)*	*Asia (17)*	*Latin America and Caribbean (12)*	*Central and Eastern Europe (25)*	*Western Europe (20)*	*Other Countries (6)*	*Total (103)*
Tax holidays	16	13	8	19	7	4	67
Accelerated depreciation	12	8	6	6	10	5	47
Investment allowances	4	5	9	3	5		26
Import duty exemption	15	13	11	13	7	4	63
Duty drawback	10	8	10	12	6	3	49

Source: UNCTAD, 1996.

research. Taxes affect the net return on capital and should, at least in the mind of numerous policymakers, influence the capital movements between countries. For this reason, the early literature attempted to evaluate if a generous tax policy could compensate for other obstacles in the business environment and, thus, attract multinational corporations. In the mid-1980s, the literature went one step further by exploring what kind of tax instruments should have the greatest impact on the location decision of multinational corporations. Special attention was also given to the motivations and tax behavior of the multinational corporation.

In recent years, the globalization process has led to the emergence of new issues. Not only have companies tended to become more mobile, but also governments have to deal with this new dimension in the design of their national tax policy. The gradual elimination of barriers to capital movements have stimulated governments to compete for FDI in global markets as well as reinforced the role of tax policy in this process. This recent competitive trend has to be offset by the increasing pressure that governments face to harmonize their tax policies within regional (or international) agreements. A second important issue has been the recognition that tax policies of the home and host countries are interconnected and that this link influences the behavior of multinationals. There has been a great deal of evidence, especially after the changes in the US tax laws during the late 1980s, that home country tax policy affects both the multinational firm's behavior and the effectiveness of tax policy in the countries where these firms operate and invest. Last, but not the least, there has been a growing attention to the costs associated with tax incentives – and not only to their possible benefits. Tax incentives are likely not only to have a direct negative impact on fiscal revenues but also, and frequently, create significant possibilities for suspicious behaviors from tax administrations and companies. This issue has become crucial in emerging countries where budgetary constraints as well as corruption are certainly more severe than in industrial countries.

This chapter proceeds as follows. The second section reviews the early literature that examined the impact of tax policy on FDI from a global perspective using investors' surveys and time-series econometric analysis. The third section explores which tax instruments have the greatest impact on FDI and what kind of foreign investors are likely to be most responsive to changes in tax policy, since these two areas have retained the attention of many researchers over the past fifteen years. The fourth section focuses on three issues that have emerged with globalization: the interconnection between the home and host countries' taxation and its subsequent impact on FDI; tax competition versus harmonization across countries and states, and the costs associated with tax incentive schemes. The last section concludes with a few remarks and ideas for future research.

Early literature: the aggregate approach

Tax policies are obviously capable of affecting the volume and location of FDI, since all other considerations are equal, higher tax rates reduce after-tax returns. Of course, all other considerations are seldom equal. Countries not only differ in their tax policies, but also in their commercial and regulatory policies, market size, natural endowments, and human capital. All these factors influence the desirability of an investment location.

Based on this perception, the early literature attempted to determine if tax policy was one of the key factors in the decision-making process of multinational corporations. Two basic approaches were and continue to be developed: (A) selective surveys of international investors, and (B) time-series econometric analysis. The majority of earlier studies focused on the aggregate FDI data by lumping together firms of all types and paid little attention to differences across sectors and industries as well as between regions and countries. A brief summary of the major findings is presented here.

Survey of investors

One of the first survey studies was conducted by Barlow and Wender in 1955. They interviewed 247 US companies on their strategies to invest abroad. One of the questions asked was about the conditions that were required before companies proceed with foreign investment. Only 10 percent of the companies listed favorable foreign taxes as a condition for FDI, while another 11 percent mentioned "host government encouragement to companies". Together, these inducements were ranked fourth after currency convertibility, guarantee against expropriation, and host country political stability.

Those findings were confirmed by the survey of 205 companies conducted by Robinson in 1961. Perhaps the most important result of Robinson's survey was the considerable difference of opinion between the business community and the governments, with regard to the major factors influencing decisions to invest. Tax concessions headed the list of government responses, while they were omitted from the list of private investor responses.

Next came the result of a field research conducted by Aharoni and published in 1966 on the way foreign investment decisions were made by US manufacturing firms. The conclusions were that host government concessions did not bring about the decisions to invest. Income tax exemption was considered a very weak stimulant. Those investors who did consider it, did it only marginally. In the word of one of the investors in the survey: "Tax exemption is like a dessert; it is good to have, but it does not help very much if the meal is not there". It should be noted that in this case, as in the case of Robinson's interviews, host government officials interviewed in the field research believed income tax exemption to be a very powerful stimulus to FDI.

In a 1984 survey of fifty-two multinational corporations, the Group of Thirty found that among nineteen factors that were identified as influencing FDI flows, inducements offered by the host country rank seventh in importance for investment in developing countries and eighth in developed countries. In recent years, several investors' surveys explored the effectiveness of tax policies on FDI using alternative samples or asking more detailed questions (e.g. JETRO (1995), Ernst & Young (1994) or Fortune/Deloitte & Touche (1997)). In general, these surveys have confirmed the conclusions summarized above: if tax policy matters it is not the most influential factor in the site selection of multinationals.[3]

Econometric analysis

The available econometric evidence on the effect of taxation used time-series estimation of the responsiveness of FDI to annual variations in tax rates. Most econometric studies have tended to confirm the results of surveys; that investors are mostly influenced in their decision by market and political factors and that tax policy appears to have little effect on the location of FDI.

A selective sample of studies has concluded in that direction: Root and Ahmed (1978), Agodo (1978), Shah and Toye (1978), and Lim (1983). In 1978, Root and Ahmed performed an econometric study with data for forty-one developing countries for the period 1966–1970. They classified countries into three categories – unattractive, moderately attractive, and highly attractive – according to their average annual per capita inflow of FDI. Forty-four variables were chosen as potentially significant discriminators of the three country groups. Among the six policy related discriminators were three relating to tax levels. Of these, corporate tax rates proved to be an effective discriminator of the three defined country groups; however tax incentives laws and liberality were not found to be effective discriminators. Agodo analyzed a sample of thirty-three US firms having forty-six manufacturing investments in twenty African countries. Tax concessions were found to be insignificant as a determinant of FDI in simple and multiple regressions.

Much of the literature of the period used highly aggregate data, evaluating the correlation between annual changes in FDI flows, and a series of factors, including movements in after-tax rates of return earned by foreign investments. The primary limitation of aggregate studies is that changes in FDI may be correlated with important omitted variables such as trade and financial liberalization as well as the elimination of barriers against FDI. Most countries embark on a reform process that includes simultaneous actions aimed at enhancing the development of private investment, including FDI promotion. As a result, it becomes very difficult to distinguish the effects of taxation from the effects of other variables that are in turn correlated with tax rates.

There is also the crucial issue of how to define tax policy changes and to measure the after-tax rate of return. Which taxes should be included in the regressions (corporate profit tax, trade taxes, domestic indirect taxes, etc.)? Should these taxes be integrated in one aggregate or several indicators? Several studies have employed nominal tax rates but they can be misleading for a variety of reasons. In particular, they do not capture the eventual tax rebates that are offered to specific investments or activities. Understanding the exact impact of tax policy on investment decisions has led to the development of the popular concept of effective tax rate, which is defined as the percentage reduction in the financial rate of return on an investment that is due to the fiscal system of the host country.[4] In principle, both the effective marginal and average tax rates[5] may be relevant in the strategic decisions made by firms. Locating production in an area with low marginal rate should lead to a high optimal level of output, while the average rate will affect the profit level.[6] In a recent econometric study on the behavior of US firms in the European Union, Devereux and Griffith (1998) have shown that the average effective tax rates seem to have a greater impact on the FDI location than the marginal tax rates.

Still, the general conclusion that emerged from the early econometric studies is that the effect of tax policy on FDI is rather limited, at least compared to other factors such as political stability, the costs and availability of labor and basic infrastructure. The importance of these other factors suggests that tax policy is a poor instrument to compensate for various negative factors in the investment climate of a country. Many countries from South America to Sub-Saharan Africa have offered investment incentives for businesses to locate in underdeveloped, more costly, and otherwise unattractive regions with little success in generating (sustainable) investment flows to those areas. This experience strongly suggests that the fiscal investment incentives popular in developing countries have not been effective in making up for fundamental weaknesses in the investment climate.

New evidence – a quest for details

The relative little importance of tax policy does not mean that it does not exert any impact on FDI. Looking at FDI figures, it is certainly not a coincidence that FDI in tax haven countries in the Caribbean and South Pacific grew more than fivefold between 1985 and 1994, to over $200 billion. Ireland's tax policy has been generally recognized as a key factor in its success to attract international investors over the past two decades. In fact, the simple position described in the preceding section was not completely accurate. It is not true that tax policy and incentives fail to attract investors; they do affect the decisions of *some* investors *some* of the time.

Even in the 1970s, there were researchers who started to look into more detailed FDI data and came out with conclusions that made the result of previous studies more vulnerable to criticism. Forsyth in his 1972 study provides support for the view that inducements and incentives may often not play a key role in influencing the decision to undertake a particular foreign investment. However, once other factors have provoked the decisions to set up production facilities in a broad area, then the more precise location decision may be strongly affected by such factors.

By the mid-1980s, understanding the exact role of incentives in attracting FDI became a new research agenda. One direction has been to explore the reaction of multinational corporations to changes in tax policy when they differ in their activities, motivations, market structure and/or financing. Others have searched to examine which tax instruments may have a greater effect on the behavior of international investors.

Tax behavior of multinational corporations

While most early studies examine the impact of taxes on the average foreign investors, there were many reasons to believe that this impact differs greatly depending on the characteristics of the multinational corporation. International investors often have at their disposal numerous alternative methods of structuring and financing their investments, arranging their transactions between related parties located in different countries, and returning profits to investors. These alternatives have important tax implications, and there is considerable anecdotal evidence that tax considerations strongly influence the choices that firms make.

One of the earlier findings of the literature is that the impact of tax rates on investment decisions is generally higher on export-oriented companies than those seeking the domestic market or location-specific advantages. In surveys, these firms are those with managers that have responded more favorably to tax incentives (see Reuber (1973)[7] and Guisinger and Associates (1985)). This finding is not really surprising because export-oriented firms such as garment manufacturers are operating in highly competitive markets with very slim margins. Moreover, these firms are often highly mobile, and more likely to compare taxes across alternative locations (Wells 1986). Hence, taxes can be an important part of their cost structure, and the firms can easily move to take advantage of more favorable tax regimes.

The impact and the nature of incentive schemes may also differ if they apply to new or existing companies. For example, Rolfe *et al.* (1993) shows, using a survey of managers of US firms, that start-up companies will prefer incentives that reduce their initial expenses (equipment and material exemption), while expanding firms will prefer tax incentives that target profit. He also reports that manufacturing industries will prefer incentives related to depreciable assets because they utilize more fixed assets than service industries.

In an interesting study, Coyne (1994) suggests that small investors are generally more responsive to tax incentives than large ones. Taxes may play a more important role in the cost structure of small companies because they do not have the financial and human capacity to developed sophisticated tax avoidance strategies. Large multinational corporations are also more likely to receive special tax treatments, whatever the tax laws applied by the host country. Oman (2000) reports some evidence that large firms, especially in the automobile sector, are more likely to negotiate secret advance agreements on how much they will pay in both industrial and emerging countries.

There exist a few studies that estimate separate equations for FDI financed by retained earnings and external funds (equity plus debt) (Hartman (1985) and Boskin and Gale (1987)). They typically found that FDI financed by retained earnings is more strongly influenced by host country tax rates. However, they do not offer any clear explanation for this result, but it is possible that equity and debt financing are also influenced by the tax policy in the home country, thereby reducing the impact of the host country's tax regimes (see the next section for more explanations).

Finally, there is growing evidence that low taxes might be a key factor for firms that are not operating in one specific market but multiple markets such as Internet related business, insurance companies and banks. Establishing a subsidiary in a low tax country gives them the opportunity to develop tax avoidance strategies. It is indeed difficult for any one country to claim the right to tax the holding company if its operations have taken place in multiple markets at the same time. A typical example is when filing tax returns in a high tax country, a multinational corporation claims that it has earned as little profits as possible. Instead, it tries to attribute as much profit as possible to its operations in low tax countries by arranging "transactions" between its subsidiaries in the two countries, and setting the "transfer price" of those transactions so that it has the desired effect on profits. Multinationals can also adjust the timing of their dividend repatriations from foreign subsidiaries (see Hines and Hubbard (1990)). In practice, such strategies may explain the success of tax haven countries in attracting subsidiaries of "global" companies and the expenses incurred by multinationals on economists and accountants to justify their transfer prices that suit their tax needs. Still, very little is known about the magnitude of such international tax evasion and how much they affect tax revenues across countries (see, for some preliminary evidence, Gruber *et al.* (1993) or the Economist (2000)).

Tax instruments used by governments

Governments have several tax instruments that they can use to attempt to influence the effective tax rates and the location decision of multinational corporations.[8] The literature has traditionally focused on the instruments linked to the corporate income tax such as tax holidays and tax allowance. Of course, these instruments are of no help to an unprofitable company and, therefore, other forms of incentives have also been widely used around the world. Exemptions from custom duties or local indirect taxes (generally to targeted sectors) do exist in many countries, even though their use has been restricted in most international and bilateral trade treaties. Outright grants are used in many industrial countries but rarely in the developing world because of their upfront costs.

Following the existing literature, our focus is on the corporate income tax and the different options used by governments to relieve companies. Governments with high corporate tax rates have a number of options to reduce them to more competitive levels. One is to give tax incentives to a selected group of firms. An alternative is to change the general fiscal system to lower the effective tax rate for all firms. There are many options between these two extremes, including the "stability premium", that have been offered to investors by countries such as Chile and Colombia. This premium consists in an option where the investor purchases the right to maintain its corporate tax rate at a given level, even if the tax regime will be modified in the future. A short review of the major options is presented below, but, at the outset, it is worth underscoring that there is certainly no clear-cut answer in favor of one or another alternative mechanism (see Mintz and Tsiopoulos (1992), for fuller details).

The first option is to generalize a low corporate tax rate on a broad base. Small countries such as Hong Kong, Lebanon or Mauritius have typically retained this option. A low corporate tax rate is, in itself, an incentive. It allows investors to keep a larger portion of profits. Governments are also able to maintain corporate tax revenues because investors have limited tax-planning opportunities and the simplicity of the system makes for a favorable investment climate. Investors look favorably on a country offering a low statutory tax rate, especially one well below the worldwide norm of 35–40 percent, since it signals that the government is interested in letting the market determine the most profitable investments without undue governmental influence. Although a broad-based low corporate tax rate is appealing, this approach has limitations. In particular, international linkages can undermine a country's efforts to make its tax system relatively neutral. In fact, a country with a corporate tax system greatly out of line with other countries might be better off having a less neutral system to minimize distortions. It has also to be recognized that the sudden change to a low, generalized tax rate can reduce tax revenues during a transition period, even though the simplicity of the tax system may attract further investors and increase the tax base in the longer run and so compensate for the initial reduction.

For these reasons, many governments rely on tax incentive schemes in their effort to lure foreign investors. This selective approach, in contrast to a generalized tax reduction, is attractive to many countries because it may minimize the initial effect on fiscal revenues and, in principle, should help to target specific industries or activities that would bring greater benefits to the country. It can also be argued that incentives may have a signaling effect on the government's commitments to stimulate FDI, as they are generally easier to implement than a general reform of the tax system (see Bond and Samuelson (1986)).

One popular form of tax incentive consists of reducing the corporate income tax rate by providing tax holidays or temporary rebates. This form of incentive has been popular in emerging countries where authorities have favored a discretionary approach. For example, several African Investment Codes have included tax holidays, with differentiated rebates and periods of abatement, depending on the government's objectives. The main benefit of tax holidays is that they provide large benefits as soon as the company begins earning income, and are thus more valuable than an incentive such as a lower corporate tax rate that accrues more slowly over a longer time. However, they primarily benefit short-term investments, which are often undertaken in so-called footloose industries characterized by companies that can quickly disappear from one jurisdiction to reappear in another. They also tend to reward the founding of a company, rather than investment in existing companies and discriminate against investments that rely on long-lived depreciable capital. Last but not the least, they can lead to large erosion of the tax base as taxpayers learn how to escape taxation of income from other sources.[9]

Many countries, especially in the industrial world, allow fast write-offs for investment expenditures – either all investments, or those they especially want to induce through tax allowances or credits.[10] Investment tax allowances have distinct advantages. The incentive is correctly targeted at the desired activity since a company receives the benefit of lower corporate taxes only if it makes capital investments (rather than formation of a new company). It encourages companies to take a long-term view when planning investments. By targeting current capital spending, the allowance causes less revenue leakage than a tax holiday would and it promotes new investment instead of giving a windfall gain to owners of old capital, as does a reduction in corporate tax rates. It can also be made refundable, allowing the government to share the investment costs and risks with the foreign entrepreneur. Still, investment tax allowances have limitations and drawbacks. If the investment tax allowance is not refundable, existing companies reap the full benefits (i.e. supporting expansion) while start-up companies must first earn enough income before they can take the allowance. Also, projects with long gestation periods suffer in comparison with those that begin earning income quickly. When inflation is high, the allowance aggravates the tax system's uneven impact on the investment behavior of companies. Companies in high-inflation countries will benefit more if they borrow to finance capital, because tax deductions for capital expenditures are more valuable. This is the reverse of the tax holiday and of lower corporate tax rates, which reduce the advantages of interest cost deductions for tax purposes during high inflation.

Finally, an extreme approach has been to reduce or simply eliminate taxes to all or specific investors. Some countries have become tax havens, especially in the Caribbean and Pacific regions. They generally chose to suppress all direct income taxes and rely on indirect consumption and employment taxes. Other countries have limited those benefits to specific areas and export oriented activities – the so-called Export Processing Zones (EPZs). These zones usually provide a number of benefits to firms that export a minimum share of total output (usually more than 70–80 percent). In virtually all of these zones there is a tax holiday for a substantial period of time (often 10 years) coupled with a reduction or elimination of import taxes on machinery and production inputs. In addition, the zones usually provide less cumbersome procedures for importing and exporting.

Tax haven countries have been successful in encouraging FDI, but this has to be qualified as they principally attracted mobile companies or activities that are relatively global such as banking and insurance as well as Internet companies. Today, the Cayman Islands claims that it is the fifth largest financial center, as it is home to subsidiaries of forty-five of the world's largest banks. It has to be noted that tax havens have been much less successful in convincing multinational firms to relocate their corporate home than establishing new subsidiaries, partly reflecting the tax and regulatory costs of doing so from the home countries (Collins and Shackelfold (1995)). The experience with EPZ has been mixed as reported by Magati (1999). It remains unclear if the benefits (employment, exports) outweigh the costs (foregone tax revenues, distortions in the allocation of resources). In many countries, such regimes have created a dichotomy between the EPZ companies and those operating under the common regime. The capacity of custom and tax administrations to properly manage and control EPZ companies has also been a crucial element in the performance of EPZ.

Recent issues in the context of globalization

In recent years, the globalization process and the gradual elimination of barriers to capital movements, including FDI, across countries have led to the emergence of new issues. The first issue that has received growing attention from researchers has been the interaction between the home and host countries' taxation regimes and its resulting impact on FDI flows. Second, the issue of tax competition between countries and across regions has also been widely debated in view of the growing importance of this phenomenon worldwide. Finally, several widely publicized recent deals have revealed that a few multinational corporations have received large, perhaps disproportionate, tax rebates, suggesting that the costs and not only the benefits of tax incentives need to be examined more closely. These three issues are reviewed below.

Home country tax policy

In the presence of international capital mobility, home-country corporate income tax rates and rules about how taxes paid in the host country are considered at home should influence FDI. In fact, such influence was recognized a long time ago by the bilateral agreements that were signed to avoid double taxation of income between countries (see UNCTAD, 1995). The current literature has emphasized two additional effects: (1) the influence of the home country's tax system on the efficacy of the tax incentives granted by the host country, and (2) its impact on the way multinationals do business abroad.

Home country's taxation rules affect the effectiveness of tax incentives in the host country. Most FDI outflows originate from OECD countries, with different regimes on how they tax the activities of their multinationals abroad. For example, the foreign tax paid by US companies can be claimed as a tax credit on the US tax liabilities (up to a rate of 35 percent). Japan and UK use similar tax credit systems, while other countries such as Australia, Canada, France, Germany and the Netherlands exempt more or less any profits earned abroad from home-taxation. In 1996, Hines compared the distribution of FDI within the United States of foreign investors whose home governments grant foreign tax credits for federal income and state income taxes, with those whose governments do not tax income earned in the United States. His findings reveal that companies with home tax-free rules (France, Canada, etc.) have invested more in low tax states that those that have to pay taxes in their home country (Japan and UK).[11] In a more recent paper of 1998, the same author found that Japanese firms have a tendency to favor investment in countries where Japan has agreements to claim foreign tax credits for income taxes that they would have paid to foreign governments in the absence of tax holidays.[12] From a policy perspective, these two findings seem to indicate that tax incentives are more effective when they apply to firms from countries whose governments do not tax their foreign activities.

Some recent evidence has shown that the home country's taxation system is likely to influence the way their multinational corporations do business abroad.

Hines and Hubbard (1990) and Grubert (1998) found that it is attractive for US firms to use debt to finance foreign investment in high tax countries (compared to the US) and equity in low tax countries. The argument is that the debt generates interest deductions for the subsidiary and so reduces its taxable income in the host country (note that the parent firm has to pay additional taxes, but at a lower rate, in the US). Harris (1993) uses firm-level data to illustrate that the Tax Reform Act of 1986 in the United States pushed US firms with higher equipment/structure ratios to invest abroad more heavily because their tax regime encouraged such an action. A series of other recent studies have found similar results for preferred stock issuances (Collins and Shakelford (1992)) or domestic versus foreign borrowing (Atshuler and Mintz (1995)). An interesting finding is that the 1986 Tax Reform has also influenced the form of business organization that the multinational will select in the foreign country. For example, since 1986, American investors have had fewer tax incentives to participate in joint ventures, particularly in low tax foreign countries, and the number for this type of foreign investments fell sharply as reported by Desai and Hines (1999).

Finally, the importance of the home-country tax system can also be illustrated by the efforts of tax authorities to prevent the transfer of multinationals' headquarters or other specific activities (such as R&D) to other countries. Many governments negotiate contractual arrangements or, and often simultaneously, impose high penalties if the multinational corporation decides to do so. For example, the costs of moving a parent company, if it is already incorporated in the United States, are prohibitive because the tax administration generally takes the view that the firm is selling off its assets, and levies a substantial capital gain tax. On the other hand, the US tax system provides incentives to local R&D if imported technology and local technology are substitutes, and thus discourages US firms to move those activities abroad (see Hines 1999).

Harmonization versus tax competition

In recent years, there has been new empirical evidence that tax rates and incentives influence the location decision of companies within regional economic groupings, such as the European Union, NAFTA or ASEAN. The location decision of foreign companies within the US has also retained the attention of several researchers (Ondrich and Wasylenko (1993) and Swensson (1994)). As an illustration of this effect, Devereux and Griffith (1998) found that the average effective tax rate plays a significant role in the choice of US companies to locate within Europe. This factor, however, does not seem to influence the choice of whether to locate in Europe compared with one of the outside options (domestic or other foreign markets).

Such findings confirm the idea that was put forward by Forsyth (1972) about thirty years ago. The potential effectiveness of fiscal incentives is that they are able to make a difference between competing jurisdictions where the basic, more important conditions, in other words the fixed locational characteristics, are more or less equivalent. These jurisdictions may be subnational or in different countries included in a supranational unified market (e.g. the European Union). Here, once a locational decision is narrowed down to a handful of alternative sites, incentives can play a decisive role in the final locational choice.

Since tax policy seems to have a greater impact on the location decision within regional markets, the argument is that it can push governments to "race to the bottom" with competitive tax reductions. The main concern is that the various countries may end up in a bidding war that results in a "prisoner's dilemma" that benefits the foreign firms at the expense of the winning State and the welfare of its citizens.

The issue of tax competition across countries or regions has led to many studies in the past few years. For example, Haaparanta (1996) shows that countries will engage in tax bidding processes to attract FDI, if their key motivation is to create jobs. The same reasoning could apply to R&D. Hauffer and Wooton (1999) suggest that the size of the host country may also matter. In principle, countries with large domestic markets are capable of taxing more FDI because they benefit from positive agglomeration effects; but this advantage decreases with lower trade costs, as may happen in regional grouping and Trade Union. Overall, the outcome of tax competition is generally ambiguous because it depends on many factors such as: Do governments enter in cooperative or non-cooperative contests? Do firms operate in a competitive or non-competitive market? What kinds of tax instruments do the governments use?

In reality, it is difficult to assess the magnitude of tax competition across countries or within a country because of the inherent difficulty of obtaining any reliable data from governments and even more so from firms (see Oman (2000) for a tentative assessment in several countries and regions). Tax competition seems to be more intensive in some sectors such as in the automotive sector and for larger firms. In any case, both the European Union and OECD have declared that tax competition is harmful to countries. However, this view has to be contrasted with the argument that variations in tax regimes are a good thing because they give tax payers more choice, and thus more chance of being satisfied, and also exert pressure on governments to compete by offering different combinations of public services and taxes.

Recent efforts to harmonize tax systems have been launched both in the industrial and developing world. For example, it has been one of the major objectives of the European Union, where member countries are discussing more stable, predictable and transparent tax rules for investors and governments alike. A first step was achieved in December 1997 with the adoption of the Code of Conduct for business taxation in which member states agree not to introduce "harmful" tax measures and to roll back existing harmful measures. Similarly, several West African countries have been undertaking a joint effort to harmonize their tax incentives for FDI in one unified Investment Code within the Monetary Union of West African States. These processes have been slow and the challenge remains great at both the political and economic levels. The fact of the matter is that the temptation to use tax incentives for attracting FDI will certainly increase as a consequence of the growing mobility of capital and companies across countries and regions as well as the homogenization of basic fundamentals across (larger) economic areas.

The costs of fiscal incentives

The debate about the effectiveness of incentives in attracting investment – the potential benefit side – has diverted the attention from the cost side. Even if tax incentive were quite effective in increasing investment flows, the costs might well outweigh the benefits. This issue has become critical in view of the increase in tax competition around the world. This competition has not only taken place in relatively wealthy industrial countries but also in emerging markets where governments generally face severe budgetary constraints.[13]

There is no doubt that tax incentives are costly. The first and most direct costs are those associated with the potential loss of revenues for the host government.[14] The argument here is to determine if the new foreign investment would have come to the country if no or lower incentives were offered. In such cases, "free rider" investors benefit, whilst the Treasury loses, and there are no net benefits to the economy. An interesting recent study on the State of South Carolina in the US (Figlio and Blonigen 1999) has shown that FDI has several important negative impacts on the State budget, in fact more than on new domestic investment. Not only did they generate more revenue losses (an average sized new foreign firm is associated with a 1.2 percent reduction in real per capita revenues while a domestic firm is associated with only 0.1 percent) but also additional expenses on infrastructure and education, even though those may have indirect benefits for the economy. These results simply illustrate that attracting foreign companies is not a "zero-sum game" from a public finance perspective.

Tax policy and incentives have many, perhaps less evident, additional costs. Indeed, the argument for their efficacy presuppose that tax authorities are capable of identifying the "positive externalities" of investments, and determine the exact level of tax incentives required to attract the investor. Most incentive programs have relied on vague assessments of potential externalities, and presumptions of policymakers about both the desirability and likelihood of attracting certain types of investments.[15] The distortionary effects of incentives on the allocation of resources can be significant as they bias the investment decisions of private companies. Incentives can be further counterproductive if they contribute to attracting more investors of the "wrong kind", which is certainly the case in countries where basic fundamentals are not yet in place.

Another problem with incentive measures relates less to whether they achieve their objectives than to the difficulty and cost of administering them effectively. Put another way, incentive regimes generally impose a significant administrative burden, and must, therefore, be more than marginally effective in order to cover the costs of implementing them and produce a net overall benefit. On this point, it is worth mentioning the difference between discretionary regimes, which depend upon case by case evaluations, and non-discretionary regimes, which grant incentives to whatever company meets clearly stated requirements. Difficult-to-administer discretionary regimes result in delays and uncertainty for investors, which can even increase the overall cost of making an investment in some countries. They have also been significant sources of corruption, effectively screening out desirable investment, and detrimental to the processes of developing competitive markets and sound policy-making. In contrast, automatic incentive regimes are easier to implement, and generally involve such incentives as investment tax credits, accelerated depreciation, and subsidies linked to indicators that can be easily measured (exports, technology imports, skilled labor). One has to keep in mind, however, that successful examples like Singapore or Ireland are rare. There have been more governments that failed to attract FDI with targeted tax incentives, explaining why the recent trend has been to eliminate and streamline tax incentive programs. In fact, it seems that multinationals give more importance to simplicity and stability in the tax system than generous tax rebates, especially in an environment with great political and institutional risks (see Ernst & Young (1994)).

Concluding remarks and next steps

In summary, incentives will generally neither make up for serious deficiencies in the investment environment, nor generate the desired externalities. Thus, advisors often counsel long-run strategies of improving human and physical infrastructure, and where necessary streamlining government policies and procedures, thereby increasing the chances of attracting investment on a genuine long-term basis. Indeed, the importance of fundamental factors like economic conditions and political climate is underlined by the fact that most serious investors are often unaware of the full range of incentives on offer when they invest, and that they often do not consider alternative locations.

Recent evidence has nevertheless shown that, when other factors such as political and economic stability, infrastructure and transport costs are more or less equal between potential locations, taxes may exert a significant impact. This is evidenced by the growing tax competition in regional groupings such as the European Union or at the sub-regional level within one country (e.g. the U.S.). This impact, however, has to be qualified on two important counts. First, the impact of tax policy may significantly depend on the tax instruments used by the authorities. For example, tax holidays and a general reduction in the statutory tax rate may have an equivalent impact on the effective tax rate but significantly different effects on FDI flows and government's revenues. Second, the effectiveness of tax policy and incentives is also likely to vary depending on the multinational firm's activity and on its motivations for investing abroad. For example, tax incentives seem to be a crucial factor for mobile firms or firms that operate in multiple markets because they can exploit better the different tax regimes across countries.

The debate around the impact of taxes and fiscal incentives on FDI is far from being over. Old questions will lead to new answers, and new questions will also emerge in the future. Among all these possibilities, we would like to focus on *five* directions that, we believe, offer ideas for future research. The first direction consists of the eventual non-linear impact of tax rates on the investment decision of multinational corporations. A look at the reality suggests that countries with excessive tax rates can kill foreign direct investment but those with reasonable tax rates may exert little or no influence on it. At the other extreme, the success of tax haven countries indicates that extremely low tax rates may also attract foreign investors, at least some of them. There is a need for a detailed econometric evidence of those non-linear effects as they may have implications for policy makers that aim at using tax policy to attract foreign investors.

The second direction for research could be to examine more closely the effect of tax policy on the composition of FDI (e.g. greenfield, reinvested earnings, and mergers and acquisitions). There have been only a few studies on this aspect, most of the authors preferring to focus on the level of total FDI in the country. However, depending on the tax policy or the fiscal incentives, foreign investors may choose alternative ways to invest abroad. For example, as mentioned in the previous section, recent changes in the US tax policy seem to have discouraged US joint ventures. By having a better understanding of how tax policies affect the composition of FDI, policy makers in host countries would have a better chance of attracting the right type of investment and maximizing its impact on the economy.

The third direction is linked to the development of new technologies. As a matter of fact the Internet has the potential to increase tax competition, not least by making it much easier for multinationals to shift their activities to low-tax regimes, that are physically a long way from their customers, but virtually are only a mouse-click away. As reported in *The Economist* (2000), "many more companies may be able to emulate Rupert Murdoch's News Corporation, which has earned profits of US2.3 billion in Britain since 1987 but paid no corporation tax there". The emergence of global companies will have a significant impact on government revenues. These companies are likely to be much sensitive to tax incentives as they will be more capable to exploit them by transferring their activities from one country to another. Additional evidence is certainly needed on this rapidly expending sector of the economy.

The fourth direction concerns the need for a global approach to the taxation of multinational corporations. Within that vision, the following areas merit further attention: (1) should countries harmonize their tax regimes and, if yes, how? (2) should "transfer pricing" or other techniques used by multinational corporations to exploit cross-country differences in tax regimes be restricted as followed recently by US tax legislators who have the possibility to force companies to repatriate their profits if the authorities consider that they attempt to avoid taxation? (3) Should a global agency calculate the profit of global companies worldwide and then allocate it to individual countries on the basis of a formula that reflect the firm's presence in that country? Today, those areas offer more questions than answers, but it has to be recognized that a global approach is increasingly needed because national boundaries are fading away, and national tax administrations are losing their control over taxpayers.

The fifth and last direction lies in the question whether tax incentives should only be directed at (foreign) investors that make the "right things" in the host country, such as environment-safe projects, or those leading to employment or transfers of technology and marketing skills. This new trend caught the attention of a few researchers in the past few years. For example, Markusen *et al.* (1995) study a model where governments compete through environmental taxes when productive activity causes local pollution (see also Rauscher (1995)). Hines (1996) found that American owned-foreign affiliates are more R&D intensive if located in countries that impose high withholding taxes on royalty payments, and similarly, that foreign firms investing in the United States are more R&D intensive if they are subject to higher royalty withholding taxes. Recently, Blonigen and Slaughter (1999) suggested that tax policy influence the magnitude of which foreign affiliates use skilled labor and transfer new technologies in the host country. These recent studies indicate that tax policy can be used not only to attract foreign investors but also to regulate some of their activities in the host economy. This issue merits further attention from research, especially as there is need for additional evidence of these possible effects both at the country and enterprise level.

Notes

1 Foreign Investment Advisory Service (FIAS), a joint service of the International Finance Corporation and the World Bank. The opinions and arguments expressed are the sole responsibility of the authors and do not necessarily reflect those of the above institutions. We would like to thank Gokhan Alkinci and Carl Aaron for their comments.

2 According to Wells (1999), the earliest reference was in 1160, when wool weavers were offered tax incentives to locate in Biella, in the Piedmont region of Northern Italy.

3 In the *Fortune*/Deloitte & Touche's survey, taxes ranked at the thirteenth position out of twenty-six factors.

4 There exists a considerable literature around this concept, which include recent developments such as uncertainty, relations between labor and capital taxes, and indirect taxes. Several studies can be found in Anwar Shah (1995).

5 The average rate can be viewed as the marginal rate multiplied by the statutory average tax rate.

6 It has to be noted that in principle the locational decision of the firm may be affected by the marginal and average rates in two opposite directions. When the average level is high in one country, it is possible that the overall profit level may be less than in another country even though its marginal rate is lower.

7 For his study, Reuber separated investors into different groups according to their type investment (market seeking or export oriented). He used eighty investment projects in various industries of thirty developing countries, made by companies from various national origin. The companies surveyed were asked to identify, among various incentives, which one was deemed so important that its absence would have caused the abandonment of the project or major changes in it. Among export-oriented projects, 48 percent named fiscal incentives (including tax holidays, duty remission and accelerated depreciation). Among market-oriented projects, 56 percent of responses named protection of the market as the prevailing factor. By using a different approach to define the problem, Reuber showed that investment incentives might not matter to all investors but they do matter to some investors having a specific investment strategy (e.g. export platform). Another merit of the study is to pose the question "do incentive matter?" in terms of the location of the projects rather than a broader decision to carry out FDI.

8 For example, an effective tax rate in the United States of about 25 percent at the end of 1994 was produced by a 38 percent corporate tax rate combined with no investment tax allowance, depreciation rates on buildings of 4.4 percent and 18.6 percent on machinery,

and a number of other assumptions about inflation, interest rates (interest is deductible) etc. Approximately the same effective tax rate was achieved in Spain with a lower corporate tax rate (35 percent), and lower rates of depreciation of buildings (3 percent) and equipment (12 percent).

9 For example, during the holiday years, companies operate at a preferential corporate tax rate. When corporate taxpayers have a choice, they have incentive to shift income into a company enjoying the tax holiday and take more deductible expenses in another company they may own that must pay taxes. They would prefer to have the taxpaying company incur interest costs on borrowed finance and the tax-holiday company to be financed with equity. In fact, the tax holiday company could hold debt in the non-holiday company. The non-holiday company can deduct interest while the tax-holiday company earns the interest tax-free.

10 These allowances take three forms: (1) accelerated depreciation, which allows companies to write off capital more quickly for tax purposes than for accounting; (2) an investment expenditure allowance that lets companies write off a percentage of qualifying investment expenditures from their taxable income; and (3) an investment tax credit that allows companies to reduce taxes paid by a percentage of investment expenditures.

11 Note that Slemrod (1990) did not find any clear pattern at the country (rather than the State) level.

12 Hines shows that Japanese firms are subject to 23 percent lower tax rates than their American counterparts in countries with whom Japan has agreements. In other words, Japanese firms have a greater propensity to invest when they can benefit from tax incentives than when they cannot because they would have to pay taxes in Japan.

13 This is certainly the main argument why tax incentives are frequently eliminated in budgetary crisis; see recent examples of East Asian countries (e.g. Indonesia) as discussed by Wells (1999).

14 It is estimated that the direct and indirect fiscal "cost-per-job" of incentives received by investors in the automobile industry often exceeds US$100,000 (see Oman (2000)).

15 Even if incentives are effective in attracting more investment, the fact is that they distort the profit signals to investors. Thus, unless the envisaged externalities can somehow be generated, the resources used by a government to fund incentive measures are being put to less than optimal use.

References

Agodo O. (1978), "The Determinants of US Private Manufacturing Investment in Africa", *Journal of International Business Studies*, 9: 95–107.

Aharoni Y. (1966), "The Foreign Investment Decision Process", Boston: Harvard Business School.

Atshuler R. and J. Mintz (1995), "US Interest-Allocation Rules: Effects and Policy", *International Tax and Public Finance*, 2(1): 7–35.

Barlow E. and I. Wender (1955), *Foreign Investment and Taxation*, Englewood Cliffs: Prentice Hall.

Blonigen B. and M. Slaughter, "Foreign-Affiliate Activity and US Skill Upgrading", NBER Working Paper, N. 7040, Cambridge Mass: NBER.

Bond E. and L. Samuelson (1986), "Tax Holidays as Signals", *American Economic Review*, 76(4): 820–6.

Boskin M. and W. Gale (1987), "New Results on the Effects of Tax Policy on the International Location of Investment", in Feldstein M. (ed), *The Effects of Taxation on Capital Accumulation*, Chicago: University of Chicago Press.

Coyne E. J. (1994), "An Articulated Analysis Model for FDI Attraction into developing Countries", Florida: Nova Southeastern University.

Collins J. and D. Shackelfold (1995), "Corporate Domicile and Average Effective Tax Rates: The Cases of Canada, Japan, the United Kingdom, and the United States", *International Tax and Public Finance*, 2(1): 55–83.

Devereux M. and R. Griffith (1998), "Taxes and the Location of Production: Evidence from a Panel of US Multinationals", *Journal of Public Economics*, 68: 335–67.

Desai M. and J. Hines (1999), "Basket Cases: Tax Incentives and International Joint Venture Participation by American Multinational Firms", *Journal of Public Economics*, 71(3): 379–402.

The Economist (2000), "Globalization and Tax", January 29.

Ernst & Young (1994), "Investment in Emerging Markets", A Surrey of the Strategic Investment of global 1000 Companies", New York.

Figlio D. and B. Blonigen (1999), "The Effects of Direct Foreign Investment on Local Communities", NBER Working Paper, N. 7274, Cambridge Mass, NBER.

Forsyth D. (1972), *US Investment in Scotland*, New York: Praeger.

Fortune/Deloitte & Touche (1997), "1997 Business Location Study", Processed.

Group of Thirty (1992), "Foreign Direct Investment: 1973–87", New York: Group of 30.

Gruber H., T. Goodspeed and D. Swensson (1993), "Explaining the Low Taxable Income of Foreign-Controlled Companies in the US", in A. Giovannini, R. Hubbard, and J. Slemrod (eds), *Studies in International Taxation*, Chicago: University of Chicago Press.

Gruber H. (1998), "Taxes and the Division of Foreign Operating Income Among Royalties, Interest, Dividends, and retained earnings", *Journal of Public Economics*, 68 (2): 285–93.

Guisinger S. and Associates (1985), *Investment Incentives and Performance Requirements*, New York: Praeger.

Haaparanta P. (1996), "Competition for Foreign Direct Investment", *Journal of Public Economics*, 63: 141–153.

Harris D. (1993), "The Impact of US Tax Law revision on Multinational corporations' capital Location and Income – Shifting Decisions", *Journal of Accounting Research*, 31: 111–40. Supplement.

Hartman D. (1985), "Tax Policy and Foreign Direct Investment", *Journal of Public Economics*, 26(1): 107–21.

Hauffer A. and I. Wooton (1999), "Country Size and Tax Competition for Foreign Direct Investment", *Journal of Public Economics*, 71: 121–39.

Hines J. and G. Hubbard (1990), "Coming Home to America: Dividend Repatriations by US Multinationals", in A. Razin and J. Slemrod (eds), *Taxation in the Global Economy*, Chicago: University Press.

Hines J. (1996), "Altered States: Taxes and the Location of Foreign Direct Investment in America", *American Economic Review* 86, N.5, December 1996: 1076–94.

Hines J. (1998), "Tax Sparing and Direct Investment in developing Countries", NBER Working Paper, N. 6728, Cambridge Mass: NBER.

Hines J. (1999), "Lessons from Behavioral Responses to International Taxation", *National Tax Journal*, 52(2): 305–22.

Japan External Trade Organization (JETRO) (1995), The Current State of Japanese Affiliated Manufacturers in ASEAN – 1994", Tokyo: Overseas Research Department, June 1995.

Lim D. (1983), "Fiscal Incentives and Direct Foreign Investment in Less Developed Countries", *Journal of Development Studies*, 19(2): 207–12.

D. Magati (1999), "A Review of the Role and Impact of Export Processing Zones", Washginton, DC: World Bank, Research Department.

Markusen J. R., E. Morey and N. Olewiler (1995), "Competition in Regional Environment Policies when Plant Location are Endogenous", *Journal of Public Economics*, 56: 55–77.

Mintz J. and T. Tsiopoulos (1992), "Corporate Income Taxation and Foreign Direct Investment", Foreign Investment Advisory Service, Occasional Paper 4, 1992.

Oman C. (2000), "Policy Competition for Foreign Direct Investment: A Study of Competition Among Governments to Attract FDI", Paris: OECD Development Centre Studies.

Ondrich J. and M. Wasylenko (1993), *Foreign Direct Investment in the United States: Issues, Magnitudes, and Location Choice of New Manufacturing Plants*, Kalamazoo: W.E. Upjohn Institute.

Phillips A. (1969), "The Significance of Nigeria's Income Tax Relief Incentives", *The Nigerian Journal of Economic and Social Studies*, 11.

Rauscher M. (1995), "Environment Regulation and the Location of Polluting Industries", *International Tax and Public Finance*, 2: 229–44.

Reuber G., *Private Foreign Investment in Development*, Clarendon Press for the OECD Development Centre: Oxford, 1973.

Robinson H. J. (1961), *The Motivation and Flow of Private Foreign Investment*, Menlo Park, California: Stanford Research Institute.

Rolfe R. J. (1993), "Determinants of FDI Incentive Preferences of MNEs", *Journal of International Business Studies*, 24(2): 335–56.

Root F. and Ahmed A. (1978), " The Influence of Policy Instruments on Manufacturing Direct Foreign Investment in developing Countries", Journal of International Business Studies, 9(3): 81–93.

Shah A. (1975), Fiscal Incentives for Investment and Innovation, Oxford: Oxford Press for the World Bank.

Shah A. and J. Toye (1978), "Fiscal Incentives for Firms in Some Developing Countries: Survey and Critique", J. Toye (ed), *Taxation and Economic Development*, London: Frank Cass.

Slemrod J. (1990), "Tax Effects on Foreign Direct Investment in the United States: Evidence from a Cross Country Comparison", in A. Razin and J. Slemrod (eds), *Taxation in the Global Economy*, Chicago: University Press.

Swensson D. (1994), "The Impact of US Tax reform on Foreign Direct Investment in the United States", *Journal of Public Economics*, 54: 243–56.

UNCTAD (1996), *Incentives and Foreign Direct Investment: Background Report*, Geneva and New York: United Nations.

Wells L. (1986), "Investment Incentives: An unnecessary Debate", *CTC Reporter*, New York: United Nations, 58–60.

Wells L. (1999), "Attracting Foreign Investment: Incentives, Institutions, and Infrastructure", Washington: Foreign Investment Advisory Service.

17 Options for collecting globalisation statistics

Australia[1]

Mark Lound and Geoff Robertson

The demand for globalisation statistics

Businesses, financial institutions, governments, individuals and households and international institutions are all players in the globalisation phenomenon. Therefore, in various ways, each requires an appropriate understanding of the factors contributing to globalisation and the issues that need to be addressed by governments. Importantly, appropriate statistics can help to provide an understanding of globalisation and serve as a base for the development of relevant policies, strategies and responses.

The pervasiveness of globalisation may require constant reassessment of the economic situation and appropriateness of strategies and responses by each of the players. At the national level, governments need to make decisions across a range of issues and for this purpose, good statistics and other information are required. Before exploring the type of statistics required it is necessary to identify some of the issues that governments need to address. These may include:

- What is the extent of foreign ownership, both within a host country and by domestic investors abroad? In what industries do foreign investment dominate and why? Are the levels of penetration changing over time? Are the levels consistent with government policy? Should government encourage or discourage further ownership? What are the public perceptions about the extent and nature of foreign ownership; are these perceptions correct and do they reinforce or inhibit government policy?
- What are the links between investment, trade in goods and services flows and employment? Does foreign investment in the domestic economy generate production, employment and exports or simply lead to greater imports? Does investment abroad lead to the transfer of production and jobs abroad and to loss of exports and increase in imports, or to greater production, employment and exports by the investing country?
- Do foreign owned businesses have different employment practices – pay relatively higher or lower salaries, have higher or lower overheads, employ mostly more skilled or less skilled staff, have higher or lower productivity, are more or less labour-intensive, employ a higher proportion of non-nationals,

have higher or lower levels of unionised staff, transfer administrative work abroad, encourage staff training and development schemes, etc?

- Does foreign investment assist or hinder competition policy, lower or increase price levels of goods and services, and breakdown or create barriers to trade? To maintain or change the status quo, should existing levels of protection, economic regulation, subsidies, etc. be maintained, increased or reduced?
- Does foreign investment encourage or discourage transfer of technical know-how, expenditure on research and development, etc? Should government policy offer incentives to foreign owned businesses to establish research and development units in the domestic economy?
- Does foreign investment lead to the discovery of new resources through, for example, mineral exploration? Again, should governments offer targeted incentives to encourage mineral exploration?
- Are the dividends and reinvested earnings yields on foreign investment commensurate with the level of investment? What are the income tax implications and what is appropriate tax policy to encourage foreign investment without too heavily subsidising such investment? Is there evidence of transfer pricing by which earnings are manipulated, usually to reduce overall taxes paid by multinationals? (Transfer pricing involves intra-firm pricing of immediate production at artificially high or low prices to keep earnings of enterprises artificially high or low in particular economies.)
- What is the relationship between foreign and domestic finance for either foreign owned companies in the domestic economy or domestically owned companies abroad?
- What is the impact of foreign ownership on particular industries and/or particular regions?
- What countries are the better sources of foreign investment and what countries provide the better investment opportunities?
- Globalisation statistics of other countries may provide much data that assist to understand the motivation and behaviour of transnational corporations. Would patterns revealed in one country be true for another, or are there different factors, influencing motivation and behaviour?

It needs to be borne in mind that statistics cannot answer all of these issues and often need to be used in conjunction with industry experience, case studies and business and political assessments. Nevertheless, they provide a framework when considering questions for a particular industry and a frame of reference against which to judge other data for a particular industry.

Limitation of current statistics

Existing statistics can provide many insights into globalisation phenomena. National Accounts statistics, for example, provide broad measures of the national production, income, consumption, investment and saving and the contributions to these aggregates by transactions with the rest of the world. However, it is not possible to determine from existing national accounts data the separate impact of foreign and domestically owned companies on production, income generation, exports and imports of goods, net income earnings from abroad, and corporate savings. In addition, because national accounts data are restricted in concept to measuring only domestic economic activity (including transactions with the rest of the world), these statistics essentially provide no data on the activities of domestic businesses abroad. The revised international standard, System of National Accounts (*SNA93*) suggests that national statisticians introduce a dissection of national accounts aggregates to provide separate data on foreign controlled and domestically controlled enterprises; however, it is unlikely that such a classification will be introduced in the statistics collections of many countries in the near future. The proposals canvassed in this chapter may provide an initial step towards further consideration of this option.

Financial Accounts publications typically provide statistics on financial flows and stocks (asset and liability positions) of financial, trading enterprises, government and household sectors. To complete the accounts, a rest of the world sector is included. These statistics provide very valuable data on aspects of globalisation. It is difficult from this type data, however to dissect the financial and trading enterprise sectors according to whether businesses are foreign or domestically owned, because the compilation methodology requires, *inter alia*, data from banks on their portfolio of loans to trading corporations and bank data would not readily distinguish whether loans are to foreign or domestic owned corporations.

International trade, balance of payments, and international investment statistics provide extensive data on transactions between domestic residents and the rest of the world. International investment statistics also provide measures on the stock of other foreign assets and liabilities such as foreign debt. International trade statistics provide very detailed data on the value and quantities of traded goods. Rarely, however, is there data on the extent of exports and imports by foreign owned businesses.

Balance of payments publications provide data on transactions between residents and non-residents classified by goods, services, income, transfers and capital. Capital transactions are in turn classified by direct investment, portfolio investment and other investment and reserves. Data is rarely collected on whether goods and services exports and imports are by foreign or domestic owned enterprises and whether such trade is with foreign affiliates or not. Income and capital transactions between domestic businesses and their foreign affiliates are separately identified as direct investment. In addition, income and capital transactions associated with ownership of companies, other than affiliates, is separately identified as part of portfolio investment.

International statistical initiatives on globalisation

Internationally, globalisation is a central concern of economic debate and statisticians worldwide are addressing how to provide appropriate statistical measures. No clear consensus has yet emerged. One aim of this chapter is to contribute to the discussions on developing an appropriate framework for globalisation statistics. To develop this framework, it is necessary to summarise some of the sources from which a conceptual framework may be drawn. The debate centres on two issues, namely what definition of foreign ownership/control to use and what globalisation indicators to use, and these are addressed in this section of the chapter.

US, Canadian, Japanese and Australian statistics all recognise the importance of the direct investment concept in defining foreign affiliates. However, the US, Canada and Australia have all adopted narrower concepts. The US provides some data in respect of 'majority owned affiliates' only. Canada has a number of definitions of control including directly controlled foreign enterprises (majority foreign ownership), minority foreign controlled and other effectively foreign controlled enterprises.

Both *BPM5* and *SNA93* address the issue of foreign ownership. *BPM5* defines direct investment and portfolio investment. *Direct investment* refers to an investor in one economy investing in an entity in another economy to obtain a lasting interest in that entity and to exercise significant influence in its management. While the direct investor may actually control the enterprise, the *BPM5* concept is less stringent and stops at *significant influence*, which allows for situations where there may be several large investors. Ownership of shares in companies by a foreign investor, other than direct investment, is referred to as *portfolio investment*. *SNA93* approaches the classification from a different perspective and uses a narrower concept, namely control, based upon majority ownership of a company. While the concepts of direct investment and control do not contradict each other, they make the task of choosing a suitable measure of ownership a little more difficult.

The other major matter on which globalisation statistics need to focus is the selection of globalisation indicators. This is not straight forward because to date there is no international definitive list of indicators. *BPM5* suggests a list as does the Organisation for Economic Co-operation and Development (OECD) Working Group on Industry Statistics. These are both described below.

BPM5 definition of direct investment

Direct investment has long been an important item within balance of payments and more recently international investment statistics. *Direct investment* is investment undertaken by an entity resident in one economy in an enterprise resident in another economy with the objective of obtaining or sustaining a lasting interest in the enterprise and exercising a significant degree of influence in the management of the enterprise. The entity undertaking the investment is referred to as the *direct investor* and the enterprise in which the investment takes place is referred to as the *direct investment enterprise*.

Direct investment is essentially defined in terms of the direct investor (an individual, a government, an enterprise, or an associated group of individuals or corporations) owning 10 per cent or more of the ordinary shares (or an equivalent ownership interest) in the direct investment enterprise. The direct investment enterprise may be a branch, subsidiary or an associate of the direct investor. Also generally included within the definition of direct investment enterprises are subsidiaries and associates of the enterprise in which the initial direct investment takes place.

Direct investors and direct investment enterprises fall within most notions of foreign owned, multinational or global corporations. Balance of payments statisticians have long recognised that investment and associated investment income flows between enterprises in one country with their direct investors (inward investment) or direct investment enterprises abroad (outward investment) are key aggregates in balance of payments analysis.

It has also been recognised for some time that, having defined direct investment enterprises, the statistician may measure the activities of these enterprises in the domestic economy and thus obtain an understanding of the impact of these enterprises in the domestic economy. Similarly, statisticians have recognised the usefulness of measuring the activities of direct investment enterprises abroad; such data may be collected from resident direct investors. In this context, it is useful to quote from *BPM5* which provides a useful summary of globalisation indicators.

> There are aspects of direct investment, other than those directly related to the balance of payments and international investment position data, that may be – particularly in the host economy – of interest from analytical and policy-making points of view. Among such aspects are those pertaining to the financial structure and operations of subsidiaries, associates, branches, and direct investors. Examples are the value of the total assets of enterprises; complete balance sheets and income statements; the composition of sales and external financing; employment; industry activity of direct investment enterprises and of direct investors; geographic allocation of activities; gross product or value added of subsidiaries in relation to total GDP of the economies involved; and country of ultimate beneficial owner.
>
> (*BPM5*, para. 384)

SNA93 definition of foreign controlled enterprises

SNA93 suggests that national statistical agencies identify separately public (Government) controlled, foreign controlled, and other privately controlled enterprises as part of the institutional sector classification. In this chapter we are not concerned with defining government controlled enterprises, but we are interested in the foreign control and other control distinction. The *SNA93* definition of foreign control is given in Table 17.1. While *SNA93* (paragraph 4.70) recognises that it is possible to secure control of a corporation with less than a majority shareholding, it recommends as a practical guideline that more than 50 per cent ownership holding be used as evidence that control exists (Table 17.1).

Table 17.1 SNA93 definition of foreign control

Foreign controlled corporations consist of all resident corporations and quasi-corporations that are controlled by non-resident institutional units. They include:

All subsidiaries of non-resident corporations (but not associates of non-resident corporations);
All corporations controlled by a non-resident institutional unit that is not itself a corporation: for example, a corporation which is controlled by a foreign government; it also includes corporations controlled by a group of non-resident units acting in concert;
All branches or other unincorporated agencies of non-resident corporate and unincorporated enterprises that are engaged in significant amounts of production on the economic territory on a long-term basis and that are, therefore, treated as quasi-resident corporations.

Extracts from *SNA93*, pp. 96–98.

Table 17.2 Globalisation indicators under consideration by the OECD Working Group on Industry Statistics

Direct investment	Share of foreign affiliates in domestic production Share of foreign affiliates abroad in domestic production of recipient country Share of foreign affiliates abroad in direct investment in recipient country
Employment	Share of foreign affiliates in domestic employment Employment in foreign affiliates abroad Foreign affiliates and foreign affiliates abroad labour costs Foreign affiliates and foreign affiliates abroad labour productivity
Technology	Share of foreign affiliates in research and development (R&D) expenditure in domestic economy R&D intensity in foreign affiliates compared to domestic enterprises R&D expenditure by foreign affiliates abroad Share of intra-firm technology transfer compared with total transfer
Trade	Import/export ratio of foreign affiliates and foreign affiliates abroad Intra-firm trade compared with total trade

Note: The OECD discussion has so far identified many measurement problems in the list of indicators identified. The list is meant to be illustrative and is not complete.

OECD Working Group on Industry Statistics

The OECD Working Group on Industry Statistics (within the Directorate for Science, Technology and Industry) has undertaken several initiatives in the area of globalisation statistics. It has established a database on available national statistics and is giving consideration to preparing a *Manual on Globalisation Indicators*. While, its work on indicators is preliminary, it has identified a number of areas in which indicators may be developed (Table 17.2).

International statistical work on trade-in-services

The General Agreement on Trade in Services (GATS), which is one of the multilateral trade agreements administered by the World Trade Organisation (WTO) has a framework of concepts, rules and principles aimed at the liberalisation of trade-in-services. What is clearly emerging from the international discussions on data requirements under the Agreement, is that existing balance of payments data on international trade-in-services do not go far enough. The WTO, which is responsible for all arrangements concluded within the framework of the Agreement, is playing an active role in this work. Work on extending international trade-in-services statistical standards is also being undertaken jointly by the OECD Statistics Directorate and the Statistical Office of the European Community, while the Interagency Task Force on Trade-in-Services Statistics, which includes OECD Statistics Directorate, WTO and a number of other international agencies, is developing a *Manual on Trade-in-Services Statistics*, which *inter alia* is likely to add a new statistical requirement on foreign affiliates trade-in-services.

To examine the barriers to trade-in-services and measure countries liberalisation commitments, data are required on the mode of service supply. Three modes of supply: cross-border supply, consumption abroad and presence of natural persons would be additional breakdowns of trade-in-services and compensation of employees (labour income) classifications in the balance of payments. A fourth category, *commercial presence*, would require additional data to be obtained.

Commercial presence is defined as services delivered within the territory of the Member, through the commercial presence of the supplier. It refers to delivery of services through any type of business or professional establishment, such as corporations, representative offices and branches, owned or controlled by persons from other countries. The provision of such services is beyond the scope of the balance of payments framework. However, the activities of foreign affiliates are reflected, to a limited degree, in the equity income and reinvested earnings reported by direct investors and direct investment enterprises published in balance of payments statistics.

It is not clear at this time how the modes of supply would be defined in practice and when WTO Members are likely to be required to supply statistical data and the nature of that data. However, it is likely that greater demands will be placed on the national statistical offices to measure service sales and trade provided by foreign affiliates, including foreign affiliates abroad and foreign owned affiliates in the domestic economy.

Work on globalisation within the Statistical Office of the European Community

The Statistical Office of the European Community established a task force in 1992 to study the feasibility of harmonising available information to describe certain aspects of globalisation and to co-ordinate activities with organisations such as the International Monetary Fund, OECD and the United Nations. The task force is currently evaluating the quality of the available information from member countries and participating in various international statistical fora. It has also commenced the publication of the *Globalisation Newsletter* and has issued a report, the *FATS (Foreign Affiliates Trade in Services) Task Force Report.*

A conceptual framework for globalisation statistics with an application to Australia

It is premature to articulate a complete conceptual framework for globalisation statistics because among official statisticians there is no consensus about the nature and measurement of globalisation statistics. As seen in previous sections of this chapter, few countries have comprehensive data collections in place and each of them has developed somewhat different measurement and collection practices. International statistical standards and recommendations can best be described as embryonic. However, there are a number of elements from which a consensus about a conceptual framework may emerge. These include how to define and classify foreign owned and domestic owned businesses; how to identify the appropriate statistical unit for the measurement of globalisation indicators; and what globalisation indicators to measure. There are a number of subsidiary issues to resolve such as whether to measure country of ultimate or immediate ownership and whether globalisation indicators, when foreign ownership of a business is less than 100 per cent, should be apportioned or allocated?

An important consideration, and one adhered to in this chapter, is that any new economic statistics, including globalisation statistics, need to build on and be consistent with existing international standards (such as *SNA93* and *BPM5*) and classifications and national statistical standards which are based upon them. This precondition, which underscores much of the thinking in this chapter, will greatly strengthen the analytical usefulness of globalisation data. This precondition would not limit globalisation statistics. For example, it may be possible to present satellite globalisation accounts to either the national accounts or balance of payments statistics, provided the links between the satellite accounts and more traditional methods of presentation are clearly understood, identified and reconciliation made explicit. In this section a conceptual framework for collecting globalisation statistics is explored, with particular reference to Australia and works that maybe undertaken by the Australian Bureau of Statistics (ABS).

Foreign ownership classification of Australian businesses

In past foreign participation studies, the ABS had two measures of foreign ownership, namely *foreign ownership* and *foreign control*. As described elsewhere in this chapter, under the first measure the percentage of foreign ownership of each business was determined from the survey of shareholdings and globalisation indicators (such as turnover, value added and employment) were apportioned between foreign and Australian ownership accordingly. For foreign control, businesses were classified to one category of control and the globalisation indicators were allocated accordingly. In any future foreign ownership statistics, do analysts need two measures of ownership: one based on apportionment and one based on allocation? One view is that there should only be one and that should be based upon foreign control, that is, allocation of globalisation indicators according to the single foreign ownership category (such as foreign, joint and Australian control) for each enterprise.

The apportionment method has been criticised on a number of grounds. First, having two measures of ownership based on different methodologies confuses rather than enlightens. Second, questions have been raised about the meaning of this type of statistic: what does it mean to say that certain percentages of Australian turnover, value added and employment may be attributed to foreign ownership; on the other hand, it is meaningful to say that certain percentages of turnover, value added and employment may be attributed to foreign owned (controlled) businesses. Third, neither other countries nor international statistical standards would seem to favour the apportionment measure. Fourth, there are additional collection and processing costs involved.

Another issue is whether, in future foreign ownership studies, the ABS should adopt the same classification of foreign ownership (control) as adopted in previous foreign participation studies. In the past, four categories of control were adopted: foreign, naturalised or naturalising, joint and Australian. Given that the naturalised and naturalising category is no longer relevant this would be dropped. For historical comparison purposes, that category could be combined with foreign control. The resulting classification (foreign, joint and Australian control) is not, however, consistent with international statistical standards such as *SNA93* and *BPM5*.

There are several classification options that analysts may wish to consider. The first is to extend the classification to include three sub-categories, *wholly foreign controlled*, *other majority foreign control* (e.g. businesses which are less than 100 per cent owned, but have a single foreign shareholder with a majority ownership held either directly or indirectly), and *other foreign control* (Table 17.3). The first two sub-categories would approximate the *SNA93* concept of majority control. The joint control category would remain unchanged. The Australian control category could be extended to provide one or two additional sub-categories. First, it could include the category *other direct investment*, which would include those businesses for which there is (or intended to be) a lasting interest and a significant

Table 17.3 Extended classification of foreign ownership

Foreign control	Wholly foreign owned
	Other majority foreign control
	Other foreign control
Joint control	Joint foreign and Australian control
Australian control	Other direct investment
	Other businesses (with 10% or more) foreign ownership
	Other businesses with little or no foreign ownership

Table 17.4 Alternative classification of foreign ownership

Majority foreign control	Wholly foreign owned Other majority foreign control
Other direct investment	Other foreign control Joint foreign and Australian control Australian control
Other businesses	With (10% or more) foreign ownership With little or no foreign ownership

influence in the management of the enterprise by a foreign investor. Second, it could also include a sub-category, *other businesses with foreign ownership*; this categorises businesses which have no direct investment but in which there is significant foreign portfolio investment. For this purpose a threshold of 10 per cent foreign ownership may be set. The last category, *other businesses with little or no foreign ownership*, would be a residual category.

This classification would facilitate historical comparability with previous foreign participation studies. It would also comply with international standards in that it would follow the *SNA93* definition of majority control (wholly foreign owned plus other majority control) and the *BPM5* definition of direct investment (majority control, other foreign control, joint control and other direct investment). Finally, it would restore some information on other foreign ownership which would be lost if the apportionment method of measuring ownership is dropped.

The extended classification may be considered to have too many categories for some purposes and analysts may prefer a different higher level classification. There is an alternative classification, which conforms to international statistical standards (Table 17.4). The alternative classification is simply a rearrangement of the categories and sub-categories in the extended classification.

A further issue that needs to be resolved is the country classification of foreign owner. In previous foreign participation studies, country of control or ownership was assigned to the country of the immediate foreign investor. One view is that data on *ultimate beneficial owner* should also be collected in respect of the largest direct investor. The country of ultimate beneficial owner would be determined by the country of location of the top company in a group of companies under common control (i.e. those companies in a global parent subsidiary relationship). US experience is that there can be significant differences in statistics based upon the two concepts, immediate foreign investor and ultimate beneficial owner.

Defining Australian owned businesses abroad

A similar range of issues present themselves in determining the definition of Australian owned businesses abroad. To be consistent with international statistical standards should majority control or the broader concept of direct investment be adopted? Should the definition be aligned to the definition used in previous ABS foreign participation studies?

One approach would be a classification that would be consistent with both the *SNA93* or *BPM5* classifications, and with the classification of foreign ownership suggested in the previous section. Additional categories could be included in a conceptual framework for joint Australian and foreign control (included in other direct investment) and for businesses which, while not direct investment enterprises, have some Australian portfolio share ownership. However, these additional categories are not considered to be warranted. There is no category for joint control, as it is not considered to be of concern to analysts, and there is no category for businesses with Australian portfolio share ownership because it would not be possible, or even that meaningful, to collect data for such companies.

A question that arises, in a conceptual discussion, is the treatment of Australian owned businesses abroad, where the Australian parent is itself foreign owned. US and Australian experience is that such businesses would account for a relatively small share of investment abroad. Furthermore their behaviour is likely to be similar to non-foreign owned businesses in Australia when it comes to their investing abroad.

The statistical units model

It is necessary to understand the statistical units that underlie the data collected to produce Australian economic statistics. The statistical units model consists of the following types of units – enterprise group, legal entity, enterprise, management unit establishment and location.

A *legal entity* is an entity that possesses some or all of the rights and obligations of individual persons or corporations. Examples of legal entities for statistical purposes include companies, partnerships, trusts, sole proprietorships, government departments and statutory authorities. Legal entities are classified to an institutional sector according to the type of institutional unit it is. An institutional unit is an economic entity that is capable, in its own right, of owning assets, incurring liabilities and engaging in economic activities and in transactions with other entities.

The *enterprise group* consists of one or more legal entities under common ownership and/or control. The *enterprise* consists of all legal entities within an enterprise group which are classified to a single institutional sub-sector. The *Standard Institutional Sector Classification of Australia* (SISCA) groups the institutional units into the following institutional sectors: non-financial corporations, financial corporations, general government, households, non-profit institutions serving households and rest of the world. Note that the financial corporations sector is split into sub-sectors which reflect the differing operations of certain groups within the financial sector.

Therefore, an enterprise group may contain enterprises that are classified to the non-financial corporations sector and the financial corporations sector depending on the legal entities within the group. Furthermore, if an enterprise group consisted of a bank, another deposit taking entity and a life insurance office then there would be at least three enterprises within that enterprise group. ABS financial surveys (i.e. both government and private) and international investment statistics are based on the enterprise unit.

The *management unit* or the *establishment* unit is the statistical unit that is used in most ABS economic censuses and surveys to collect industry or production data. These units are classified according to the *Australian and New Zealand Standard Industry Classification* (ANZSIC) which classifies units based on the main economic activity undertaken by the unit.

The *management unit* is the highest level production unit (consistent with two digit ANZSIC) within an enterprise group which controls its productive activities and for which a set of management accounts is maintained quarterly. In most cases it coincides with the legal entity owning the business. However, in the case of large diversified businesses there are often a number of management units, each coinciding with a division or line of business which undertakes different activities and where separate and comprehensive quarterly accounts are maintained. Therefore, for large diversified businesses, the management unit may be a lower level unit compared with the enterprise.

The *establishment* is the lowest level unit within an enterprise group within a State or Territory of Australia which controls its productive activities and a specified range of detailed data is maintained. It allows for four digit ANZSIC classification. Again, in large businesses structures, the establishment may be a lower level unit compared with the management unit.

Therefore, ABS data on the production value added, compensation of employees and employment, and research and development may be based on either management units or establishments.

Not all ABS economic statistics are provided by the actual business but rather as a result of some administrative by-product. For example, international trade data are collected from the exporters and importers (or their agents) registered with the Australian Customs Service. Consequently, the data are received from a reporting unit as distinct from the statistical unit. This will add a complication when attempting to link data from collections, which are based on statistical units with those that are based on some other reporting unit. For example, because the reporting unit used in international trade statistics is not a standard statistical unit, it has not been possible to date to link international trade to data collected in other ABS economic statistics collections. (Obviously it can be linked for many businesses but for many others there is no ready correspondence possible.)

Data on foreign ownership are determined at the legal entity level and, therefore, any classification of foreign ownership, based on legal entities, will be applied to the enterprise unit. However, where the data are collected from management units, establishments or another reporting unit, this classification will need to be reflected down from the enterprise level.

The statistical unit used in any measurement of Australian owned businesses abroad would be the enterprise, that is, legal entities in the same country, in the same institutional sub-sector, in the same enterprise group. This unit is chosen, because it is consistent with the unit adapted in the survey of international investment and it is not considered practical to adopt a lower level unit. Again, this may make comparison of data on Australian resident businesses and their overseas affiliates somewhat difficult because different types of units may be compared.

Globalisation indicators

Globalisation indicators are any business, accounting or economic variables that may help to measure the extent of foreign ownership, business behaviour, sources of finance, foreign affiliates trade, and industry and commodity classifications. There is no consensus about just what data items should be used; this will develop with data use. However, there are several broad headings under which data items may be considered. These include business accounting data, economic data, financial data and foreign affiliates trade data. Data items under each of these headings may overlap.

Business accounting data, such as income and expenditure accounts and balance sheets provide a useful starting point to measure business activity. The ABS' *Businesses Operations and Industry Performance* publication (Catalogue no. 8140.0), based upon the ABS economic activity survey, includes the main data items from income and balance sheet statements for businesses in Australia. These data items are used to calculate a number of business averages and industry ratios. This type of data would make a useful starting point for analysis of the behaviour of foreign and Australian owned businesses in Australia (if the foreign ownership classification was available) and Australian owned businesses abroad (if a new collection of such businesses was introduced). However, like all business accounting data, even though accounts may comply with international and national accounting standards, there may be differences in accounting policy and practices across businesses and industries which may lead to some data inconsistencies. Also, in the case of the economic activity survey data, the ABS has expressed some reservations about the appropriateness of the use of the management unit to collect balance sheet data, although it recognises that such data can, nevertheless, serve some useful analytical purposes.

As most analysts of globalisation statistics would want data in the context of monitoring and developing industry policy, it would be desirable that data be classified by industry. In Australian studies this would mean using ANZSIC. For foreign ownership studies in Australia it is envisaged that industry data would be provided at the two, or sometimes four, digit ANZSIC level, while for studies of Australian owned businesses abroad, the aim would be to provide data at the two digit level, though confidentiality limitations may restrict data to industry division only.

While economic statistics largely come from business accounting records, attempts are made to compile economic statistics more rigorously to obtain measures on a consistent basis. Key economic variables such as gross output, gross product or value added, compensation of employees and employment, international trade in goods and services, capital expenditure, mineral exploration expenditure, and expenditure on research and development would all be key globalisation indicators. These data items should be measured according to the definitions used in economic statistics. Again, these data should be classified by industry.

Financial data would measure the flows and stocks of financial assets and liabilities. Of particular interest are data on the sources (increases in liabilities and decrease in assets) and uses (increases in assets and decreases in liabilities) of funds of foreign owned businesses. In respect of foreign owned businesses in Australia it would be useful to know the counter party to the change in liabilities (affiliates abroad, other non-resident entities and Australian resident sectors) and the instrument of finance (shares, debt securities, loans, etc) used. In terms of change in assets it would be useful to know their disposition in terms of fixed assets, inventories, other non-financial assets and financial assets; counter party and instrument should also classify the latter. For Australian owned enterprises abroad a similar range of data would be useful. *SNA93* makes recommendations about defining and classifying financial and non-financial flows and stocks which should provide the basis for an emerging consensus for international standards about the precise data items to be collected.

For foreign affiliate trade in goods and services analysis, it is necessary to link data on trade, sales and purchases of goods and services at various levels. For example, the data items ideally required to measure the sales, purchases and trade of foreign owned businesses in Australia are shown in Table 17.5. Likewise, the data required in respect of Australian owned businesses abroad is shown in Table 17.6. Data on goods and services should be classified by broad commodity to enable any detailed analysis. A stricter analysis would require identifying those foreign owned businesses in Australia which themselves own businesses abroad, and undertaking a suitable adjustment; few foreign owned businesses in Australia themselves own businesses abroad.

Linking data on trade, sales and purchases needs to be treated with caution. Data are not necessarily collected on a consistent basis. For example, international trade in economic statistics is usually valued at the national border, whereas sales and purchases may be measured at the factory door or at a number of other valuation points, depending upon individual business accounting practices.

A moment's reflection will indicate that the provision of such data may be difficult for many businesses, especially supplying a split of domestic sales and

Table 17.5 Theoretical data items required to measure trade of foreign owned businesses in Australia

Sales	Purchases
Exports to	Imports from
Affiliates	Affiliates
Others	Others
Domestic sales to	Domestic sales from
Affiliates	Affiliates
Other foreign owned businesses*	Other foreign owned businesses*
Others	Others

* That is affiliates of other non-resident entities.

Table 17.6 Theoretical data items required to measure foreign affiliates trade of Australian owned businesses abroad

Sales	Purchases
Exports to	Imports from
Australia	Australia
Affiliates	Affiliates
Non-affiliates	Non-affiliates
Elsewhere	Elsewhere
Affiliates*	Affiliates#
Affiliates of other Australian entities**	Affiliates of other Australian entities##
Other***	Other###
Domestic sales to	Domestic purchases from
Affiliates*	Affiliates#
Affiliates of other Australian entities**	Affiliates of other Australian entities##
Other***	Other###

Note: Items marked with the same numbers of asterisks or hashes signs may be combined. Therefore, the numbers of items in each column could be reduced from eight to five.

purchases according to whether customers or suppliers are, or are not, foreign owned businesses. Therefore, in practice it may be difficult to collect data for the full range of categories.

Once again, the theoretical complexity of the data will be apparent and will restrict what businesses could be expected to provide. It is likely that data could only be collected in respect of an affiliates and non-affiliates split.

An important consideration is whether data already exist or new data sources need to be developed. In the case of foreign owned businesses in Australia, much of the data already exist and a major advance could be achieved by classifying these data by a foreign ownership classification. However, some analysis would not be possible, especially more detailed studies on sources and uses of funds and foreign affiliates trade, unless new data collections were established. Such collections are not currently being contemplated. Establishing a new collection for Australian owned businesses abroad would enable the collection of a broad range of data, however, it would not be possible to provide the fine levels of detail that may be possible in respect of foreign owned businesses in Australia.

Possible initiatives on globalisation statistics

This chapter has detailed some of the issues involved in the context of improving the collection of globalisation statistics. In this concluding section some initiatives are put forth on how globalisation statistics may be developed. Again, the focus is on Australia as a practical example. Nevertheless, the initiatives can serve as a model or guideline for other national statistical agencies.

Survey of shareholdings linked to other ABS economic collections

The first initiative is to classify data in existing ABS collections by whether businesses are foreign owned or Australian owned. To identify the foreign ownership characteristics of Australian businesses it would be necessary to introduce a survey of shareholdings and link the data collected with other ABS business collections.

The survey would approach all direct investment enterprises in the survey of international investment and collect data from them on their foreign and Australian shareholders, their ownership of subsidiaries in Australia, and their shareholdings above 10 per cent in other Australian companies. Companies in which direct investment enterprises and their subsidiaries have 10 per cent or more equity holding would in turn be approached to collect similar data. This would enable companies in Australia to be classified according to the classification of foreign ownership such as foreign control, joint foreign and Australian control, and Australian control, or whatever other classification may be adopted. Companies which have some portfolio investment shareholders and are not direct investment enterprises could also be included in the survey of shareholdings if it were decided to include other businesses with 10 per cent or more foreign ownership in the foreign ownership classification. It should be noted that the survey of international investment collects data on country of residence of foreign shareholders through its special nominee collection. Therefore, the ABS is able to identify Australian companies with foreign direct and portfolio shareholdings.

It should be noted that data collected in the survey of shareholdings would relate to legal entities which are only one of the statistical units in ABS collections; therefore, the linking process would result in the foreign ownership classification being applied to all types of statistical and other reporting units in ABS collections. As only a minority of Australian businesses have some degree of foreign ownership, the foreign ownership classification would only be applied to a limited number of units; those not identified as having foreign ownership would be regarded as Australian owned. Therefore, the survey should not be regarded as an exhaustive survey, but past validation work suggests that the survey methodology identifies most of the Australian businesses with foreign ownership.

Annual ABS economic censuses and surveys which are based on the ABS business register would be able to draw on these data and cross classify other variables according to whether businesses in those collections were foreign or Australian owned. However, as each of these ABS collections and the survey of shareholdings would be running in parallel, the linking of survey and other collection data would take place in the latter stages of the processing of economic censuses and surveys. Therefore, the survey of shareholdings would need to adhere to strict timetables so that the inclusion of foreign ownership classifications in normal annual ABS economic censuses and surveys publications would not delay those publications.

The ABS' *Business Operations and Industry Performance* publication (Catalogue no. 8140.0) publishes data at the broad level of industry on the number of businesses, employment, sales of goods and services, labour costs, various items of profits, balance sheet items, capital expenditure, gross operating surplus, industry gross product, and various business and industry ratios for large and medium and small businesses. Industry data, at two digit level, and some State data are available on request. These data come from the annual economy activity survey and data are collected at the management unit level. These data as well as other data collected in these surveys could be classified by whether businesses in these surveys are foreign or Australian owned.

The ABS economic collections include mining, manufacturing and selected service industries; these comprise both censuses and sample surveys. Again, these collections collect similar data and, if conducted in the same year as the survey of shareholdings, businesses in these censuses and surveys could be classified as being either foreign or Australian owned.

In addition the ABS undertakes a number of activity based surveys, such as research and development, mineral exploration, and growth and performance surveys of medium and small businesses. It would be possible to publish the results of these surveys by whether the reporting businesses are foreign or Australian owned. The research and development collection is not based on the ABS business register, so matching of units for this collection would involve an added cost.

It should be noted that where sampling is involved in ABS business surveys, no account has been taken in the sample design to date of whether the selected businesses are foreign or Australian owned. This may mean that a foreign ownership classification in business surveys may have a higher sample error compared with other data. In the longer term, if sample errors are considered too high, the ABS might need to adjust the sample size and or stratification to accommodate the foreign ownership classification if the cost could be justified. In addition, the treatment of certain business units, for example, unincorporated joint ventures, while acceptable in current business collections may need to be re-examined for purposes of publishing foreign ownership classifications.

It would be possible to publish economic statistics not based on the ABS business register according to whether the businesses reporting in those collections are foreign or Australian owned. In the 1980s, the ABS conducted studies of foreign control of Australian exports and imports (of goods). To undertake these studies, a sample of exporters and importers data using foreign trade statistics was used and linked to data from the survey of shareholdings.

Previous ABS foreign participation studies included studies of financial enterprises such as banks, insurance companies and registered financial corporations. These studies examined the assets and liabilities of financial institutions classified by foreign ownership and control. Similar studies could be repeated, but again, as these are not ABS business register based collections, an additional matching task is required.

The final issue that needs to be addressed is whether, if a survey of shareholdings is introduced, it should be run on a regular or irregular basis.

Survey of Australian owned businesses abroad

The second initiative would be to institute a collection on Australian owned businesses abroad and collect business accounting, economic, source and use of funds and foreign affiliates trade data. In addition it would be possible to publish business averages and industry ratios. It might also be possible to add different types of questions which seek qualitative data. User views on the approach outlined here and what data items should be included would be welcome. Readers need to consider that business reporting burden and costs are constraints.

The statistical unit in this collection would be the enterprise, all legal entities within the one enterprise group in a single country, which have the same institutional sub-sector classification. Foreign affiliates would be classified by ANZSIC at the two digit level. It is envisaged that foreign owned affiliates would include all direct investment enterprises abroad. The definition of the statistical unit and the availability of data would need to be discussed with the Australian owners of direct investment enterprises.

Foreign affiliates trade

Some economists have argued that the work on foreign affiliates trade undertaken by the BEA, and promoted by the WTO and others, should be undertaken by the ABS. This requires linking cross-border trade and foreign affiliates sales of goods and services data. Such data would need to be collected from foreign owned businesses in Australia and Australian owned businesses abroad. The proposals in this chapter do not include the collection of additional data from foreign owned businesses in Australia, except for shareholding data. However, they do address the collection of foreign affiliates trade data from Australian owned businesses abroad.

Note

1 This is a revised and shortened version of a more detailed and Australian-specific paper entitled 'Australian Globalisation Statistics: Past, Present and Future', *Australian Economic Indicators*, March (1998), Catalogue no. 1350.

18 Multilateral investment rules

David Robertson

Introduction

Until 1998, enthusiasm for multilateral rules for investment protection and liberalisation was spreading. It has dissipated since the collapse of the Organisation for Economic Co-operation and Development (OECD) negotiations for the multilateral agreement on investment (MAI).

The first multilateral step was the inclusion of trade-related investment measures (TRIMs) on the Uruguay Round agenda in 1986. Later negotiations resulted in other investment-related provisions being incorporated into WTO agreements. Progress in multilateral agencies continued in 1995 with the granting of the OECD mandate to begin the MAI negotiations. Then the first WTO ministerial meeting in December 1996, established a working group on the relationship between trade and investment, coupled with a parallel working group on the interaction between trade and competition policy. While these multilateral initiatives were getting under way, bilateral investment treaties (BITs) were becoming widespread (over 1,500 existed by 1996).

The reason for this interest in investment rules was alleged to come from the strong increase in cross-border investment activity which was growing faster than international trade in 1986–89 and in the mid-1990s (WTO, 1996). In addition, the different negotiations on multilateral investment rules, coupled with unilateral relaxations of foreign investment restrictions, adoption of 'voluntary' investment guidelines (World Bank, 1992 and APEC, 1994), and the spread of regional investment regimes (European Union (EU) and NAFTA) were adding to the complexity of investment rules. Not surprisingly, governments and international officials proposed and pursued the idea of multilateral rules to clarify and promote investment. Multinational corporations (MNCs) showed less interest, being concerned in exploiting investment opportunities, and probably preferring the buccaneer opportunities that lack of regulations provided. Since conflicts over investments and national policies were decreasing, the case for a multilateral agreement was not really made. It is not surprising, therefore, that since the collapse of the MAI negotiations, investment rules have slipped down the international agenda.

The MAI mandate called for a comprehensive and fully binding multilateral agreement (open to non-OECD countries to join when it was finalised) to liberalise investment regimes and to protect investments, which would contain effective dispute settlement procedures. These objectives were to build on the OECD's existing instruments and expertise. However, this ambitious programme was frustrated because eagerness had overcome prudence and negotiating difficulties were neglected. It was quickly realised that taxation regimes were too complicated to be negotiated. Further hurdles arose from the comprehensive definition of investment which included all owned assets with economic value (direct and portfolio investments, real estate, tangible and intangible property). When member governments began to seek specific exemptions and reservations from these ambitious commitments, the negotiations became bogged down. The rising protests from non-governmental organisations (NGOs) against even a watered-down MAI provided a welcome excuse for OECD governments to close the negotiations in 1998.

After the collapse of the MAI negotiations (officially acknowledged in December 1998), the WTO working group on the relationship between trade and investment became the only forum left where multilateral investment issues were being discussed. However, some OECD countries were discouraged by the difficulties exposed during the MAI negotiations. Many of these same issues arose in the working group and were magnified by non-OECD countries' sensitivities to MNCs and perceptions that rules on investment policies would impede development strategies. At the WTO Ministerial meeting in Seattle, the only major players to include investment in their negotiating positions were the EU and Japan. The difficulties brought to light in the MAI negotiations warned off many governments, while rising dissatisfaction with globalisation expressed by militant NGOs increased opposition to multilateral economic agreements, generally (UNDP Annual Report, 1999).

The collapse of the MAI generated some reviews of why the initiative failed, including triumphalist claims from the NGOs. However, careful analyses of the economic reasons for the failure and assessments of the political forces that came into conflict in the negotiations have been few. Pro-MAI and anti-MAI lobbies tend to argue from positions where they have been entrenched since the UN Centre for transnational corporations (TNCs) was established in the 1970s.

This chapter will review some of the recent contradictions between trade and investment policies to indicate important areas where research is needed if new negotiations on multilateral investment rules are to have sound foundations.

Defining 'investment'

The MAI definition of investment covered all kinds of asset owned or controlled, directly or indirectly, by a non-resident investor, including direct investment, portfolio investments (debt or equity), real estate, intellectual property rights (IPRs), rights under contracts and rights conferred by authorisations or permits (OECD, 1997). In addition, the MAI was to apply to established and future investments. Defining items on the capital account of the balance of payments has been a perennial statistical problem and the MAI was intended to bring all types of foreign asset ownership under one umbrella. This comprehensive definition raised serious differences among the OECD countries, especially in connection with rights of establishment, non-discrimination and national treatment across all forms of assets.

The French authorities' statement that scuttled the MAI in October 1998 set conditions for the continuation of negotiations that would safeguard national sovereignty (Lalumiére Report, 1998). This included restricting the scope of negotiations to exclude portfolio investment and financial market operations (short-term capital flows). Problems defining 'investment' were exacerbated by requirements that once investment restrictions were liberalised they could not be re-introduced (the ratchet effect), which some regarded as an infringement of national sovereignty.

Discussions in the WTO working group have also failed to suggest a suitable definition of investment. Financial crises in Asia and Latin America since 1997 have increased sensitivity to short-term capital flows, and some countries introduced restraints on such inflows and against potential outflows (Malaysia, Chile). This new sensitivity to speculative financial flows has influenced perceptions of the scope of any investment agreement.

Proposals to limit an agreement to foreign direct investment (FDI) was rejected in the WTO working group because the character of investment varies according to economic circumstances. Many developing countries' representatives in the working group have expressed concerns about the development consequences of foreign ownership and technology transfers that have been familiar in UNCTAD meetings for thirty years. However, the working group recognised that national investment policies were about competing for the location of foreign investment. Lacking domestic competition policies, some developing countries have used investment regulations to manage domestic markets as part of their development strategies. Using border measures to promote domestic economic objectives is not unusual, but like the use of tariffs in the presence of domestic market distortions, it is second best (Bhagwati, 1971).

Using International Monetary Fund (IMF) balance-of-payments' definitions to identify foreign investment flows is inappropriate because, like any financial transaction, these flows are fungible. A portfolio investment may be held indefinitely and even a small equity holding can represent a controlling influence equivalent to an FDI. At the same time, corporate equity can be bought and sold in a few days, making it a short-term capital flow. This fungibility was one motive for the initial comprehensive definition of investment in the MAI. It has become evident, however, that many governments prefer a limited definition, which requires practical definitions of ownership, control and location to be found.

The competition to attract foreign investment of all kinds is not about net effects on the current or capital accounts of the balance of payments (or indeed, external debt or net external payments), but about economic growth and efficiency arising from competition, technology transfers, economic 'spillovers' (social external economies), access to overseas markets, etc.

Investment in the WTO

The Uruguay Round negotiations introduced several specific provisions on trade-related investment flows, as well as new agreements that are indirectly relevant to proposed investment agreements.

TRIMs were included in the Uruguay Round at the insistence of some OECD countries, though opposed by many developing countries. At that time a wide range of investment issues was meant to be included, including rights of establishment, national treatment and investment incentives and performance requirements. In the final act, however, the TRIMs agreement merely reaffirmed existing GATT disciplines relating to national treatment (article III) and the prohibition of quantitative restrictions (article XI), recognising that countries were in violation of GATT obligations. The TRIMs introduced a standstill and roll-back applied only to local content rules, trade balancing and foreign exchange balancing. Export performance requirements were not addressed because several OECD countries, as well as some developing countries, used investment incentives and performance requirements.

The General Agreement on Trade in Services (GATS) includes several provisions affecting investment. Cross-border trade in services often requires location in the country of sale and non-discrimination applies, with some notified exceptions. National treatment and 'commercial presence' provisions in the GATS represent a step towards liberalisation of investment for service industries (limited by the positive listing of sectors covered). Negotiations continued in major sectors after the Uruguay Round final act (financial services, professional services, telecommunications). The GATS provisions on market access (commercial presence and national treatment) created an anomaly between treatment of investment in service sectors and its treatment in goods industries under the GATT (1994). The OECD countries have a major interest in service industries as their comparative advantage shifts away from manufacturing which was one reason for pursuing the MAI and rights of establishment in all sectors (Sauvé, 1994).

The trade-related aspects of intellectual property rights (TRIPs) agreement had indirect significance for liberalising investment policies, because IPRs (patents, copyright, etc.) internalise assets that can be exploited using foreign investment (Casson, 1979; Dunning, 1981). The new protection of property rights reduces uncertainties, promotes FDI and encourages joint ventures and other forms of corporate participation.

Three of the less effective WTO agreements are also relevant to an investment agreement, because they affect the trade/investment interface.

i the antidumping agreement (ADA)
ii the agreement on subsidies and countervailing measures (ASCM)
iii the agreement on government procurement (GPA) (a plurilateral agreement).

The ADA provides import protection which may promote FDI inflows to establish local production (Brewer and Young, 1997). The ASCM could apply directly to investment incentives, although they were not specifically mentioned in the

Uruguay Round and many exceptions are provided (Sauvé, 1994). The GPA attracted only limited interest from governments where state governments insisted on their independence. Renegotiation of this agreement in 1999 was intended to establish GPA as part of the WTO 'single undertaking' in the new negotiating Round. All these agreements were highly contentious in the Uruguay Round negotiations, as in earlier GATT rounds, because OECD countries use 'contingent' protection to insulate politically sensitive sectors from foreign competition (Robertson, 1992). In general, the investment aspects of these agreements were not acknowledged as relevant to the TRIMs negotiations, because some governments did not want the links to investment incentives and performance requirements to be acknowledged.

The complexity of multilateral investment rules, whether in the OECD or the WTO, will require a dispute settlement mechanism. In this context, WTO experience with its understanding on dispute settlement is relevant. However, investment disputes would be more complex. WTO disputes are between governments and about implementation of policies (e.g. quarantine regulations, administrative barriers that impede trade, etc.). In an investment agreement there may be instances where governments would dispute interpretations, but disputes are more likely to be between MNCs and governments. Most bilateral investment treaties, which establish a network of rules centred on major OECD countries, designate the World Bank's ICSID[1] as the arbiter in disputes between MNCs and governments. Despite ICSID's widespread acceptance, it has seldom been called upon to adjudicate, because it is a costly process. Only major cases reach ICSID, though its establishment has probably encouraged resolution of disputes. Firm-to-firm disputes are usually resolved in national courts.

International disputes over foreign investment are rare. Disputes have mostly been about obtaining compensation for confiscation or nationalisation of foreign-owned assets. Now the problems often relate to allowing foreigners to participate in privatisation of state-owned enterprises – how much? And at what price?

Trade-investment cross currents

After the MAI negotiations and the Uruguay Round outcomes, it has become recognised that trade policy measures can influence investment decisions. Any analysis of investment incentives or performance requirements needs to be considered within a broad conceptual framework encompassing all influences on locational decisions.

Hence, existing WTO agreements might be extended in ways that include investment rules. Some OECD countries see dangers in this approach, because the term 'incentive' could be understood to cover any government actions that give financial advantage, which would include subsidies and, therefore, the ASCM. Similarly, performance requirements affect the protection provided by antidumping duties, which are based on rules of origin.

It is one of the paradoxes of *The MAI Affair* (Henderson, 1999) that, while apparently negotiating a far reaching agreement on investment policies, many

OECD countries were competing to attract FDI inflows using investment incentives and disguised performance requirements. A few years earlier WTO members had been asked to relinquish similar measures in the TRIMs negotiations. The OECD countries were exploiting loop-holes in other General Agreement on Tariffs and Trade (GATT) provisions by using preferential rules of origin, regional free trade agreements, antidumping protection and gaps in the subsidies agreement (ASCM). Moreover, the OECD countries excluded taxation from the MAI negotiations at an early stage, which left scope for fiscal incentives too. Given the resources available to OECD governments, these investment-related trade measures can be very effective.

As globalisation led MNCs to locate in low-cost locations in non-OECD economies, because of ready access to markets in an open trading system, many OECD governments launched a counter-offensive to attract foot-loose investments back home (Moran, 1998). This included protectionist and investment-diverting measures that could be slipped past the WTO provisions – and regional and state subsidies not covered by existing agreements. In terms of the 'eclectic' model of MNCs, the focus of national investment policies was 'locational' (Dunning, 1998).

This counter-offensive deserves a thorough examination, not only as an investment issue but also in terms of the multilateral trading system. It is misleading not to consider investment incentives alongside performance requirements because they are linked and should be negotiated together in trade and investment agreements. Local content, trade balancing and export requirements were included in the TRIMs' negotiations, but investment incentives were not. Yet financial grants in Ireland for operations that export outside the Irish market have the same effect as export incentives. By restricting the TRIMs negotiations in the Uruguay Round, new distortions were introduced, whereas a broader agreement covering all locational incentives (incorporating the ASCM) would have been less discriminatory and more beneficial. (Why is a regional subsidy provided by the European Commission, which is consistent with the ASCM, better than a local content requirement that leads to additional employment in a developing country (Brewer and Young, 1997)?)

Another inconsistency between the treatment of trade and investment in the Uruguay Round agreements is evident in the GATS. 'Commercial presence' in the GATS is not matched by investment access for goods' production. On the other hand, the ASCM applies only to subsidies affecting trade in goods, not to trade in services. The ASCM does not consider rights of establishment (commercial presence) which are included in the GATS. Yet, if trade and investment flows are complementary (WTO, 1996), this results in inconsistencies. So far, the effects of multilateral trade rules on competitive bidding for investment have not been considered.[2]

The relevance of trade policies to investment decisions was ignored in the MAI negotiations. Many negotiators came from non-trade government departments and were not familiar with the relevant WTO agreements. Hence the relevance of trade measures to competitive bidding for investment was neglected, in the same way that the investment policies were ignored in the TRIMs negotiations.

Investment and development

As discussed in Chapter 11 in the context of East Asia and in Chapter 19, FDI has played a key role in economic growth and development; raising the investment rate and introducing resources and knowledge that are internalised by the MNC (non-marketed services such as technology, management, marketing networks and services). Trade and investment are inter-dependent and must be considered together. The trade effects of FDI depend on whether the investment is for locational advantage (resource-exploiting or an export platform based on labour costs), which is export biased, or for access to consumer markets, which is import replacing. That trade measures and investment strategies are important was acknowledged in reports from the WTO working group on the relationship between trade and investment.

FDI can also result in negative effects in the host economy, such as reduced competition in certain markets, restrictive business practices or distorted transfer prices. These negative effects can be exaggerated because benefits and costs from FDI are often difficult to assess (Wells, 1998). Uncertainties are augmented by some commentators who confuse FDI by profit-seeking MNCs with 'no-strings' official development assistance.[3] This leads to demands for corporate social responsibility and environmental protection, and for technology transfers without charge. Such attitudes have been evident in the WTO working group and at the WTO High-Level Symposium on Trade and Development (March 1999). Some NGOs condemn MNCs' failure in such social responsibilities. Ultimately, the contribution of FDI to development depends on social and economic conditions in the receiving countries and on host governments' domestic policies, as well as their trade and investment policies.

Most host governments go beyond purely economic criteria when assessing the effects of FDI on MNC activities. The effects of capital formation and economic growth are likely to be qualified by concerns about income distribution. Host government policies can increase benefits from FDI, although costs must also be considered (e.g. tax incentives may promote FDI but lost revenue could increase budget deficits). These policies will influence MNCs' managements and investment decisions in developing countries.

Recently, foreign investment flows to developing countries (including from non-OECD countries) increased strongly in response to market reform and trade and investment liberalisation strategies (UNCTAD, 1999). However, little attention has been given to the impact on MNCs and host governments. How have MNCs responded to market reforms? Why did developing countries forsake their commitments to import substitution strategies? What have been the consequences for developing countries of lower trade barriers and easier access for FDI (financial deregulation, dismantling investment rules and screening)?

Benefits of increased FDI flows occur though externalities and spillovers, but little has been done to measure these effects. Beyond the uncertain economic effects, still less is known about the social and political effects in developing countries. These used to be major sources of tension between MNCs and host governments in the context of economic development and some tensions must remain.

Since the 1997–98 financial crises in South-East Asia, Mexico and Brazil, foreign capital is being treated with more suspicion, with some governments controlling short-term capital flows (Malaysia, Chile) and portfolio investment being monitored. With the value of development assistance declining, the long-term commitment of FDI is attractive. These observations deserve supporting analysis. Host governments have become more tolerant of MNCs as their investment flows have increased, but as the scope of such resource inflows increases the potential for conflict with local competitors must increase.

The developing countries' honeymoon with FDI has been supported by complex BITs with the OECD countries that supply most investments. These BITs are often clustered to give strength to the commitments. A developing country's government will be reluctant to infringe a BIT if this would hand a competitive advantage to a neighbouring capital importer that is party to a similar accord. The success of BITs may be one reason for the declining interest in multilateral agreements on rules to govern FDI. After all, multilateral rules might impose new restrictions that restrict host governments' policy freedom. For similar reasons many MNCs might not support a new international regime either. While economists exalt the benefits of the open trading system, support for a multilateral investment regime is more circumspect. This asymmetry is evident in the cross-currents between trade and investment in WTO trade rules. The WTO working group has identified 'investment-related trade measures' for special attention, with any consideration of WTO rules on investment to take account of existing agreements, such as GATS, TRIMs and ASCM. Discussions in the working group are restricted by its information-gathering and non-negotiating mandate, but it is evident there are differences of opinion even over proposals to categorise instruments.

Difficulties in multilateral treaties

Any multilateral agreement depends on finding enough common ground to allow balanced trade-offs over controversial matters. In the MAI negotiations, difficulties arose because the scope of the proposals was too broad. Ultimately participants wanted so many exclusions and reservations that the value of the agreement came into doubt. And yet, the final breakdown of the negotiations contained a paradox. Non-government organisations objected to losses of national sovereignty from rights of establishment, and national treatment for potential investors, and yet they wanted to extend the scope of the draft agreement to include provisions on environmental protection, human rights, labour standards, cultural protection and development interests. It is small wonder that MNCs prefer the existing patchwork of BITs, and a low profile to escape NGOs' interest.

A belief had grown up that any problem or conflict of interests could be solved by high-level negotiations, but recent experience suggests that international negotiations can become a focus for dispute rather than a means to a solution. The increasing numbers of countries represented at negotiating tables bring distractions (the WTO now has 135 members compared with original GATT membership of 23) – though the 26 OECD members could not claim that excuse for the MAI collapse. In addition, UN meetings are handicapped further by allowing affiliated NGOs into conferences. The questionable claim of 'international civil society' (a collective term for NGOs) that it blocked the MAI using coordinated demonstrations and lobbying has encouraged more protests against globalisation and the obstruction of intergovernmental meetings (WTO in Geneva and Seattle, Global Economic Forum in Davos, World Bank/IMF in Washington).

NGOs are single-issue lobby groups that are anti-business, anti-market and anti-liberal; whether in fact any group of NGOs could establish a common position on, say, multilateral investment rules has not been tested, though it seems unlikely. The declared goal of NGOs is 'to construct new, effective and democratic governance beyond the nation state' (Scholte *et al.*, 1999). This concept of global governance was evident at the European Commission's meeting with 'civil society' in April 1999. NGO representatives argued that the objective of an MAI should be 'sustainable development' rather than liberalisation and that the most appropriate forum for negotiations would be the UN. They argued that the precautionary principle (an axiom for most NGOs) required assessment of the costs of investment liberalisation before establishing investment rules (EC, 1999). The same sentiments were evident at UNCTAD X in Bangkok in February 2000 (UNCTAD, 2000). Many speakers identified globalisation as 'increasing uncertainty and marginalising many developing countries', and called for 'a new global order'. Similar demands were made at the WTO High-Level Symposium in March 1999. Anti-globalisation, presented as the defence of national sovereignty, has become the catchcry at recent NGO demonstrations. (It is paradoxical that these groups also demand 'global governance' as the preferred prophylactic!)

The NGOs would prefer to negotiate in the UN because they have status under UN Charter article 71, which provides arrangements for consultations with NGOs. With 29,000 NGOs accredited to the UN (1997), it is difficult to believe that any agreement could be achieved. This does explain why MNCs and many OECD governments are losing interest in multilateral investment rules.

Regional trade agreements introduce yet another political dimension into the negotiation of new multilateral investment rules. Investment rules in North American Free Trade Agreement (NAFTA) and the EU stimulated interest in a comprehensive agenda for the MAI mandate. One reason for the failure of the MAI was that these regional economic blocks within the OECD wanted special dispensations to maintain discriminatory treatment among their members, while calling for most-favoured-nation rules and national treatment in the MAI. This double standard carried over into the matter of 'subsidiarity', where member states in a federation may not be required constitutionally to follow the requirements of international treaties.

The EU (and Japan) remain committed to a multilateral framework of rules on international investment within the WTO, 'to secure a stable and predictable climate for investment worldwide' (EC, 2000). In reality, however, this is severely circumscribed from the MAI proposal. The rules would apply only to FDI and would exclude short-term capital flows. Moreover, host countries would be free to regulate investors' behaviour in their territory, including social responsibilities. While acknowledging that WTO trade disciplines are relevant to investment decisions, the EU Commission does not mention the existing exemptions provided for regional trade agreements (GATT, article XXIV), antidumping (ADA) or subsidies (ASCV). The EU support for multilateral investment rules could be a tactical ploy in the context of a new WTO round.

MNCs are under selective attack by NGOs with demands for 'corporate social responsibility'. The threat of 'naming and shaming' in the media forces corporations to seek low public profiles, or face economic damage to their reputations (e.g. Brent Spar platform and Shell). However inaccurate NGO claims prove to be, such blackmail gets publicity that helps to raise funds and to open new opportunities for NGOs. The new OECD Principles of Corporate Governance put new requirements on MNCs. Ironically, while corporations are expected to be socially accountable, NGOs are self-elected, financially unaccountable and non-transparent. A code of conduct for NGOs is overdue (Robertson, 2000).

At another level, governments are not unambiguously committed to new multilateral rules. Foreign investment policies are designed to extract maximum national income and efficiency gains, and to optimise income distributions. Most governments focus on distributional issues because of utility-maximising electoral behaviour. Such strategies discriminate against MNCs, because they do not have a vote (Caves, 1996). In negotiating multilateral investment rules, governments will not neglect their interest in maintaining policy freedom. This seems to have shifted from a focus on distribution of economic rents and technology transfers towards providing incentives for knowledge-based FDI. However, cross-hauling of FDI flows has altered government–business relations so that policies and instruments have become pragmatic, generally not favouring inflows or outflows.

International agencies also play a role in multilateral negotiations, providing secretarial support but also having interests in the outcomes. Many international organisations have succumbed to NGOs' pressures, partly to avoid bad publicity but also because including NGOs on their committees expands their work and their influence. The OECD is reviewing its relations with NGOs since the MAI collapsed. UN agencies use NGOs to promote their interests at international meetings; World Health Organisation (WHO) and United Nations High Commissioner for Refugees (UNHCR) use NGOs to deliver services in remote areas. Empire-building is not restricted to national governments or MNCs.

The increasing complexity of trade and investment interactions makes difficult the determination of precise rules for an international investment agreement. But this is not simply an analytical question because new interventionism has been introduced into domestic and international policies by NGOs. These bellicose lobbies are not susceptible to rational analysis.

Agenda for research

To establish the case for or against multilateral investment rules, the focus of research is rather different from the traditional research on MNCs' activities in national and global markets, their motives, instruments and returns. There are many learned studies into research agendas for theoretical and analytical assessments of MNCs and foreign investment flows (Dunning, 1997; Caves, 1996). Most relate to industrial organisation, sectoral studies, location decisions and host government policies (Guisinger and Brewer, 1998).

In recent years most major international economic agencies have convened conferences or produced their own studies on foreign investment and public policies. The reports are constrained by the international bureaucrats' requirement not to offend any member government, which often prevents objective conclusions. This was evident in the MAI negotiations and discussions in the WTO working group, where the compartmentalised interests of different government departments create lacunae in reports. In particular, narrow national politics have plagued discussions in international meetings; US and EC domestic 'lobbies' have proscribed discussions on antidumping and subsidies because of their value as investment incentives.

The agenda for a multilateral framework of investment rules suffered major setbacks with the collapse of the MAI negotiations and the delay in opening the new WTO negotiating Round in December 1999. Furthermore, anti-globalisation propagated by the NGOs makes any new initiative on investment rules a dangerous undertaking, fraught with risks and multifarious issues.

Statistics

Reliable and standardised statistical data is always difficult to access because global, aggregate figures for bilateral flows provide nothing for most industry- or firm-based research on trade, investment or financial flows. Most official information is collected by periodic surveys, where even categories may change between collections. Moreover, for all but the very large economies, detailed breakdowns by industry can expose commercial information that is provided in confidence. In consequence, much traditional research proceeds using individual research surveys (sometimes within firms) to obtain data. Without statistical data, policies may be mistaken and claims made without supporting evidence.

Statistical information is collected by national authorities (albeit according to international standards defined by the UN or IMF). Historically, this data has had an official purpose – national accounts, balance-of-payments. Such data are seldom appropriate for assessing MNC management strategies or the influences on MNCs of government policies.

A notable gap in present economic statistics is in the area of services. One of the reasons given for the sharp increase in FDI flows has been the transboundary transmission of services. The GATS was initiated by the need to facilitate trade in services, yet the data on services remain highly speculative and the hypothetical production chains are not verifiable. A major effort is required.

WTO agreements and investment policies

The prospects for a new initiative on multinational investment rules has receded. This places pressure on existing agreements. Serious amendments to OECD Codes on Liberalisation of Capital Movements, Current Invisible Transactions (1961) and the National Treatment instrument are unlikely in present circumstances. Only existing WTO agreements offer scope for influencing government policies on investment.

The potential for WTO agreements to override investment distorting measures such as investment incentives and performance requirements has been explained. By removing exceptions in the ASCV introduced by OECD countries and tightening the TRIMs agreement in the five year review, significant distortions in investment flows could be eliminated. In the same way, tightening the ADA and clarifying GATS provisions on commercial presence, in reviews as part of the 'built-in agenda', could make substantial contributions to investment liberalisation. The spread of investment incentives and requirements has quickened since 1995 when OECD governments began negotiating for multilateral investment rules, but little research has yet occurred to measure these effects. Does this OECD counterattack divert direct investment away from developing countries? Or does it simply redistribute FDI flows among OECD economies? Some research on the effects of increasing incentives would help analysis, and that in turn would provide a foundation on which to build liberalisation of these trade measures and make a positive contribution to an open multilateral investment framework.

Obtaining governments support for extending WTO trade disciplines to investment policies will not be easy, but exposure is the first step. The EU has recently complained that the 1916 US antidumping legislation is not compatible with the ADA. This dispute will focus attention on the ADA and could provide a trigger for wider reviews. In addition, several dispute cases have already ruled on subsidies (e.g. US complaint against Australia's Howe Leather subsidies).

There is scope for progressing WTO trade disciplines to cover investment policies under the 'built-in agenda', if the will can be found.

Other instruments of liberalisation

Enthusiasm for multilateral investment rules, offering harmonised conditions in all markets, pushed bilateral investment treaties (and double tax agreements) into the background. Over 1,500 BITs have similar contents and requirements, and many are clustered around major OECD markets. By collecting data on these treaties and comparing their contents, it may be possible to show that BITs are harmonising conditions for investment among many economies.

Regional trade agreements have also been increasing and these usually involve investment liberalisation among members, though with discrimination against third countries. The nature of reciprocal regional liberalisation should be considered alongside BITs.

Unilateral market reforms and capital market deregulations have spread rapidly in the 1990s. These uncoordinated liberalisations have contributed to the growth in all kinds of international capital flows, especially FDI. It seems conceivable that actual access for FDI is now largely free of restraints in most non-OECD countries, although not all economies attract capital inflows. So negotiating new multilateral rules may not be necessary. Some research into the scope of remaining investment regulations would be useful.

Globalisation and non-economic arguments

The major barrier to opening new negotiations on multilateral investment rules – or on trade liberalisation for that matter – is the rising opposition to globalisation arriving from several directions. The media impact of NGOs cannot be ignored, and their self-appointed leaders are experts in propaganda and misinformation. So far these groups have been strong on organisation but their agenda has been 'against' things, which makes them impossible to draw into negotiations.

Information about some of the NGOs is now appearing on the internet, but their agendas show little overlap, while their unifying force is anti-capitalist and anti-authority (governments, international agencies, MNCs, etc.). Much more needs to be known before negotiation can have meaning. One strand in the NGO network wants to replace democratic governments with some new form of 'global governance' which is 'more representative' than the present democratic process. In general, the NGOs are about politics, focusing on means but not ends. Until their goals are defined, meaningful negotiation on technical matters like multilateral investment rules will not be possible.

It is inappropriate to pursue multilateral investment rules without recognising that trade policies significantly influence investment decisions. This accords with the latest view that trade and investment flows are complementary. Notwithstanding fifty years of GATT, there are many anomalies in trade rules that allow distortions in investment decisions. In view of the political forces marshalled against new multilateral agreements, and the progress of unilateral, bilateral and regional liberalisation of investment regulations, the most effective means to facilitate foreign investment flows and to remove policy anomalies will be to increase the effectiveness of existing agreements.

The WTO offers the most accessible instrument, because even if the new negotiating round is blocked by the Seattle hiatus, there remain effective avenues within the Uruguay Round agreements to pursue liberalisation using mandated reviews of agreements that make up the Uruguay Round's 'built-in agenda'. The ASCM and the ADA (together with the safeguards clause (GATT, article XIX)), preserve 'contingency protection' (trade remedies) for OECD countries against imports that damage domestic industries. Incidentally, they offer opportunities for investment incentives and performance requirements (e.g. local content). Hence, tightening these agreements would bring double returns by liberalising trade and investment flows.

The GATS contains another anomaly, by allowing 'commercial presence' in markets for services without extending the equivalent treatment in the GATT (1994) for manufacturing activities. Yet services account for a major and growing share of global production and soon differentiating between manufacturing and services will become arbitrary.

Apart from the investment incentive/performance requirement dimensions of these 'contingent protection' exceptions to most-favoured-nation treatment and national treatment, these policy instruments are major barriers to developing countries' manufactured exports, and so to their structural adjustment and economic development. When the agreement on textiles and clothing is fully implemented (2005), these 'contingent' measures will be the only protectionist devices available against these competitive exports from developing countries. Any genuine commitment to economic development within a globalising economy must dismantle these 'trade remedies'. Developing countries already identify these rules as impediments to their achieving expected benefits from the Uruguay Round. Now these instruments are also regarded as sources of investment distortions, which need to be dismantled before any effective new multilateral investment rules are introduced.

The moment for a frontal attack on investment regulations seems to have passed. The political forces against globalisation mean that a subtle approach to investment liberalisation will be necessary using existing multilateral instruments. But even that flanking movement requires full support from major players as negotiations of policy reviews proceed in the multilateral agencies.

Notes

1 ICSID is the International Centre for Settlement of Investment Disputes, established in 1966 under the auspices of The World Bank. The Multilateral Investment Guarantee Agency (MIGA) was added in 1988, to promote FDI in developing countries.

2 In Australia, tariffs on PMV imports were retained in 1997, because the subsidy component provided to domestic output attracted new investment from overseas parent companies. On the other hand, a production subsidy to Howe Leather was declared incompatible with ASCM by a dispute panel in February 2000.

3 OECD 'aid fatigue' has sharply reduced official development assistance in the past twenty years which has increased the dependence of developing countries on FDI and other financial flows.

References

Brewer, T.L. and S. Young (1997), 'Investment incentives and the international agenda', *The World Economy*, 20(2): 175–197.

Bhagwati, J.D. (1971), 'The generalised theory of distortions and welfare', in J. Bhagwati *et al.* (eds) *Trade, Balance of Payments and Growth*, Amsterdam, North-Holland.

Casson, M. (1979), *Alternatives to the Multinational Enterprise*, London: Macmillan.

Caves, R.E. (1996), *Multilateral Enterprise and Economic Analysis*, Cambridge: Cambridge University Press.

Dunning, J.H. (1981), *International Production and the Multinational Enterprise*, London: Allen and Unwin.

—— (ed.) (1997), *Governments, Globalisation and International Business*, Oxford: Oxford University Press.

Dunning (1998), 'Location and the multinational enterprise: a neglected factor', *Journal of International Business Studies*, 29(1): 45–66.

European Commission (1999), Civil society dialogue meeting on trade and investments (28 April in Brussels): http://europa.eu.int/comm/trade/2000_round/csdmti.htm

—— (2000), 'EC approach to trade and investment' (April, 2000): http://europa.eu.int/comm/trade/2000_round/180bti.htm

Guisinger, S. and T.L. Brewer (1998), 'Symposium: multinational enterprise and economic analysis', *Journal of International Business Studies*, 29(1): 1–136.

Henderson, J.D. (1999), *The MAI Affair: A Story and its Lessons*, Melbourne Business School, Pelham Paper No. 5, Melbourne: Melbourne Business School.

Lalumiére Report, (1998), Rapport sur L'Accord multilatéral sur l'investissement. Paris, September.

Moran, T.H. (1998), 'Foreign direct investment and development: a reassessment of the evidence and policy implications', paper presented at OECD Conference on the Role of International Investment in Development. Paris, 20–21 September, 1999.

OECD (1997), Report by MAI Negotiating Group, May.

Robertson, D. (1992), *GATT Rules for Emergency Protection*, (Trade Policy Research Centre, Thames Essay No. 5): London: Harvester-Whatsheaf.

—— 2000, 'Civil society and the WTO', *The World Economy*, 23(9): 1119–1134.

Sauvé, P. (1994), 'A first look at investment in the Final Act of the Uruguay Round', *Journal of World Trade*, 28(5): 5–16.

Scholte, J.A., R. O'Brian and M. Williams (1999), 'The WTO and Civil Society', *Journal of World Trade*, 33(1): 107–123.

UNCTAD (1999), *World Investment Report: FDI and the Challenge of Development*, New York and Geneva: United Nations.

—— (2000), Summary of General Debate, Plenary UNCTAD X, February 2000, http://www.unctad-10.org/general_debate/gc_12_18feb.en.htm

UNDP (1999), *Human Development Report*, New York: United Nations.

Wells, L.T. (1998), 'Multinationals and developing countries', *Journal of International Business Studies*, 29(1): 101–114.

World Trade Organisatsion (1996), *Annual Report Vol. I: Special Topic: Trade and Foreign Direct Investment*, Geneva: WTO Secretariat.

19 FDI and development

Research issues in the emerging context

Sanjaya Lall

The new context for FDI

The large literature on foreign direct investment (FDI) and development reveals more than its fair share of controversy, large parts of it unedifying and unscientific. Until the 1980s, the general approach to transnational corporations (TNCs) and developing host countries reflected considerable suspicion and reservation. As Caves (1982) put it,

> MNEs have encountered hostility and resentment in all countries that host substantial foreign investment, but nowhere more than in LDCs, where they get blamed for the national economy's manifest shortcomings, not to mention that historical sins of colonial domination. Economic analysis has played no great part in resolving disputes between critics and defenders of the MNE's role in development processes. There is little consensus on what institutions and policies most effectively promote the goal of economic development, and writings on the economic development, and writings on the economic role of MNEs have correspondingly run a high ratio of polemic to documented evidence.
>
> Caves (1982: 252)

In recent years, however, the heat of the debate has subsidised considerably. By the closing years of the 1980s, there was a general warming of attitudes to FDI not just in the development literature but also on the part of the national governments traditionally strongly hostile to TNCs.[1] There are many explanations for this change. There was a 'maturing' of the theory of international production, with a better appreciation of the nature and advantages of TNCs in host countries. The experience of developing countries, with some exceptionally successful countries drawing heavily on FDI and many regimes restrictive to TNCs faring poorly, led to serious rethinking of their role. Host developing countries improved their capabilities to deal with TNCs The more advanced ones showed the ability to absorb leading-edge technologies transferred by TNCs, and to even attract R&D facilities. TNCs themselves changed their patterns of behaviour, and many new sources of FDI emerged, reducing the threat of domination by a handful of giant enterprises. The debt crisis – Asian financial crisis – showed that FDI was more stable in difficult periods than other forms of capital inflows.

Two other factors induced even greater changes in attitudes. The first was the accelerating pace of technological change and the rising costs of innovation. Reinforced by the growing reluctance of TNCs (the technological leaders) to part with valuable technologies to unrelated firms, this meant greater reliance on FDI to obtain new technologies. The second was the emergence of integrated production networks under the aegis of TNCs. Participating in these large, technology intensive and dynamic areas of activity necessarily meant that countries had to invite TNCs. This has to be considered in the context of the pattern of world trade over the past two decades. Manufactured products grew much faster (four times faster) than primary products. Within manufactured products, growth was driven by technology. High-technology exports were the fastest growing group and resource-based products the slowest (Lall, 1998). In high-technology exports, TNCS played the dominant role in most countries: thus, their participation was almost a *sine qua non* of entering the most dynamic areas of export growth.

All these developments coincided with growing liberalisation on trade and a more general reduction in the role of the state in economic activity. Liberalisation was generally beneficial, removing many inefficient and uneconomic interventions. However, in some cases, the shift to market forces may have been carried too far. Possible deficiencies in free markets were ignored or glossed over. In the context of TNCs, some long-standing concerns were forgotten, some legitimately but others not. In its strong form, the neoliberal approach (the 'Washington Consensus') led many governments not only to remove all restraints to FDI flows but also to abrogate tools to attract, target, guide and bargain with TNCs. In the presence of market failures, the objectives of TNCs can differ from those of host governments: governments seek to spur development and TNCs to enhance their profitability and competitiveness. There is much overlap between the two, but there can also be differences.

A vital part of the emerging context is the need on the part of host countries to improve *national competitiveness*.[2] 'Competitiveness' is taken here to mean the ability of economies to sustain income growth in an open setting. In a globalised world, growth can be sustained only if countries can create new, higher value-added activities that hold their own in free (domestic or export) markets. This requires many things, but central to them is the ability to use new technologies efficiently, furnishing the requisite skills and institutions.[3] Globalisation also affects the TNCs themselves. Their ownership advantages change in line with technical progress and shrinking economic space. Rapid innovation and deployment of new technologies to take advantage of changing costs, logistical needs and specific market demands become more important. The rising complexity of information flows means that TNCs have to organise and manage their activities differently, changing relations with suppliers, buyers and competitors to manage better processes of technical change and innovation. They also have to strike closer links with institutions dealing with technology and skills. New TNCs are constantly entering the arena to challenge established ones. Many are small firms or previously publicly owned enterprises and utilities that were traditionally confined to home markets. A significant number are enterprises from developing countries.

A striking feature of the new context is how TNCs are increasingly shifting their portfolios of mobile assets across the globe to find the best match with the immobile assets of different locations. In the process, they are also shifting some functions that create their ownership assets like R&D, training and strategic management (the process of 'deep integration') within an internationally integrated production and marketing system. The ability to provide the necessary immobile assets thus becomes a critical part of FDI – and competitiveness – strategy for developing countries. While a large domestic market remains a powerful magnet for investors, TNCs serving global markets increasingly look for other attributes, which are changing in response to policy liberalisation and technical change. The opening of markets creates new opportunities and challenges for TNCs and gives them a broader choice of modes with which to access those markets. It also makes them more selective in their choices of potential investment sites.

Apart from primary resources, the most attractive immobile assets for export-oriented TNCs are now world-class infrastructure, skilled and productive labour, and an agglomeration of efficient suppliers, competitors, support institutions and services.[4] Cheap unskilled labour still remains a source of competitive advantage, but its importance is diminishing. Moreover, it is not a base for sustainable growth, since rising incomes erode the edge it provides. Natural resources are similar, providing a rent as long as the particular commodities are in demand; however, without upgrading technologies or setting up downstream industries, they face the risk of stagnant prices or substitution. In both cases, attracting TNCs' mobile assets requires host countries to improve the quality of their immobile assets.

There is no conflict between exploiting static sources of comparative advantage and developing new sources: existing advantages provide the resources with which to develop new advantages. The steady evolution from one to the other provides the basis for sustained growth. What is needed is a policy framework to facilitate and accelerate the process: this is the essence of competitiveness 'strategy'. The need for such strategy does not disappear with growth; it merely changes its form and focus. This is why competitiveness remains a concern of governments in advanced industrial nations as much as (if not more than) in developing ones; the former produce more competitiveness strategies, at more regular intervals, than the latter.

MNCs in developing countries[5]

Most developing countries consider FDI a vital resource for development. However, the economic effects of FDI are very difficult, if not impossible, to measure accurately. TNCs represent a complex package of attributes that vary over time and from one host country to another. They are difficult to separate and quantify. Where their entry has large (non-marginal) effects, measurement is even more difficult. There is no precise method of specifying a 'counter-factual' – what would happen if a TNC had not made a particular investment. As a consequence, the analysis of the effects of FDI resorts to one of two general approaches. The first is econometric analysis of the relationships between inward FDI and various measures of economic performance. The second is a qualitative analysis of particular aspects of TNC contribution, without any attempt at calculating a net rate of return.

The econometric analysis of FDI and development is of long standing, but its conclusions remain unclear. Some analyses show a positive impact while others remain agnostic.[6] Since growth depends on many factors whose effects are difficult to disentangle, and since FDI itself affects several of these factors, an agnostic conclusion is probably the most sensible. As one leading analyst notes, most statistical analysis 'has suffered both from the lack of theoretical guidance and in some cases from a surfeit of special pleading by the researchers' (Caves, 1996, p. 275).

The qualitative analysis of FDI, taking its different components separately, is more appealing and practical. The premise is FDI it offers host countries a mixture of positive and negative effects. The challenge is to disentangle these effects, taking measures to maximise one and minimise the other. If TNCs operated in 'efficient' markets and acted with full information, there would be no need for policy intervention. If markets were not efficient, or TNCs did not have full information on investment opportunities in particular locations, there would be a case for interventions in markets and the investment decisions of TNCs. It is likely that markets and information are deficient in developing countries – underdevelopment is typified by a lack of efficient markets and institutions.

There is another analytical issue. The existence of TNCs is itself a manifestation of market failure. Large oligopolistic firms can operate over national boundaries precisely because they are 'imperfect', with firm-specific ownership advantages over other firms, scale and scope economies and internalised markets for information and skills. All these violate the requirements of perfect competition. It is not clear, therefore, that the interaction between the efficient internalised markets of TNCs with the deficient ones of host developing countries will lead *automatically* to mutual benefit.

Policies on FDI are needed to counter two sets of market failures. The first arises from information or coordination failures in the investment process, which can lead a country to attract insufficient FDI or the wrong quality of FDI. The second arises from divergences between the private interests of investors and the economic interests of the host country. This can lead FDI to have negative effects on development, or to positive but static benefits. Private and social interests may of course diverge for any investment, local or foreign. However, some divergences are specific to *foreign* investment. FDI differs from local investment in that the locus of decision-making and sources of competitiveness in the former lie abroad. The foreign investor has less commitment to the host economy and is also more mobile. Many governments feel that foreign ownership has to be controlled on non-economic grounds, for instance, to keep cultural or strategic activities in national hands. Let us consider how TNC and host country interests may diverge under various headings.

What FDI offers

Foreign direct investment comprises a bundle of assets, some proprietary to the investor and others not. The proprietary assets are what are termed the 'ownership advantages' of TNCs. These give TNCs an edge over other firms (local and foreign) and allow them to overcome the transaction costs of operating across national boundaries. The non-proprietary assets – finance, capital goods, intermediate inputs and the like – can be obtained from the market by any firm, though large TNCs may have privileged access to some markets. Proprietary assets reside in the firms that create them. They can be copied or reproduced by others, but the cost can be very high (particularly in developing countries and where advanced technologies are involved). TNCs are reluctant to sell their most valuable proprietary assets to unrelated firms that can become competitors or 'leak' them to others. These advantages mean that TNCs can provide assets to host developing countries that other firms cannot – if the host country can induce them to transfer their advantages in appropriate forms. The assets FDI comprises are:

- *Capital.* FDI brings in investible financial resources to capital scarce countries. The inflows are more stable, and are easier to service, than commercial debt or portfolio investment. In distinction to other sources of capital, TNCs invest in long-term projects, taking risks and repatriating profits only when the projects yield returns.
- *Technology.* Developing countries tend to lag in the use of technology. Many of the technologies deployed even in mature industries may be outdated. More importantly, the efficiency with which they use given technologies is often relatively low. Even if part of their productivity gap is compensated for by lower wages, technical inefficiency and obsolescence affect the quality of their products and handicap their ability to cope with new market demands. TNCs can bring modern technologies (many not available without FDI) and raise the efficiency with which technologies are used. They adapt technologies to local conditions, drawing on their experience in other developing countries. They may, in some cases, set up local R&D facilities. They can upgrade technologies as innovations emerge and consumption patterns change. They can stimulate technical efficiency in local firms, both suppliers and competitors, by providing assistance, acting as role models and intensifying competition.
- *Skills and management.* TNCs possess advanced skills and can transfer these to host countries by bringing in experts and by setting up training facilities (the need for training is often not recognised by local firms). They also possess new, presumably among the best, management techniques, whose transfer to host countries offers enormous competitive benefits. Where affiliates are integrated into TNC networks, they can develop capabilities to service the regional or global system in specific tasks or products.

- *Market access.* TNCs can provide access to export markets, both for existing activities (that switch from domestic to international markets) and for new activities. More important is the fact that they are by definition the only way to enter the international production systems that increasingly dominate trade in sophisticated and high-tech products. Export activity in turn offers many important benefits: technical information, realisation of scale economies, competitive stimulus and market intelligence.
- *Environment.* TNCs often possess advanced environmental technologies and can use them in all countries in which they operate.

While TNCs offer the *potential* for accessing these benefits in one package, this does not mean that simply 'opening up' to FDI is the best way of obtaining them. As noted, there may be market failures in the investment process and possible divergences between TNC and national interests. This raises the following issues for host government policy:

- Information and coordination failures in the international investment process.
- Infant industry considerations in the development of local enterprises, which can lead inward FDI to 'crowd out' these enterprises.
- Static nature of advantages transferred by TNCs where domestic capabilities are low and do not improve over time, or where TNCs fail to invest sufficiently in raising the relevant capabilities.
- Weak bargaining and regulatory capabilities on the part of host governments, resulting in the unequal distribution of benefits or abuse of market power by TNCs.

The complexity of the FDI package also means that there may be *trade-offs* between different benefits and objectives. For instance, countries may have to choose between investments that offer short as opposed to long-term benefits; the former may lead to static gains but not necessarily to dynamic ones. A large inflow of FDI can add to foreign exchange and investment resources in a host economy, but it may lead to a crowding out of local firms or create exchange rate problems. The desire to generate employment may lead governments to favour labour-intensive, low-technology investments, while that to promote technology development may favour more sophisticated investors. Similarly, the desire to upgrade technology may call for heavy reliance on technology transfer by TNCs, while the desire to promote local innovation and deepening may require more emphasis on arm's length transfers to indigenous firms. There can be many such trade-offs, and there is no universal answer to how they should be made. As noted, there is no 'ideal' policy on FDI that applies to all countries at all times.

The international investment process

The factors affecting the TNC choice of location relate increasingly to efficiency and competitiveness. Resource-based investments apart, the sites that will receive most FDI are those that allow TNCs to set up facilities able to withstand global competition. This means that the host country has to provide competitive immobile assets – skills, infrastructure, services, supply networks and institutions – to complement the mobile assets of TNCs (Narula and Dunning, 1999). While transport costs and taste differences mean that large markets will continue to attract more investment than small ones, few countries can afford to take a continued inflow of FDI – especially high quality, export-oriented FDI – for granted. This means that the ultimate draw for FDI is the economic base of the host country: just offering incentives for investors cannot compensate for the lack of such a base.

This being said, however, there remains a strong case for proactive policies to attract FDI. Countries may not be able to attract the volume and quality of FDI they desire, and that their economic base merits, for one or more of three reasons. These are high transaction costs; deficient information on the potential of the host economy; and insufficient coordination between the needs of TNCs, the assets of the host economy and the potential to improve those assets.

High transaction costs. While FDI regimes are converging on a common (reasonably welcoming) set of rules and incentives, there remain large differences in how these rules are implemented. The FDI approval process can take several times longer, and entail costs many times greater, in one country than another with similar policies. After approval, the cost of setting up facilities, operating them, importing and exporting goods, paying taxes, hiring and firing workers and generally dealing with the authorities, can differ enormously. Such costs can affect significantly the competitive position of a host economy. An important part of competitiveness strategy thus consists of reducing unnecessary, distorting and wasteful business costs. One important measure that many countries are taking to ensure that international investors face minimal costs is to set up one-stop promotion agencies able to guide and assist them in getting necessary approvals. However, unless the agencies have the authority needed to negotiate the regulatory system, and unless the rules themselves are simplified, this may not help. On the contrary, there is a risk that a 'one-stop shop' becomes 'one more stop'.

Market failures in information. Despite their size and international exposure, TNCs have imperfect information on potential sites, and the decision-making process can be subjective and biased.

> Prospective investors, even the largest firms, do not always conduct systematic world-wide searches for opportunities. The search for opportunities is a bureaucratic process whose initiation and direction may be swayed by many factors, including imperfect information and skewed risk perceptions. Most companies consider only a small range of potential investment locations. Many other countries are not even on their map.
>
> (IFC/FIAS, p. 49)

Taking economic fundamentals as given, it may be worthwhile for a country to invest in altering the perception of potential investors by improving its 'image'

(Wells and Wint, 1990). Such promotion efforts are highly skill-intensive and potentially expensive. They need to be carefully mounted, and they must be targeted to maximise their impact. Targeting can be general (aimed at countries with which there are trade or other connections, or that lack past connections but are ripe for establishing them), industry specific (investors in industries in which the host economy has an actual or potential competitive edge), or investor specific. Investment promotion is *not* the same as giving subsidies or fiscal incentives: incentives play a relatively minor role in a good promotion programme, and good long-term investors are not the ones most susceptible to short-term inducements. The experience Ireland, Singapore and more recently Costa Rica (Spar, 1998), suggests that promotion can be extremely effective in raising the inflow of investment and of raising its quality.

Coordination. Effective promotion should go beyond simply 'marketing a country' into *coordinating the supply of immobile assets with the specific needs of targeted investors*. This addresses potential failures in markets and institutions for skills, technical services or infrastructure in relation to the specific needs of new activities targeted via FDI. A developing country may not be able to meet such needs, particularly in activities with advanced skill and technology requirements. The attraction of FDI in such industries can be greatly helped if the host government discovers the TNC's needs and meets them. As Costa Rica illustrates, the fact that it was prepared to invest in training to meet Intel's skill needs was a major point in attracting the investment (Spar, 1998). Singapore goes further, and involves TNC managers in designing its on-going training and infrastructure programmes, ensuring that it remains attractive for their future high-technology investments. The information and skill needs of such coordination and targeting exceed those of promotion *per se*, requiring the agency involved to have detailed knowledge of the technologies involved (their skill, logistical, infrastructural, supply and institutional needs) as well as of the strategies of the relevant TNCs.

Domestic enterprise development and FDI

The development of domestic enterprise is a policy objective of most countries, and the risk of 'crowding out' by FDI remains an important concern. Crowding out can take two forms: in product markets by adversely affecting learning and growth by local firms in competing activities, and in factor markets, by reducing access for local firms (particularly to finance).

The first issue reflects 'infant industry' considerations (Bruton, 1998), though it differs from the usual connotation of protecting new activities against import competition. Here it takes the form of fostering incipient learning in domestic *vis-à-vis* foreign firms. FDI can abort or distort the growth of domestic capabilities in competing industries when direct exposure to foreign competition prevents local enterprises former from undertaking lengthy and costly learning processes. TNC affiliates also undergo learning locally, to master and adapt technologies and train employees in new skills. However, they have much greater resources to undertake this learning, and considerably more experience of how to go about learning in different conditions. In these cases, 'crowding out' can be said to occur if potentially competitive local firms cannot compete with affiliates *at a given time*.

The infant industry argument for trade protection differs from that for domestic enterprise protection. Without trade protection, consumers benefit from cheaper imports but some domestic production, employment and so on are lost. Without local enterprise protection, there is still domestic production but less indigenous entrepreneurial development particularly in sophisticated activities. The net cost is that local linkages may be less and technological deepening constricted. As with all infant industry arguments, crowding out is economically undesirable if three conditions are met. First, infant local enterprises are able to mature to full competitiveness if sheltered against foreign competition. Second, the maturing process does not take so long that the discounted present social costs outweigh the social benefits. Third, even if there are net social costs, there must be external benefits that outweigh them.

Crowding out can impose a long-term cost on the host economy if it holds back the development of domestic capabilities and retards the growth of a local innovative base. This can make technological upgrading and deepening dependent on decisions taken by TNCs, and in some cases hold the host economy at lower technological levels than would otherwise happen. However, it is important to distinguish between crowding out potentially efficient enterprises from affiliates out-competing inefficient local firms that cannot achieve full competitiveness. One of the greatest benefits of FDI is the injection of new technologies and competition that leads to the exit of inefficient enterprises and the raising of efficiency in others. Without such a process, the economy can lack dynamism and flexibility, and lose competitiveness over time, unless competition between local firms is intense and they face international competition (say, in export markets). TNCs can also *crowd in* local firms if they strike strong linkages with domestic suppliers, subcontractors and institutions (discussed further).

The second form of crowding out reflects an uneven playing field for domestic firms because of segmentation in local factor markets. TNCs may gain privileged access to such inputs as finance and skilled personnel because of their reputation and size. They can raise entry costs for local firms, or simply deprive them of the best factors. They may also have stronger bargaining positions with the government and so garner larger favours. The same argument may apply if TNCs have privileged access to *foreign* factor markets, for instance if they can raise capital in world markets at lower rates than local competitors.

Both forms of crowding out raise legitimate concerns. Most governments wish to promote local enterprises, particularly in complex and dynamic industrial activities. Many feel that deepening capabilities in local firms yields greater benefits than receiving the same technologies from TNCs. Knowledge is not 'exported' to be exploited abroad, linkages with local suppliers are stronger, there is more interaction with local institutions, and so on. The few developing countries that have developed advanced indigenous technological capabilities, like Korea and

Taiwan, have restricted foreign entry. Without building such capabilities, countries may languish at the bottom of the technology ladder. The possession of a strong indigenous technology base is not just vital for building the competitiveness of local enterprises – it is also important for attracting high-technology FDI and for R&D investments by TNCs. As noted further, the level of local capabilities determines the benefits of spillovers from foreign presence.

At the same time, there are risks in restricting FDI to promote local enterprises. For one thing, it is very difficult in practice to draw the distinction between crowding out and legitimate competition. If policy makers cannot do this efficiently and flexibly, they may simply prop up uneconomic, rent-seeking local firms, at heavy cost to domestic consumers and economic growth. For another, the context is itself changing. The danger of technological lags if TNCs are kept out in sophisticated activities is much greater now than, say, three decades ago. So is the risk of being unable to enter export markets for activities with high product differentiation and internationally integrated production processes. Few domestic firms from developing countries have a significant international presence in complex manufacturing activities. Since most countries are liberalising their trade regimes in any case, FDI may provide the most effective way to develop industry since TNCs face lower learning costs than local enterprises. It is very likely that in a liberal trade regime, it is mainly large international firms with that will be able to undertake advanced industrial activities.

The right balance between regulating foreign entry and permitting competition depends on the context. As noted, some countries have built impressive competitive capabilities and world-class innovative systems by restricting the access of TNCs, but the number of successes is low. Many others have restricted foreign entry without being able to promote competitive domestic enterprises in complex manufacturing activities. Success clearly depends on several things apart from sheltering learning. The most important are the competitive climate in which learning takes place and the availability of complementary inputs. If firms face intense competition, both locally and in international markets (say, through export activity), they have an incentive to invest in constant learning and upgrading. If they have access to ample human (particularly technical and managerial) resources, a strong science and technology infrastructure, and efficient suppliers, consultants and institutions, they are able to learn. Without a competitive setting and responsive factor markets, however, learning is likely to be stunted. Since many high-technology sectors have significant economies of scale and scope, the size of the domestic market is also important. In sum, the infant enterprise argument remains valid, and provides a case for policy intervention to promote local capability development. However, restrictions have to be very carefully and selectively applied, monitored and reversed where necessary.

As far as access to factor markets is concerned, TNCs can crowd in as well as crowd out domestic firms. Crowding in can take place when foreign entry increases business opportunities and local linkages, raises investible resources or makes factor markets more efficient. Such stimulating effects are most likely when FDI concentrates in sectors that are undeveloped in host countries. Where local firms are well developed, however, but face difficulties in raising capital or other resources because of TNC entry, there can be harmful crowding out.

Similar considerations apply to *mergers and acquisitions* (M&As) by TNCs. M&As are becoming a common form of foreign entry in Latin America and Africa, and more recently in Asian countries affected by the financial crisis (UNCTAD, 1999). Some M&As may be of dubious developmental value. If, for instance, they only lead to a change of ownership without adding to productive capacity or productivity, they just add to the foreign exchange drain on the host economy. Some take-overs lead to asset stripping and large M&A inflows can become large outflows when the investments are liquidated, giving rise to exchange rate volatility and discouraging productive investment. Many countries, including developed ones, are concerned about the adverse impact on employment, though this may be part of a rationalisation effort that can raise productivity. They also worry about the effects of M&As on competition and market structure. In the absence of effective competition policy, a liberal stance on M&As may lead to undue concentration or suppression of competition in the domestic market.

On the other hand, M&As may yield significant economic benefits (Harzing, 1999). Where the investor makes a long-term commitment to the acquired firm and invests in upgrading and restructuring its technology and management, the impact is very similar to a green-field investment. In Thailand, for instance, M&As in the automobile sector are leading to restructuring and increased competitiveness, with a surge in commercial vehicle exports. FDI can play an important role in modernising privatised utilities like telecommunications and public utilities, as in many instances in Latin America. Foreign acquisitions can prevent viable assets of local firms from being wiped out; this can be particularly important in transition and financially distressed developing countries (Maucher, 1998).

The benefits of M&As depend on the circumstances of the country and the conditions under which enterprises are acquired. Several countries feel the need control M&As, in developed countries in particular for reasons of competition policy. The correct policy is not a blanket prohibition of M&As; this would involve the loss of large potential benefits in terms of foreign exchange, productivity and export growth (in any case, prohibition may not be permissible). However, there may be value in monitoring M&As, instituting effective competition policies, and placing limits on their amount when the macroeconomic situation justifies this.

This raises a related question: the effects of FDI on *market structure* in host countries. There has been a long-standing concern that the entry of large TNCs raises concentration levels within an economy and so leads to the abuse of market power. The risk is certainly present. TNCs tend to congregate in highly concentrated industries. Whether this means the abuse of market power is not clear. The correlation between foreign presence and concentration owes more to the nature of TNC ownership advantages than to anti-competitive behaviour. In small economies, efficient deployment of modern scale-intensive technologies is bound to lead to highly concentrated market structures. If these economies have liberal trade regimes, the danger of anti-competitive behaviour in such structures is largely mitigated. However, it remains true that effective competition policy becomes more and more important in a world in which very large transnational firms can easily dominate an industry in a host country – we take up competition policy further.

Static versus dynamic benefits

Many important issues concerning the benefits of FDI to technology, skills and competitiveness revolve around their static or dynamic nature. TNCs are highly efficient vehicles for the transfer of technologies and skills suited to existing factor endowments in host economies (i.e. *static* benefits). They adapt the same technology to very different levels of scale and complexity in different locations, depending on market orientation and size, labour skills, technical capabilities and supplier networks. Where the trade regime is conducive (and infrastructure adequate), they use the endowments to expand exports from the host country. Such an activity can create new capabilities in the host economy and have beneficial spillover effects. In low-technology assembly activities, the skills and linkage benefits may be low; in high-technology activities, however, they may be considerable.

Unless they operate in highly protected regimes, pay unduly low wages (as in some EPZs in low-skill assembly) or benefit from expensive infrastructure while paying no taxes, there is a strong presumption that FDI contributes positively to using host country resources efficiently and productively. This constitutes one major step up the development ladder, and it can apply to each host country depending on where it is located on that ladder.

In this context, one of the main benefits of TNCs to export growth is not simply their ability to provide the technology and skills to complement local resources or labour, but to provide access to large foreign markets. TNCs are increasingly important players in world trade (UNCTAD, 1999). They have large internal (intra-firm) markets, access to which is available only to affiliates: these markets comprise some of the most dynamic and technology-intensive products in world trade. They also control or have access to large markets in unrelated parties. They have established brand names and distribution channels, with supply facilities spread over several national locations. They can influence the granting of trade privileges in their home markets. All these factors mean that they enjoy considerable advantages in creating an initial export base for new entrants on the basis of their static resource endowments.

The development impact of FDI depends, however, on more than this. It also depends on the *dynamics* of the transfer of technology and skills by TNCs: how much upgrading of local capabilities takes place over time, how far local linkages deepen, and how closely affiliates integrate themselves to the local 'learning system'. As noted, sustainable growth is more the outcome of dynamic sequences than the static ones, though there need be no necessary conflict between the two. However, TNCs may simply exploit the existing advantages of a host economy and move on as those advantages erode. Static advantages may not automatically transmute into dynamic advantages. This possibility looms particularly large where the host economy's main advantage is cheap unskilled labour and the main TNC export activity is low-technology assembly. The extent to which TNCs dynamically upgrade their technology and skill transfer and raise local capabilities and linkages depends on the interaction of *four factors*. These are the trade and competition regime; government policies on TNC operations; the corporate strategy and resources of the TNC; and development and responsiveness of local factor markets and institutions.

The *trade and industrial policy regime* in the host economy provides the incentives for enterprises, local and foreign, to invest in developing local capabilities. In general, the more competitive and outward-oriented the regime, the more dynamic is the upgrading process. A highly protected regime, or one with stringent constraints on local entry and exit, deters technological upgrading, isolating the economy from international trends. This is not to say that completely free trade is the best setting. Infant industry considerations deem that some protection of new activities can promote technological learning and deepening. However, even protected infants must be subjected to the rigours of international competition fairly quickly – otherwise, they will never grow up. This applies to affiliates as well as to local firms, though, as noted, their learning processes are likely to differ. A strongly export-oriented setting with selective trade interventions provides the best setting for rapid technological upgrading.

The second is *policies on TNC operations*: local content requirements, incentives for local training or R&D, pressures to diffuse technologies and so on. Most host countries have used such policies. The results have been poor when they were not integrated into a wider strategy for upgrading capabilities. However, where countries used them as part of a coherent strategy, as in the mature newly industrializing economies (NIEs), the results were highly beneficial: TNCs enhanced the technology content of their activities and of their linkages to local firms, which were supported in raising their efficiency and competitiveness. Much of the effort needed by the TNC to upgrade local capabilities involves extra cost and effort; they will not undertake this effort unless persuaded or induced to do so. For the host economy, it is only worth doing so if it leads to efficient outcomes. If upgrading is forced beyond this limit it will not survive in a competitive and open environment. While there are good reasons for pressing for greater market orientation and level playing fields, it is important to retain policies to correct for market failures – in this case in information, linkage and cluster formation, and learning.

The third factor is *TNC strategies*. Firms differ between themselves in the extent to which they assign responsibility to different affiliates and decide their position in the global value chain. TNCs are changing their strategies in response to technological change and policy liberalisation, and much of this is outside the scope of influence of developing host countries. Nevertheless, host governments can influence aspects of TNC location decisions by such measures as targeting investors, inducing upgrading by specific tools and incentives and improving local factors and institutions (discussed later). This requires them to have a clear understanding of TNC strategies and their evolution; they cannot formulate effective strategies otherwise.

The fourth factor, the state and responsiveness of *local factor markets and institutions*, is probably the most important. Since TNCs respond rationally to competitive pressures and market signals, they will upgrade their affiliates where it is cost efficient to do so. Moreover, since firms prefer their suppliers to be nearby, they will deepen local linkages if the suppliers can respond to new demands efficiently. Both depend upon the efficacy and development of local skills and technological capabilities, supplier networks and support institutions. Without improvements in factor markets, TNCs can improve the skills and capabilities of their employees, but only to a limited extent. They cannot displace the local education, training and technology system; in the absence of rising skills and capabilities generally, it will be too costly for them to import advanced technologies and complex, linkage-intensive operations.

Education, training and technology markets have well-known public good characteristics which lead to market failures. Individuals may invest too little in education because of myopia, risk aversion, lack of information or the lack of finance. Institutions may not provide the right kinds of skills, or may be absent altogether. Other firms may under-invest in training and knowledge creation. Small and medium enterprises (SMEs) may not receive adequate technical, training and marketing support. Raising local skills and capabilities requires widespread policy support. Some are pure public goods that only governments can provide. Others need governments to catalyse private provision (including by TNCs themselves) and to regulate its quality and delivery. Whatever the nature of such improvements, there is no doubt that they are critical to realising the dynamic benefits of foreign (and domestic) investment.

At the same time, there exists the risk that TNCs *inhibit technological development* in the host economy. TNCs are highly efficient at transferring the results of innovation performed in advanced industrial countries, but less so in transferring the innovation process itself. While there are notable exceptions, foreign affiliates tend to do relatively little R&D apart from that needed for local absorption and adaptation. For US TNCs, for instance, R&D by developing country affiliates in 1994 came to only 7.6 per cent of total overseas, or 1 per cent of parent company, R&D. Even this was very concentrated. Brazil accounted for over one-quarter of affiliate R&D in the developing world; the top four countries, with Mexico, Singapore and Taiwan Province, accounted for 77.4 per cent. Least developed countries had no significant affiliate R&D.

The absence of affiliate R&D may be acceptable in host countries at very low levels of industrial development. However, it becomes a constraint on technology development and competitiveness as countries approach maturity and need to deepen local capabilities and institutions. At the stage reached by many newly industrialising countries, the presence of powerful TNCs with ready-made technology can inhibit local technology development, especially when local competitors are too far behind to gain from their presence. Their technology spillovers may, in other words, be negative; there is evidence of this even in advanced host economies such as the UK or Italy (Perez, 1998). It is widely known, nevertheless, that countries with strong domestic research capabilities and institutions attract considerable R&D by TNCs. This is the 'asset seeking' form of FDI that plays an increasing role in globalisation by large firms.

More important, even countries without a strong research base can attract considerable TNC R&D if they are target FDI in technology-intensive activities and furnish the skills needed for sophisticated research work. For instance, in 1995 TNCs accounted for nearly 70 per cent of R&D in Ireland; in that year, total firm-financed R&D in Ireland was higher than in the UK (OECD, 1999). Their role in Singapore is similar: it has the third highest ratio of enterprise-financed R&D to GDP in the developing world, with most of it coming from foreign affiliates (Wong, 1995). The strategy it used was to target technology intensive TNCs, give incentives for the transfer of advanced functions and invest heavily in advanced education and training.

The appropriate policy response, as before, is not to rule out FDI but to use it so to promote local learning. In countries that have technological ambitions for local firms and strong technological capabilities, selective restriction of FDI may be justifiable. In others, it may be possible to induce advanced TNC technological activity by FDI targeting, incentives and building skills and institutions. As before, there are no general prescriptions – FDI strategy is an art not a science.

Bargaining and regulation

In several cases, the outcome of FDI depends on how well the host government bargains with TNCs. However, the capacity of developing host countries to negotiate with TNCs is often limited. The skills and information available to the TNC tend to be of better quality. With growing competition for TNC resources, the need of many developing countries for the assets of TNCs is often more acute than the need of TNCs for the locational advantages offered by a specific country. In many cases, particularly in export-oriented investment projects where natural resources are not a prime consideration, TNCs have several alternative locations. Host countries may also have alternative foreign investors, but they are often unaware of them.

It is, therefore, a distinct possibility that where the outcome of an FDI project depends on astute bargaining, developing host countries do poorly compared to TNCs. The risk is particularly large for lumpy resource extraction projects and the privatisation of large public utilities and industrial companies. Considerable bargaining also takes place in manufacturing projects where incentives, grants and so on are negotiated on a case-by-case basis (there is intense and prolonged bargaining for large manufacturing investments in developed countries). Though the general trend is towards non-discretionary incentives, considerable scope for bargaining still exists.

The need for regulation is growing in importance. The capacity of host developing countries to regulate enterprises in terms of competition or environment policy is emerging as the most active area of policy making in this area. With globalisation and liberalisation, there are few tools left to ensure competitive conduct by foreign and local firms: effective competition policy is an absolute necessity. However, most developing countries lack effective *competition policy*. Many, in fact, are not aware of the need for such policy. Mounting such policy is a complex task, with needs for specialised skills and expertise that are often scarce in developing countries. It is important for host countries to start the process of developing these.

Similar concerns arise with respect to the *environment*. Many developing host countries have lax regulations on the environment, or lack the capacity to enforce effectively the regulations they have on paper. TNCs are often accused of exploiting these to evade tougher controls in the developed world; some host countries are accused of using lax enforcement to attract FDI in pollution intensive activities. The evidence on the propensity of TNCs to locate their investments to evade environmental regulations is mixed (UNCTAD, 1999). Some firms may well do so; others enforce uniformly strict standards in all their affiliates and even require their local suppliers to observe those standards. TNCs are under growing pressure to conform to high environmental standards from home country environmental regulations, consumers, and environment groups in the developed world (and some in the developing world). Many thus see environment management not only as necessary but also as commercially desirable. However, it is up to host governments to ensure that other TNCs and domestic firms follow the example set by these 'green' TNCs.

Another important regulation problem is that of *transfer pricing* to evade taxes or restrictions on profit remission. TNCs can now use transfer pricing over very large volumes of trade and service transactions. The problem is not restricted to dealings between affiliates, and may also arise in joint ventures. However, it is likely that the deliberate abuse of transfer pricing has declined as tax rates have fallen and remittances liberalised in much of the developing world. Double taxation treaties between host and home countries also lower the risk of transfer pricing abuses. However, this does not mean that the problem has disappeared. It remains a widespread concern among Organisation for Economic Co-operation and Development (OECD) countries and tackling it needs considerable expertise and information. Developing country tax authorities are generally ill equipped to do this, and can benefit greatly from technical assistance and information from OECD governments.

Managing effective FDI policy in the context of broader competitiveness strategy is a demanding task. A passive *laissez faire* approach is unlikely to be sufficient because of deficiencies in free markets and existing institutions. Such an approach may not attract sufficient FDI, extract all the benefits it offers or regulate it well by best practice standards. However, the desirability of any strategy depends critically on the ability of the government to 'deliver'. If administrative capabilities are not appropriate to the skill, information, negotiation and implementation abilities needed, it may be best to minimise interventions with the market: to simply reduce obstacles in the way of FDI, minimise business costs and leave resource allocation to the market. As noted, there is no ideal universal strategy on FDI. Strategy has to suit the particular conditions of the country at the particular time, and evolve as its needs change and its competitive position in the world alters.

Finally, to return to the new context: what is different today in the FDI scene from three decades ago? Perhaps the most important change is technological: the world is more closely knit, using very different means of organisation, communication and production, and more subject to rapid change, than ever before because of constant and pervasive technical change. The leaders in the innovation process are TNCs. Countries are responding to the technological challenge, and to past development experience, by liberalising their economies. However, the spread of technological benefits is highly uneven, and the activities of TNCs do not reduce this unevenness – they may exacerbate it. Part of the reason for this is that many countries lack the capabilities and institutions to cope with a globalised world. The past thirty years show striking – and growing – differences between countries in their ability to compete and grow. They also show how markets by themselves are not enough to promote sustained and rapid growth: there is a large role for government policies, but not in the earlier mould of widespread intervention behind high protective barriers. This change in the perception of the role of government is another major change, and it applies to FDI as to development more generally.

Implications for further research

Recent development experience, a disillusionment with interventionist policies, growing government sophistication and adverse international economic circumstances, have combined to produce a much more favourable, and less controversial, environment for direct investment flows. The 'maturing' of the literature on TNCs in development reflects this shift. This maturity is to be welcomed, since many of the heated debates of the past were arid and irrelevant. It does not mean, however, that all important issues have been resolved as far as FDI and development is concerned.

At the margin, TNCs are rather similar in behaviour to large local firms but have much to offer in terms of their ownership advantages: with sensible trade and industrial policies, therefore, their effects are likely, on balance, to be beneficial. When non-marginal differences are considered, however, their effects are more ambiguous. Much depends on the economy's initial and evolving conditions. A strategy of restricting TNC entry may provide a period of protection to capability building, if domestic market failures are efficiently tackled, skills promoted and local enterprise encouraged. TNCs can then be selected according to the dynamic rather than the static comparative advantages of domestic firms. This strategy may, on the other hand, be economically costly if local enterprises and capabilities are not developed and if corrective policies are not taken in hand. A choice between these alternatives is often one of degree, but recent experience suggests that in practice there can be very real differences in the strategies pursued.

What then are current research issues? Here are some ideas from a development economist who believes that the main need is for research to help developing countries cope with rapid and relentless globalisation and with the competitive pressures generated.

At the most *general level*, what is lacking is a *sound theoretical base*: a theory of development that can take market failures into account and suggest practical remedies for structural problems. Existing theories are often rooted in equilibrium systems where market failures are absent or trivial. They tend to end with simple solutions (liberalise and 'get prices right'). The proper consideration of TNCs in development requires a more complex framework for analysing the development process, taking account of market and institutional imperfections and their correction. This is clearly an area of future research, considerably broader than FDI but directly relevant to it.

At the *narrower level* of FDI issues directly, some important questions are as follows:

- The *scope for effective policy* on FDI and for *bargaining* between TNCs and host countries. The trend of policy liberalisation, reinforced by the World Trade Organisation (WTO) and new rules like trade related investment measures (TRIMs), is towards reducing the power of host governments to intervene in the market-determined investment process. How much scope will be left if something like the failed multilateral agreement on investment (MAI) by the OECD is concluded in the future? How will such agreements affect bargaining between governments and TNCs? Will they affect governments of countries of different sizes and incomes differently? What tools of FDI attraction, guidance and control on FDI will be left?
- The *impact of technological changes* on FDI and TNC strategies. Technical change is altering patterns of national and corporate comparative advantages constantly, shifting some activities back to advanced countries and others to developing ones. There are large shifts under way within the developing world, with increasing divergences between the NIEs and least developed countries. A number of important issues arise. To what extent is FDI accelerating these shifts? Can it be made to reduce divergences rather than exacerbate them? What are the effects on developing host countries of the trend to strategic alliances between the leading TNCs? Will technical change and increased competition lead to more technological effort being located in developing countries or less? At the corporate level, how do new information and communication technologies affect the location of strategic activities? Do they lead to greater centralisation or otherwise (what UNCTAD, 1999, terms 'deep integration')?
- The new drivers of *FDI location*. It is clear that in a liberalised world the factors attracting TNCs are different from before, but what are the main motive forces in investment location? How important are large domestic markets? The availability of skilled manpower? Physical infrastructure? Investment incentives? Belonging to large regional groups? Answers to this set of questions are vital to the formulation of FDI policies in developing countries. There are many reports based on rankings of factors by TNC executives, but these are analytically unsatisfactory. Econometric analyses of

investment patterns are better but they also fail to provide the kinds of detailed and industry-specific issues governments have to face.

- *FDI promotion*. The examples of Ireland and Singapore are often cited as best practice, and the broad nature of their strategies is known. However, the details are less well understood, and the steps that less advanced countries need to take to set up efficient promotion agencies are not clear. What are the emerging best practices in promotion and targeting? What sorts of skills are needed? What sort of information? How is investor targeting and monitoring operated? Which TNCs respond best to promotion? Which industries are most amenable?
- The impact of FDI on *domestic technological effort and entrepreneurship* remains a controversial and important area. The 'stylised fact' is that the countries that have built up the strongest domestic technological capabilities have restricted FDI. However, countries like Singapore and Ireland are attracting considerable R&D effort from TNCs; there are indications that Malaysia and Mexico are following some distance behind. What are the trade-offs between attracting FDI and deepening technological activity? What are the limits of depending on TNC-led R&D especially if the domestic technological base is weak? There are also issues related to linkages between TNC affiliates and local suppliers and buyers. Are these growing stronger or weaker with trade liberalisation and the removal of local content rules? What can be done to raise the intensity of vertical linkages?
- The nature and scope of emerging *integrated production systems*. At this time, these are expanding very rapidly but will they continue to do so? Which countries will they embrace and which not? What are their linkages with the economies of the host countries? What are their industry-specific characteristics? How much of world trade will be covered by these systems? What can host governments do to break into these systems?
- How can TNCs contribute to *human capital formation* in host countries? What is the best way of inducing training and skill transfer? Do strict rules on the use of expatriate experts constrain FDI and skill development? How can TNCs co-operate with host firms and institutions in training?
- What is the recent evolution of *developing country TNCs*, and what are the prospects for increasing FDI flows among developing countries? How are comparative advantages of first and third world TNCs evolving?
- How can the *international community* help developing countries attract, regulate and extract the maximum benefits from FDI? What, in other words, are the 'global public goods' in the form of rules, information, advice and technical assistance that may strengthen their position?

This is clearly not an exhaustive list, but it does reflect the author's experience of policy-related work in recent years. There must be many interesting theoretical issues on which research can also be done, but in view of current priorities I would plead for the above.

Notes

1 In the revised edition to the book, Caves (1996) notes a similar shift in sentiment towards MNCs, but points out that the issues are controversial without the political background (p. 214).

2 Some economists (Krugman, 1994) question whether national competitiveness is a legitimate policy concern for governments. They argue that firms compete with each other, not countries: all countries need do is provide a level playing field and let competitive firms and activities emerge in response to market signals. However, this is valid only to the extent that markets work perfectly. Market failures may lead agents to fail to exploit endowments or to develop new endowments. Where markets are weak and supporting institutions absent, information may not flow efficiently, risky projects may never be undertaken, costly learning may not be undergone, and externalities and linkages with other agents may result in under-investment (Stiglitz, 1996). It then becomes necessary for governments to intervene to strengthen markets and institutions.

3 For a recent review of the significance of technology to development, see Radosevic (1999).

4 As Narula and Dunning (1999) put it, 'Globalisation has influenced both the nature of the comparative or location-specific advantages of countries and the competitive or ownership specific advantages of corporations, and also the opportunity sets facing the governments of the former and the managers of the latter. *Inter alia*, value-adding activities have become increasingly knowledge- or information-intensive, not just in high-technology sectors, but also in those that were previously regarded as natural resource- or labour-intensive. Both sets of institutions have thus adjusted their strategies and policies to the realities of the new global environment. First, the nature and content of MNC activity has undergone a marked shift, as their ownership specific intangible assets – especially intellectual capital – have become more mobile. Second, national governments are now increasingly competing with each other to attract mobile investment' (Narula and Dunning, 1999, pp. 1–2). On the importance of agglomeration economies for development, see Puga and Venables (1999).

5 This section is based in part on chapter XI of UNCTAD (1999).

6 For a recent published analysis, see Borensztein *et al.* (1998).

References

Borensztein, E., de Gregorio, J. and Lee, J.-W. (1998) 'How does foreign investment affect economic growth?', *Journal of International Economics*, 45: 115–35.

Bruton, H. (1998) 'A reconsideration of import substitution', *Journal of Economic Literature*, 36: 903–36.

Caves, R. E. (1982) *Multinational Enterprise and Economic Analysis*, Cambridge: Cambridge University Press.

——(1996) *Multinational Enterprise and Economic Analysis*, 2nd edn, Cambridge: Cambridge University Press.

Dunning, J. H. (ed.) (1997) *Governments, Globalisation and International Business*, Oxford: Oxford University Press.

Harzing, A.-W. (1999) 'Acquisitions versus greenfield investments: both sides of the picture', Draft: University of Bradford Management Centre.

IFC/FIAS (1997) *Foreign Direct Investment*, Washington, DC: International Finance Corporation and Foreign Investment Advisory Service, World Bank.

Krugman, P. R. (1994) 'Competitiveness: a dangerous obsession', *Foreign Affairs*, 73(2): 28–44.

Lall, S. (1996) *Learning from the Asian Tigers*, London: Macmillan.

——(1998) 'Exports of manufactures by developing countries: emerging patterns of trade and location', *Oxford Review of Economic Policy*, 14(2): 54–73.

Maucher, H. O. (1998) 'View: mergers and acquisitions as a means of restructuring and repositioning in the global market – business, macroeconomic and political aspects', *Transnational Corporations*, 7(3): 153–83.

Narula, R. and Dunning, J. H. (1999) 'Industrial development, globalisation and multinational enterprises: new realities for developing countries', Draft, Universities of Oslo and Reading.

OECD (1999) *OECD Science, Technology and Industry Scoreboard 1999: Benchmarking Knowledge-Based Economies*, Paris: OECD.

Perez, T. (1998) *Multinational Enterprises and Technological Spillovers*, Amsterdam: Harwood Academic Publishers.

Puga, D. and Venables, A. J. (1999) 'Agglomeration and economic development: import substitution versus trade liberalisation', *Economic Journal*, 109: 292–311.

Radosevic, S. (1999) *International Technology Transfer and Catch-Up in Economic Development*, Cheltenham: Edward Elgar.

Spar, D. (1998) *Attracting High Technology Investment: Intel's Costa Rican Plant*, Washington, DC, Foreign Investment Advisory Service, IFC and World Bank, FIAS Occasional Paper 11.

Stiglitz, J. E. (1996) 'Some lessons from the East Asian miracle', *The World Bank Research Observer*, 11(2): 151–77.

UNCTAD (1999) *World Investment Report 1999*, Geneva and New York: UNCTAD.

Wells, L. T. and Wint, A. G. (1990) *Marketing a Country: Promotion as a Tool for Attracting Foreign Investment*, Washington, DC: Foreign Investment Advisory Service of the International Finance Corporation and the Multilateral Investment Guarantee Agency.

Wong, P.-K. (1995) 'Singapore's technology strategy', in D. F. Simon (ed.), *The Emerging Technological Strategy of the Pacific Rim*, New York: M. E. Sharpe.

Index

Academy of International Business (AIB) 41
activities, effects of FDI on MNCs 316
Activity of Foreign Affiliates in OECD Countries 247
Africa 175; countries 273; US firms in 276
African Investment Codes 280
Andersson, T. 12, 159–60
ASEAN 80, 283; countries 170, 174
ASEAN Investment Area (AIA) 170
Asia 79; companies in 39; crisis in mid-1997 175; economies, major economic reform packages 267; financial crisis 80, 168, 236
Asia Pacific Economic Cooperation (APEC) 252, 254; Economic Integration 246; members' Individual Action Plans 253, 259, 267; Investment Guide 265; member economies, FDI policies in 253
Asia Pacific region 17, 58, 224
Australia 21, 55, 216, 255, 257–8, 263–4, 266, 268, 282, 295, 299; control category 300; enterprise bargaining 136, 144; FDI 39; FDI model 270; GDP 39; governments 40; industry policy 21; inward investment 246; manufacturing exporters 31; policy of tariff reductions 136; researchers 40
Australian and New Zealand Standard Industry Classification (ANZSIC) 303–4, 309
Australian Bureau of Statistics (ABS) 246, 299, 309; annual economic censuses 307; Business Operations and Industry Performance publication 307; business register 308; data base of firms 41; economic activity survey 304; economic collections 306–8; economic statistics 302–3; financial surveys 302–3; firms 31, 37, 39, 248; foreign participation studies 308
Australian business: alternative classification of foreign ownership 301; extended classification of foreign ownership 300; foreign ownership classification of 299–301; foreign ownership statistics 300
Australian Customs Service 303
Australian owned businesses abroad 305; defining 301–2; survey of 308–9

Balance of Payments and International Investment Position 246
balance of payments data 52
Balance of Payments Manual (*BPM5*) 295–6, 300–1
balance of payments: publications 294; statisticians 296; type data collection 58
Bank of Japan (BOJ) 80
Barrel, R. 51–2
barriers to FDI: economic impact of different types 258; information base 253; measuring and modelling 252; modelling economic effects of 258; modelling gains from removal of 267–70; modelling requirements 270–1; quantifying 254; tariff equivalents for 254–7
Bartlett, C.A. 20, 34, 39
Beamish, P.W. 13, 17
beggar-thy-neighbour approach to world economic growth 234
behaviour among the crisis countries 175
Benito, G.R.G. 17, 51, 53–4
Bertrand conjecture 116
bilateral investment treaties (BITs) 310, 317, 321

Blomström, M. 51, 58, 136, 155–6, 159–60
Bora, B. 2, 50, 57–61, 83, 89, 232, 250
Brainard, S.L. 51–7, 95
Braunerhjelm, P. 156, 163
Brazil 197, 200, 219, 338
Brown, D. 244, 248
Buckley, P.J. 13, 31
Bureau of Economic Analysis (BEA) 63–5, 72, 309
Bureau of Industry Economics 39

Calof, J.L. 13, 17
Cambodia 219
Cameroon 219
Canada 54, 58, 171, 216, 282, 295; Census of Manufacturers 19–20; Chemical Producers' Association 221
Caribbean 277, 281
Caves, R.E. 12–13, 16, 18, 52, 139, 325
Cayman Islands 281
Central America 175
Chandler, A.D. 20
Cheshire cat: phenomenon 137; unions 132
Chia, S.-Y. 178, 180
Chile 222, 279
China 80, 170–1, 174, 181, 197, 263–4; index for financial services 266
Code of Conduct for business taxation 284
Colombia 279
Congo 219
contagion, theory of 237
conventional models 133
copyrights 197
cost characteristics, specification of 55
cost structure of MNC 242
Costa Rica 220, 224, 332
Côte d'Ivoire 222
Coughlin, C.C. 50–1
Cournot, A. 116; conjecture 116–17; duopoly solutions 118; equilibria 116–19; oligopoly models 114; standard model 114
Coyne, E.J. 278
cross-border investment 113, 121, 125–9
cross-border mergers and acquisitions 152
Culem, C.G. 51–3, 55, 57
cultural distance 54

data: and policy 21; collection 58; FDI and services trade 269–70; problems and constraints 244–7
data on the scale and activity of MNC 63
Davis, E.M. 137
Davis, J. 39
decentralisation: collective bargaining 133–4, 137; environmental issues 213
Department of Industry, Science and Technology 39
Deutsche Telekom (DT) 113
Devereux, M. 277, 283
direct investment 18, 295; capital flows 64; enterprise 295–6
divestment 7, 16
Dobson, W. 178, 180
Dunning, J.H. 8, 29, 94, 188; eclectic paradigm 29–30, 238

earnings before interest, taxes and depreciation (EBITD) 241
East Asian economic development 189–90
East Asia: net resource flows to 175; countries 78; developing countries 219; economic dynamism in 168; economies 171, 174; NIEs 182, 187; share of foreign affiliates 181
Eastern ASEAN (BIMP-EAGA) initiative 171
EC affiliates 158, 160
eclectic model of MNC 315
eco-labelling 222
econometric analysis of FDI 276–7, 328
effects of MNC operations on home-country 179
electronics activity of MNC 186
Employment Contracts Act of 1991 137
enterprise bargaining (EB) 136–7
enterprise-financed R&D, ratio to GDP 339
entry mode choice 10, 18, 31, 39
environment 234; and development, 211; host country regulations on 340
environmental accounting 225
environmental damage: definition of 211; valuation of 212
environmental footprint 211, 215
environmental management 212–13, 221
environmental strategies of MNCs 212–15
Ericsson 159
Erramilli, M.K. 10, 12
Ethier, W.J. 95, 244
Europe 80, 168, 174; businesses in 39; industrial firms 33
European Commission 315, 318

European International Business Academy conferences 41
European Single Market 158
European Union (EU) 152, 283–4; Commission 319; Direct Investment Yearbook 245; domestic lobby 320; US firms in 277
exit 7, 16
Exon–Florio legislation 113
export: expansion, role of FDI in 180; export performance 179–89
export processing zones (EPZs) 184, 281
Export–Import (EXIM): Bank of Japan (BOJ) 82; surveys 82

factor: costs, role of 56; intensity 96
factor endowments 49
FATS (Foreign Affiliates Trade in Services) Task Force Report 299
FDI 114
FDI and development 325
FDI and the environment 211
FDI data 277–81
FDI flows 316, 319
FDI–trade nexus 168, 177–9
Federal award conditions 136
Feenstra, R. 142
Financial Accounts publications 294
financial crises: in Asia and Latin America 312; in South-East Asia, Mexico and Brazil 317
firms: characteristics 94; types 97
firm specific asset 329–30
firm-specific ownership advantages 18
fiscal incentives, costs of 285–6
Fisher quantity index 68–70
fixed costs, factor composition 98
forestry management 219
Forsyth, D. 277, 283
France 171, 282
Franko, L.G. 33, 39
free trade (export) zones 21
Freeman, R.T. 154
free-trade zones 224
Friedman, M. 120

Gabon 219
Gaston, N. 132, 139
Gatignon, H. 12
GATS-based tariff equivalents 258
General Agreement on Tariffs and Trade (GATT) 318, 322; obligations 313; provisions 315; rounds 314; Uruguay Round 152
General Agreement on Trade in Services (GATS) 252–3, 264, 298, 313, 315, 317, 320–1; schedule 258, 267
general equilibrium (GE) framework: adding FDI into a 240; incorporating MNCs, database and model theory 244
general equilibrium modelling framework 247–8, 267
general equilibrium (GE) models 93, 233–49; input–output table 237–8
Germany 171, 282; manufacturing affiliates 67; mark 67
Ghoshal, S. 20, 34
globalisation 7, 48; and non-economic arguments 322–3; and organisational design 17; processes of 152; FDI issues 282–6; international statistical initiatives on 294–9; issues for governments 292–3
globalisation indicators 296; 304–6; OECD Working Group on Industry Statistics 297; statistical unit for the measurement of 299
Globalisation Newsletter 299
globalisation statistics: conceptual framework for 299–306; framework for 295; options for collecting 292; possible initiatives on 306
Global Trade Analysis Project (GTAP): database 269; input–output data 270
Goldsworthy Report 21
Graham, E. 8, 16
Greater Mekong initiative 171
greenfield 10
Griffith, R. 277, 283
Gripsrud, G. 51, 53–4
gross domestic product (GDP) 54
gross operating surplus (GOS) 241
gross product 63; estimates, method for computing 65
Group of Thirty 275
growth, patterns of MNC 16
growth, studies of MNC 11
Guyana 219

Hardin, A. 253, 259, 261
harmonization: of global minimum standards 202; versus tax competition 283–6
Harvard: Database on American and Foreign MNCs 16, 19–20; management

or process approach 20; University 41
Heckscher-Ohlin: model 108; theorem 49
Helpman, E. 49, 95
Hennart, J.-F. 8, 12–13, 17, 19,
Hill, C. 34
Hines, J. 50–1, 56, 283, 288
Hoekman, B. 257; estimates 258–9;
Hollings, Senator Ernest 113; bill 113–14
Holmes, L. 253, 259, 261
home country: effects of FDI, literature on 152; tax policy 274, 282
Hong Kong 169, 171, 174, 178–82, 187, 263–4, 266, 280; communications sector 264
host-country: gross domestic product (GDP) 63; impact of FDI 162, 168; investment 171; tax regimes 278
host-policy regimes 168–71
Hymer, S. 7–8, 16, 115

impact of tax policy and incentives 273
incentives: for inward FDI 207; role in attracting FDI 277; schemes 278
index of the degree of restrictiveness of FDI regimes 259–67
India 199, 220
Indonesia 169, 171, 179, 181, 200, 220, 245, 263
Industrial Institute for Economic and Social Research (IUI) 19–20, 155
Industrial Relations Commission 136
Industrial Relations Reform Act of 1993 136
Industry Commission Reports 21
infant industry argument for trade protection 332–3
inflows 40, 172–3
insider status within the regional trade area (RTAs) 37
instruments of liberalisation 321–2
Interagency Task Force on Trade-in-Services Statistics 298
international capital flows 233–4
International Councils on Metals and the Environment 221
International Direct Investment Statistics Yearbook 246
international distribution of FDI 49
international investment: process 330–2; statistics 294
International Monetary Fund (IMF) 267, 298; balance-of-payments' definitions 312
international trade: economics 93; level of 40; standard oligopoly model of 98; theory of 93, 105
internationalisation: behavioural models of 40; of firms, theoretical and applied research on 7; of the Australian economy 38; pattern of 33; process school 31; theories 40
internationalisation process model *see* Uppsala model
internationalisation, theory of intra-firm (or intra-affiliate) trade (IFT) of MNC 179
Internet 287; related business 279
intra-regional trade 177–9
investment: and IPRs 196–202; climate of country 56; defining 311–12; decisions, relevance of trade policies to 315; environment, deficiencies in 286; regulations 206; regulatory agencies, role of 169
Investment Code 284
investment liberalization 109; and factor prices 107; volume and direction of trade 104–7
investors, survey of 275–6
intellectual property rights (IPRs) 205; and FDI 195, 208; and FDI, econometric evidence on 202–4; global system of 195; index of perceived weakness of 203; law and enforcement 202; research in 208; systems 201
Ireland 286, 332; market 315; tax policy 277
ISO 14000 environmental management standards 221–2
Italy 338

Japan 161, 168, 174, 245, 264, 266, 269, 282, 295, 318; affiliates 70–1; auto producers 180; banks, expansion of 78; bubble economy in 80; deregulation in 76; electronic firms 15; Foreign Exchange Law in 82; index for telecommunications 265; industry, internationalisation of 83–8; investment in US, database on 19; JVs 12, 17; manufacturing firms 79–80; MNCs 12, 17, 179, 199
Japan Company Handbook 19
Japan Economic Institute 19

Japanese FDI 75–6: and trade flows 80; annual statistics of 82; Asia's share of 177; changing industrial distribution of 80; cumulative 77; data 88; database of 83; evolving nature of 88; greenfield 17; industrial categories of 75; in manufacturing, distribution of 79; outflows 88; pattern of investment 76–80; research issues in 75; statistics 82; surveys of outward investment 270
Johanson, J. 30, 39
joint ventures (JV) 10–11, 236
Jones, S.R.G. 141

Knickerbocker, F.T. 8, 16
knowledge-based 319
knowledge-based assets (KBAs) 197
knowledge capital 95; approach 93–7
Kogut, B. 12–13, 15, 18
Kojima, Professor Kiyoshi 174
Korea 169, 171, 174–5, 180, 182, 187, 200, 263, 266, 333; foreign investment 19; investment 177; labour-intensive growth phase of 182; MNCs 20; technology imports 186
Kravis, I.B. 56, 57, 154
Krugman, P. 58, 244

labour demand elasticity 235
labour markets 235; effects of globalisation on 133; institutions 140; outcomes 134–6; performances 133; standards 234–5
laissez faire approach 340
Lansbury, R.D. 137
Latin America 335
Lawrence, R.Z. 142
Leamer, E. 83
licensing: agreements 236; costs 200
Lindbeck, A. 133
Linder effect 54
link between FDI and country characteristics, 95
Lipsey, R.E. 48, 51, 56, 57, 66, 154
literature on FDI 325
locational theorists in economics 48
location choices 41
London 38
Low, P. 236

macroeconomic level 42
majority-owned-foreign affiliates (MOFAs) 65, 68; components of the gross product of 66; of US multinationals 183, 189, 216
Malaysia 171, 175, 179, 181, 186, 200; home-country export shares of 184; investments in palm oil plantations 170; telecommunications sector in 265
managements and investment decisions of MNCs' 316
management strategies of MNC 21
market: access 47; characteristics, specification of 53; clearing condition 117; entry mode 11; exchange rates 70; failures in information 331; for telecommunications services 114; liberalisation 36, 208; share strategy 119; structure, effects of FDI on 335; transactions, concept of internalising 8
Markusen, J. 46–8, 143, 234, 248, 268, 288; formal model of multinational corporations 47
Maskus, K. 2, 4, 111, 195, 197, 200–4, 209–10
Mauritius 280
McKinsey and Company 31, 39; born global firms 39
Mehra, S.K. 12, 18
Mexico 200, 203, 220–2, 235, 264, 338
Mezzetti, C. 139
mode choice 34–5
models of labour markets, 134
models: with endogenous multinationals 13, 97–9, 132, 248
modelling: divestment and exit decision 17; FDI in a general equilibrium framework 233
Mody, A. 51–2, 54–5, 57, 135
monopoly: effect 197; in the United States 114; prices 120; rents 128;
Monetary Union of West African States 284
Montero-Muñoz, M. 154
Mortimer Report 21
multilateral agreement on investment (MAI) 310, 313; mandate 318; negotiations, collapse of the 311
multilateral investment rules 310; agenda for research 320–3
multilateral treaties, difficulties in 317–19
multinational corporations (MNCs) 310, 315, 319; activity 41, 99–104, 244; global operations 36; global system 35; and governments 314; home country 96; in developing countries 327–41; investment 176; location decisions 38,

219; operations in East Asia 178; parents and affiliates 157; profitability 157; R&D 160, 163
multinationals: theory of 106; data collection on 110; effects of 104 Murkowski, Senator Frank 113; bill 113

Nash: bargaining condition 140; equilibrium 119–20, 125; non-cooperative equilibrium 129; solution 138
National Accounts data 88
National Accounts statistics 293
National Bureau of Economic Research website 59
natural monopolies 121, 169
Nayyar, D. 181
Nelson, D. 132
Netherlands 101, 161, 245, 282
New York 38
New Zealand 136, 255, 265–6; Broadcasting Commission budget 265
NIEs 174; first generation 187
non-governmental organisations (NGOs) 311, 316, 318; code of conduct for 319; media impact of 322
non-OECD countries 72, 136, 188
Nordstrom, K.A. 31
North American Free Trade Agreement (NAFTA) 283; investment rules in 318
North American Free Trade Area 236
NTBs, removal of 206

Oceania 80
OECD 54, 59, 68, 252, 284, 310, 318; countries 68, 70, 159, 201, 245, 282, 312–14, 317, 321, 340; economies 182; governments 311; investors 174; markets 321; R&D norms 186;
OECD Codes on Liberalisation of Capital Movements 18, 321
OECD Principles of Corporate Governance 319
OECD Statistics Directorate 298
OECD Working Group on Industry Statistics 295, 297
oligopoly: competition model 115–21; markets 121; theory 116
outsourcing: jobs 132; of production facilities 133, 140

Papua New Guinea 219, 220; mining projects in 224; telecommunications sector in 265
Park, Y.-R. 12–13, 19
patents 197, 200–1; in developing countries 204
Pearce, R.D. 51
Penn World Database 59
Penubarti, M. 197, 204
Petri, P.A. 58, 80, 177, 248, 259, 267; approach 269; model of trade liberalisation 247; multiregional model of FDI 268
Pfaffermayr, M. 154
Philippines 170, 175–6, 179, 181, 220, 263–4, 266
Plaza Accord 78
policy 170, 187, 340
pollution: abatement practices 213; abatement technology 222; intensity of FDI 215–20; intensive industries 213, 216–17
pollution haven hypothesis 219–20, 236
pre-1939 British MNCs 16, 20
predatory pricing 113
price: cut 120; setters 116; wedges 257
profits, tax on FDI 269
psychic dispersion 41
psychic distance 30
purchasing-power-parity (PPP) exchange rates 68; data 72; development of 64; economy-wide 70

qualitative analysis 328
quality of data 19
quantifying investment barriers 269
quantitative import restrictions (QRs) 182

R&D: in Ireland 339; in the parent company 162; spillovers 163
race to the bottom 234, 284
Ramstetter, E.D. 171, 180–1
Rao, C.P. 10, 12
RASing 241
real gross product estimates 68–71
recycled material, use of 211
Reddy, S. 12–13, 19
Rolfe, R.J. 50–1, 53, 57, 278

Sato, Y. 187
SC Johnson 212
Scandinavian firms, studies of 33
Scaperlanda, A. 51, 53, 57
sequential entry and investment clustering 15–16
Simon, H. 122

Singapore 171, 175–6, 178–81, 187–8, 258, 286, 332, 338–9; home-country export shares of 184
Singh, H. 13
Singh, S. 12
Single Market area 161
single-issue lobby groups 318
Sisson, K. 133
Sjoholm, S. 185
Slaughter, M. 288
small island host countries 219
Solomon Islands 219
Solow, R.M. 138
Song, L. 83
South America 277
South Korea 181
South Pacific 277
specialisation: effects of increasing 161–3; of home country production 160; trend to 31
stability premium 279
stages models of internationalisation 39
standard HOS trade model 142
Standard Institutional Sector Classification of Australia (SISCA) 302
standard oligopoly theory 114
state: and MNCs 18; opportunism 19
state-owned enterprises (SOEs) 185
Statistical Office of the European Community 298; work on globalisation 298–9
statistics on the foreign activities of MNC 64–5
static versus dynamic benefits 336
stocks 241–2
Stolper-Samuelson Theorem 142
Stone, G. 65
Stone, R. 65
Stopford, J.M. 11–12, 32–3, 39
strategic issues 28
strategy: and strategic management definitions 28; restricting TNC entry 341
Structure-Conduct-Performance paradigm 52
structure of home country production 152
studies of structure and coordination of MNCs 40
sub-Saharan Africa 197, 277
subsidiary–parent relationship literature 18
survey of FDI 55
Svensson, R. 12, 155–6
Sweden 58, 101, 107, 152, 157; database 20; economy 152–3; exports and employment 153; FDI–trade relationship 155; firms 31, 136, 154; income tax rates 161; investment abroad 153; MNCs 152, 155, 157–9, 161–2; surveys of direct investment abroad 156
Swedenborg, B. 155–6
Switzerland 101, 161
System of National Accounts (*SNA93)* 294–5, 297, 300–1, 305

Taiwan 171, 174–5, 178–82, 187–8, 334, 338; investment in Southeast Asia 178; labour-intensive growth phase of 182
tariff equivalents: frequency-based measures 257; price effects 208
tariff protection 21
tax: allowance 279; and tariffs 234–5; behavior of multinational corporations 278–9; competition across countries 284; havens 235, 281; holiday 273, 279–80; incentives 274, 280; instruments used by governments 279–81; policies and FDI 273–5, 277; policy changes 276; rate, average effective 283
taxation: effects of 50; of multinational corporations, global approach to 287
tax haven countries 277
technology and FDI 184–9
technology: development policies 208; development programs 207; life cycle model 236; spillovers 237, 268, 338; transfers 18, 234, 236–7
technology transfer and FDI 204–7
Teece, D.J. 11, 13
telecommunications: cost structures typical of 114; industry 159; sector 113, 117; services sector 116
telecoms: sector 121–5; services, provision of 121
Telstra 257, 264
tension between MNCs and host governments 316
Thailand 171, 179–81, 263–4, 266
theory of the MNC 93
transnational corporations (TNCs) 325, 336; affiliates 332; choice of location 330; issues for host government policy 330; mergers and acquisitions (M&As) by 335; mobile assets 327; R&D 339; strategies 337; training and infrastructure programmes 332
trends and patterns of FDI 171–7

Town and Village Enterprises, TVEs 185
trade and FDI 93
trade: and industrial policy regime 337; and investment liberalisation 211; and investment liberalization, studies of 259; barriers to 195; costs, changes in 108–9; direction of 101; industrial-organization approach to 93; in services (GATS) 233; liberalisation 109, 132, 195, 234; secrets 197; theorists 49
trade effects of FDI 316
trade-in-services 298
trade-investment cross currents 314–16
trademarks 197
trade-related aspects of intellectual property rights (TRIPs) 195, 233, 313
trade-related investment measures (TRIMs) 310, 313, 317; agreement 321; negotiations 314–15
transaction cost model 18; of the MNC 15
transaction cost-agency: economics 16; model 8; theory 9; theory of the MNC 21
transport costs 48–9; bias 54
Trefler, D. 139

UN Centre for transnational corporations (TNCs) 311
UN Charter article 71 318
union: membership 136, 142; preferences 138
United Kingdom (UK) 132, 163, 171, 255, 282, 338–9; labour market flexibility in 142
United Nations Conference on Environment and Development 213
United Nations Conference on Trade and Development (UNCTAD) 56, 59, 253, 273, 312; definition of FDI stock 245; World Investment Report 246
United Nations High Commissioner for Refugees (UNHCR) 319
United States (US) 50, 54–5, 58, 78, 132, 160, 163, 168, 171, 174, 204, 215, 235, 245–6, 263–4, 266, 269, 282, 288, 295; Census of Manufacturers 19; companies' majority-owned foreign affiliates (MOFA) 64; direct investment 64–5, 203; domestic lobby 320; economic accounts 64; economy, model for 154; firms 180, 248; firms, survey of managers of 278; foreign-owned firms in 34; implicit price deflator for GDP 69; manufacturing firms 32; MNCs 63–5, 72, 157; MNCs 183, 202; multinationals 179, 183; surveys of outward FDI investment 270; tax laws 274; tax policy 287; Tax Reform Act of 1986 283; TNCs, R&D 338
University of Melbourne 19
University of New South Wales (UNSW) 19
UNTCMD 181
Uppsala model 29–32
Uruguay Round 206, 310, 313–14, 322–3; agreements 315;
US Council of Economic Advisors 114
US Department of Commerce 63

Vahlne, J.E. 30, 39, 153
Venables, A.J. 95, 143
Venezuela 222, 235
Vernon, R. 29, 39; product life cycle model 29
Veugels, R. 51–5
Vishwasrao, S. 201
Voice Stream 113

wage: and employment bargains 138; bargaining, centralised 133;
wage-setting by MNCs 235
dispersion 132; spillover effects 135
Washington Consensus 326
Wasylenko, M. 51, 55
web of contractual arrangements of MNCs 8
Welch, L. 17, 31
Wells, L.T. 11–12, 32–3, 39
Wheeler, D. 51, 52, 54–5, 57, 135
Wiedersheim-Paul, F. 30
Williamson, O. 8, 14, 18
Woodward, D.P. 50, 51, 53, 57
World Bank: International Centre for Settlement of Investment Disputes (ICSID) 314
world Edgeworth box 99
World Health Organisation (WHO) 319
World Investment Report 245
World Trade Organisation (WTO) 1, 195, 252–4, 298, 309, 314, 318; agreement on government procurement (GPA) 313–14;

World Trade Organisation (WTO) (*Continued*)
agreement on subsidies and countervailing measures (ASCM) 313–15, 317, 321–2; agreements 310, 313–14, 321; antidumping agreement (ADA) 313, 321–2; investment in 313–14; provisions 315; rules 317; trade agreements 18; trade disciplines 321; working group 316
WTO High-Level Symposium on Trade and Development 316, 318

Yamamura, K. 178
Yang, G. 201

Zander, U. 15, 18